Deep Learning on Graphs

Deep learning on graphs has become one of the hottest topics in machine learning. The book consists of four parts to best accommodate the readers with diverse backgrounds and purposes of reading. Part I introduces basic concepts of graphs and deep learning; Part II discusses the most-established methods from the basic to advanced settings; Part III presents the most typical applications including natural language processing, computer vision, data mining, biochemistry, and health care; and Part IV describes advances of methods and applications that tend to be important and promising for future research. The book is self-contained, making it accessible to a broader range of readers including (1) senior undergraduate and graduate students; (2) practitioners and project managers who want to adopt graph neural networks into their products and platforms; and (3) researchers without a computer science background who want to use graph neural networks to advance their disciplines.

Yao Ma is a PhD student of the Department of Computer Science and Engineering at Michigan State University (MSU). He is the recipient of the Outstanding Graduate Student Award and FAST Fellowship at MSU. He has published papers in top conferences such as WSDM, ICDM, SDM, WWW, IJCAI, SIGIR, and KDD, which have been cited hundreds of times. He is the leading organizer and presenter of tutorials on GNNs at AAAI'20, KDD'20 and AAAI'21, which received huge attention and wide acclaim. He has served as Program Committee Members/Reviewers in many well-known conferences and magazines such as *AAAI, BigData, IJCAI, TWEB, TKDD*, and *TPAMI*.

Jiliang Tang is Assistant Professor in the Department of Computer Science and Engineering at Michigan State University. Previously, he was a research scientist in Yahoo Research. He received the 2020 SIGKDD Rising Star Award, 2020 Distinguished Withrow Research Award, 2019 NSF Career Award, the 2019 IJCAI Early Career Invited Talk and 7 best paper (runner-up) awards. He has organized top data science conferences including KDD, WSDM, and SDM, and is an associate editor of the *TKDD* journal. His research has been published in highly ranked journals and top conferences, and received more than 12,000 citations with h-index 55 and extensive media coverage.

Deep Learning on Graphs

YAO MA
Michigan State University

JILIANG TANG
Michigan State University

CAMBRIDGE
UNIVERSITY PRESS

University Printing House, Cambridge CB2 8BS, United Kingdom

One Liberty Plaza, 20th Floor, New York, NY 10006, USA

477 Williamstown Road, Port Melbourne, VIC 3207, Australia

314–321, 3rd Floor, Plot 3, Splendor Forum, Jasola District Centre,
New Delhi – 110025, India

103 Penang Road, #05–06/07, Visioncrest Commercial, Singapore 238467

Cambridge University Press is part of the University of Cambridge.

It furthers the University's mission by disseminating knowledge in the pursuit of
education, learning, and research at the highest international levels of excellence.

www.cambridge.org
Information on this title: www.cambridge.org/9781108831741
DOI: 10.1017/9781108924184

First published 2021

Printed in the United Kingdom by TJ Books Ltd, Padstow Cornwall

A catalogue record for this publication is available from the British Library.

ISBN 978-1-108-83174-1 Hardback

Contents

Preface

Graphs have been leveraged to denote data from various domains ranging from social science and linguistics to chemistry, biology, and physics. Meanwhile, numerous real-world applications can be treated as computational tasks on graphs. For examples, air quality forecasting can be regarded as a node classification task, friends, recommendations in social networks can be solved as a link prediction task, and protein interface prediction can be regarded as a graph classification task. To better take advantage of modern machine learning models for these computational tasks, effectively representing graphs plays a key role. There are two major ways to extract features to represent graphs: feature engineering and representation learning. Feature engineering relies on hand-engineered features, which is time consuming and often not optimal for given downstream tasks. Representation learning is to learn features automatically, which requires minimal human effort and is adaptive to given downstream tasks. Thus, representation learning on graphs has been extensively studied.

The field of graph representation learning has been greatly developed over the past decades and can be roughly divided into three generations: traditional graph embedding, modern graph embedding, and deep learning on graphs. As the first generation of graph representation learning, traditional graph embedding has been investigated under the context of classic dimension reduction techniques on graphs such as IsoMap, LLE, and eigenmap. Word2vec is to learn word representations from a large corpus of text, and the generated word representations have advanced many natural language processing tasks. The successful extensions of word2vec to the graph domain have started the second generation of representation learning on graphs, that is, modern graph embedding. Given the huge success of deep learning techniques in representation learning in the domains of images and text, efforts have been

made to generalize them to graphs, which have opened a new chapter of graph representation learning, that is, deep learning on graphs.

More and more evidence has demonstrated that the third generation of graph representation learning, especially graph neural networks (GNNs), has tremendously facilitated computational tasks on graphs including both node-focused and graph-focused tasks. The revolutionary advances brought by GNNs have also immensely contributed to the depth and breadth of the adoption of graph representation learning in real-world applications. For the classical application domains of graph representation learning, such as recommender systems and social network analysis, GNNs result in state-of-the-art performance and bring them into new frontiers. Meanwhile, new application domains of GNNs have been continuously emerging, such as combinational optimization, physics, and health care. These wide applications of GNNs enable diverse contributions and perspectives from disparate disciplines and make this research field truly interdisciplinary.

Graph representation learning is a rapidly growing field. It has attracted significant amounts of attention from different domains and consequently accumulated a large body of literature. Thus, it is a propitious time to systematically survey and summarize this field. This book is our diligent attempt to achieve this goal by taking advantage of our many years of teaching and research experience in this field. In particular, we aim to help researchers acquire essential knowledge of graph representation learning and its wide range of applications and understand its advances and new frontiers.

An Overview of the Book. This book provides a comprehensive introduction to graph representation learning with a focus on deep learning on graphs, especially GNNs. It consists of four parts: Foundations, Methods, Applications, and Advances. The Foundations part introduces the necessary background and basic concepts of graphs and deep learning. Topics covered by the Methods part include modern graph embedding, GNNs for both simple and complex graphs, the robustness and scalability issues of GNNs, and deep graph models beyond GNNs. Each of these topics is covered by a chapter with fundamental concepts and technical details on representative algorithms. The Applications part presents GNN applications in the most typical domains, including natural language processing, computer vision, data mining, biochemistry, and health care. One chapter is used to cover the most representative subfields advanced by GNNs for each domain. New emerging methods and application domains are discussed by the Advances part. For each chapter, further reading is included at the end for readers who are interested in more advanced topics and recent trends.

Target Audience. This book is designed to be as self-contained as possible, though the basic background of graph theory, calculus, linear algebra, probability, and statistics can help better understand its technical details. Thus, it is suitable for a wide range of readers with diverse backgrounds and different purposes of reading. This book can serve as both a learning tool and a reference for students at the senior undergraduate or graduate levels who want to obtain a comprehensive understanding of this research field. Researchers who wish to pursue this research field can consider this book as a starting point. Project managers and practitioners can learn from GNN applications in the book on how to adopt GNNs in their products and platforms. Researchers outside of computer science can find an extensive set of examples in this book on how to apply GNNs to different disciplines.

Acknowledgments

We start by acknowledging our families to whom this book is dedicated. This book would not have been possible without their selfless support and encouragement.

Graph representation learning has grown tremendously in the past decade from traditional graph embedding to modern graph embedding and graph neural networks. We have had the fortune to witness these three generations. This evolution is impossible without pioneering research performed by numerous researchers. Meanwhile, increasing efforts have been made to take advantage of graph representation learning to advance applications from many domains. Graph representation learning has become a truly interdisciplinary research field. We would like to acknowledge all people contributing to this field. Their efforts not only enable us to have a book on this field but also make it one of the most popular topics in machine learning.

The idea of writing this book is strongly inspired by Huan Liu (Arizona State University). He has been working on feature selection for decades. We began the journey on graph representation learning by his ingenious suggestion on feature selection on graphs in 2010. We would like to thank Charu Aggarwal (IBM Research) and Shiyu Chang (University of California, Santa Barbara) with whom we started the research of modern graph embedding in 2014. We have worked in this field since 2010 and we got immense support from our collaborators. In particular, we would like to express our tremendous gratitude to Salem Alelyani (King Khalid University), Yi Chang (Jilin University), Ken Frank (Michigan State University), Huiji Gao (LinkedIn), Xia Hu (Texas A&M University), Anil Jain (Michigan State University), Shuiwang Ji (Texas A&M University), Jundong Li (University of Virginia), Zitao Liu (TAL Education Group), Sinem Mollaoglu (Michigan State University), Shin-Han Shiu (Michigan State University), Kai Shu (Illinois Institute of Technology), Pang-Ning Tan (Michigan State University), Lei Tang (Lyft), Guanhua Tu (Michigan

State University), Suhang Wang (Pennsylvania State University), Lingfei Wu (JD.com), Yuying Xie (Michigan State University), Ming Yan(Michigan State University), Dawei Yin (Baidu, Inc.), Mi Zhang (Michigan State University) and Jiayu Zhou (Michigan State University).

We would like to thank the current and former members of the Data Science and Engineering Laboratory at Michigan State University. They include Meznah Almutairy, Norah Alfadhli, Aaron Brookhouse, Jamell Dacon, Daniel K.O-Dankwa, Tyler Derr, Jiayuan Ding, Wenqi Fan, Haoyu Han, Jiangtao Huang, Hamid Karimi, Wei Jin, Juanhui Li, Yaxin Li, Haochen Liu, Hua Liu, Xiaorui Liu, Jie Ren, Namratha Shah, Harry Shomer, Yuxuan Wan, Wentao Wang, Yiqi Wang, Xochitl Weiss, Hongzhi Wen, Xiaoyang Wang, Xin Wang, Zhiwei Wang, Han Xu, and Xiangyu Zhao. They provided invaluable comments and feedback for the early drafts of this book.

We would like to thank Xavier Sumba (Heyday.ai), Shunshi Hu (Hunan Normal University), Kannan Presanna Kumar (SAP), and Chen Chen (Ningxia Normal University) for their suggestions for the preprint of the book.

The computer science and engineering department at Michigan State University provided us a fantastic atmosphere for this book. Our research on graph representation learning has been, in part, supported by National Science Foundation, Army Research Office, NEC Labs America, Snap Inc., The Ford Motor Company, JD.com, Criteo Labs, and TAL Education Group. In particular, Hector Munoz-Avila, Zhengchang Chen, Wei Ding, Purush S. Iyer, Balakrishnan Prabhakaran, Neil Shah, Finbarr Sloane, Maria Zemankova, and Aidong Zhang have been supportive of our research in graph representation learning. It was a pleasure working with Cambridge University Press. We would like to acknowledge Lauren Cowles, a senior editor of Mathematics and Computer Sciences at Cambridge, for her support, and the helpful staff at Cambridge, Amy He and Mark Fox, as well as Harshavardhanan Udhayakumar and his colleagues at SPi Global for their efforts on the production of the book.

1

Deep Learning on Graphs
An Introduction

1.1 Introduction

We start the chapter by answering a few questions about the book. First, we discuss why we should pay attention to deep learning on graphs. In particular, why do we represent real-world data as graphs, why do we want to bridge deep learning with graphs, and what are the challenges for deep learning on graphs? Second, we introduce the content that will be covered by this book, specifically, which topics we will discuss and how we organize these topics. Third, we provide guidance about who should read this book; in particular, who our target audience is and how to read this book for readers with different backgrounds and purposes for reading. To help better understand deep learning on graphs, we briefly review the history under the more general context of feature learning on graphs.

1.2 Why Deep Learning on Graphs?

Because data from real-world applications have very diverse forms, from matrix and tensor to sequence and time series, a natural question that arises is why we attempt to represent data as graphs. There are two main motivations. First, graphs provide a universal representation of data, as shown in Figure 1.1. Data from many systems across various areas can be explicitly denoted as graphs such as social networks, transportation networks, protein–protein interaction networks, knowledge graphs, and brain networks. In addition as indicated by Figure 1.1, numerous other types of data can be transformed into the form of graphs. Second, a huge number of real-world problems can be addressed as a small set of computational tasks on graphs. For example, inferring node attributes, detecting anomalous nodes (e.g., spammers or terrorists),

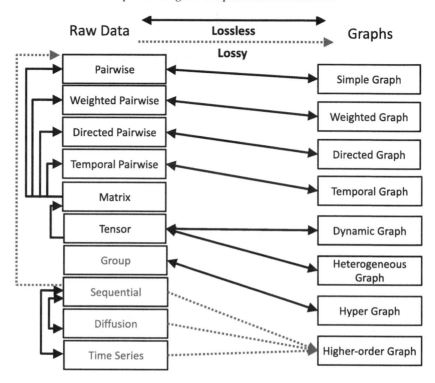

Figure 1.1 Representing real-world data as graphs. The figure is reproduced with permission from J. Xu (2017). Solid lines are utilized to denote lossless representations and dotted lines are used to indicate lossy representations. Note that we replace "network" in the original figure with "graph."

identifying genes relevant to diseases, and suggesting medications for patients can be summarized as problems of node classification, and recommendations, polypharmacy side effect prediction, drug–target interaction identification, and knowledge graph completion are essentially problems of link prediction.

Nodes on graphs are inherently connected, which suggests that nodes are not independent and identically distributed. Thus, traditional machine learning techniques cannot be directly applied for the computational tasks on graphs. There are two main directions to develop solutions. As shown in Figure 1.2, we will use node classification as an illustrative example to discuss these two directions. One direction is to build a new mechanism specific to graphs. The classification problem designed for graphs is known as collective classification (Sen et al., 2008) as demonstrated in Figure 1.2a. Different from traditional classification, collective classification for a node considers not only the mapping between its features and its label but also the mapping for its neighborhood. The other direction is to flat a graph by constructing a set of features to denote its nodes where traditional classification techniques can be applied as illustrated in Figure 1.2b. This direction can take advantage of traditional machine learning techniques; thus it has become increasingly popular and dominant. The key to the success of this direction is how to construct a set of features for nodes (or how to construct node representations). Deep learning has been proven to be powerful in representation learning, which has greatly advanced various domains such as computer vision, speech recognition, and natural language processing. Therefore, bridging deep learning with graphs presents unprecedented opportunities. However, deep learning on graphs also faces immense challenges. First, traditional deep learning has been designed for regular data such as images and sequences where the size is fixed, whereas graphs can have varied sizes and nodes in a graph are unordered and can have distinct neighborhoods. Second, the structural information for regular data is simple, whereas that for graphs is complicated, especially given that there are various types of complex graphs, as shown in Figure 1.1, and nodes and edges can associate with rich side information; thus traditional deep learning is not sufficient to capture such rich information. Embracing the unprecedented opportunities as well as the immense challenges, a new research field has been cultivated – deep learning on graphs.

1.3 What Content Is Covered?

The high-level organization of the book is illustrated in Figure 1.3. The book consists of four parts to best accommodate readers with diverse backgrounds and purposes for reading. Part I introduces basic concepts, Part II discusses the most established methods, Part III presents the most representative applications, and Part IV describes advances of methods and applications that are believed to be important and promising for future research. In each chapter, we first motivate the content that will be covered, then present the content with necessary examples or technical details, and finally provide more relevant content as further reading. Next, we briefly elaborate on each chapter.

- Part I: Foundations. These chapters focus on the basics of graphs and deep learning that will lay foundations for deep learning on graphs. In Chapter 2, we introduce the key concepts and properties of graphs, graph Fourier transform, and graph signal processing and formally define various types of complex graphs and computational tasks on graphs. In Chapter 3, we

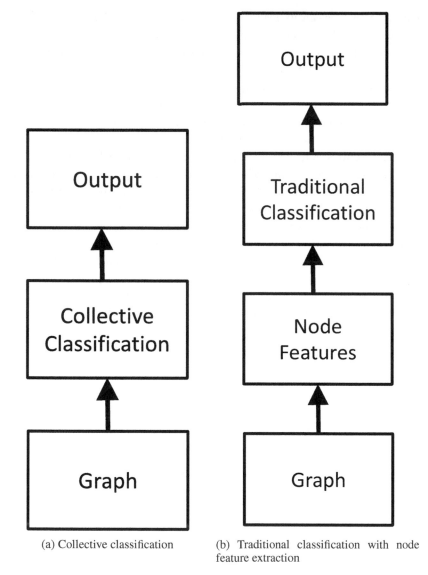

(a) Collective classification

(b) Traditional classification with node feature extraction

Figure 1.2 Two major directions to develop solutions for node classification on graphs.

discuss a variety of basic neural network models, key approaches to training deep models, and practical techniques to prevent overfitting during training.

- Part II: Methods. These chapters cover the most established methods of deep learning on graphs from the basic to advanced settings. In Chapter 4,

1. Introduction

Part I : Foundations

2. Foundations of Graphs

3. Foundations of Deep Learning

Part II: Methods

4. Graph Embedding

5. Graph Neural Networks

6. Robust Graph Neural Networks

7. Scalable Graph Neural Networks

8. Graph Neural Networks on Complex Graphs

9. Beyond GNNs: More Deep Models on Graphs

Part III: Applications

10. Graph Neural Networks in Natural Language Processing

11. Graph Neural Networks in Computer Vision

12. Graph Neural Networks in Data Mining

13. Graph Neural Networks in Biochemistry and Health Care

Part IV: Advances

14. Advanced Topics in Graph Neural Networks

15. Advanced Applications in Graph Neural Networks

Figure 1.3 The high-level organization of the book.

we introduce a general graph embedding framework from the information preservation perspective, provide technical details on representative algorithms to preserve numerous types of information on graphs, and present embedding approaches specifically designed for complex graphs. A typical graph neural network (GNN) model consists of two important operations, that is, the graph filter operation and the graph pooling operation. In Chapter 5, we review the state-of-the-art graph filter and pooling operations and discuss how to learn the parameters of GNNs for a given downstream task. As generalizations of traditional deep models to graphs, GNNs inherit the drawback of traditional deep models and are vulnerable to adversarial examples. In Chapter 6, we focus on concepts and definitions of graph adversarial attacks and detail representative adversarial attack and defense techniques. GNNs perform the recursive expansion of neighborhoods across layers. The expansion of the neighborhood for a single node can rapidly involve a large portion of the graph or even the whole graph. Hence, scalability is a pressing issue for GNNs. We provide detailed representative techniques to scale GNNs in Chapter 7. In Chapter 8, we discuss GNN models that have been designed for more complicated graphs. To enable deep learning techniques to advance more graph tasks under wider settings, we introduce numerous deep graph models beyond GNNs in Chapter 9.

- Part III: Applications. Graphs provide a universal representation for real-world data; thus methods of deep learning on graphs have been applied to various fields. These chapters present the most representative applications of GNNs, including natural language processing in Chapter 10, computer vision in Chapter 11, data mining in Chapter 12, and biochemistry and health care in Chapter 13.
- Part IV: Advances. These chapters focus on recent advances in both methods and applications. In Chapter 14, we introduce advanced GNNs in terms of expressiveness, depth, fairness, interpretability, and self-supervised learning. We discuss more areas to which GNNs have been applied, including combinatorial optimization, physics, program representation, reinforcement learning, and computer networks in Chapter 15.

1.4 Who Should Read This Book?

This book is easily accessible to readers with a computer science background. Basic knowledge of calculus, linear algebra, probability, and statistics can aid in understanding its technical details. This book has a wide range of target audiences. One target audience is senior undergraduate and graduate students

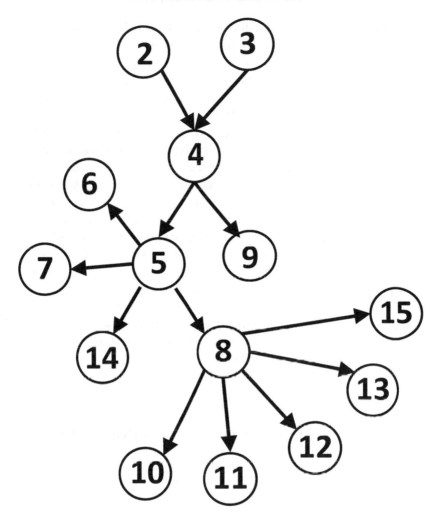

Figure 1.4 The guidance on how to read this book. Note that the number in the circle indicates the corresponding chapter as shown in Figure 1.3.

who are interested in data mining, machine learning, and social network analysis. This book can be independently used for a graduate seminar course on deep learning on graphs. It also can be utilized as a part of a course. For example, Parts II and IV can be considered as advanced topics in courses on data mining, machine learning, and social network analysis; and Part III can be used as advanced methods in solving traditional tasks in computer vision, natural language processing, and health care. Practitioners and project managers who want to learn the basics and tangible examples of deep learning on graphs and adopt GNNs into their products and platforms are also our target audience. Graph neural networks have been applied to benefit numerous disciplines beyond computer science. Thus, another target audience is researchers who do not have a computer science background but want to apply GNNs to advance their disciplines.

Readers with different backgrounds and purposes for reading should go through the book differently. Suggested guidance on how to read this book is illustrated in Figure 1.4. If readers aim to understand GNN methods for simple graphs (Chapter 5), knowledge about foundations of graphs and deep learning and graph embedding is necessary (Chapters 2–4). If readers want to apply GNNs to advance health care (Chapter 13), they should first read prerequisite materials on foundations of graphs and deep learning, graph embedding, and GNN methods for simple and complex graphs (Chapters 2–5, and 8). For Part III, we do assume that the readers have the necessary background in the corresponding fields of application. In addition, readers should feel free to skip some chapters if they are equipped with the corresponding background. For example, if readers have knowledge regarding foundations of graphs and deep learning, they can skip Chapters 2 and 3 and only read Chapters 4 and 5 to understand GNNs for simple graphs.

1.5 Feature Learning on Graphs: A Brief History

As aforementioned, to take advantage of traditional machine learning for computational tasks on graphs, finding vector node representations is desired. As shown in Figure 1.5, there are two main ways to achieve this goal: feature engineering and feature learning. Feature engineering relies on hand-designed features such as node degree statistics, whereas feature learning is automatic learning of node features. On the one hand, we often do not have prior knowledge of what features are important especially for a given downstream task; thus features from feature engineering could be suboptimal for the downstream task and the process requires an immense amount of human effort. On the other hand, feature learning is automatic learning of features and the process can be guided by the downstream task; consequently, the learned features are likely to be suitable for the downstream task and often obtain better performance than those obtained via feature engineering. Furthermore, the process requires minimal human intervention and can be easily adapted to new tasks. Thus, feature learning on graphs has been extensively studied and various types of

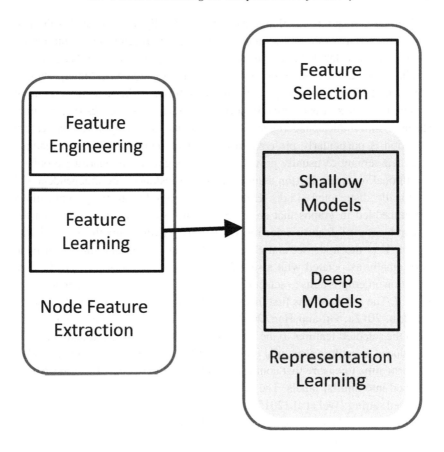

Figure 1.5 Node feature extraction.

feature learning techniques have been proposed to meet different requirements and scenarios. We roughly divide these techniques into feature selection on graphs, which aims to remove irrelevant and redundant node features, and representation learning on graphs, which targets the generation of a set of new node features. In this section, we briefly review these two groups of techniques that provide a general and historical context for readers to understand deep learning on graphs.

1.5.1 Feature Selection on Graphs

Real-world data are often high-dimensional and there exist noisy, irrelevant, and redundant features (or dimensions), particularly when considering a given task. Feature selection aims to automatically select a small subset of features that have minimal redundancy but maximal relevance to the target, such as the class labels under the supervised setting. In many applications, the original features are crucial for knowledge extraction and model interpretation. For example, in genetic analysis for cancer studies in addition to differentiating cancerous tissues, it is of great importance to identify the genes (i.e., original features) that induce cancerogenesis. In these demanding applications, feature selection is particularly preferred because it maintains the original features and their semantics usually provide critical insights to the learning problem. Traditional feature selection assumes that data instances are independent and identically distributed (i.i.d.). However, data samples in many applications are embedded in graphs that are inherently not i.i.d. This has motivated the research area of feature selection on graphs. Given a graph $\mathcal{G} = \{\mathcal{V}, \mathcal{E}\}$, where $\mathcal{V}$ is the node set and $\mathcal{E}$ is the edge set, we assume that each node is originally associated with a set of d features $\mathcal{F} = \{f_1, f_2, \ldots, f_d\}$. Feature selection on graphs aims to select K features from $\mathcal{F}$ to denote each node where $K \ll d$. The problem was first investigated under the supervised setting (Tang and Liu, 2012a; Gu and Han, 2011). A linear classifier is employed to map from the selected features to the class labels and a graph regularization term is introduced to capture structural information for feature selection. In particular, the term aims to ensure that connected nodes with the selected features can be mapped into similar labels. The problem was further studied under the unsupervised setting (Wei et al., 2015, 2016; Tang and Liu, 2012b). In Tang and Liu (2012b), pseudo labels are extracted from the structural information that serves as the supervision to guide the feature selection process. In Wei et al. (2016), both the node content and structural information are assumed to be generated from a set of high-quality features that can be obtained by maximizing the likelihood of the generation process. The problem has also been extended from simple graphs to complex graphs such as dynamic graphs (Li et al., 2016), multidimensional graphs (Tang et al., 2013b), signed graphs (Cheng et al., 2017; Huang et al., 2020), and attributed graphs (Li et al., 2019b).

1.5.2 Representation Learning on Graphs

Different from feature selection on graphs, representation learning on graphs is to learn a set of new node features. It has been extensively studied for decades and has been greatly accelerated by deep learning. In this subsection, we will give it a brief historical review from shallow models to deep models.

At the early stage, representation learning on graphs was studied under the context of spectral clustering (Shi and Malik, 2000; Ng et al., 2002), graph-based dimension reduction (Belkin and Niyogi, 2003; Tenenbaum et al., 2000;

Roweis and Saul, 2000), and matrix factorization (Zhu et al., 2007; Tang et al., 2013a; Koren et al., 2009). In spectral clustering (Shi and Malik, 2000; Ng et al., 2002), data points are considered as nodes of a graph and then clustering is used to partition the graph into communities of nodes. One key step for spectral clustering is spectral embedding. It aims to embed nodes into a low-dimensional space where traditional clustering algorithms such as k-means can be applied to identify clusters. Techniques of graph-based dimension reduction can be directly applied to learn node representations. These approaches typically build an affinity graph using a predefined distance (or similarity) function based on the raw features of data samples and then they aim to learn node representations to preserve structural information of this affinity graph. For example, IsoMap (Tenenbaum et al., 2000) preserves the global geometry via geodesics, locally linear embedding (Roweis and Saul, 2000) and eigenmap (Belkin and Niyogi, 2003) preserve local neighborhoods in the affinity graph. The aforementioned methods often need to perform eigendecomposition on the affinity matrix (or adjacency matrix or Laplacian matrix). Thus, they are often computationally expensive. Matrix is one of the most popular approaches to denote graphs such as adjacency matrices, incidence matrices, and Laplacian matrices. As a result, matrix factorization can be naturally applied to learn node representations. Using the adjacency matrix to denote a graph as an example, it aims to embed nodes into a low-dimensional space where the new node representations can be utilized to reconstruct the adjacency matrix. A document corpus can be denoted as a bipartite graph where documents and words are nodes and an edge exists between a word and a document if the word appears in the document. Latent semantic indexing has employed truncated singular value decomposition to learn representations of documents and words (Deerwester et al., 1990). In recommender systems, interactions between users and items can be captured as a bipartite graph and matrix factorization has been employed to learn representations of users and items for recommendations (Koren et al., 2009). Matrix factorization is also leveraged to learn node representations for node classification (Zhu et al., 2007; Tang et al., 2016a), link prediction (Menon and Elkan, 2011; Tang et al., 2013a), and community detection (Wang et al., 2011). Actually, a family of modern graph embedding algorithms we will introduce later can also be unified as matrix factorization (Qiu et al., 2018b).

Word2vec is a technique to generate word embeddings (Mikolov et al., 2013). It takes a large corpus of text as input and produces a vector representation for each unique word in the corpus. The huge success of Word2vec in various natural language processing tasks has motivated increasing efforts to apply Word2vec, especially the SkipGram model, to learn node representations in the graph domain. DeepWalk (Perozzi et al., 2014) takes the first step to achieve this goal. Specifically, nodes in a given graph are treated as words of an artificial language and sentences in this language are generated by random walks on the graph. Then, it uses the SkipGram model to learn node representations, which preserves co-occurring nodes in these random walks. A large body of works have been developed in three major directions: (1) Developing advanced methods to preserve co-occurring nodes (Tang et al., 2015; Grover and Leskovec, 2016; Cao et al., 2015); (2) Preserving other types of information such as a node's structural role (Ribeiro et al., 2017), community information (Wang et al., 2017c), and node status (Ma et al., 2017; Lai et al., 2017; Gu et al., 2018); and (3) Designing frameworks for complex graphs such as directed graphs (Ou et al., 2016), heterogeneous graphs (Chang et al., 2015; Dong et al., 2017), bipartite graphs (Gao et al., 2018b), multidimensional graphs (Ma et al., 2018d), signed graphs (Wang et al., 2017b), hyper graphs (Tu et al., 2018), and dynamic graphs (Nguyen et al., 2018; Li et al., 2017a).

Given the power and the success of deep neural networks (DNNs) in representation learning, increasing efforts have been made to generalize DNNs to graphs. These methods are known as graph neural networks and can be roughly divided into spatial approaches and spectral approaches. Spatial approaches explicitly leverage the graph structure, such as spatially close neighbors, and the first spatial approach was introduced by Scarselli et al. in 2005. Spectral approaches utilize the spectral view of graphs by taking advantage of graph Fourier transform and the inverse graph Fourier transform (Bruna et al., 2013). In the era of deep learning, GNNs have been rapidly developed in the following aspects:

- A huge number of new GNN models have been introduced, including spectral approaches (Defferrard et al., 2016; Kipf and Welling, 2016a) and spatial approaches (Atwood and Towsley, 2016; Niepert et al., 2016; Gilmer et al., 2017; Monti et al., 2017; Veličković et al., 2017; Hamilton et al., 2017a).

- For graph-focused tasks such as graph classification, representation of the whole graph is desired. Thus, numerous pooling methods have been introduced to obtain the graph representation from node representations (Li et al., 2015; Ying et al., 2018c; Gao and Ji, 2019; Ma et al., 2019b).

- Traditional DNNs are vulnerable to adversarial attacks. GNNs inherit this drawback. A variety of graph adversarial attacks have been studied (Zügner et al., 2018; Zügner and Günnemann, 2019; Dai et al., 2018; Ma et al., 2020a) and various defense techniques have been developed (Dai et al., 2018; Zhu et al., 2019a; Tang et al., 2019; Jin et al., 2020b).

- As aforementioned, scalability is a pressing issue for GNNs. Many strategies have been studied to allow GNNs scale to large graphs (Chen et al., 2018a,b; Huang et al., 2018).
- GNN models have been designed to handle complex graphs such as heterogeneous graphs (Zhang et al., 2018b; Wang et al., 2019i; Chen et al., 2019b), bipartite graphs (He et al., 2019), multidimensional graphs (Ma et al., 2019c), signed graphs (Derr et al., 2018), hyper graphs (Feng et al., 2019b; Yadati et al., 2019), and dynamic graphs (Pareja et al., 2019).
- Diverse deep architectures have been generalized for graphs, such as autoencoder (Wang et al., 2016; Cao et al., 2016), variational autoencoder (Kipf and Welling, 2016b), recurrent neural networks (Tai et al., 2015; Liang et al., 2016), and generative adversarial networks (Wang et al., 2018a).
- Because graphs are a universal data representation, GNNs have been applied to advance a number of fields, such as natural language processing, computer vision, data mining, and health care.

1.6 Conclusion

In this chapter, we discuss the opportunities and challenges when we bridge deep learning with graphs that have motivated the focus of this book deep learning on graphs. The book will cover the essential topics of deep learning on graphs, which are organized into four parts to accommodate readers with diverse backgrounds and purposes for reading, including foundations, methods, applications, and advances. This book can benefit a wide range of readers, including senior undergraduate students, graduate students, practitioners, project managers, and researchers from various disciplines. To provide more context for readers, we give a brief historical review on the area of feature learning on graphs.

1.7 Further Reading

In this chapter, we have briefly reviewed the history of feature selection on graphs. If readers want to know more about feature selection, there are quite a few books (Liu and Motoda, 2007, 2012) and comprehensive surveys (Tang et al., 2014a). An open source feature selection repository scikit-feature has been developed that consists of most of the popular feature selection algorithms (Li et al., 2017b). This is the first comprehensive book on the topic of deep learning on graphs. There are books on the general topics of deep learning (Goodfellow et al., 2016; Aggarwal, 2018), deep learning on speech recognition (Yu and Deng, 2016; Kamath et al., 2019), and deep learning in natural language processing (Deng and Liu, 2018; Kamath et al., 2019).

Part I

Foundations

2

Foundations of Graphs

2.1 Introduction

Graphs, which describe pairwise relations between entities, are essential representations for real-world data from many different domains, including social science, linguistics, chemistry, biology, and physics. Graphs are widely utilized in social science to indicate the relations between individuals. In chemistry, chemical compounds are denoted as graphs with atoms as nodes and chemical bonds as edges (Bonchev, 1991). In linguistics, graphs are utilized to capture the syntax and compositional structures of sentences. Specifically, parsing trees are leveraged to represent the syntactic structure of a sentence according to some context-free grammar, and abstract meaning representation encodes the meaning of a sentence as a rooted and directed graph (Banarescu et al., 2013). Hence, research on graphs has attracted immense attention from multiple disciplines. In this chapter, we first introduce basic concepts of graphs and discuss the matrix representations of graphs including adjacency matrix and Laplacian matrix (Chung and Graham, 1997) and their key properties. Then we introduce attributed graphs where each node is associated with attributes and provide a new understanding on such graph by regarding the attributes as functions or signals on the graph (Shuman et al., 2013). We present the concepts of graph Fourier analysis and graph signal processing, which lay important foundations for deep learning on graphs. Next, we describe various complex graphs that are frequently utilized to capture complicated relations among entities in real-world applications. Finally, we discuss representative computational tasks on graphs that have been broadly served as downstream tasks for deep learning on graphs.

2.2 Graph Representations

In this section, we introduce the definition of graphs. We focus on simple unweighted graphs and will discuss more complex graphs in the following sections.

Definition 2.1 (Graph)   *A graph can be denoted as $G = \{V, \mathcal{E}\}$, where $V = \{v_1, \ldots, v_N\}$ is a set of $N = |V|$ nodes and $\mathcal{E} = \{e_1, \ldots, e_M\}$ is a set of M edges.*

Nodes are essential entities in a graph. In social graphs, users are viewed as nodes, whereas in chemical compound graphs, chemical atoms are treated as nodes. The size of a given graph G is defined by its number of nodes; i.e., $N = |V|$. The set of edges $\mathcal{E}$ describes the connections between nodes. An edge e_i connects two nodes $v_{e_i}^1$ and $v_{e_i}^2$; thus, the edge e_i can be also represented as $(v_{e_i}^1, v_{e_i}^2)$. In directed graphs, the edge is directed from node $v_{e_i}^1$ to node $v_{e_i}^2$. In undirected graphs, the order of the two nodes does not make a difference; i.e., $e_i = (v_{e_i}^1, v_{e_i}^2) = (v_{e_i}^2, v_{e_i}^1)$. Note that without specific mention, we limit our discussion to undirected graphs in this chapter. The nodes $v_{e_i}^1$ and $v_{e_i}^2$ are incident to the edge e_i. A node v_i is said to be adjacent to another node v_j if and only if there exists an edge between them. In social graphs, different relations such as friendship can be viewed as edges between nodes, whereas chemical bonds are considered as edges in chemical compound graphs (we simply regard all chemical bonds as edges while ignoring their different types). A graph $G = \{V, \mathcal{E}\}$ can be equivalently represented as an adjacency matrix, which describes the connectivity between the nodes.

Definition 2.2 (Adjacency Matrix)   *For a given graph $G = \{V, \mathcal{E}\}$, the corresponding adjacency matrix is denoted as $\mathbf{A} \in \{0, 1\}^{N \times N}$. The i, jth entry of the adjacency matrix $\mathbf{A}$, indicated as $\mathbf{A}_{i,j}$, represents the connectivity between two nodes v_i and v_j. More specifically, $\mathbf{A}_{i,j} = 1$ if v_i is adjacent to v_j; otherwise, $\mathbf{A}_{i,j} = 0$.*

In an undirected graph, a node v_i is adjacent to v_j if and only if v_j is adjacent to v_i; thus, $\mathbf{A}_{i,j} = \mathbf{A}_{j,i}$ holds for all v_i and v_j in the graph. Hence, for an undirected graph, its corresponding adjacency matrix is symmetric.

Example 2.3   An illustrative graph with five nodes and six edges is shown in Figure 2.1. In this graph, the set of nodes is represented as $V = \{v_1, v_2, v_3, v_4, v_5\}$, and the set of edges is $\mathcal{E} = \{e_1, e_2, e_3, e_4, e_5, e_6\}$. Its adjacency matrix can be denoted as follows:

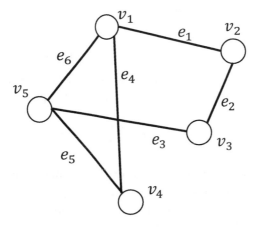

Figure 2.1 A graph with five nodes and six edges.

$$\mathbf{A} = \begin{pmatrix} 0 & 1 & 0 & 1 & 1 \\ 1 & 0 & 1 & 0 & 0 \\ 0 & 1 & 0 & 0 & 1 \\ 1 & 0 & 0 & 0 & 1 \\ 1 & 0 & 1 & 1 & 0 \end{pmatrix}. \qquad (2.1)$$

.

2.3 Properties and Measures

Graphs can have varied structures and properties. In this section, we discuss basic properties and measures for graphs.

2.3.1 Degree

The degree of a node v in a graph G indicates the frequency at which a node is adjacent to other nodes. We have the following formal definition.

Definition 2.4 (Degree) *In a graph $G = \{\mathcal{V}, \mathcal{E}\}$, the degree of a node $v_i \in \mathcal{V}$ is the number of nodes that are adjacent to v_i.*

$$d(v_i) = \sum_{v_j \in \mathcal{V}} \mathbb{1}_{\mathcal{E}}(\{v_i, v_j\}), \qquad (2.2)$$

where $\mathbb{1}_{\mathcal{E}}(\cdot)$ is an indicator function:

$$\mathbb{1}_{\mathcal{E}}(\{v_i, v_j\}) = \begin{cases} 1 & \text{if } (v_i, v_j) \in \mathcal{E}, \\ 0 & \text{if } (v_i, v_j) \notin \mathcal{E}. \end{cases} \tag{2.3}$$

The degree of a node v_i in G can also be calculated from its adjacency matrix. More specifically, for a node v_i, its degree can be computed as

$$d(v_i) = \sum_{j=1}^{N} \mathbf{A}_{i,j}. \tag{2.4}$$

Example 2.5   In the graph shown in Figure 2.1, the degree of node v_5 is 3, because it is adjacent to three other nodes (i.e., v_1, v_3, and v_4). Furthermore, the fifth row of the adjacency matrix has three nonzero elements, which also indicates that the degree of v_5 is 3.

Definition 2.6 (Neighbors)   *For a node v_i in a graph $G = \{V, \mathcal{E}\}$, the set of its neighbors $N(v_i)$ consists of all nodes that are adjacent to v_i.*

Note that for a node v_i, the number of nodes in $N(v_i)$ equals to its degree; i.e., $d(v_i) = |N(v_i)|$.

Theorem 2.7   *For a graph $G = \{V, \mathcal{E}\}$, its total degree–i.e., the summation of the degree of all nodes–is twice the number of edges in the graph:*

$$\sum_{v_i \in V} d(v_i) = 2 \cdot |\mathcal{E}|. \tag{2.5}$$

Proof

$$\sum_{v_i \in V} d(v_i) = \sum_{v_i \in V} \sum_{v_j \in V} \mathbb{1}_{\mathcal{E}}(\{v_i, v_j\})$$

$$= \sum_{\{v_i, v_j\} \in \mathcal{E}} 2 \cdot \mathbb{1}_{\mathcal{E}}(\{v_i, v_j\})$$

$$= 2 \cdot \sum_{\{v_i, v_j\} \in \mathcal{E}} \mathbb{1}_{\mathcal{E}}(\{v_i, v_j\})$$

$$= 2 \cdot |\mathcal{E}|$$

□

Corollary 2.8   *The number of nonzero elements in the adjacency matrix is also twice the number of the edges.*

Proof   The proof follows Theorem 2.7 by using Eq. (2.4).   □

Example 2.9   For the graph in Figure 2.1, the number of edges is six. The total degree is 12 and the number of nonzero elements in its adjacent matrix is also 12.

2.3.2 Connectivity

Connectivity is an important property of graphs. Before discussing connectivity in graphs, we first introduce some basic concepts such as walk and path.

Definition 2.10 (Walk)   *A walk on a graph is an alternating sequence of nodes and edges, starting with a node and ending with a node where each edge is incident with the nodes immediately preceding and following it.*

A walk starting at node u and ending at node v is called a u–v walk. The length of a walk is the number of edges in this walk. Note that u–v walks are not unique because there exist various u–v walks with different lengths.

Definition 2.11 (Trail)   *A trail is a walk whose edges are distinct.*

Definition 2.12 (Path)   *A path is a walk whose nodes are distinct.*

Example 2.13   In the graph shown in Figure 2.1, $(v_1, e_4, v_4, e_5, v_5, e_6, v_1, e_1, v_2)$ is a v_1–v_2 walk of length 4. It is a trail but not a path because it visits node v_1 twice. Meanwhile, $(v_1, e_1, v_2, e_2, v_3)$ is a v_1–v_3 walk. It is a trail as well as a path.

Theorem 2.14   *For a graph $\mathcal{G} = \{\mathcal{E}, \mathcal{V}\}$ with the adjacency matrix $\mathbf{A}$, we use $\mathbf{A}^n$ to denote the nth power of the adjacency matrix. The i, jth element of the matrix $\mathbf{A}^n$ equals to the number of v_i–v_j walks of length n.*

Proof   We can prove this theorem by induction. For $n - 1$, according to the definition of the adjacency matrix, when $\mathbf{A}_{i,j} = 1$, there is an edge between nodes v_i and v_j, which is regarded as a v_i–v_j walk of length 1. When $\mathbf{A}_{i,j} = 0$, there is no edge between v_i and v_j; thus, there is no v_i–v_j walk of length 1. Hence, the theorem holds for $n = 1$. Assume that the theorem holds when $n = k$. In other words, the i, hth element of $\mathbf{A}^k$ equals to the number of v_i–v_h walks of length k. We then proceed to prove the case when $n = k + 1$. Specifically, the i, jth element of $\mathbf{A}^{k+1}$ can be calculated by using $\mathbf{A}^k$ and $\mathbf{A}$ as

$$\mathbf{A}_{i,j}^{k+1} = \sum_{h=1}^{N} \mathbf{A}_{i,h}^k \cdot \mathbf{A}_{h,j}. \tag{2.6}$$

For each h in Eq. (2.6), the term $\mathbf{A}_{i,h}^k \cdot \mathbf{A}_{h,j}$ is nonzero only if both $\mathbf{A}_{i,h}^k$ and $\mathbf{A}_{h,j}$ are nonzero. We already know that $\mathbf{A}_{i,h}^k$ denotes the number of v_i–v_h walks of length k and $\mathbf{A}_{h,j}$ indicates the number of the v_h–v_j walk of length 1. Hence, the

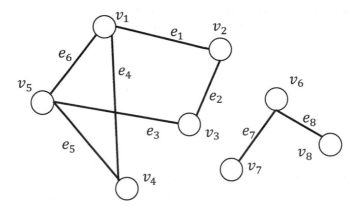

Figure 2.2 A graph with two connected components.

term $\mathbf{A}^k_{i,h} \cdot \mathbf{A}_{h,j}$ counts the number of v_i–v_j walks of length $k+1$ with v_h as the second to last node in the walk. Thus, when summing over all possible nodes v_h, the i, jth element of $\mathbf{A}^{k+1}$ equals to the number of v_i–v_j walks of length $k+1$, which completes the proof. $\qquad\qquad\qquad\qquad\qquad\qquad\qquad\qquad\qquad\square$

Definition 2.15 (Subgraph)   *A subgraph $\mathcal{G}' = \{\mathcal{V}', \mathcal{E}'\}$ of a given graph $\mathcal{G} = \{\mathcal{V}, \mathcal{E}\}$ is a graph formed with a subset of nodes $\mathcal{V}' \subset \mathcal{V}$ and a subset of edges $\mathcal{E}' \subset \mathcal{E}$. Furthermore, the subset $\mathcal{V}'$ must contain all of the nodes involved in the edges in the subset $\mathcal{E}'$.*

Example 2.16   For the graph in Figure 2.1, the subset of nodes $\mathcal{V}' = \{v_1, v_2, v_3, v_5\}$ and the subset of edges $\mathcal{E}' = \{e_1, e_3, e_3, e_6\}$ form a subgraph of the original graph $\mathcal{G}$.

Definition 2.17 (Connected Component)   *Given a graph $\mathcal{G} = \{\mathcal{V}, \mathcal{E}\}$, a subgraph $\mathcal{G}' = \{\mathcal{V}', \mathcal{E}'\}$ is said to be a connected component if there is at least one path between any pair of nodes in the subgraph and the nodes in $\mathcal{V}'$ are not adjacent to any nodes in $\mathcal{V}/\mathcal{V}'$.*

Example 2.18   A graph with two connected components is shown in Figure 2.2, where the left and right connected components are not connected to each other.

Definition 2.19 (Connected Graph)   *A graph $\mathcal{G} = \{\mathcal{V}, \mathcal{E}\}$ is said to be connected if it has exactly one component.*

Example 2.20   The graph in Figure 2.1 is a connected graph, whereas the graph in Figure 2.2 is not a connected graph.

Given a pair of nodes in a graph, there may exist multiple paths with different lengths between them. For example, there are three paths from node v_5 to node v_2 in the graph in Figure 2.1: $(v_5, e_6, v_1, e_1, v_2)$, $(v_5, e_5, v_4, e_4, v_1, e_1, v_2)$, and $(v_5, e_3, v_3, e_2, v_2)$. Among them, $(v_5, e_6, v_1, e_1, v_2)$ and $(v_5, e_3, v_3, e_2, v_2)$ with length 3 are the shortest paths from v_5 to v_2.

Definition 2.21 (Shortest Path) *Given a pair of nodes v_s, $v_t \in \mathcal{V}$ in graph $\mathcal{G}$, we denote the set of paths from node v_s to node v_t as $\mathcal{P}_{st}$. The shortest path between node v_s and node v_t is defined as*

$$p_{st}^{sp} = \arg\min_{p \in \mathcal{P}_{st}} |p|, \tag{2.7}$$

where p denotes a path in $\mathcal{P}_{st}$ with $|p|$ its length and p_{st}^{sp} indicates the shortest path. Note that there could be more than one shortest path between any given pair of nodes.

The shortest path between a pair of nodes describes important information between them. Collective information on the shortest paths between any pairs of nodes in a graph indicates important characteristics of the graph. Specifically, the diameter of a graph is defined as the length of the longest shortest path in the graph.

Definition 2.22 (Diameter) *Given a connected graph $\mathcal{G} = \{\mathcal{V}, \mathcal{E}\}$, its diameter is defined as follows:*

$$diameter(\mathcal{G}) = \max_{v_s, v_t \in \mathcal{V}} \min_{p \in \mathcal{P}_{st}} |p|. \tag{2.8}$$

Example 2.23 For the connected graph shown in Figure 2.1, its diameter is 3. In detail, the longest shortest paths are between node v_2 and node v_4.

2.3.3 Centrality

In a graph, the centrality of a node measures the importance of the node in the graph. There are different ways to measure the importance. In this section, we introduce various definitions of centrality.

Degree Centrality
Intuitively, a node can be considered important if there are many other nodes connected to it. Hence, we can measure the centrality of a given node based on its degree. In particular, for node v_i, its degree centrality can be defined as follows:

$$c_d(v_i) = d(v_i) = \sum_{j=1}^{N} \mathbf{A}_{i,j}. \tag{2.9}$$

Example 2.24 For the graph in Figure 2.1, the degree centrality for node v_1 and v_5 is 3, and the degree centrality for nodes v_2, v_3, and v_4 is 2.

Eigenvector Centrality

Though degree-based centrality considers a node with many neighbors as important, it treats all neighbors equally. However, the neighbors themselves can have different importance; thus, they could affect the importance of the central node differently. The eigenvector centrality (Bonacich, 1972, 2007) defines the centrality score of a given node v_i by considering the centrality scores of its neighboring nodes as

$$c_e(v_i) = \frac{1}{\lambda} \sum_{j=1}^{N} A_{i,j} \cdot c_e(v_j), \tag{2.10}$$

which can be rewritten in matrix form as

$$\mathbf{c}_e = \frac{1}{\lambda} \mathbf{A} \cdot \mathbf{c}_e, \tag{2.11}$$

where $\mathbf{c}_e \in \mathbb{R}^N$ is a vector containing the centrality scores of all nodes in the graph. We can rewrite Eq. (2.11) as

$$\lambda \cdot \mathbf{c}_e = \mathbf{A} \cdot \mathbf{c}_e. \tag{2.12}$$

Clearly, $\mathbf{c}_e$ is an eigenvector of the matrix $\mathbf{A}$ with its corresponding eigenvalue λ. However, given an adjacency matrix $\mathbf{A}$, there exist multiple pairs of eigenvectors and eigenvalues. Usually, we want the centrality scores to be positive. Hence, we wish to choose an eigenvector with all positive elements. According to the Perron–Frobenius theorem (Perron, 1907; Frobenius et al., 1912; Pillai et al., 2005), a real squared matrix with positive elements has a unique largest eigenvalue and its corresponding eigenvector has all positive elements. Thus, we can choose λ as the largest eigenvalue and its corresponding eigenvector as the centrality score vector.

Example 2.25 For the graph shown in Figure 2.1, its largest eigenvalue is 2.481 and its corresponding eigenvector is $[1, 0.675, 0.675, 0.806, 1]$. Hence, the eigenvector centrality scores for the nodes $[v_1, v_2, v_3, v_4, v_5]$ are $[1, 0.675, 0.675, 0.806, 1]$. Note that the degree of nodes v_2, v_3, and v_4 is 2; however, the eigenvector centrality of node v_4 is higher than that of the other two nodes because it directly connects to nodes v_1 and v_5, whose eigenvector centrality is high.

Katz Centrality

The Katz centrality is a variant of the eigencentrality, which not only considers the centrality scores of the neighbors but also includes a small constant for the central node itself. Specifically, the Katz centrality for a node v_i can be defined as:

$$c_k(v_i) = \alpha \sum_{j=1}^{N} \mathbf{A}_{i,j} c_k(v_j) + \beta, \qquad (2.13)$$

where β is a constant. The Katz centrality scores for all nodes can be expressed in matrix form as

$$\mathbf{c}_k = \alpha \mathbf{A} \mathbf{c}_k + \boldsymbol{\beta}$$
$$(I - \alpha \cdot \mathbf{A})\mathbf{c}_k = \boldsymbol{\beta}, \qquad (2.14)$$

where $\mathbf{c}_k \in \mathbb{R}^N$ denotes the Katz centrality score vector for all of the nodes and $\boldsymbol{\beta}$ is the vector containing the constant term β for all of the nodes. Note that the Katz centrality is equivalent to the eigencentrality if we set $\alpha = \frac{1}{\lambda_{max}}$ and $\beta = 0$, with λ_{max} the largest eigenvalue of the adjacency matrix $\mathbf{A}$. The choice of α is important: A large α may make the matrix $I - \alpha \cdot \mathbf{A}$ ill-conditioned but small α may make the centrality score useless because it will assign very similar scores close to β to all nodes. In practice, $\alpha < \frac{1}{\lambda_{max}}$ is often selected, which ensures that the matrix $I - \alpha \cdot \mathbf{A}$ is invertible and $\mathbf{c}_k$ can be calculated as

$$\mathbf{c}_k = (I - \alpha \cdot \mathbf{A})^{-1} \boldsymbol{\beta}. \qquad (2.15)$$

Example 2.26 For the graph shown in Figure 2.1, if we set $\beta = 1$ and $\alpha = \frac{1}{5}$, the Katz centrality score for nodes v_1 and v_5 is 2.16, for nodes v_2 and v_3 it is 1.79, and for node v_4 it is 1.87.

Betweenness Centrality

The aforementioned centrality scores are based on the connections to neighboring nodes. Another way to measure the importance of a node is to check whether it is at an important position in the graph. Specifically, if there are many paths passing through a node, it is at an important position in the graph. Formally, we define the betweenness centrality score for a node v_i as

$$C_b(v_i) = \sum_{v_s \neq v_i \neq v_t} \frac{\sigma_{st}(v_i)}{\sigma_{st}}, \qquad (2.16)$$

where σ_{st} denotes the total number of shortest paths from node v_s to node v_t and $\sigma_{st}(v_i)$ indicates the number of these paths passing through node v_i.

As suggested by Eq. (2.16), we need to compute the summation over all possible pairs of nodes for the betweenness centrality score. Therefore, the magnitude of the betweenness centrality score scales as the size of graph scales. Hence, to make the betweenness centrality score comparable across different graphs, we need to normalize it. One effective way is to divide the betweenness score by the largest possible betweenness centrality score given a graph. The maximum of the betweenness score in Eq. (2.16) can be reached when all of the shortest paths between any pair of nodes passing through the node v_i. That is, $\frac{\sigma_{st}(v_i)}{\sigma_{st}} = 1$, $\forall v_s \neq v_i \neq v_t$. There are, in total, $\frac{(N-1)(N-2)}{2}$ pairs of nodes in an undirected graph. Hence, the maximum betweenness centrality score is $\frac{(N-1)(N-2)}{2}$. We then define the normalized betweenness centrality score $c_{nb}(v_i)$ for the node v_i as

$$c_{nb}(v_i) = \frac{2 \sum\limits_{v_s \neq v_i \neq v_t} \frac{\sigma_{st}(v_i)}{\sigma_{st}}}{(N-1)(N-2)}. \tag{2.17}$$

Example 2.27   For the graph shown in Figure 2.1, the betweenness centrality score for nodes v_1 and v_5 is $\frac{3}{2}$ and their normalized betweenness score is $\frac{1}{4}$. The betweenness centrality score for nodes v_2 and v_3 is $\frac{1}{2}$ and their normalized betweenness score is $\frac{1}{12}$. The betweenness centrality score for node v_4 is 0 and its normalized score is also 0.

2.4 Spectral Graph Theory

Spectral graph theory studies the properties of a graph through analyzing the eigenvalues and eigenvectors of its Laplacian matrix. In this section, we first introduce the Laplacian matrix of a graph and then discuss the key properties of the Laplacian matrix and its eigenvalues and eigenvectors.

2.4.1 Laplacian Matrix

In this subsection, we introduce the Laplacian matrix of a graph, which is another matrix representation for graphs in addition to the adjacency matrix.

Definition 2.28 (Laplacian Matrix)   *For a given graph $G = \{V, \mathcal{E}\}$ with $\mathbf{A}$ as its adjacency matrix, its Laplacian matrix is defined as*

$$\mathbf{L} = \mathbf{D} - \mathbf{A}, \tag{2.18}$$

where $\mathbf{D}$ is a diagonal degree matrix $\mathbf{D} = diag(d(v_1), \ldots, d(v_{|V|}))$.

Another definition of the Laplacian matrix is a normalized version of Eq. (2.18).

Definition 2.29 (Normalized Laplacian Matrix)   *For a given graph $\mathcal{G} = \{\mathcal{V}, \mathcal{E}\}$ with $\mathbf{A}$ as its adjacency matrix, its normalized Laplacian matrix is defined as*

$$\mathbf{L} = \mathbf{D}^{-\frac{1}{2}}(\mathbf{D} - \mathbf{A})\mathbf{D}^{-\frac{1}{2}} = \mathbf{I} - \mathbf{D}^{-\frac{1}{2}}\mathbf{A}\mathbf{D}^{-\frac{1}{2}}. \qquad (2.19)$$

Next, we focus on the discussion of the (unnormalized) Laplacian matrix as defined in Definition 2.28. However, in some later chapters of this book, the normalized Laplacian matrix will also be utilized. Unless specifically mentioned, we refer to the Laplacian matrix as the unnormalized one defined in Definition 2.28.

Note that the Laplacian matrix is symmetric because both the degree matrix $\mathbf{D}$ and the adjacency matrix $\mathbf{A}$ are symmetric. Let $\mathbf{f}$ denote a vector where its ith element $\mathbf{f}[i]$ is associated with node v_i. Multiplying $\mathbf{L}$ by $\mathbf{f}$, we can get a new vector $\mathbf{h}$ as

$$\mathbf{h} = \mathbf{Lf}$$
$$= (\mathbf{D} - \mathbf{A})\mathbf{f}$$
$$= \mathbf{Df} - \mathbf{Af}.$$

The ith element of $\mathbf{h}$ can be represented as

$$\mathbf{h}[i] = d(v_i) \cdot \mathbf{f}[i] - \sum_{j=1}^{N} \mathbf{A}_{i,j} \cdot \mathbf{f}[i]$$
$$= d(v_i) \cdot \mathbf{f}[i] - \sum_{v_j \in \mathcal{N}(v_i)} \mathbf{A}_{i,j} \cdot \mathbf{f}[i]$$
$$= \sum_{v_j \in \mathcal{N}(v_i)} (\mathbf{f}[i] - \mathbf{f}[j]). \qquad (2.20)$$

As informed by Eq. (2.20), $\mathbf{h}[i]$ is the summation of the differences between node v_i and its neighbors. We next calculate $\mathbf{f}^T\mathbf{Lf}$ as follows:

$$\mathbf{f}^T\mathbf{Lf} = \sum_{v_i \in \mathcal{V}} \mathbf{f}[i] \sum_{v_j \in \mathcal{N}(v_i)} (\mathbf{f}[i] - \mathbf{f}[j])$$
$$= \sum_{v_i \in \mathcal{V}} \sum_{v_j \in \mathcal{N}(v_i)} (\mathbf{f}[i] \cdot \mathbf{f}[i] - \mathbf{f}[i] \cdot \mathbf{f}[j])$$
$$= \sum_{v_i \in \mathcal{V}} \sum_{v_j \in \mathcal{N}(v_i)} (\frac{1}{2}\mathbf{f}[i] \cdot \mathbf{f}[i] - \mathbf{f}[i] \cdot \mathbf{f}[j] + \frac{1}{2}\mathbf{f}[j] \cdot \mathbf{f}[j])$$
$$= \frac{1}{2} \sum_{v_i \in \mathcal{V}} \sum_{v_j \in \mathcal{N}(v_i)} (\mathbf{f}[i] - \mathbf{f}[j])^2. \qquad (2.21)$$

Thus, $\mathbf{f}^T\mathbf{Lf}$ is the sum of the squares of the differences between adjacent nodes. In other words, it measures how different the values of adjacent nodes are. It is easy to verify that $\mathbf{f}^T\mathbf{Lf}$ is always nonnegative for any possible choice of a non-zero real vector **f**, which indicates that the Laplacian matrix is positive semi-definite.

2.4.2 The Eigenvalues and Eigenvectors of the Laplacian Matrix

In this subsection, we discuss main properties of eigenvalues and eigenvectors of the Laplacian matrix.

Theorem 2.30   *For a graph $G = \{V, E\}$, the eigenvalues of its Laplacian matrix **L** are nonnegative.*

Proof   Suppose that λ is an eigenvalue of the Laplacian matrix **L** and **u** is the corresponding normalized eigenvector. According to the definition of eigenvalues and eigenvectors, we have $\lambda\mathbf{u} = \mathbf{L}\mathbf{u}$. Note that **u** is a nonzero unit vector and we have $\mathbf{u}^T\mathbf{u} = 1$. Then,

$$\lambda = \lambda\mathbf{u}^T\mathbf{u} = \mathbf{u}^T\lambda\mathbf{u} = \mathbf{u}^T\mathbf{L}\mathbf{u} \geq 0. \tag{2.22}$$

□

For a graph G with N nodes, there are, in total, N eigenvalues/eigenvectors (with multiplicity). According to Theorem 2.30, all of the eigenvalues are non-negative. Furthermore, there always exists an eigenvalue that equals 0. Let us consider the vector $\mathbf{u}_1 = \frac{1}{\sqrt{N}}(1, \ldots, 1)$. Using Eq. (2.20), we can easily verify that $\mathbf{L}\mathbf{u}_1 = \mathbf{0} = 0\mathbf{u}_1$, which indicates that $\mathbf{u}_1$ is an eigenvector corresponding to the eigenvalue 0. For convenience, we arrange these eigenvalues in non-decreasing order as $0 = \lambda_1 \leq \lambda_2 \leq, \ldots, \leq \lambda_N$. The corresponding normalized eigenvectors are denoted as $\mathbf{u}_1, \ldots, \mathbf{u}_N$.

Theorem 2.31   *Given a graph G, the number of 0 eigenvalues of its Laplacian matrix **L** (the multiplicity of the 0 eigenvalue) equals the number of connected components in the graph.*

Proof   Suppose that there are K connected components in the graph G. We can partition the set of nodes V into K disjoint subsets $V_1, \ldots, V_K$. We first show that there exist at least K orthogonal eigenvectors that correspond to the eigenvalue 0. Construct K vectors $\mathbf{u}_1, \ldots, \mathbf{u}_K$ such that $\mathbf{u}_i[j] = \frac{1}{\sqrt{|V_i|}}$ if $v_j \in V_i$ and 0 otherwise. We have that $\mathbf{L}\mathbf{u}_i = 0$ for $i = 1, \ldots, K$, which indicates that all of the K vectors are the eigenvectors of **L** corresponding to eigenvalue 0. Furthermore, it is easy to validate that $\mathbf{u}_i^T\mathbf{u}_j = 0$ if $i \neq j$, which means that these K eigenvectors are orthogonal to each other. Hence, the multiplicity of the 0 eigenvalue is at least K. We next show that there are at most K orthogonal eigenvectors corresponding to the eigenvalue 0. Assume that there exists another eigenvector $\mathbf{u}^*$ corresponding to the eigenvalue 0, which is orthogonal to all of the K aforementioned eigenvectors. Because $\mathbf{u}^*$ is nonzero, there must exist an element in $\mathbf{u}^*$ that is nonzero. Let us assume that the element is $\mathbf{u}^*[d]$ associated with node $v_d \in \mathcal{V}_i$. Furthermore, according to Eq. (2.21), we have

$$\mathbf{u}^{*T}\mathbf{L}\mathbf{u}^* = \frac{1}{2} \sum_{v_i \in \mathcal{V}} \sum_{v_j \in \mathcal{N}(v_i)} (\mathbf{u}^*[i] - \mathbf{u}^*[j])^2. \tag{2.23}$$

To ensure $\mathbf{u}^{*T}\mathbf{L}\mathbf{u}^* = 0$, the values of nodes in the same component must be the same. This indicates that all nodes in $\mathcal{V}_i$ have the same value $\mathbf{u}^*[d]$ as node v_d. Hence, $\mathbf{u}_i^T\mathbf{u}^* > 0$. This means $\mathbf{u}^*$ is not orthogonal to $\mathbf{u}_i$, which leads to a contradiction. Therefore, there is no more eigenvector corresponding to the eigenvalue 0 beyond the K vectors we have constructed. $\square$

2.5 Graph Signal Processing

In many real-world graphs, there are often features or attributes associated with the nodes. This kind of graph structured data can be viewed as graph signals, which capture both the structure information (or connectivity between nodes) and data (or attributes at nodes). A graph signal consists of a graph $\mathcal{G} = \{\mathcal{V}, \mathcal{E}\}$ and a mapping function f defined on the node domain, which maps the nodes to real values. Mathematically, the mapping function can be represented as

$$f : \mathcal{V} \to \mathbb{R}^d, \tag{2.24}$$

where d is the dimension of the value (vector) associated with each node. Without loss of generality, in this section, we set $d - 1$ and denote the mapped values for all nodes as $\mathbf{f}$ with $\mathbf{f}[i]$ corresponding to node v_i.

Example 2.32   A graph signal is shown in Figure 2.3, where the color of a node represents its associated value with smaller values tending toward blue and larger values tending toward red.

A graph is smooth if the values in connected nodes are similar. A smooth graph signal is low frequency, because the values change slowly across the graph via the edges. The Laplacian matrix quadratic form in Eq. (2.21) can be utilized to measure the smoothness (or the frequency) of a graph signal $\mathbf{f}$ because it is the summation of the square of the difference between all pairs of connected nodes. Specifically, when a graph signal $\mathbf{f}$ is smooth, $\mathbf{f}^T\mathbf{L}\mathbf{f}$ is small. The value $\mathbf{f}^T\mathbf{L}\mathbf{f}$ is called the smoothness (or the frequency) of the signal $\mathbf{f}$.

In the classical signal processing setting, a signal can be denoted in two domains; i.e., the time domain and the frequency domain. Similarly, the graph

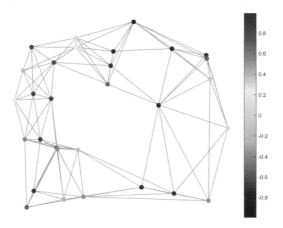

Figure 2.3 A one-dimensional graph signal.

signal can also be represented in two domains; i.e., the spatial domain, which we just introduced, and the spectral domain (or frequency domain). The spectral domain of graph signals is based on the graph Fourier transform. It is built upon the spectral graph theory that we introduced in the previous section.

2.5.1 Graph Fourier Transform

The classical Fourier transform (Bracewell, n.d.)

$$\hat{f}(\xi) =< f(t), \exp(-2\pi it\xi) >= \int_{\infty}^{\infty} f(t)\exp(-2\pi it\xi)dt \qquad (2.25)$$

decomposes a signal $f(t)$ into a series of complex exponentials $\exp(-2\pi it\xi)$ for any real number ξ, where ξ can be viewed as the frequency of the corresponding exponential. These exponentials are the eigenfunctions of the one-dimensional Laplace operator (or the second-order differential operator) because we have

$$\nabla(\exp(-2\pi it\xi)) = \frac{\partial^2}{\partial t^2}\exp(-2\pi it\xi)$$

$$= \frac{\partial}{\partial t}(-2\pi i\xi)\exp(-2\pi it\xi)$$

$$= -(2\pi i\xi)^2\exp(-2\pi it\xi). \qquad (2.26)$$

Analogously, the graph Fourier transform for a graph signal $\mathbf{f}$ on graph $\mathcal{G}$ can be represented as

$$\hat{\mathbf{f}}[l] = <\mathbf{f}, \mathbf{u}_l> = \sum_{i=1}^{N} \mathbf{f}[i]\mathbf{u}_l[i], \qquad (2.27)$$

where $\mathbf{u}_l$ is the lth eigenvector of the Laplacian matrix $\mathbf{L}$ of the graph. The corresponding eigenvalue λ_l represents the frequency or the smoothness of the eigenvector $\mathbf{u}_l$. The vector $\hat{\mathbf{f}}$ with $\hat{\mathbf{f}}[l]$ as its lth element is the graph Fourier transform of $\mathbf{f}$. The eigenvectors are the graph Fourier basis of the graph $\mathcal{G}$, and $\hat{\mathbf{f}}$ consists of the graph Fourier coefficients corresponding to this basis for a signal $\mathbf{f}$. The graph Fourier transform of $\mathbf{f}$ can be also denoted in matrix form as

$$\hat{\mathbf{f}} = \mathbf{U}^T\mathbf{f}, \qquad (2.28)$$

where the lth column of the matrix $\mathbf{U}$ is $\mathbf{u}_l$.

As suggested by the following equation:

$$\mathbf{u}_l^T\mathbf{L}\mathbf{u}_l = \lambda_l \cdot \mathbf{u}_l^T\mathbf{u}_l = \lambda_l, \qquad (2.29)$$

the eigenvalue λ_l measures the smoothness of the corresponding eigenvector $\mathbf{u}_l$. More specifically, the eigenvectors associated with small eigenvalues vary slowly across the graph; i.e., the values of the eigenvector at connected nodes are similar. Thus, these eigenvectors are smooth and change with low frequency across the graph. However, the eigenvectors corresponding to large eigenvalues may have very different values on two nodes even if they are connected. An extreme example is the first eigenvector $\mathbf{u}_1$ associated with the eigenvalue 0: It is constant over all of the nodes, which indicates that its value does not change across the graph. Hence, it is extremely smooth and has extremely low frequency 0. These eigenvectors are the graph Fourier basis for the graph G and their corresponding eigenvalues indicate their frequencies. The graph Fourier transform as shown in Eq. (2.28) can be regarded as a process to decompose an input signal $\mathbf{f}$ into graph Fourier basis with different frequencies. The obtained coefficients $\hat{\mathbf{f}}$ denote how much the corresponding graph Fourier basis contributes to the input signal.

Example 2.33 Figure 2.4 shows the frequencies of the Fourier basis of the graph shown in Figure 2.3.

The graph Fourier coefficients $\hat{\mathbf{f}}$ are the representation of the signal $\mathbf{f}$ in the spectral domain. There is also the inverse graph Fourier transform, which can transform the spectral representation $\hat{\mathbf{f}}$ to the spatial representation $\mathbf{f}$ as

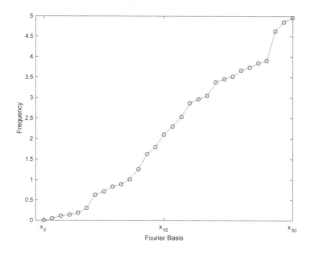

Figure 2.4 Frequencies of Fourier basis.

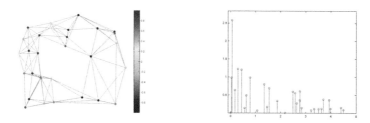

(a) A graph signal in the spatial domain   (b) A graph signal in the spectral domain

Figure 2.5 Representations of a graph signal in both spatial and spectral domains.

$$\mathbf{f}[i] = \sum_{l=1}^{N} \hat{f}[l]\mathbf{u}_l[i]. \qquad (2.30)$$

This process can also be represented in the matrix form as follows

$$\mathbf{f} = \mathbf{U}\hat{\mathbf{f}}. \qquad (2.31)$$

In summary, a graph signal can be denoted in two domains; i.e., the spatial domain and the spectral domain. The representations in the two domains can be transformed to each other via the graph Fourier transform and the inverse graph Fourier transform, respectively.

Example 2.34 Figure 2.5 shows a graph signal in both the spatial and spectral domains. Specifically, Figure 2.5a shows the graph signal in the spatial domain and Figure 2.5b illustrates the same graph signal in the spectral domain. In Figure 2.5b, the x-axis is the graph Fourier basis and the y-axis indicates the corresponding graph Fourier coefficients.

2.6 Complex Graphs

In the earlier sections, we introduced simple graphs and their key properties. However, graphs in real-world applications are much more complicated. In this section, we briefly describe popular complex graphs with formal definitions.

2.6.1 Heterogeneous Graphs

The simple graphs we have discussed are homogeneous, which only contain one type of node as well as a single type of edge. However, in many real-world applications, we want to model multiple types of relations between multiple types of nodes. As shown in Figure 2.6, in an academic network describing publications and citations, there are three types of nodes, including authors, papers, and venues. There are also various kinds of edges describing different relations between the nodes. For example, there exist edges describing the citation relations between papers or edges denoting the authorship relations between authors and papers. Next, we formally give a definition of heterogeneous graphs.

Definition 2.35 (Heterogeneous Graphs) *A heterogeneous graph $\mathcal{G}$ consists of a set of nodes $\mathcal{V} = \{v_1, \ldots, v_N\}$ and a set of edges $\mathcal{E} = \{e_1, \ldots, e_N\}$ where each node and each edge are associated with a type. Let $\mathcal{T}_n$ denote the set of node types and $\mathcal{T}_e$ indicate the set of edge types. There are two mapping functions $\phi_n : \mathcal{V} \to \mathcal{T}_n$ and $\phi_e : \mathcal{V} \to \mathcal{T}_e$ that map each node and each edge to their types, respectively.*

2.6.2 Bipartite Graphs

In a bipartite graph $\mathcal{G} = \{\mathcal{V}, \mathcal{E}\}$, its node set $\mathcal{V}$ can be divided into two disjoint subsets $\mathcal{V}_1$ and $\mathcal{V}_2$ where every edge in $\mathcal{E}$ connects a node in $\mathcal{V}_1$ to a node in $\mathcal{V}_2$. Bipartite graphs are widely used to capture interactions between different objects. For example, as shown in Figure 2.7, in many e-commerce platforms

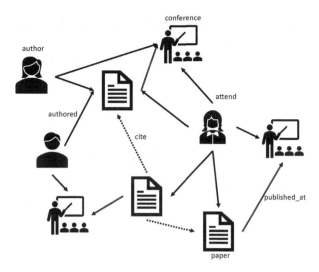

Figure 2.6 A heterogeneous academic graph.

such as Amazon, the click history of users can be modeled as a bipartite graph where the users and items are the two disjoint node sets and users' click behaviors form the edges between them. Next, we formally define bipartite graphs.

Definition 2.36 (Bipartite Graph)   *Given a graph $\mathcal{G} = \{\mathcal{V}, \mathcal{E}\}$, it is bipartite if and only if $\mathcal{V} = \mathcal{V}_1 \cup \mathcal{V}_2$, $\mathcal{V}_1 \cap \mathcal{V}_2 = \emptyset$ and $v_e^1 \in \mathcal{V}_1$ and $v_e^2 \in \mathcal{V}_2$ for all $e = (v_e^1, v_e^2) \in \mathcal{E}$.*

2.6.3 Multidimensional Graphs

In many real-world graphs, multiple relations can simultaneously exist between a pair of nodes. One example of such graph can be found at the popular video-sharing site YouTube, where users can be viewed as nodes. YouTube users can subscribe to each other, which can be viewed as one relation. Users can be connected via other relations such as "sharing" or "commenting" on videos from other users. Another example is from e-commerce sites such as Amazon where users can interact with items through various types of behaviors such as "click," "purchase," and "comment." These graphs with multiple relations can be naturally modeled as multidimensional graphs by regarding each type of relation as one dimension.

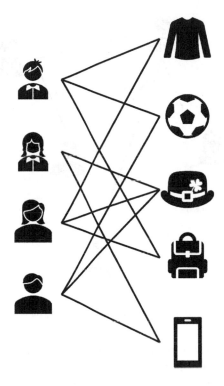

Figure 2.7 An e-commerce bipartite graph.

Definition 2.37 (Multidimensional graph) *A multidimensional graph consists of a set of N nodes $\mathcal{V} = \{v_1, \ldots, v_N\}$ and D sets of edges $\{\mathcal{E}_1, \ldots, \mathcal{E}_D\}$. Each edge set $\mathcal{E}_d$ describes the dth type of relation between the nodes in the corresponding dth dimension. These D types of relations can also be expressed by D adjacency matrices $\mathbf{A}^{(1)}, \ldots, \mathbf{A}^{(D)}$. In the dimension d, its corresponding adjacency matrix $\mathbf{A}_d \in \mathbb{R}^{N \times N}$ describes the edges $\mathcal{E}_d$ between nodes in $\mathcal{V}$. Specifically, the i, jth element of $\mathbf{A}_d$, denoted as $\mathbf{A}_d[i, j]$, equals 1 only when there is an edge between nodes v_i and v_j in the dimension d (or $(v_i, v_j) \in \mathcal{E}_d$) and otherwise 0.*

2.6.4 Signed Graphs

Signed graphs, which contain both positive and negative edges, have become increasingly ubiquitous with the growing popularity of online social networks. Examples of signed graphs are from online social networks such as Facebook and Twitter, where users can block or unfollow other users. The behavior

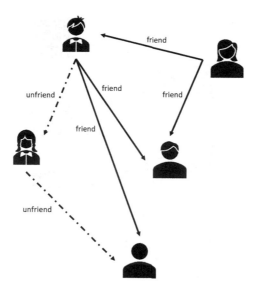

Figure 2.8 An illustrative signed graph.

of "block" can be viewed as negative edges between users. In addition, the behavior of "unfriend" can also be treated as negative edges. An illustrative example of a signed graph is shown in Figure 2.8, where users are nodes and unfriend and friend relations are the "negative" and "positive" edges, respectively. Next, we give the formal definition of signed graphs.

Definition 2.38 (Signed Graphs)   *Let $\mathcal{G} = \{\mathcal{V}, \mathcal{E}^+, \mathcal{E}^-\}$ be a signed graph, where $\mathcal{V} = \{v_1, \ldots, v_N\}$ is the set of N nodes and $\mathcal{E}^+ \subset \mathcal{V} \times \mathcal{V}$ and $\mathcal{E}^- \subset \mathcal{V} \times \mathcal{V}$ denote the sets of positive and negative edges, respectively. Note that an edge can only be either positive or negative; i.e., $\mathcal{E}^+ \cap \mathcal{E}^- = \emptyset$. These positive and negative edges between nodes can also be described by a signed adjacency matrix $\mathbf{A}$, where $\mathbf{A}_{i,j} = 1$ only when there is a positive edge between node v_i and node v_j and $\mathbf{A}_{i,j} = -1$ denotes a negative edge; otherwise, $\mathbf{A}_{i,j} = 0$.*

2.6.5 Hypergraphs

The graphs we introduced so far only encode pairwise information via edges. However, in many real-world applications, relations are beyond pairwise associations. Figure 2.9 demonstrates a hypergraph describing the relations between papers. A specific author can publish more than two papers. Thus, the author can be viewed as a hyperedge connecting multiple papers (or nodes).

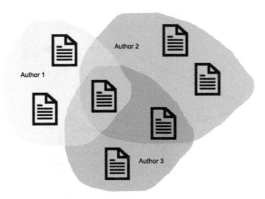

Figure 2.9 An illustrative hypergraph.

Compared with edges in simple graphs, hyperedges can encode higher-order relations. The graphs with hyperedges are called hypergraphs. Next, we give the formal definition of hypergraphs.

Definition 2.39 (Hypergraphs)   *Let $G = \{V, \mathcal{E}, \mathbf{W}\}$ be a hypergraph, where V is a set of N nodes, $\mathcal{E}$ is a set of hyperedges, and $\mathbf{W} \in \mathbb{R}^{|\mathcal{E}| \times |\mathcal{E}|}$ is a diagonal matrix with $\mathbf{W}[j, j]$ denoting the weight of the hyperedge e_j. The hypergraph G can be described by an incidence matrix $\mathbf{H} \in \mathbb{R}^{|V| \times |\mathcal{E}|}$, where $\mathbf{H}_{i,j} = 1$ only when the node v_i is incident to the edge e_j. For a vertex v_i, its degree is defined as $d(v_i) = \sum_{j=1}^{|\mathcal{E}|} \mathbf{H}_{i,j}$, and the degree for a hyperedge is defined as $d(e_j) = \sum_{i=1}^{|V|} \mathbf{H}_{i,j}$. Furthermore, we use $\mathbf{D}_e$ and $\mathbf{D}_v$ to denote the diagonal matrices of the edge and vertex degrees, respectively.*

2.6.6 Dynamic Graphs

The aforementioned graphs are static where the connections between nodes are fixed when observed. However, in many real-world applications, graphs are constantly evolving as new nodes are added to the graph and new edges are continuously emerging. For example, in online social networks such as friendship on Facebook, users can constantly establish friendships with others and new users can also join Facebook at anytime. These kinds of evolving graphs can be modeled as dynamic graphs where each node or each edge in the graph is associated with a timestamp. An illustrative example of dynamic graphs is shown in Figure 2.10, where each edge is associated with a timestamp

Foundations of Graphs

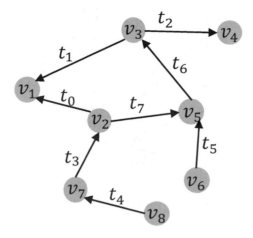

Figure 2.10 An illustrative example of dynamic graphs.

and the timestamp of a node is when the very first edge involves the node. Next, we give a formal definition of dynamic graphs.

Definition 2.40 (Dynamic Graphs) *A dynamic graph $G = \{\mathcal{V}, \mathcal{E}\}$ consists of a set of nodes $\mathcal{V} = \{v_1, \ldots, v_N\}$ and a set of edges $\mathcal{E} = \{e_1, \ldots, e_M\}$ where each node and/or each edge is associated with a timestamp indicating the time it emerged. Specifically, we have two mapping functions ϕ_v and ϕ_e mapping each node and each edge to their emerging timestamps, respectively.*

In reality, we may not be able to record the timestamp of each node and/or each edge. Instead, we only check from time to time to observe how the graph evolves. At each observation timestamp t, we can record the snapshot of the graph G_t as the observation. We refer to this kind of dynamic graph as a discrete dynamic graph, which consists of multiple graph snapshots. We formally define the discrete dynamic graph as follows.

Definition 2.41 (Discrete Dynamic Graphs) *A discrete dynamic graph consists of T graph snapshots, which are observed along with the evolution of a dynamic graph. Specifically, T graph snapshots can be denoted as $\{G_0, \ldots, G_T\}$ where G_0 is the graph observed at time 0.*

2.7 Computational Tasks on Graphs

There are a variety of computational tasks proposed for graphs. These tasks can be mainly divided into two categories: (1) node-focused tasks where the entire data are usually represented as one graph with nodes as the data samples; and (2) graph-focused tasks, where data often consist of a set of graphs and each data sample is a graph. In this section, we briefly introduce representative tasks for each group.

2.7.1 Node-Focused Tasks

Numerous node-focused tasks have been extensively studied, such as node classification, node ranking, link prediction, and community detection. Next we discuss two representative tasks including node classification and link prediction.

Node classification

In many real-world graphs, nodes are associated with useful information, which is often treated as labels of these nodes. For example, in social networks, such information can be demographic properties of users such as age, sex, and occupation or users' interests and hobbies. These labels usually help characterize the nodes and can be leveraged for many important applications. For example, on social media such as Facebook, labels related to interests and hobbies can be utilized to recommend relevant items (i.e., news and events) to their users. However, in reality, it is often difficult to get a full set of labels for all nodes. For example, less than 1% of Facebook users provide their complete demographic profiles. Hence, we are likely given a graph where only a part of the nodes are associated with labels and we want to infer the labels for those nodes without labels. This motivates the problem of node classification on graphs.

Definition 2.42 (Node classification) *Let $\mathcal{G} = \{\mathcal{V}, \mathcal{E}\}$ denote a graph with $\mathcal{V}$ the set of nodes and $\mathcal{E}$ the set of edges. Some of nodes in $\mathcal{V}$ are associated with labels, and the set of these labeled nodes is represented as $\mathcal{V}_l \subset \mathcal{V}$. The remaining nodes do not have labels, and this set of unlabeled nodes is denoted as $\mathcal{V}_u$. Specifically, we have $\mathcal{V}_l \cup \mathcal{V}_u = \mathcal{V}$ and $\mathcal{V}_l \cap \mathcal{V}_u = \emptyset$. The goal of the node classification task is to learn a mapping ϕ by leveraging $\mathcal{G}$ and labels of $\mathcal{V}_l$, which can predict the labels of unlabeled nodes (or $v \in \mathcal{V}_u$).*

The above definition is for simple graphs and can be easily extended to graphs with attributes and complex graphs introduced in Section 2.6.

Example 2.43 (Node Classification in Flickr) Flickr is an image-hosting platform that allows users to host their personal photos. It also serves as an online social community where users can follow each other. Hence, users on Flickr and their connections form a graph. Furthermore, users on Flickr can subscribe to interest groups such as Black and White, The Fog and The Rain, and Dog World. These subscriptions indicate the interest of users and can be used as their labels. A user can subscribe to multiple groups. Hence, each user can be associated with multiple labels. A multilabel node classification problem on graphs can help predict the potential groups that users are interested in but have not yet subscribed to. Such data sets for Flickr can be found in Tang and Liu (2009).

Link Prediction

In many real-world applications, graphs are not complete with missing edges. On the one hand, some of the connections exist but they are not observed or recorded, which leads to missing edges in the observed graphs. On the other hand, many graphs are naturally evolving. On social media such as Facebook, users can always become friends with other users. In academic collaboration graphs, a given author can always build new collaboration relations with other authors. Inferring or predicting these missing edges can benefit many applications such as friend recommendations (Adamic and Adar, 2003), knowledge graph completion (Nickel et al., 2015), and criminal intelligence analysis (Berlusconi et al., 2016). Next, we give the formal definition of the link prediction problem.

Definition 2.44 (Link Prediction) *Let $G = \{\mathcal{V}, \mathcal{E}\}$ denote a graph with $\mathcal{V}$ its set of nodes and $\mathcal{E}$ its set of edges. Let M denote all possible edges between the nodes in $\mathcal{V}$. Then, we denote the complementary set of $\mathcal{E}$ with respect to M as $\mathcal{E}' = M - \mathcal{E}$. The set $\mathcal{E}'$ contains the unobserved edges between the nodes. The goal of the link prediction task is to predict the most likely edges. Specifically, a score can be assigned to each of the edges in $\mathcal{E}'$, which indicates how likely it exists or will emerge in the future.*

Note that the definition is stated for simple graphs and can be easily extended to complex graphs introduced in Section 2.6. For example, for signed graphs, in addition to the existence of an edge, we want to predict its sign. For hypergraphs, we want to infer hyperedges that describe the relations between multiple nodes.

Example 2.45 (Predicting Emerging Collaboration in the DBLP website) DBLP is an online computer science bibliography website that hosts a comprehensive list of research papers in computer science. A co-authorship graph can be constructed from the papers in DBLP where the authors are the nodes and authors can be considered as connected if they have co-authored at least one paper as recorded in DBLP. Predicting what new collaborations between authors who never co-authored before is an interesting link prediction problem. A large DBLP collaboration data set for link prediction research can be found in Yang and Leskovec (2015).

2.7.2 Graph-Focused Tasks

There are numerous graph-focused tasks such as graph classification, graph matching, and graph generation. Next we discuss the most representative graph-focused task; i.e., graph classification.

Graph Classification

Node classification treats each node in a graph as a data sample and aims to assign labels to these unlabeled nodes. In some applications, each sample can be represented as a graph. In chemoinformatics, chemical molecules can be denoted as graphs where atoms are the nodes and chemical bonds between them are the edges. These chemical molecules may have different properties such as solubility and toxicity, which can be treated as their labels. In reality, we may want to automatically predict these properties for newly discovered chemical molecules. This goal can be achieved by the task of graph classification, which aims to predict the labels for unlabeled graphs. Due to the complexity of graph structures, graph classification cannot be carried out by traditional classification, which calls for dedicated efforts. Next, we provide a formal definition of graph classification.

Definition 2.46 (Graph Classification) *Given a set of labeled graphs $\mathcal{D} = \{(\mathcal{G}_i, y_i)\}$ with y_i as the label of the graph $\mathcal{G}_i$, the goal of the graph classification task is to learn a mapping function ϕ with $\mathcal{D}$, which can predict the labels of unlabeled graphs.*

In the definition above, we did not specify additional information potentially associated with the graphs. For example, in some scenarios, each node in a graph is associated with certain features that can be utilized for graph classification.

Example 2.47 (Classifying Protein Structure into Enzymes or Nonenzymes) Proteins can be represented as graphs, where amino acids are the nodes and edges between two nodes can be formed if they are less than 6Å apart. Enzymes are a type of proteins that serve as biological catalysts to catalyze biochemical reactions. Given a protein, predicting whether it is an enzyme or not can be treated as a graph classification task where the label for each protein is either enzyme or nonenzyme.

2.8 Conclusion

In this chapter, we briefly introduce the concepts of graphs, the matrix representations of graphs, and the important measures and properties of graphs, including degree, connectivity, and centrality. We then discuss graph Fourier transform and graph signal processing, which lay foundations for spectral-based graph neural networks. We introduce a variety of complex graphs. Finally, we discuss representative computational tasks on graphs including both node-focused and graph-focused tasks.

2.9 Further Reading

We briefly introduce many basic concepts in graphs. There are also other more advanced properties and concepts in graphs such as flow and cut. Furthermore, there are a lot problems defined on graphs, including graph coloring problems, route problems, network flow problems, and covering problems. The book *Graph Theory with Applications* (Bondy et al., n.d.) covers these concepts and topics. More spectral properties and theories on graphs can be found in the book *Spectral Graph Theory* (Chung and Graham, 1997). Applications of graphs in different areas can be found in (Borgatti et al., 2009; Nastase et al., 2015; Trinajstic, 2018). The Stanford Large Network Dataset Collection (Leskovec and Krevl, 2014) and the Network Data Repository (Rossi and Ahmed, 2015), host large amounts of graph data sets from various areas. The python libraries networks (Hag-berg et al., 2008), graph-tool (Peixoto, 2014), and SNAP (Leskovec and Sosič, 2016) can be used to analyze and visualize graph data. The Graph Signal Processing Toolbox (Perraudin et al., 2014) can be employed to perform graph signal processing.

3

Foundations of Deep Learning

3.1 Introduction

Machine learning is the research field of allowing computers to learn to act properly from sample data without being explicitly programmed. Deep learning is a class of machine learning algorithms that is built upon artificial neural networks. In fact, most of the key building components of deep learning have existed for decades, though deep learning has only gained popularity in recent years. The idea of artificial neural networks dates back to the 1940s when the McCulloch–Pitts Neuron (McCulloch and Pitts, 1943) was first introduced. This linear model can recognize inputs from two categories by linearly aggregating information from inputs and then making the decision. Later on, Rosenblatt (1958) developed the perceptron, which is able to learn its parameters given training samples. Research on neural networks was revived in the 1980s. One of the major breakthroughs during this period is the successful use of the back-propagation algorithm (Rumelhart et al., 1986; Le Cun and Fogelman-Soulié, 1987) to train deep neural network models. Note that the back-propagation algorithm has many predecessors dating to the 1960s and was first mentioned by Werbos to train neural networks (Werbos, 1994). The back-propagation algorithm is still the dominant algorithm to train deep models in the modern ages of deep learning. Research on deep learning was revived and gained unprecedented attention with the availability of "big data" and powerful computational resources in recent years. The emergence of fast GPUs allows us to train deep models of extremely large sizes and the increasingly large data ensure that these models can generalize well. These two advantages led to the tremendous success of deep learning techniques in various research areas and resulted in immense real-world impact. Deep neural networks have outperformed state-of-the-art traditional methods by a large margin in various applications. Deep learning has significantly advanced the performance of the image recognition task. The ImageNet Large-Scale Visual Recognition Challenge is the largest contest in image recognition and was held yearly from 2010 to 2017. In 2012, the convolutional neural network (CNN) won this challenge for the first time by a large margin, reducing the top-5 error rate from 26.1% to 15.3% (Krizhevsky et al., 2012). Since then, CNNs have won the competition consistently, which has further decreased the error rate to 3.57% (He et al., 2016). Deep learning has also dramatically improved the performance of speech recognition systems (Dahl et al., 2010; Deng et al., 2010; Seide et al., 2011). The introduction of deep learning techniques to speech recognition led to a huge drop in error rates, which have stagnated for years. The research field of natural language processing has also been heavily accelerated by deep learning techniques. Recurrent neural networks such as LSTM (Hochreiter and Schmidhuber, 1997) have been broadly used in sequence-to-sequence tasks such as machine translation (Sutskever et al., 2014; Bahdanau et al., 2014) and dialogue systems (Vinyals and Le, 2015). Because research on "deep learning on graphs" has its root in deep learning, understanding some basic deep learning techniques is essential. Hence, in this chapter, we briefly introduce important deep learning techniques that will serve as the foundations for studying deep learning on graphs, including feedforward networks, convolutional networks, recurrent networks, and autoencoders. While focusing on basic deep models in this chapter, we will expand our discussion to more advanced deep models such as variational autoencoders and generative adversarial networks in later chapters.

3.2 Deep Feedforward Networks

Feedforward networks are the basis for many important deep learning techniques. A feedforward network approximates a certain function $f^*(\mathbf{x})$ using given data. For example, for the classification task, an ideal classifier $f^*(\mathbf{x})$ maps an input $\mathbf{x}$ to a target category y. In this case, a feedforward network is supposed to find a mapping $f(\mathbf{x}|\boldsymbol{\Theta})$ such that it can approximate the ideal classifier $f^*(\mathbf{x})$ well. More specially, the goal of training the feedforward network is to learn the values of the parameters θ that can result in the best approximation to $f^*(\mathbf{x})$.

In feedforward networks, the information $\mathbf{x}$ flows from the input, through some intermediate computations, and finally to the output y. The intermediate computational operations are in the form of networks, which can typically be represented as the composition of several functions. For example, the feedforward network shown in Figure 3.1 has four functions $f^{(1)}, f^{(2)}, f^{(3)}, f^{(4)}$ connected in a chain and $f(\mathbf{x}) = f^{(4)}(f^{(3)}(f^{(2)}(f^{(1)}(\mathbf{x}))))$. In the feedforward network shown in Figure 3.1, $f^{(1)}$ is the first layer, $f^{(2)}$ is the second layer, $f^{(3)}$ is the third layer, and the final layer $f^{(4)}$ is the output layer. The number of computational layers in the network defines the depth of the network. During training of the neural network, we try to push the output $f(\mathbf{x})$ to be close to the ideal output; i.e., $f^*(\mathbf{x})$ or y. In particular, during the training process, the results from the output layer are directly guided by the training data and all of the intermediate layers do not obtain direct supervision from the training data. Thus, to approximate the ideal function $f^*(\mathbf{x})$ well, the learning algorithm decides the parameters of the intermediate layers using the indirect supervision signal passing back from the output layer. Because no desired output is given for the intermediate layers from the training data during the training procedure, these intermediate layers are called hidden layers. The networks are

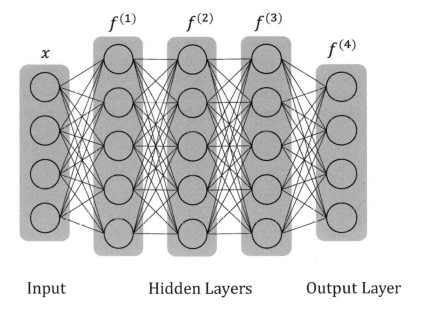

Figure 3.1 An illustrative example of feedforward networks.

called neural networks because they are loosely inspired by neuroscience. As discussed before, each layer of the neural network can be viewed as a vector-valued function, where both the input and output are vectors. The elements in the layer can be viewed as nodes (or units). Thus, each layer can be viewed as a set of vector to scalar functions where each node is a function. The operation in a node loosely mimics what happens in a neuron in the brain, which gets activated when it encounters sufficient stimuli. A node gathers and transforms information from all of the nodes in the previous layer and then passes the information through an activation function, which determines to what extent the information can pass through to the next layer. The operation of gathering and transforming information is typically linear, and the activation function adds nonlinearity to the neural network, which largely improves its approximation capability.

3.2.1 The Architecture

In a fully connected feedforward neural network, nodes in consecutive layers form a complete bipartite graph; i.e., a node in one layer is connected to all nodes in the other layer. A general view of this architecture is demonstrated in Figure 3.1. Next we introduce the details of the computation involved in the neural network. To start, we focus on a single node in the first layer. The input of the neural network is a vector $\mathbf{x}$ where we use $\mathbf{x}_i$ to denote its ith element. All of these elements can be viewed as nodes in the input layer. A node in the second layer (or the one after the input layer) is connected to all of the nodes in the input layer. These connections between the nodes in the input layer and an arbitrary node in the second layer are illustrated in Figure 3.2. The operations in one node consist of two parts: (1) combining the elements

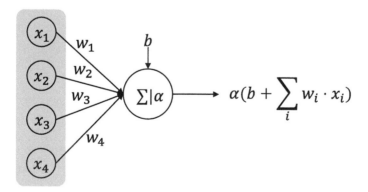

Figure 3.2 Operations in one node.

of the input linearly with various weights (or $\mathbf{w}_i$) and (2) passing the value obtained in the previous step through an activation function. Mathematically, it can be represented as

$$h = \alpha\left(b + \sum_{i=1}^{4} \mathbf{w}_i \cdot \mathbf{x}_i\right), \tag{3.1}$$

where b is a bias term and $\alpha(\cdot)$ is a nonlinear activation function, which will be introduced in later sections. We now generalize the operation to an arbitrary hidden layer. Assume that in the kth layer of the neural network we have N^k nodes and the output of the layer can be represented as $\mathbf{h}^k$ with $\mathbf{h}_i^k$ its ith element. Then, to compute $\mathbf{h}_j^{k+1}$ in the $(k + 1)$st layer, the following operation is conducted:

$$\mathbf{h}_j^{(k+1)} = \alpha\left(b_j^{(k)} + \sum_{i=1}^{N^{(k)}} \mathbf{W}_{ji}^{(k)}\mathbf{h}_i^{(k)}\right). \tag{3.2}$$

Note that we use $\mathbf{W}_{ji}^k$ to denote the weight corresponding to the connection between $\mathbf{h}_i^k$ and $\mathbf{h}_j^{(k+1)}$ and b_j^k is the bias term for calculating $\mathbf{h}_j^{(k+1)}$. The operations to calculate all the elements in the $(k+1)$st layer can be summarized in matrix form as

$$\mathbf{h}^{(k+1)} = \alpha(\mathbf{b}^{(k)} + \mathbf{W}^{(k)}\mathbf{h}^{(k)}), \tag{3.3}$$

where $\mathbf{W}^k \in \mathbb{R}^{N^{k+1} \times N^k}$ contains all weights and its j, ith element is $\mathbf{W}_{ji}^k$ in Eq. (3.2) and $\mathbf{b}^k$ consists of all bias terms. Specifically, for the input layer, we have $\mathbf{h}^0 = \mathbf{x}$. Recall that we use $f^{(k+1)}$ to represent the operation of the $(k + 1)$st layer in the neural network; thus, we have

$$\mathbf{h}^{(k+1)} = f^{(k+1)}(\mathbf{h}^{(k)}) = \alpha(\mathbf{b}^{(k)} + \mathbf{W}^{(k)}\mathbf{h}^{(k)}). \tag{3.4}$$

Note that the introduced operations are typical for hidden layers. The output layer usually adopts a similar structure but different activation functions to transform the obtained information. We next introduce activation functions and the design of the output layers.

3.2.2 Activation Functions

An activation function decides whether or to what extent the input signal should pass. The node (or neuron) is activated if there is information passing through the node. As introduced in the previous section, the operations of a neural network are linear without the activation functions. The activation function introduces the nonlinearity into the neural network that can improve its approximation capability. In the following, we introduce some commonly used activation functions.

Rectifier

Rectifier is one of the most commonly used activation functions. As shown in Figure 3.3, it is similar to linear functions and the only difference is that the rectifier outputs 0 on the negative half of its domain. In the neural network, the units employ this activation function are called rectifier linear units (ReLUs). The rectifier activation function is linear (identity) for all positive input values and 0 for all negative values. Mathematically, it is defined as

$$\text{ReLU}(z) = \max\{0, z\}. \tag{3.5}$$

At each layer, only a few of the units are activated, which ensures efficient computation. One drawback of the ReLU is that its gradient is 0 on the negative half of the domain. Hence, during training, once the unit is not activated, no supervision information can be passed back for training that unit. Some generalizations of ReLU have been proposed to overcome this drawback. Instead of setting the negative input to 0, leaky ReLU (Maas et al., 2013) performs a linear transformation with a small slope to the negative values as shown in Figure 3.4a. More specifically, the leaky ReLU can be mathematically represented as

$$\text{LeakyReLU}(z) = \begin{cases} 0.01z & z < 0 \\ z & z \geq 0. \end{cases} \tag{3.6}$$

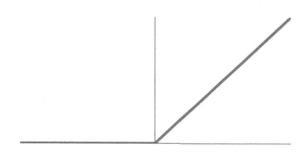

Figure 3.3 ReLU.

Another generalization of ReLU is the exponential linear unit (ELU). It still has linear transform for the positive values but it adopts an exponential transform for the negative values, as shown in Figure 3.4b. Mathematically, the ELU activation function can be represented as

$$\text{ELU}(z) = \begin{cases} c \cdot (\exp(z - 1)) & z < 0 \\ z & z \geq 0, \end{cases} \tag{3.7}$$

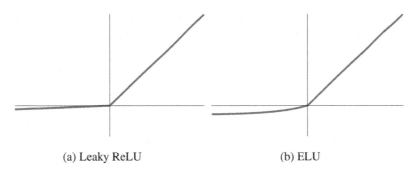

(a) Leaky ReLU   (b) ELU

Figure 3.4 Generalizations of ReLU

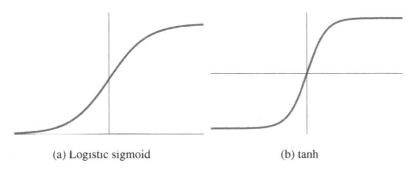

(a) Logistic sigmoid   (b) tanh

Figure 3.5 Logistic sigmoid and hyperbolic tangent.

where c is a positive constant controlling the slope of the exponential function for the negative values.

Logistic Sigmoid and Hyperbolic Tangent

Prior to the ReLU, logistic sigmoid and hyperbolic tangent functions were the most commonly adopted activation functions. The sigmoid activation function can be mathematically represented as follows:

$$\sigma(z) = \frac{1}{1 + \exp(-z)}. \tag{3.8}$$

As shown in Figure 3.5a, the sigmoid function maps the input in the range of 0 to 1. Specifically, the more negative the input is, the closer the output is to 0 and the more positive the input is, the closer the output is to 1.

The hyperbolic tangent activation function is highly related to the sigmoid function with the following relation:

$$\tanh(z) = \frac{2}{1 + \exp(-2z)} - 1 = 2 \cdot \sigma(2z) - 1. \tag{3.9}$$

As shown in Figure 3.5b, the hyperbolic tangent function maps the input in the range of -1 to 1. Specifically, the more negative the input is, the closer the output is to -1 and the more positive the input is, the closer the output is to 1.

These two activation functions face the same saturation issue (Nwankpa et al., 2018). They saturate when the input z is a very large positive number or a very negative number. They are only sensitive to values that are close to 0. The phenomenon of the widespread saturation makes gradient based training very difficult, because the gradient will be around 0 when z is either very positive or very negative. For this reason, these two activation functions are becoming less popular in feedforward networks.

3.2.3 Output Layer and Loss Function

The choice of the output layer and loss function varies according to the applications. Next, we introduce some commonly used output units and loss functions.

In regression tasks, a neural network needs to output continuous values. A simple way to achieve this is to perform an affine transformation (or an affinity) without the nonlinear activation. Given input features (or features from previous layers) $\mathbf{h} \in \mathbb{R}^{d_{in}}$, a layer of linear units outputs a vector $\hat{\mathbf{y}} \in \mathbb{R}^{d_{ou}}$ as

$$\hat{\mathbf{y}} = \mathbf{W}\mathbf{h} + \mathbf{b}, \tag{3.10}$$

where $\mathbf{W} \in \mathbb{R}^{d_{ou} \times d_{in}}$ and $\mathbf{b} \in \mathbb{R}^{d_{ou}}$ are the parameters to be learned. For a single sample, we can use a simple squared loss function to measure the difference between the predicted value $\hat{\mathbf{y}}$ and the ground truth $\mathbf{y}$ as follows:

$$l(\mathbf{y}, \hat{\mathbf{y}}) = (\mathbf{y} - \hat{\mathbf{y}})^2. \tag{3.11}$$

For classification tasks, the neural network needs to predict the labels of the classes of given samples. Instead of directly producing a discrete output indicating the predicted labels of a given sample, we usually produce a discrete probability distribution over the labels. Different output layers and loss functions are used depending on whether the prediction is binary or multiway. Next, we discuss the details in these two scenarios.

Binary Targets

For binary classification, we assume that a sample is labeled either 0 or 1. Then, to perform the prediction, we first need a linear layer to project the input (results from previous layers) to a single value. Following this, a sigmoid function is applied to map this value in the range of 0 to 1, which indicates the probability of the sample with label 1. In summary, this process can be modeled as

$$\hat{y} = \sigma(\mathbf{W}h + b), \tag{3.12}$$

where $\mathbf{h} \in \mathbb{R}^{d_{in}}$ and $\mathbf{W} \in \mathbb{R}^{1 \times d_{in}}$. Specifically, $\hat{y}$ denotes the probability of predicting the input sample with label 1 and $1 - \hat{y}$ indicates the probability for label 0. With the output $\hat{y}$, we can employ the cross-entropy loss to measure the difference between the ground truth and the prediction as

$$l(y, \hat{y}) = -y \cdot \log(\hat{y}) - (1 - y) \cdot \log(1 - \hat{y}). \tag{3.13}$$

During the inference, an input sample is predicted with label 1 if the predicted $\hat{y} > 0.5$ and with label 0 otherwise.

Categorical Targets

For the n-class classification task, we assume that the ground truth is denoted as integers between 0 and $n - 1$. Thus, we use a one-hot vector $\mathbf{y} \in \{0, 1\}^n$ to indicate the label where $\mathbf{y}_i = 1$ indicates that the sample is labeled as $i - 1$. To perform the prediction, we first need a linear layer to transform the input $\mathbf{h}$ to an n-dimensional vector $\mathbf{z} \in \mathbb{R}^n$ as

$$\mathbf{z} = \mathbf{W}h + b, \tag{3.14}$$

where $\mathbf{W} \in \mathbb{R}^{n \times d_{in}}$ and $\mathbf{b} \in \mathbb{R}^n$. We then apply the softmax function to normalize $\mathbf{z}$ into a discrete probability distribution over the classes as

$$\hat{\mathbf{y}}_i = \text{softmax}(z)_i = \frac{\exp(\mathbf{z}_i)}{\sum_j \exp(\mathbf{z}_j)}, i = 1, \ldots, n, \tag{3.15}$$

where $\mathbf{z}_i$ denotes the ith element of the vector $\mathbf{z}$ and $\hat{\mathbf{y}}_i$ is the ith element of the output of the softmax function. Specifically, $\hat{\mathbf{y}}_i$ indicates the probability of the input sample with label $i - 1$. With the predicted $\hat{y}$, we can employ the cross-entropy loss to measure the difference between the ground truth and the prediction as

$$l(y, \hat{y}) = -\sum_{i=0}^{n-1} \mathbf{y}_i \log(\hat{\mathbf{y}}_i). \tag{3.16}$$

During the inference, an input sample is predicted with label $i - 1$ if $\hat{y}_i$ is the largest among all output units.

3.3 Convolutional Neural Networks

A convolutional neural network is a popular kind of neural network model that is best known for processing regular grid-like data such as images. It is similar to a feedforward neural network in many aspects. A CNN also consists of neurons that have trainable weights and biases. Each neuron receives and transforms some information from previous layers. The difference is that some of the neurons in CNNs may have different designs compared to the ones we introduced for feedforward networks. More specifically, the convolution operation is introduced to design some of the neurons. The layers with the convolution operation are called convolutional layers. The convolution operation typically only involves a small number of neurons in the previous layers, which enforces sparse connections between layers. Another important operation in CNNs is the pooling operation, which summarizes the output of nearby neurons as the new output. The layers consisting of the pooling operations are called the pooling layers. In this section, we first introduce the convolution operation and convolutional layers, then discuss the pooling layers, and finally present an overall framework of CNNs.

3.3.1 The Convolution Operation and Convolutional Layer

In general, the convolution operation is a mathematical operation on two real functions to produce a third function (Widder and Hirschman, 2015). The convolution operation between two functions $f(\cdot)$ and $g(\cdot)$ can be defined as

$$(f * g)(t) = \int_{-\infty}^{\infty} f(\tau)g(t - \tau)d\tau. \tag{3.17}$$

As an example of motivation, let us consider a continuous signal $f(t)$, where t denotes time and $f(t)$ is the corresponding value at time t. Suppose that the signal is somewhat noisy. To obtain a less noisy signal, we would like to average the value at time t with its nearby values. Furthermore, values of time closer to t may be more similar to that at time t and they should contribute more. Hence, we would like to take a weighted average over a few values that are close to time t as its new value. This can be modeled as a convolution operation between the signal $f(t)$ and a weight function $w(c)$, where c represents the closeness to the target t. The smaller c is, the larger the value of $w(c)$ is. The signal after the convolution operation can be represented as

$$s(t) = (f * w)(t) = \int_{-\infty}^{\infty} f(\tau)w(t - \tau)d\tau. \tag{3.18}$$

Note that to ensure that the operation does a weighted average, $w(c)$ is constrained to integrate to 1, which makes $w(c)$ a probability density function. In general, the convolution operation does not need to be a weighted average operation and the function $w(t)$ does not need to meet these requirements.

In reality, data are usually discrete with fixed intervals. For example, the signal $f(t)$ may only sample at integer values of time t. Assume that $f(\cdot)$ and $w(\cdot)$ in the previous example are both defined on integer values of time t. Then the convolution can be written as

$$s(t) = (f * w)(t) = \sum_{\tau=-\infty}^{\infty} f(\tau)w(t - \tau). \qquad (3.19)$$

We further consider that in most cases, the function $w(\cdot)$ is only nonzero within a small window. In other words, only local information contributes to the new value of a target position. Suppose that the window size is $2n + 1$; i.e., $w(c) = 0$ for $c < -n$ and $c > n$. Then the convolution can be further modified as

$$(f * w)(t) = \sum_{\tau=t-n}^{t+n} f(\tau)w(t - \tau). \qquad (3.20)$$

In the scenario of neural networks, t can be considered as the indices of the units in the input layer. The function $w(\cdot)$ is called a kernel or filter. The convolution operation can be represented as a sparse connected graph. The convolutional layers can be explained as sliding the kernel over the input layer and calculating the output correspondingly. An example of the layers consisting of the convolution operation is shown in Figure 3.6.

Example 3.1 Figure 3.6 shows a convolutional layer, where the input and output have the same size. To maintain the size of the output layer, the input layer is padded with two additional units (the dashed circles) with value 0. The kernel of the convolution operation is shown on the right of the figure. For simplicity, the nonlinear activation function is not shown. In this example, $n = 1$, and the kernel function is defined only at three nearby locations.

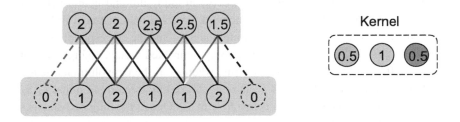

Figure 3.6 An example of a convolutional layer.

In the practical machine learning scenario, we often deal with data with more than one dimension, such as images. The convolution operation can be extended to data with high dimensions. For example, for a two-dimensional image I, the convolution operation can be performed with a two-dimensional kernel K as

$$S(i,j) = (I * K)(i,j) = \sum_{\tau=i-n}^{i+n} \sum_{j=\gamma-n}^{\gamma+n} I(\tau,\gamma)K(i-\tau,j-\gamma). \qquad (3.21)$$

Next we discuss some key properties of the convolutional layer. Without loss of generality, we consider the convolutional layer for single-dimensional data. These properties can be also applied to high-dimensional data. Convolutional layers mainly have three key properties, including *sparse connections*, *parameter sharing*, and *equivariant representation*.

Sparse Connection

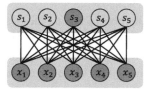 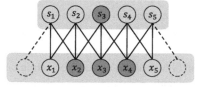

(a) Traditional neural network layers   (b) Convolutional neural network layers

Figure 3.7 Dense and sparse connectivity.

In traditional neural network layers, the interactions between the input units and the output units can be described by a matrix. Each element of this matrix defines an independent parameter for the interaction between each input unit and each output unit. However, the convolutional layers usually have sparse connections between layers when the kernel is only nonzero on a limited number of input units. A comparison between the traditional neural network layers and the convolutional neural network layers is demonstrated in Figure 3.7. In this figure, we highlight one output unit S_3 and the corresponding input units that affect S_3. Clearly, in the densely connected layers, a single output unit is affected by all of the input units, whereas in the convolutional neural network layers, the output unit S_3 is only affected by three input units, x_2, x_3 and x_4, which are called the *receptive field* of S_3. One of the major advantages of the sparse connectivity is that it can largely improve the computational efficiency. If there are N input units and M output units, there are $N \times M$ parameters in the traditional neural network layers. The time complexity for a single computation pass of this layer is $O(N \times M)$. The convolutional layers with the same number of input and output units only have $K \times M$ parameters (we discuss parameter sharing in the next subsection), when its kernel size is

K. Correspondingly, the time complexity is reduced to $O(K \times M)$. Typically, the kernel size K is much smaller than the number of input units N. In other words, the computation of convolutional neural networks is much more efficient than that of traditional neural networks.

Parameters Sharing

As aforementioned, there are $K \times M$ parameters in the convolutional layers. However, this number can be much smaller due to *parameter sharing* in the convolutional layers. Parameter sharing means sharing the same set of parameters when performing the calculation for different output units. In the convolutional layers, the same kernel is used to calculate the values of all of the output units, which naturally leads to parameter sharing. An illustrative example is shown in Figure 3.8, where we use the color to denote different parameters. In this example, we have a kernel size of 3, which results in three parameters. In general, for convolutional layers with a kernel size K, there are K parameters. Comparing with $N \times M$ parameters in the traditional neural network layers, K is much smaller and consequently the requirement for memory is much lower.

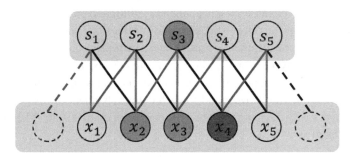

Figure 3.8 Parameter sharing.

Equivariant Representation

The parameter sharing mechanism naturally introduces another important property of CNNs, which is called *equivariant* to translation. A function is said to be equivariant if the output changes in the same way as the input changes. More specifically, a function $f(\cdot)$ is equivariant to another function $g(\cdot)$ if $f(g(x)) = g(f(x))$. In the case of the convolution operation, it is not difficult to verify that it is equivariant to translation functions such as shifts. For example, if we shift the input units in Figure 3.8 to the right by one unit, we can still find the same output pattern that is also shifted to the right by one unit. This property is important in many applications where we care more about whether a certain feature appears than where it appears. For example, when recognizing whether an image is of a cat or not, we care whether there are some important features in the image indicating the existence of a cat instead of where these features show in the image. The property of equivariant to translation of CNNs is crucial to their success in the area of image classification (Krizhevsky et al., 2012; He et al., 2016).

3.3.2　Convolutional Layers in Practice

In practice, when we discuss convolution in CNNs, we do not refer to the exact convolution operation as it is defined mathematically. The convolutional layers used in practice differ from the definition slightly. Typically, the input is not only a grid of real values. Instead, it is a grid of vector-valued input. For example, in a colored image consisting of $N \times N$ pixels, there are three values associated with each pixel, representing red, green, and blue. Each color denotes a *channel* of the input image. Generally, the ith channel of the input image consists of the ith element of the vectors at all positions of the input. The length of the vector at each position (e.g., pixel in the case of image) is the number of channels. Hence, the convolution typically involves three dimensions, though it only "slides" in two dimensions (or it does not slide in the dimension of channels). Furthermore, in typical convolutional layers, multiple distinct kernels are applied in parallel to extract features from the input layer. As a consequence, the output layer is also multichannel where the results for each kernel correspond to each output channel. Let us consider an input image I with L channels. The convolution operation with P kernels can be formulated as

$$S(i, j, p) = (I * K_p)(i, j) = \sum_{l=1}^{L} \sum_{\tau=i-n}^{i+n} \sum_{j=\gamma-n}^{\gamma+n} I(\tau, \gamma, l) K_p(i - \tau, j - \gamma, l), \quad (3.22)$$

where K_p is the pth kernel with $(2n + 1)^2 \cdot L$ parameters. The output clearly consists of P channels.

In many cases, to further reduce computational complexity, we can regularly skip some positions when sliding the kernel over the input. The convolution can be only performed every s positions, where the number s is usually called the *stride*. We call the convolutions with stride strided convolutions. An illustrative example of strided convolutions is illustrated in Figure 3.9a, where the stride is $s = 2$. The strided convolution can be also viewed as a downsampling over the results of the regular convolution as shown in Figure 3.9b. The strided convolution with stride s can be represented as

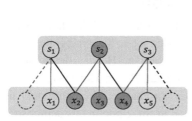 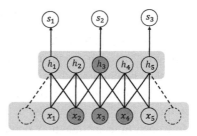

(a) Strided convolutions   (b) Convolutions with downsampling

Figure 3.9 Strided convolutions can be viewed as convolutions with downsampling.

$$S(i, j, p) =$$

$$\sum_{l=1}^{L} \sum_{\tau=i-n}^{i+n} \sum_{j=\gamma-n}^{\gamma+n} I(\tau, \gamma, l) K_p((i-1) \cdot s + 1 - \tau, (j-1) \cdot s + 1 - \gamma, l). \quad (3.23)$$

When stride is $s = 1$, the strided convolution operation is equivalent to the nonstrided convolution operation as described in Eq. (3.22). As mentioned before, zero padding is usually applied to the input to maintain the size of the output. The size of the padding, the size of the receptive field (or the size of the kernel), and the stride determine the size of the output when the input size is fixed. More specifically, consider a one-dimensional input with size N. Suppose that the padding size is Q, the size of the receptive field is F, and the size of stride is s. Then the size of the output O can be calculated with the following formulation:

$$O = \frac{N - F + 2Q}{s} + 1. \quad (3.24)$$

Example 3.2 The input size of the strided convolution shown in Figure 3.9a is $N = 5$. Its kernel size is $F = 3$. Clearly, the size of zero-padding is $Q = 1$. Together with stride $s = 2$, we can calculate the output size using Eq. (3.24):

$$O = \frac{N - F + 2Q}{s} + 1 = \frac{5 - 3 + 2 \times 1}{2} + 1 = 3. \quad (3.25)$$

3.3.3 Nonlinear Activation Layer

Similar to feedforward neural networks, nonlinear activation is applied to every unit after the convolution operation. The activation function widely used in CNNs is the ReLU. The process of applying nonlinear activation is also called the *detector* stage or the *detector* layer.

3.3.4 Pooling Layer

A *pooling* layer usually follows the convolution layer and the detector layer. The pooling function summarizes the statistic of a local neighborhood to denote this neighborhood in the resulting output. Hence, the width and height of the data are reduced after the pooling layer. However, the depth (the number of channels) of the data does not change. The commonly used pooling operations include max pooling and average pooling as demonstrated in Figure 3.10. These pooling operations take the values in a 2 × 2 local neighborhood as input and output a single value based on them. As the names indicate, the max pooling operation takes the maximum value in the local neighborhood as the output and the average pooling takes the average value of the local neighborhood as its output.

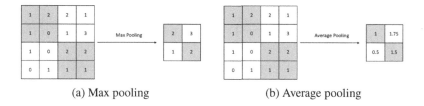

(a) Max pooling   (b) Average pooling

Figure 3.10 Pooling methods in CNNs.

3.3.5 An Overall CNN Framework

With the convolution and pooling operations introduced, we now introduce an overall framework of convolutional neural networks with classification as the downstream task. As shown in Figure 3.11, the overall framework for classification can be roughly split to two components – the feature

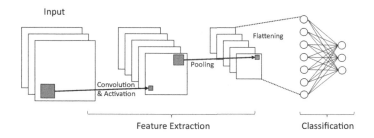

Figure 3.11 An overall framework of convolutional neural networks.

extraction component and the classification component. The feature extraction component, which consists of convolution and pooling layers, extracts features from the input. The classification component is built upon fully connected feedforward neural networks. These two components are connected by a flattening operation. It flattens the feature matrices in multiple channels extracted by the feature extraction component to a single feature vector, which serves as the input to the classification component. Note that in Figure 3.11, only a single convolutional layer and a single pooling layer are illustrated. However, in practice, we usually stack multiple convolutional and pooling layers. Similarly, in the classification component, the feedforward neural networks can consist of multiple fully connected layers.

3.4 Recurrent Neural Networks

Many tasks such as speech recognition, machine translation, and sentiment classification need to handle sequential data, where each data sample is represented as a sequence of values. Given a sentence (a sequence of words) in one language, machine translation aims to translate it in to another language. Thus, both the input and output are sequences. Sentiment classification predicts the sentiment of a given sentence where the input is a sequence and the output is a value to indicate the sentiment class. We may try to use standard neural network models to deal with sequential data, where each element in the sequence can be viewed as an input unit in the input layer. However, this strategy is not sufficient for sequential data for two main reasons. First, standard network models often have fixed input and output size; however, sequences (either input or output) can have different lengths for different data samples. Second, and more important, standard network models do not share parameters to deal with input from different positions of the sequence. For example, in language-related tasks, given two sentences – "I went to Yellow-stone National Park last summer" and "Last summer, I went to Yellow-stone National Park" – we expect the model to figure out that the time is "last summer" in both sentences, although it appears in different positions. A natural way to achieve this is the idea of parameter sharing as similar to CNNs. Recurrent neural networks (RNNs) have been introduced to solve the two challenges. RNNs recurrently apply the same functions to each element of the sequence one by one. Because all positions in the sequence are processed using the same functions, parameter sharing is naturally realized among different positions. Meanwhile, the same functions can be repeatedly applied regardless of the length of the sequence, which can inherently handle sequences with varied lengths.

3.4.1 The Architecture of Traditional RNNs

A sequence with length n can be denoted as $(\mathbf{x}^{(1)}, \mathbf{x}^{(2)}, \ldots, \mathbf{x}^{(n)})$. As shown in Figure 3.12, the traditional RNN model takes one element of the sequence at a time and processes it with a block of neural networks. The block of neural networks often takes not only the element as input but also the information that flowed from the previous block. As a result, the information in the early positions of the sequence can flow through the entire sequence. The blocks of neural networks are identical. The RNN model in Figure 3.12 has an output $\mathbf{y}^{(i)}$ at each position i, which is not mandatory for RNN models.

The block of neural networks has two inputs and also produces two outputs. We use $\mathbf{y}^{(i)}$ to denote the output and $\mathbf{h}^{(i)}$ to denote the information flowing to the next position. To process the first element, $\mathbf{h}^{(0)}$ is often initialized as $\mathbf{0}$. The procedure for dealing with the ith element can be formulated as

$$\mathbf{h}^{(i)} = \alpha_h(\mathbf{W}_{hh} \cdot \mathbf{h}^{(i-1)} + \mathbf{W}_{hx}\mathbf{x}^{(i-1)} + \mathbf{b}_h)$$
$$\mathbf{y}^{(i)} = \alpha_y(\mathbf{W}_{yh}\mathbf{h}^{(i)} + \mathbf{b}_y),$$

where $\mathbf{W}_{hh}$, $\mathbf{W}_{hx}$, and $\mathbf{W}_{yh}$ are the matrices to perform linear transformations; $\mathbf{b}_h$ and $\mathbf{b}_y$ are the bias terms; and $\alpha_h(\cdot)$ and $\alpha_y(\cdot)$ are two activation functions for generating $\mathbf{h}$ and $\mathbf{y}$, respectively.

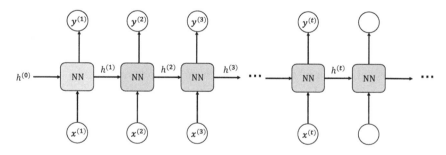

Figure 3.12 The architecture of traditional RNNs.

When dealing with sequential data, it is important to capture the long-term dependency in the sequence. For example, in language modeling, two words that appear far from each other in a sentence can be tightly related. However, it turns out that the traditional RNN model is not good at capturing long-term dependency. The major issue is that the gradients propagated over many stages tend to either vanish or explode. Both phenomena cause problems for the training procedure. The gradient explosion will damage the optimization process, and the vanishing gradient makes it difficult for the guidance information in the later positions to affect the computations in the earlier positions. To solve these issues, gated RNN models have been proposed. Long short-term memory (LSTM) (Hochreiter and Schmidhuber, 1997) and gated recurrent unit (GRU; Cho et al., 2014a) are two representative gated RNN models.

3.4.2 Long Short-Term Memory

The overall structure of the LSTM is the same as the traditional RNN model. It also has a chain structure that has identical neural network blocks applying to the elements of the sequence. The key difference is that a set of gating units is utilized to control the information flow in LSTM. As shown in Figure 3.13, the information flowing through consecutive positions in a sequence includes the *cell state* $\mathbf{C}^{(t-1)}$ and the *hidden state* $\mathbf{h}^{(t-1)}$. The cell state serves as the information from the previous states that are propagated to the next position and the hidden state helps decide how the information should be propagated. The hidden state $\mathbf{h}^{(t)}$ also serves as the output of this position if necessary.

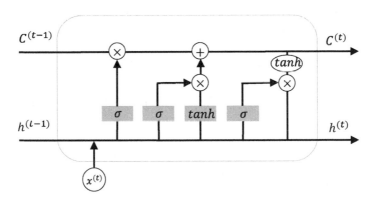

Figure 3.13 A block of LSTM.

The first step of the LSTM is to decide what information from previous cell states we are going to discard. The decision is made by a *forget gate*. The forget gate considers the previous hidden state $\mathbf{h}^{(t-1)}$ and the new input $\mathbf{x}^{(t)}$ and outputs a value between 0 to 1 for each of the elements in the cell state $\mathbf{C}^{(t-1)}$. The corresponding value of each element controls how the information in each element is discarded. The outputs can be summarized as a vector $\mathbf{f}_t$, which has the same dimension as the cell state $\mathbf{C}^{(t-1)}$. More specifically, the forget gate can be formulated as

$$\mathbf{f}_t = \sigma(\mathbf{W}_f \cdot \mathbf{x}^{(t)} + \mathbf{U}_f \cdot \mathbf{h}^{(t-1)} + \mathbf{b}_f), \tag{3.26}$$

where $\mathbf{W}_f$ and $\mathbf{U}_f$ are the parameters, $\mathbf{b}_f$ is the bias term, and $\sigma(\cdot)$ is the sigmoid activation function, which maps values in the range between 0 and 1.

The next step is to determine what information from the new input $\mathbf{x}^{(t)}$ should be stored in the new cell state. Similar to the forget gate, an *input gate* is designed to make the decision. The input gate is formulated as

$$\mathbf{i}_t = \sigma(\mathbf{W}_i \cdot \mathbf{x}^{(t)} + \mathbf{U}_i \cdot \mathbf{h}^{(t-1)} + \mathbf{b}_i). \tag{3.27}$$

The input information $\mathbf{x}^{(t)}$ is processed by a few layers of neural networks to generate candidate values $\tilde{\mathbf{C}}^{(t)}$, which are used to update the cell state. The process of generating $\tilde{\mathbf{C}}^{(t)}$ is

$$\tilde{\mathbf{C}}^{(t)} = tanh(\mathbf{W}_c \cdot \mathbf{x}^{(t)} + \mathbf{U}_c \cdot \mathbf{h}^{(t-1)} + \mathbf{b}_c). \tag{3.28}$$

Then, we generate the new cell state $C^{(t)}$ by combining the old cell state $\mathbf{C}^{(t-1)}$ and the new candidate cell $\tilde{\mathbf{C}}^{(t)}$ as

$$\mathbf{C}^{(t)} = \mathbf{f}_t \odot \mathbf{C}^{(t-1)} + \mathbf{i}_t \odot \tilde{\mathbf{C}}^{(t)}, \tag{3.29}$$

where the notation $\odot$ denotes the Hadamard product; i.e., element-wise multiplication.

Finally, we need to generate the hidden state $\mathbf{h}^{(t)}$, which can flow to the next position and serve as the output for this position at the same time if necessary. The hidden state is based on the updated cell state $\mathbf{C}^{(t)}$ with an output gate determining which parts of the cell state to preserve. The output gate is formulated in the same way as the forget gate and the input gate as

$$\mathbf{o}_t = \sigma(\mathbf{W}_o \cdot \mathbf{x}^{(t)} + \mathbf{U}_o \cdot \mathbf{h}^{(t-1)} + \mathbf{b}_o). \tag{3.30}$$

The new hidden state $\mathbf{h}^{(t)}$ is then generated as follows:

$$\mathbf{h}^{(t)} = \mathbf{o}_t \odot tanh(\mathbf{C}^{(t)}). \tag{3.31}$$

The entire process of the LSTM is shown in Figure 3.13 and can be summarized as

$$\mathbf{f}_t = \sigma(\mathbf{W}_f \cdot \mathbf{x}^{(t)} + \mathbf{U}_f \cdot \mathbf{h}^{(t-1)} + \mathbf{b}_f)$$
$$\mathbf{i}_t = \sigma(\mathbf{W}_i \cdot \mathbf{x}^{(t)} + \mathbf{U}_i \cdot \mathbf{h}^{(t-1)} + \mathbf{b}_i)$$
$$\mathbf{o}_t = \sigma(\mathbf{W}_o \cdot \mathbf{x}^{(t)} + \mathbf{U}_o \cdot \mathbf{h}^{(t-1)} + \mathbf{b}_o)$$
$$\tilde{\mathbf{C}}^{(t)} = tanh(\mathbf{W}_c \cdot \mathbf{x}^{(t)} + \mathbf{U}_c \cdot \mathbf{h}^{(t-1)} + \mathbf{b}_c)$$
$$\mathbf{C}^{(t)} = \mathbf{f}_t \odot \mathbf{C}^{(t-1)} + \mathbf{i}_t \odot \tilde{\mathbf{C}}^{(t)}$$
$$\mathbf{h}^{(t)} = \mathbf{o}_t \odot tanh(\mathbf{C}^{(t)}). \tag{3.32}$$

For convenience, we summarize the block of neural networks in LSTM for processing the tth position described in Eq. (3.32) as

$$\mathbf{C}^{(t)}, \mathbf{h}^{(t)} = \text{LSTM}(\mathbf{x}^{(t)}, \mathbf{C}^{(t-1)}, \mathbf{h}^{(t-1)}). \tag{3.33}$$

3.4.3 Gated Recurrent Unit

The GRU as shown in Figure 3.14 can be viewed as a variant of the LSTM where the forget gate and the input gate are combined as the *update gate* and the cell state and the hidden state are merged as the same one. These changes lead to a simpler gated RNN model that is formulated as:

$$\mathbf{z}_t = \sigma(\mathbf{W}_z \cdot \mathbf{x}^{(t)} + \mathbf{U}_z \cdot \mathbf{h}^{(t-1)} + \mathbf{b}_z)$$
$$\mathbf{r}_t = \sigma(\mathbf{W}_r \cdot \mathbf{x}^{(t)} + \mathbf{U}_r \cdot \mathbf{h}^{(t-1)} + \mathbf{b}_r)$$
$$\tilde{\mathbf{h}}^{(t)} = tanh(\mathbf{W} \cdot \mathbf{x}^{(t)} + \mathbf{U} \cdot (\mathbf{r}_t \odot \mathbf{h}^{(t-1)}) + \mathbf{b})$$
$$\mathbf{h}^{(t)} - (1 - \mathbf{z}_t) \odot \tilde{\mathbf{h}}^{(t)} + \mathbf{z}_t \odot \mathbf{h}^{(t-1)}, \tag{3.34}$$

where $\mathbf{z}_t$ is the update gate and $\mathbf{r}_t$ is the reset gate. For convenience, we summarize the process in Eq. (3.34) as

$$\mathbf{h}^{(t)} = \text{GRU}(\mathbf{x}^{(t)}, \mathbf{h}^{(t-1)}). \tag{3.35}$$

3.5 Autoencoders

An autoencoder can be viewed as a neural network that tries to reproduce the input as its output. Specifically, it has an intermediate hidden representation $\mathbf{h}$, which describes a *code* to denote the input. An autoencoder consists of two

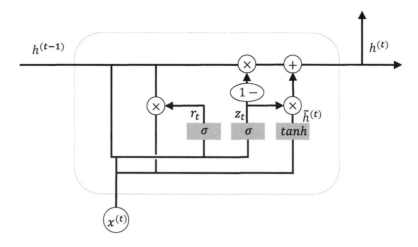

Figure 3.14 A block of GRU.

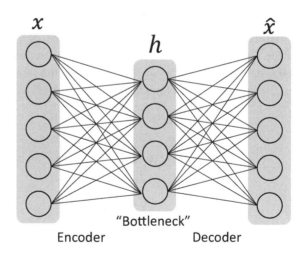

Figure 3.15 A general framework of an autoencoder.

components: (1) an encoder $\mathbf{h} = f(\mathbf{x})$, which encodes the input $\mathbf{x}$ into a code $\mathbf{h}$, and (2) a decoder that aims to reconstruct $\mathbf{x}$ from the code $\mathbf{h}$. The decoder can be represented as $\hat{\mathbf{x}} = g(\mathbf{h})$. If an autoencoder works perfectly in reproducing the input, it is not especially useful. Instead, autoencoders are to approximately reproduce the input by including some restrictions. More specifically, they are to compress necessary information of the input in the hidden code $\mathbf{h}$ to

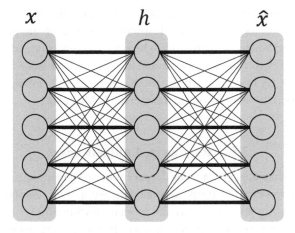

Figure 3.16 An autoencoder memorizes the input to the output. The bold connection indicates the memorization from the input to the output and the other connections are not used (with weights 0) in the autoencoder.

reproduce satisfactory output. A general framework of autoencoders is shown in Figure 3.15. The input **x** is pushed through a "bottleneck," which controls the information that can be preserved in the code **h**. Then, a decoder network utilizes the code **h** to output $\hat{\mathbf{x}}$, which reconstructs the input **x**. The network of an autoencoder can be trained by minimizing the reconstruction error:

$$l(\mathbf{x}, \hat{\mathbf{x}}) = l(\mathbf{x}, g(f(\mathbf{x}))), \tag{3.36}$$

where $l(\mathbf{x}, \hat{\mathbf{x}})$ measures the difference between **x** and $\hat{\mathbf{x}}$. For example, we can use the mean squared error l. The design of the bottleneck is important for autoencoders. Ideally, as shown in Figure 3.16, without a bottleneck, an autoencoder can simply learn to memorize the input and pass it through the decoder to reproduce it, which can render the autoencoder useless. There are different ways to design the bottleneck (i.e., adding constraints to the autoencoder). A natural way is to constrain the number of dimensions of the code **h**, which leads to an *undercomplete autoencoder*. We can also add a regularizer term to discourage memorization between input and output, which leads to a *regularized autoencoder*.

3.5.1 Undercomplete Autoencoders

Constraining the number of dimensions in the *code* **h** to be smaller than the input **x** is a simple and natural way to design the bottleneck. An autoencoder whose code dimension is smaller than the input dimension is called an undercomplete autoencoder. An illustrative example of an undercomplete autoencoder is shown in Figure 3.15, where both the encoder and decoder only contain a single layer of the network and the hidden layer has fewer units than the input layer. By minimizing the reconstruction error, the model can preserve the most important features of the input in the hidden code.

3.5.2 Regularized Autoencoders

We can also make the autoencoder deeper by stacking more layers for both the encoder and decoder. For deep autoencoders, we must be careful to limit the their capacity. Autoencoders may fail to learn anything useful if the encoder and decoder are given too much capacity. To prevent the autoencoder from learning an identity function, we can include a regularization term in the loss function of the autoencoder as

$$l(\mathbf{x}, g(f(\mathbf{x}))) + \eta \cdot \Omega(\mathbf{h}), \tag{3.37}$$

where $\Omega(\mathbf{h})$ is the regularization term applied to code $\mathbf{h}$ and η is a hyper-parameter controlling the impact of the regularization term.

In Olshausen and Field (1997), the L_1 norm of the code $\mathbf{h}$ is adopted as the regularization term as follows:

$$\Omega(\mathbf{h}) = \|\mathbf{h}\|_1. \tag{3.38}$$

The L_1 norm–based regularization term enforces the code $\mathbf{h}$ to be sparse. In this case, the autoencoder is also named a *sparse autoencoder*.

Another way to enforce the sparsity in the code is to constraint the neurons in the code $\mathbf{h}$ to be inactive most of the time. By *inactive* we mean that the value of a neuron in $\mathbf{h}$ is small. We use $\mathbf{h}$ to denote the hidden code so far, which does not explicitly show what input leads to this code. Hence, to explicitly express the relation, for a given input $\mathbf{x}$, we use $\mathbf{h}(\mathbf{x})$ to denote its code learned by the autoencoder. Then, the average hidden code over a set of samples $\{\mathbf{x}_{(i)}\}_{i=1}^m$ is

$$\bar{\mathbf{h}} = \sum_{i=1}^m \mathbf{h}(\mathbf{x}_{(i)}). \tag{3.39}$$

Then, we would like to enforce each element in the hidden code to be close to a small value ρ. For example, ρ could be set to 0.05. In Ng et al. (n.d.), each element in the hidden code is treated as a Bernoulli random variable with its corresponding value in $\bar{\mathbf{h}}$ as the mean. These random variables are constrained to be close to the Bernoulli random variable with ρ as mean by Kullback – Leibler divergence as follows:

$$\Omega(\mathbf{h}) = \sum_j \left(\rho \log \frac{\rho}{\bar{\mathbf{h}}[j]} + (1 - \rho) \log \frac{1 - \rho}{1 - \bar{\mathbf{h}}[j]} \right). \tag{3.40}$$

The autoencoder with the regularization term in Eq. (3.40) can also be called as *sparse autoencoder*. Though the regularization term can be applied to *under-complete autoencoder*, it can also work alone to serve as the bottleneck. With the regularization terms, the hidden code **h** does not have to have a smaller dimension than the input.

3.6 Training Deep Neural Networks

In this section, we discuss the training procedure of deep neural networks. Particularly, we briefly introduce gradient descent and its variants, which are popular approaches to train neural networks. We then detail the backprop-agation algorithm, which is an efficient dynamic algorithm to calculate the gradients of the parameters of the neural networks.

3.6.1 Training with Gradient Descent

To train the deep learning models, we need to minimize a loss function $\mathcal{L}$ with respect to the parameters we want to learn. Generally, we denote the loss function as $\mathcal{L}(\mathbf{W})$, where $\mathbf{W}$ denotes all parameters that need to be optimized. Gradient descent and its variants are commonly adopted to minimize the loss function in deep learning. Gradient descent (Cauchy, n.d.) is a first-order iterative optimization algorithm. At each iteration, we update the parameters $\mathbf{W}$ by taking a step toward the direction of the negative gradient as follows:

$$\mathbf{W}' = \mathbf{W} - \eta \cdot \nabla_{\mathbf{W}} \mathcal{L}(\mathbf{W}), \tag{3.41}$$

where $\nabla_{\mathbf{W}} \mathcal{L}(\mathbf{W})$ denotes the gradient and η is the learning rate, which is a positive scalar determining how much we want to go in this direction. The learning rate η is commonly fixed to a small constant in deep learning.

The loss function is usually a summation of penalty over a set of training samples. Therefore, we write the loss function as follows:

$$\mathcal{L}(\mathbf{W}) = \sum_{i=1}^{N_s} \mathcal{L}_i(\mathbf{W}), \tag{3.42}$$

where $\mathcal{L}_i(\mathbf{W})$ is the loss for the ith sample and N_s denotes the number of samples. In many cases, directly calculating $\nabla_{\mathbf{W}} \mathcal{L}(\mathbf{W})$ over all samples could

Foundations of Deep Learning

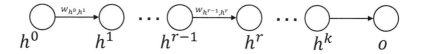

Figure 3.17 A sequence of neurons from consecutive layers.

be both space- and time-consuming. Mini-batch gradient descent comes to the rescue and is very popular in training deep neural networks. Instead of evaluating the gradient over all training samples, the mini-batch gradient descent method draws a small batch of samples out of the training data and uses them to estimate the gradients. This estimated gradient is then utilized to update the parameters. Specifically, the gradient can be estimated as $\sum_{j\in M} \nabla_{\mathbf{W}}\mathcal{L}_j(\mathbf{W})$, where M denotes the set of samples in the mini-batch. Other variants of gradient descent have also been developed to train deep neural networks, such as Adagrad (Duchi et al., 2011), Adadelta (Zeiler, 2012), and Adam (Kingma and Ba, 2014). They typically have better convergence than standard gradient descent methods.

3.6.2 Backpropagation

One crucial step to perform gradient-based optimization methods is to calculate the gradients with respect to all parameters. The backpropagation algorithm (Rumelhart et al., 1986; Le Cun and Fogelman-Soulié, 1987) provides an efficient way to calculate the gradients using dynamic programming. It consists of two phases: (1) a *forward phase* in which the inputs are fed into and pass through the neural networks and the outputs are calculated using the current set of parameters, which are then used to evaluate the value of the loss function, and (2) a *backward phase*, whose goal is to calculate the gradients of the loss function with respect to the parameters. According to the chain rule, the gradients for all parameters can be calculated dynamically in a backward direction starting from the output layer. Next we detail the backward pass.

Figure 3.17 illustrates a sequence of connected neural units $h^0, h^1, \ldots, h^k, o$ from different layers where h^i denotes a unit from the ith layer with h^0 from the input layer and o from the output layer. Assuming that this is the only path going through the edge (h^{r-1}, h^r), we can calculate the derivative using the chain rule as follows:

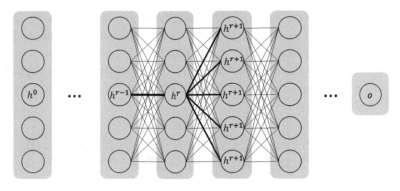

Figure 3.18 Decomposition of paths.

$$\frac{\partial \mathcal{L}}{\partial w_{(h^{r-1}, h^r)}} = \frac{\partial \mathcal{L}}{\partial o} \cdot \left[\frac{\partial o}{\partial h^k} \prod_{i=r}^{k-1} \frac{\partial h^{i+1}}{\partial h^i} \right] \cdot \frac{\partial h^r}{\partial w_{(h^{r-1}, h_r)}} \forall r \in 1 \ldots k, \quad (3.43)$$

where $w(h^{r-1}, h^r)$ denotes the parameter between the neural units h^{r-1} and h^r.

In multilayer neural networks, we often have several paths going through the edge (h^{r-1}, h^r). Hence, we need to sum up the gradients calculated through different paths as follows:

$$\frac{\partial \mathcal{L}}{\partial w_{(h^{r-1}, h^r)}} = \frac{\partial \mathcal{L}}{\partial o} \cdot \underbrace{\left[\sum_{[h^r, h^{r+1}, \ldots, h^k, o] \in \mathcal{P}} \frac{\partial o}{\partial h^k} \prod_{i=r}^{k-1} \frac{\partial h^{i+1}}{\partial h^i} \right]}_{\text{Backpropagation computes } \Delta(h^r, o) = \frac{\partial \mathcal{L}}{\partial h^r}} \frac{\partial h^r}{\partial w_{(h^{r-1}, h^r)}}, \quad (3.44)$$

where $\mathcal{P}$ denotes the set of paths starting from h^r to o, which can be extended to pass the edge (h^{r-1}, h^r). There are two parts on the right-hand side of Eq. (3.44), where the second part is trouble-free (will be discussed later in this section) to calculate and the first part (annotated as $\Delta(h^r, o)$) can be calculated recursively. Next, we discuss how to recursively evaluate the first term. Specifically, we have

$$\Delta(h^r, o) = \frac{\partial \mathcal{L}}{\partial o} \cdot \left[\sum_{[h^r, h^{r+1}, \ldots, h^k, o] \in \mathcal{P}} \frac{\partial o}{\partial h^k} \prod_{i=r}^{k-1} \frac{\partial h^{i+1}}{\partial h^i} \right]$$

$$= \frac{\partial \mathcal{L}}{\partial o} \cdot \left[\sum_{[h^r, h^{r+1}, \ldots, h^k, o] \in \mathcal{P}} \frac{\partial o}{\partial h^k} \prod_{i=r+1}^{k-1} \frac{\partial h^{i+1}}{\partial h^i} \cdot \frac{\partial h^{r+1}}{\partial h^r} \right]. \quad (3.45)$$

As shown in Figure 3.18, we can decompose any path $P \in \mathcal{P}$ into two parts: the edge (h^r, h^{r+1}) and the remaining path from h^{r+1} to o. Then, we can categorize the paths in $\mathcal{P}$ using the edge (h^r, h^{r+1}). Specifically, we denote the set of paths in $\mathcal{P}$ that share the same edge (h^r, h^{r+1}) as $\mathcal{P}_{r+1}$. Because all paths in $\mathcal{P}_{r+1}$ share the same first edge (h^r, h^{r+1}), any path in $\mathcal{P}_{r+1}$ can be characterized by the remaining path (i.e., the path from h^{r+1} to o) besides the first edge. We denote the set of remaining paths as $\mathcal{P}'_{r+1}$. Then, we can continue to simplify Eq. (3.45) as follows:

$$\Delta(h^r, o) = \frac{\partial \mathcal{L}}{\partial o} \cdot \left[\sum_{(h^r, h^{r+1}) \in \mathcal{E}} \frac{\partial h^{r+1}}{\partial h^r} \cdot \left[\sum_{[h^{r+1}, \ldots, h_k, o] \in \mathcal{P}'_{r+1}} \frac{\partial o}{\partial h_k} \prod_{i=r+1}^{k-1} \frac{\partial h^{i+1}}{\partial h^i} \right] \right]$$

$$= \sum_{(h^r, h^{r+1}) \in \mathcal{E}} \frac{\partial h^{r+1}}{\partial h^r} \cdot \frac{\partial \mathcal{L}}{\partial o} \cdot \left[\sum_{[h^{r+1}, \ldots, h_k, o] \in \mathcal{P}'_{r+1}} \frac{\partial o}{\partial h_k} \prod_{i=r+1}^{k-1} \frac{\partial h^{i+1}}{\partial h^i} \right]$$

$$= \sum_{(h^r, h^{r+1}) \in \mathcal{E}} \frac{\partial h^{r+1}}{\partial h^r} \cdot \Delta(h^{r+1}, o), \tag{3.46}$$

where $\mathcal{E}$ denotes the set containing all existing edges pointing from the unit h^r to a unit h^{r+1} from the $(r + 1)$st layer. Note that, as shown in Figure 3.18, any unit in the $r + 1$st layer is connected to h^r; hence, all units from the $r + 1$st layer are involved in the first summation in Eq. (3.46). Because each h^{r+1} is from a layer later than h^r, $\Delta(h^{r+1}, o)$ was evaluated during the previous backpropagation process and can be directly used. We still need to compute $\frac{\partial h^{r+1}}{\partial h^r}$ to complete evaluation of Eq. (3.46). To evaluate $\frac{\partial h^{r+1}}{\partial h^r}$, we need to take the activation function into consideration. Let a^{r+1} denote the values of unit h^{r+1} right before the activation function $\alpha(\cdot)$; that is, $h^{r+1} = \alpha(a^{r+1})$. Then, we can use the chain rule to evaluate $\frac{\partial h^{r+1}}{\partial h^r}$ as follows:

$$\frac{\partial h^{r+1}}{\partial h^r} = \frac{\partial \alpha(a^{r+1})}{\partial h^r} = \frac{\partial \alpha(a^{r+1})}{\partial a^{r+1}} \cdot \frac{\partial a^{r+1}}{\partial h^r} = \alpha'(a^{r+1}) \cdot w(h^r, h^{r+1}), \tag{3.47}$$

where $w(h^r, h^{r+1})$ is the parameter between the two units h^r and h^{r+1}. Then, we can rewrite $\Delta(h^r, o)$ as follows:

$$\Delta(h^r, o) = \sum_{(h^r, h^{r+1}) \in \mathcal{E}} \alpha'(a^{r+1}) \cdot w(h^r, h^{r+1}) \cdot \Delta(h^{r+1}, o). \tag{3.48}$$

Now, we return to evaluate the second part of Eq. (3.45) as follows:

$$\frac{\partial h_r}{\partial w_{(h^{r-1}, h_r)}} = \alpha'(a^r) \cdot h^{r-1}. \tag{3.49}$$

With Eq. (3.48) and Eq. (3.49), we can now efficiently evaluate Eq. (3.44) recursively.

3.6.3 Preventing Overfitting

Deep neural networks can easily overfit the training data because of their extremely high model capacity. In this section, we introduce some practical techniques to prevent neural networks from overfitting.

Weight Regularization

A common technique to prevent models from overfitting in machine learning is to include a regularization term on model parameters in the loss function. The regularization term constrains the model parameters to be relatively small, which generally enables the model to generalize better. Two commonly adopted regularizers are the L_1 and L_2 norms of the model parameters.

Dropout

Dropout is one effective technique to prevent overfitting (Srivastava et al., 2014). The idea of dropout is to randomly ignore some units in the networks during each batch of the training procedure. There is a hyperparameter called *dropout rate p* controlling the probability of ignoring each unit. Then, in each iteration, we randomly determine which neurons in the network to drop according to the probability p. Instead of using the entire network, the remaining neurons and network structure are then used to perform the calculation and prediction for this iteration. Note that the dropout technique is usually only utilized in the training procedure; in other words, the full network is always used to perform predictions in the inference procedure.

Batch Normalization

Batch normalization (Ioffe and Szegedy, 2015) was initially introduced to solve the problem of the internal covariate shift. It can also help mitigate overfitting. Batch normalization normalizes the activation from the previous layer before feeding the activation values into the next layer. Specifically, during the training procedure, if a mini-batch training procedure is adopted, this normalization is conducted by subtracting the batch mean and dividing the batch standard deviation. During the inference stage, we use the population statistics to perform the normalization.

3.7 Conclusion

In this chapter, we introduced a variety of basic deep architectures, including feedforward networks, convolutional neural networks, recurrent neural networks, and autoencoders. We then discussed gradient-based methods and the backpropagation algorithm for training deep architectures. Finally, we reviewed some practical techniques to prevent overfitting during the training procedure of these architectures.

3.8 Further Reading

To better understand deep learning and neural networks, proper knowledge on linear algebra, probability, and optimization is necessary. There are quite a few high-quality books on these topics, such as *Linear Algebra* (Hoffman and Kunze, 1971), *An Introduction to Probability Theory and Its Applications* (Feller, 1957) ,*Convex Optimization* (Boyd et al., 2004), and *Linear Algebra and Optimization for Machine Learning* (Aggarwal, 2018). These topics are also usually briefly introduced in machine learning books such as *Pattern Recognition and Machine Learning* (Bishop, 2006). There are dedicated books providing more detailed knowledge and content on deep neural networks such as *Deep Learning* (Goodfellow et al., 2016) and *Neural Networks and Deep Learning: A Textbook* (Aggarwal, 2018). In addition, various deep neural network models can be easily constructed with libraries and platforms such as Tensorflow (Abadi et al., 2015) and PyTorch (Paszke et al., 2017).

Part II

Methods

Part II

4

Graph Embedding

4.1 Introduction

Graph embedding aims to map each node in a given graph into a low-dimensional vector representation (or commonly known as node embedding) that typically preserves some key information of the node in the original graph. A node in a graph can be viewed from two domains: (1) the original graph domain, where nodes are connected via edges (or the graph structure), and (2) the embedding domain, where each node is represented as a continuous vector. Thus, from this two-domain perspective, graph embedding targets mapping each node from the graph domain to the embedding domain so that the information in the graph domain can be preserved in the embedding domain. Two key questions naturally arise: (1) What information needs to be preserved? and (2) How do we preserve this information? Different graph embedding algorithms often provide different answers to these two questions. For the first question, many types of information have been investigated, such as a node's neighborhood information (Perozzi et al., 2014; Tang et al., 2015; Grover and Leskovec, 2016), a node's structural role (Ribeiro et al., 2017), node status (Ma et al., 2017; Lai et al., 2017; Gu et al., 2018), and community information (Wang et al., 2017c). There are various methods proposed to answer the second question. Though the technical details of these methods vary, most of them share the same idea, which is to reconstruct the graph domain information to be preserved by using the node representations in the embedding domain. The intuition is that those good node representations should be able to reconstruct the information we desire to preserve. Therefore, the mapping can be learned by minimizing the reconstruction error. We illustrate an overall framework in Figure 4.1 to summarize the general process of graph embedding. As shown in Figure 4.1, there are four key components in the general framework:

75

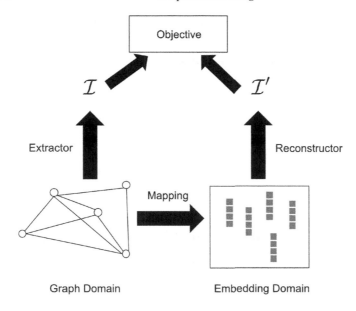

Figure 4.1 A general framework for graph embedding.

- A mapping function, which maps the node from the graph domain to the embedding domain.

- An information extractor, which extracts the key information $\mathcal{I}$ we want to preserve from the graph domain.

- A reconstructor to construct the extracted graph information $\mathcal{I}$ using the embeddings from the embedding domain. Note that the reconstructed information is denoted as $\mathcal{I}'$ as shown in Figure 4.1.

- An objective based on the extracted information $\mathcal{I}$ and the reconstructed information $\mathcal{I}'$. Typically, we optimize the objective to learn all parameters involved in the mapping and/or reconstructor.

In this chapter, we introduce representative graph embedding methods, which preserve different types of information in the graph domain, based on the general framework in Figure 4.1. Furthermore, we introduce graph embedding algorithms designed specifically for complex graphs, including heterogeneous graphs, bipartite graphs, multidimensional graphs, signed graphs, hypergraphs, and dynamic graphs.

4.2 Graph Embedding for Simple Graphs

In this section, we introduce graph embedding algorithms for simple graphs that are static, undirected, unsigned, and homogeneous, as introduced in Section 2.2. We organize algorithms according to the information they attempt to preserve, including node co-occurrence, structural role, node status, and community structure.

4.2.1 Preserving Node Co-occurrence

One of the most popular ways to extract node co-occurrence in a graph is via performing random walks. Nodes are considered similar to each other if they tend to co-occur in these random walks. The mapping function is optimized so that the learned node representations can reconstruct the "similarity" extracted from random walks. One representative network embedding algorithm preserving node co-occurrence is DeepWalk (Perozzi et al., 2014). Next, we introduce the DeepWalk algorithm under the general framework by detailing its mapping function, extractor, reconstructor, and objective. Then, we present more node co-occurrence preserving algorithms such as node2vec (Grover and Leskovec, 2016) and LINE (Tang et al., 2015).

Mapping Function
A direct way to define the mapping function $f(v_i)$ is using a lookup table. This means that we retrieve node v_i's embedding $\mathbf{u}_i$ given its index i. Specifically, the mapping function is implemented as

$$f(v_i) = \mathbf{u}_i = \mathbf{e}_i^\top \mathbf{W}, \qquad (4.1)$$

where $\mathbf{e}_i \in \{0, 1\}^N$ with $N = |\mathcal{V}|$ is the one-hot encoding of the node v_i. In particular, $\mathbf{e}_i$ contains a single element $\mathbf{e}_i[i] = 1$ and all other elements are 0. $\mathbf{W}^{N \times d}$ are the embedding parameters to be learned, where d is the dimension of the embedding. The ith row of the matrix $\mathbf{W}$ denotes the representation (or the embedding) of node v_i. Hence, the number of parameters in the mapping function is $N \times d$.

Random Walk–Based Co-occurrence Extractor
Given a starting node $v^{(0)}$ in a graph $\mathcal{G}$, we randomly walk to one of its neighbors. We repeat this process from the node until T nodes are visited. This random sequence of visited nodes is a random walk of length T on the graph. We formally define a random walk as follows.

Definition 4.1 (Random Walk)   *Let $G = \{V, \mathcal{E}\}$ denote a connected graph. We now consider a random walk starting at node $v^{(0)} \in V$ on the graph G. Assume that at the t-th step of the random walk, we are at node $v^{(t)}$ and then we proceed with the random walk by choosing the next node according to the following probability:*

$$p(v^{(t+1)}|v^{(t)}) = \begin{cases} \frac{1}{d(v^{(t)})}, & \text{if } v^{(t+1)} \in \mathcal{N}(v^{(t)}) \\ 0, & \text{otherwise}, \end{cases}$$

where $d(v^{(t)})$ denotes the degree of node $v^{(t)}$ and $\mathcal{N}(v^{(t)})$ is the set of neighbors of $v^{(t)}$. In other words, the next node is randomly selected from the neighbors of the current node following a uniform distribution.

We use a random walk generator to summarize the above process as follows:

$$\mathcal{W} = \text{RW}(G, v^{(0)}, T),$$

where $\mathcal{W} = (v^{(0)}, \ldots, v^{(T-1)})$ denotes the generated random walk, where $v^{(0)}$ is the starting node and T is the length of the random walk.

Random walks have been employed as a similarity measure in various tasks such as content recommendation (Fouss et al., 2007) and community detection (Andersen et al., 2006). In DeepWalk, a set of short random walks is generated from a given graph, and node co-occurrence is extracted from these random walks. Next, we detail the process of generating the set of random walks and extracting co-occurrence from them.

To generate random walks that can capture the information of the entire graph, each node is considered as a starting node to generate γ random walks. Therefore, there are $N \cdot \gamma$ random walks in total. This process is shown in Algorithm 1. The input of the algorithm includes a graph G, the length T of the random walk, and the number of random walks γ for each starting node. From line 4 to line 8 in Algorithm 1, we generate γ random walks for each node in V and add these random walks to $\mathcal{R}$. In the end, $\mathcal{R}$, which consists of $N \cdot \gamma$ generated random walks, is the output of the algorithm.

Algorithm 1: Generating Random Walks

---

1 **Input:** $\mathcal{G} = \{\mathcal{V}, \mathcal{E}\}, T, \gamma$

2 **Output:** $\mathcal{R}$

3 **Initialization:** $\mathcal{R} \leftarrow \emptyset$

4 **for** *i in range(1,γ)* **do**

5   **for** $v \in \mathcal{V}$ **do**

6          $\mathcal{W} \leftarrow RW(\mathcal{G}, v^{(0)}, T)$

7          $\mathcal{R} \leftarrow \mathcal{R} \cup \{\mathcal{W}\}$

8   **end**

9 **end**

These random walks can be treated as sentences in an "artificial language" where the set of nodes $\mathcal{V}$ is its vocabulary. The Skip-gram algorithm (Mikolov et al., 2013) in language modeling tries to preserve the information in sentences by capturing the co-occurrence relations between words in these sentences. For a given center word in a sentence, those words within a certain distance w away from the center word are treated as its "context." Then the center word is considered to co-occur with all words in its context. The Skip-gram algorithm aims to preserve such co-occurrence information. These concepts are adopted to the random walks to extract co-occurrence relations between nodes (Perozzi et al., 2014). Specifically, we denote the co-occurrence of two nodes as a tuple (v_{con}, v_{cen}), where v_{cen} denotes the center node and v_{con} indicates one of its context nodes. The process of extracting the co-occurrence relations between nodes from the random walks is shown in Algorithm 2. For each random walk $\mathcal{W} \in \mathcal{R}$, we iterate over the nodes in the random walk (line 5). For each node $v^{(i)}$, we add $(v^{(i-j)}, v^{(i)})$ and $(v^{(i+j)}, v^{(i)})$ into the list of co-occurrence $\mathcal{I}$ for $j = 1, \ldots, w$ (from line 6 to line 9). Note that for the cases where $i - j$ or $i + j$ is out of the range of the random walk, we simply ignore them. For a given center node, we treat all of its context nodes equally regardless of the distance between them. In Cao et al. (2015), the context nodes are treated differently according to their distance to the center node.

Algorithm 2: Extracting Co-occurrence

---

1 **Input:** $\mathcal{R}$, w
2 **Output:** $\mathcal{I}$
3 **Initialization:** $\mathcal{I} \leftarrow []$
4 **for** $\mathcal{W}$ **in** $\mathcal{R}$ **do**
5   **for** $v^{(i)} \in \mathcal{W}$ **do**
6   **for** j *in range(1,w)* **do**
7               $\mathcal{I}.append((v^{(i-j)}, v^{(i)}))$
8               $\mathcal{I}.append((v^{(i+j)}, v^{(i)}))$
9   **end**
10   **end**
11 **end**

Reconstructor and Objective

With the mapping function and the node co-occurrence information, we discuss the process of reconstructing the co-occurrence information using the representations in the embedding domain. To reconstruct the co-occurrence information, we try to infer the probability of observing the tuples in $\mathcal{I}$. For any given tuple $(v_{con}, v_{cen}) \in \mathcal{I}$, there are two roles of nodes; i.e., the center node v_{cen} and the context node v_{con}. A node can play both roles; i.e., the center node and the context node of other nodes. Hence, two mapping functions are employed to generate two node representations for each node corresponding to its two roles. They can be formally stated as

$$f_{cen}(v_i) = \mathbf{u}_i = e_i^\top \mathbf{W}_{cen}$$
$$f_{con}(v_i) = \mathbf{v}_i = e_i^\top \mathbf{W}_{con}.$$

For a tuple (v_{con}, v_{cen}), the co-occurrence relation can be explained as observing v_{con} in the context of the center node v_{cen}. With the two mapping functions f_{cen} and f_{con}, the probability of observing v_{con} in the context of v_{cen} can be modeled using a softmax function as follows:

$$p(v_{con}|v_{cen}) = \frac{exp(f_{con}(v_{con})^\top f_{cen}(v_{cen}))}{\sum_{v \in \mathcal{V}} exp(f_{con}(v) f_{cen}^\top(v_{cen}))}, \qquad (4.2)$$

which can be regarded as the reconstructed information from the embedding domain for the tuple (v_{con}, v_{cen}). For any given tuple (v_{con}, v_{cen}), the reconstructor *Rec* can return the probability in Eq. (4.2), which is summarized as:

$$Rec((v_{con}, v_{cen})) = p(v_{con}|v_{cen}).$$

If we can accurately infer the original graph information of $\mathcal{I}$ from the embedding domain, the extracted information $\mathcal{I}$ can be considered well-reconstructed. To achieve the goal, the *Rec* function should return high probabilities for extracted tuples in the $\mathcal{I}$ and low probabilities for randomly generated tuples. We assume that these tuples in the co-occurrence $\mathcal{I}$ are independent of each other as in the Skip-gram algorithm (Mikolov et al., 2013). Hence, the probability of reconstructing $\mathcal{I}$ can be modeled as follows:

$$\mathcal{I}' = Rec(\mathcal{I}) = \prod_{(v_{con}, v_{cen}) \in \mathcal{I}} p(v_{con}|v_{cen}). \tag{4.3}$$

There may exist duplicate tuples in $\mathcal{I}$. To remove these duplicates in Eq. (4.3), we reformulate it as follows:

$$\prod_{(v_{con}, v_{cen}) \in set(\mathcal{I})} p(v_{con}|v_{cen})^{\#(v_{con}, v_{cen})}, \tag{4.4}$$

where $set(\mathcal{I})$ denotes the set of unique tuples in $\mathcal{I}$ without duplicates and $\#(v_{con}, v_{cen})$ is the frequency of tuples (v_{con}, v_{cen}) in $\mathcal{I}$. Therefore, the tuples that are more frequent in $\mathcal{I}$ contribute more to the overall probability in Eq. (4.4). To ensure better reconstruction, we need to learn the parameters of the mapping functions such that Eq. (4.4) can be maximized. Thus, the node embeddings $\mathbf{W}_{con}$ and $\mathbf{W}_{cen}$ (or parameters of the two mapping functions) can be learned by minimizing the following objective:

$$\mathcal{L}(\mathbf{W}_{con}, \mathbf{W}_{cen}) = - \sum_{(v_{con}, v_{cen}) \in set(\mathcal{I})} \#(v_{con}, v_{cen}) \cdot \log p(v_{con}|v_{cen}), \tag{4.5}$$

where the objective is the negative logarithm of Eq. (4.4).

Speeding Up the Learning Process

In practice, calculating the probability in Eq. (4.2) is computationally unfeasible due to the summation over all nodes in the denominator. To address this challenge, two main techniques have been employed: hierarchical softmax and negative sampling (Mikolov et al., 2013).

Hierarchical Softmax

In hierarchical softmax, nodes in a graph $\mathcal{G}$ are assigned to the leaves of a binary tree. A toy example of the binary tree for hierarchical softmax is shown in Figure 4.2 where there are eight leaf nodes; i.e., there are eight nodes in the original graph $\mathcal{G}$. The probability $p(v_{con}|v_{cen})$ can now be modeled through the path to node v_{con} in the binary tree. Given the path to node v_{con} identified

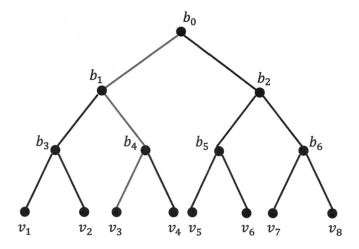

Figure 4.2 An illustrative example of hierarchical softmax. The path to node v_3 is highlighted in red.

by a sequence of tree nodes $(p^{(0)}, p^{(1)}, \ldots, p^{(H)})$ with $p^{(0)} = b_0$ (the root) and $p^{(H)} = v_{con}$, the probability can be obtained as

$$p(v_{con}|v_{cen}) = \prod_{h=1}^{H} p_{path}(p^{(h)}|v_{cen}),$$

where $p_{path}(p^{(h)}|v_{cen})$ can be modeled as a binary classifier that takes the center node representation $f(v_{cen})$ as input. Specifically, for each internal node, a binary classifier is built to determine the next node for the path to proceed.

We use the root node b_0 to illustrate the binary classifier where we are calculating the probability $p(v_3|v_8)$ (i.e., $(v_{con}, v_{cen}) = (v_3, v_8)$)) for the toy example shown in Figure 4.2. At the root node b_0, the probability of proceeding to the left node can be computed as

$$p(left|b_0, v_8) = \sigma(f_b(b_0)^\top f(v_8)),$$

where f_b is a mapping function for the internal nodes, f is the mapping function for the leaf nodes (or nodes in graph $\mathcal{G}$), and σ is the sigmoid function. Then the probability of the right node at b_0 can be calculated as

$$p(right|b_0, v_8) = 1 - p(left|b_0, v_8) = \sigma(-f_b(b_0)^\top f(v_8)).$$

Hence, we have

$$p_{path}(b_1|v_8) = p(left|b_0, v_8).$$

Note that the embeddings of the internal nodes can be regarded as the parameters of the binary classifiers, and the input of these binary classifiers is the embedding of the center node in (v_{con}, v_{cen}). By using hierarchical softmax instead of the conventional softmax in Eq. (4.2), the computational cost can be greatly reduced from $O(|\mathcal{V}|)$ to $O(\log |\mathcal{V}|)$. Note that in hierarchical softmax, we do not learn two mapping functions for nodes in $\mathcal{V}$. Instead, we learn a mapping function f for nodes in $\mathcal{V}$ (or leaf nodes in the binary tree) and a mapping function f_b for the internal nodes in the binary tree.

Example 4.2 (Hierarchical Softmax) Assume that (v_3, v_8) is a tuple describing co-occurrence information between nodes v_3 and v_8 with v_3 the context node and v_8 the center node in a given graph $\mathcal{G}$; the binary tree of hierarchical softmax for this graph is shown in Figure 4.2. The probability of observing v_3 in the context of v_8 – i.e., $p(v_3|v_8)$ – can be computed as follows:

$$p(v_3|v_8) = p_{path}(b_1|v_8) \cdot p_{path}(b_4|v_8) \cdot p_{path}(v_3|v_8)$$
$$= p(left|b_0, v_8) \cdot p(right|b_1, v_8) \cdot p(left|b_4, v_8).$$

Negative Sampling

Another popular approach to speed up the learning process is negative sampling (Mikolov et al., 2013). It is simplified from noise contrastive estimation (NCE; Gutmann and Hyvärinen, 2012), which has been shown to approximately maximize the log probability of softmax. However, our ultimate goal is to learn high-quality node representations instead of maximizing the probabilities. It is reasonable to simplify NCE as long as the learned node representations retain good quality. Hence, the following modifications are made to NCE and negative sampling is defined as follows. For each tuple (v_{con}, v_{cen}) in I, we sample k nodes that do not appear in the context of the center node v_{cen} to form the negative sample tuples. With these negative sample tuples, we define negative sampling for (v_{con}, v_{cen}) by the following objective:

$$\log \sigma \left(f_{con}(v_{con})^\top f_{cen}(v_{cen}) \right) + \sum_{i=1}^{k} E_{v_n \sim P_n(v)} \left[\log \sigma \left(-f_{con}(v_n)^\top f_{cen}(v_{cen}) \right) \right],$$

$$(4.6)$$

where the probability distribution $P_n(v)$ is the noise distribution to sample the negative tuples, which is often set to $P_n(v) \sim d(v)^{3/4}$ as suggested in Mikolov et al. (2013) and Tang et al. (2015). By maximizing Eq. (4.6), the probabilities between the nodes in the true tuples from I are maximized and those between the sample nodes in the negative tuples are minimized. Thus, it tends to ensure that the learned node representations preserve the co-occurrence information.

The objective in Eq. (4.6) is used to replace $\log p(v_{con}|v_{cen})$ in Eq. (4.5), which results in the following overall objective:

$$\mathcal{L}(\mathbf{W}_{con}, \mathbf{W}_{cen}) = \sum_{(v_{con}, v_{cen}) \in set(I)} \#(v_{con}, v_{cen}) \cdot \left(\log \sigma \left(f_{con}(v_{con})^\top f_{cen}(v_{cen}) \right) \right.$$
$$\left. + \sum_{i=1}^{k} E_{v_n \sim P_n(v)} \left[\log \sigma \left(-f_{con}(v_n)^\top f_{cen}(v_{cen}) \right) \right] \right).$$
$$(4.7)$$

By using negative sampling instead of the conventional softmax, the computational cost can be greatly reduced from $O(|\mathcal{V}|)$ to $O(k)$.

Training Process in Practice

We have introduced the overall objective function in Eq. (4.5) and two strategies to improve the efficiency of calculating the loss function. The node representations can now be learned by optimizing the objective in Eq. (4.5) (or its alternatives). However, in practice, instead of evaluating the entire objective function over the whole set of I and performing gradient descent–based updates, the learning process is usually done in a batch-wise way. Specifically, after generating each random walk $\mathcal{W}$, we can extract its corresponding co-occurrence information $I_{\mathcal{W}}$. Then, we can formulate an objective function based on $I_{\mathcal{W}}$ and evaluate the gradient based on this objective function to perform the updates for the involved node representations.

Other Co-occurrence Preserving Methods

There are other methods that aim to preserve co-occurrence information such as node2vec (Grover and Leskovec, 2016) and LINE (second-order; Tang et al., 2015). They are slightly different from DeepWalk but can still be fitted to the general framework in Figure 4.1. Next, we introduce these methods with a focus on their differences from DeepWalk.

node2vec

node2vec (Grover and Leskovec, 2016) introduces a more flexible way to explore the neighborhood of a given node through the biased random walk, which is used to replace the random walk in DeepWalk to generate I. Specifically, a second-order random walk with two parameters p and q is proposed. It is defined as follows.

Definition 4.3 *Let $G = \{\mathcal{V}, \mathcal{E}\}$ denote a connected graph. We consider a random walk starting at node $v^{(0)} \in \mathcal{V}$ in the graph G. Assume that the random walk has just walked from node $v^{(t-1)}$ to node $v^{(t)}$ and now resides* *at node $v^{(t)}$. The walk needs to decide which node to go for the next step. Instead of choosing $v^{(t+1)}$ uniformly from the neighbors of $v^{(t)}$, a probability sample is defined based on both $v^{(t)}$ and $v^{(t-1)}$. In particular, an unnormalized "probability" to choose the next node is defined as follows:*

$$\alpha_{pq}(v^{(t+1)}|v^{(t-1)}, v^{(t)}) = \begin{cases} \frac{1}{p} & \text{if } dis(v^{(t-1)}, v^{(t+1)}) = 0 \\ 1 & \text{if } dis(v^{(t-1)}, v^{(t+1)}) = 1 \\ \frac{1}{q} & \text{if } dis(v^{(t-1)}, v^{(t+1)}) = 2 \end{cases} \tag{4.8}$$

where $dis(v^{(t-1)}, v^{(t+1)})$ measures the length of the shortest path between node $v^{(t-1)}$ and $v^{(t+1)}$. The unnormalized probability in Eq. (4.8) can then be normalized as a probability to sample the next node $v^{(t+1)}$.

Note that the random walk based on this normalized probability is called a second-order random walk because it considers both the previous node $v^{(t-1)}$ and the current node $v^{(t)}$ when determining the next node $v^{(t+1)}$. The parameter p controls the probability to revisit the node $v^{(t-1)}$ immediately after stepping to node $v^{(t)}$ from node $v^{(t-1)}$. Specifically, a smaller p encourages the random walk to revisit, whereas a larger p ensures that the walk is less likely backtrack to visited nodes. The parameter q allows the walk to differentiate the "inward" and "outward" nodes. When $q > 1$, the walk is biased to nodes that are close to node $v^{(t-1)}$, and when $q < 1$, the walk tends to visit nodes that are distant from node $v^{(t-1)}$. Therefore, by controlling the parameters p and q, we can generate random walks with different focuses. After generating the random walks according to the normalized version of the probability in Eq. (4.8), the remaining steps of node2vec are the same as DeepWalk.

LINE

The objective of LINE (Tang et al., 2015) with second-order proximity can be expressed as follows:

$$- \sum_{(v_{con}, v_{cen}) \in \mathcal{E}} \left(\log \sigma \left(f_{con}(v_{con})^\top f_{cen}(v_{cen}) \right) \right.$$

$$\left. + \sum_{i=1}^{k} E_{v_n \sim P_n(v)} \left[\log \sigma \left(-f_{con}(v_n)^\top f_{cen}(v_{cen}) \right) \right] \right), \tag{4.9}$$

where $\mathcal{E}$ is the set of edges in the graph $\mathcal{G}$. Comparing Eq. (4.9) with Eq. (4.7), we can find that the major difference is that LINE adopts $\mathcal{E}$ instead of $\mathcal{I}$ as the information to be reconstructed. In fact, $\mathcal{E}$ can be viewed as a special case of $\mathcal{I}$ where the length of the random walk is set to 1.

A Matrix Factorization View

In Qiu et al. (2018b), it is shown that these aforementioned network embedding methods can be viewed from a matrix factorization perspective. For example, we have the following theorem for DeepWalk.

Theorem 4.4 (Qiu et al., 2018b) *In matrix form, DeepWalk with negative sampling for a given graph $\mathcal{G}$ is equivalent to factoring the following matrix:*

$$\log\left(\frac{\text{vol}(\mathcal{G})}{T}\left(\sum_{r=1}^{T}\mathbf{P}^{r}\right)\mathbf{D}^{-1}\right) - \log(k),$$

where $\mathbf{P} = \mathbf{D}^{-1}\mathbf{A}$ *with* $\mathbf{A}$ *the adjacency matrix of graph* $\mathcal{G}$ *and* $\mathbf{D}$ *its corresponding degree matrix,* T *is the length of random walk,* $\text{vol}(\mathcal{G}) = \sum_{i=1}^{|V|}\sum_{j=1}^{|V|}\mathbf{A}_{i,j}$, *and* k *is the number of negative samples.*

The matrix factorization form of DeepWalk can be also fitted into the general framework introduced in above. Specifically, the information extractor is

$$\log\left(\frac{\text{vol}(\mathcal{G})}{T}\left(\sum_{r=1}^{T}\mathbf{P}^{r}\right)\mathbf{D}^{-1}\right).$$

The mapping function is the same as that introduced for DeepWalk, where we have two mapping functions, $f_{cen}()$ and $f_{con}()$. The parameters for these two mapping functions are $\mathbf{W}_{cen}$ and $\mathbf{W}_{con}$, which are also the two sets of node representations for the graph $\mathcal{G}$. The reconstructor, in this case, can be represented in the following form: $\mathbf{W}_{con}\mathbf{W}_{cen}^{\top}$. The objective function can then be represented as follows:

$$\mathcal{L}(\mathbf{W}_{con}, \mathbf{W}_{cen}) = \left\|\log\left(\frac{\text{vol}(\mathcal{G})}{T}\left(\sum_{r=1}^{T}\mathbf{P}^{r}\right)\mathbf{D}^{-1}\right) - \log(b) - \mathbf{W}_{con}\mathbf{W}_{cen}^{\top}\right\|_{F}^{2}.$$

The embeddings $\mathbf{W}_{con}$ and $\mathbf{W}_{cen}$ can thus be learned by minimizing this objective. Similarly, LINE and node2vec can also be represented in matrix form (Qiu et al., 2018b).

4.2.2 Preserving Structural Role

Two nodes close to each other in the graph domain (e.g., nodes d and e in Figure 4.3) tend to co-occur in many random walks. Therefore, the co-occurrence preserving methods are likely to learn similar representations for these nodes in the embedding domain. However, in many real-world

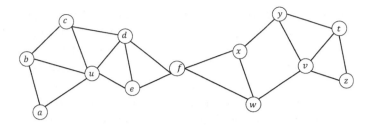

Figure 4.3 An illustration of two nodes that share similar structural roles.

applications, we want to embed nodes u and v in Figure 4.3 to be close in the embedding domain because they share a similar structural role. For example, if we want to differentiate hubs from non-hubs in airport networks, we need to project the hub cities, which are likely to be distant from each other but share a similar structural role, into similar representations. Therefore, it is vital to develop graph embedding methods that can preserve structural roles.

The method struc2vec was proposed to learn node representations that can preserve structural identity (Ribeiro et al., 2017). It has the same mapping function as DeepWalk but it extracts structural role similarity from the original graph domain. In particular, a degree-based method is proposed to measure the pairwise structural role similarity, which is then adopted to build a new graph. Therefore, the edge in the new graph denotes structural role similarity. Next, the random walk–based algorithm is utilized to extract co-occurrence relations from the new graph. Because struc2vec shares the same mapping and reconstructor functions as Deepwalk, we only detail the extractor of struc2vec. It includes the structural similarity measure, the newly built graph, and the biased random walk to extract the co-occurrence relations based on the new graph.

Measuring Structural Role Similarity

Intuitively, the degree of nodes can indicate their structural role similarity. In other words, two nodes with similar degree can be considered structurally similar. Furthermore, if their neighbors also have similar degree, these nodes can be even more similar. Based on this intuition, a hierarchical structural similarity measure was proposed in Ribeiro et al. (2017). We use $R_k(v)$ to denote the set of nodes that are k-hop away from node v. We order the nodes in $R_k(v)$ according to their degree to the degree sequence $s(R_k(v))$. Then, the structural distance $g_k(v_1, v_2)$ between two nodes v_1 and v_2 considering their k-hop neighborhoods can be recursively defined as follows:

$$g_k(v_1, v_2) = g_{k-1}(v_1, v_2) + \text{dis}(s(R_k(v_1)), s(R_k(v_2))),$$

where $\text{dis}(s(R_k(v_1)), s(R_k(v_2))) \geq 0$ measures the distance between the ordered degree sequences of v_1 and v_2. In other words, it indicates the degree similarity of k-hop neighbors of v_1 and v_2. Note that $g_{-1}(\cdot, \cdot)$ is initialized with 0. Both $\text{dis}(\cdot, \cdot)$ and $g_k(\cdot, \cdot)$ are distance measures. Therefore, the larger they are, the more dissimilar the two compared inputs are. The sequences $s(R_k(v_1))$ and $s(R_k(v_2))$ can be of different lengths and their elements are arbitrary integers. Thus, dynamic time warping (Sailer, 1978; Salvador and Chan, 2007) is adopted as the distance function $\text{dis}(\cdot, \cdot)$ because it can deal with sequences of different sizes. The dynamic time warping algorithm finds the optimal alignment between two sequences such that the sum of the distance between the aligned elements is minimized. The distance between two elements a and b is measured as

$$l(a, b) = \frac{\max(a, b)}{\min(a, b)} - 1.$$

Note that this distance depends on the ratio between the maximum and minimum of the two elements; thus, it can regard $l(1, 2)$ as much different from $l(100, 101)$, which is desired when measuring difference between degrees.

Constructing a Graph Based on Structural Similarity

After obtaining the pairwise structural distance, we can construct a multi-layer weighted graph that encodes the structural similarity between the nodes. Specifically, with k^* as the diameter of the original graph $\mathcal{G}$, we can build a k^* layer graph where the kth layer is built upon the weights defined as follows:

$$w_k(u, v) = \exp(-g_k(u, v)).$$

Here, $w_k(u, v)$ denotes the weight of the edge between nodes u and v in the k-th layer of the graph. The connection between nodes u and v is stronger when the distance $g_k(u, v)$ is smaller. Next, we connect different layers in the graph with directed edges. In particular, every node v in layer k is connected to its corresponding node in layers $k - 1$ and $k + 1$. We denote node v in the k-th layer as $v^{(k)}$ and the edge weights between layers are defined as follows:

$$w(v^{(k)}, v^{(k+1)}) = \log(\Gamma_k(v) + e), k = 0, \ldots, k^* - 1,$$
$$w(v^{(k)}, v^{(k-1)}) = 1, k = 1, \ldots, k^*,$$

where

$$\Gamma_k(v) = \sum_{v_j \in \mathcal{V}} \mathbb{1}(w_k(v, v_j) > \bar{w}_k),$$

with $\bar{w}_k = \sum_{(u,v) \in \mathcal{E}_k} w_k(u, v) / \binom{N}{2}$ denoting the average edge weight of the complete graph ($\mathcal{E}_k$ is its set of edges) in layer k. Thus, $\Gamma_k(v)$ measures the similarity of node v to other nodes in layer k. This design ensures that a node has a strong connection to the next layer if it is very similar to other nodes in the current layer. As a consequence, it is likely to guide the random walk to the next layer to acquire more information.

Biased Random Walks on the Built Graph

A biased random walk algorithm is proposed to generate a set of random walks, which are used to generate co-occurrence tuples to be reconstructed. Assume that the random walk is now at node u in layer k. For the next step, the random walk stays at the same layer with probability q and jumps to another layer with probability $1 - q$, where q is a hyperparameter.

If the random walk stays at the same layer, the probability of stepping from the current node u to another node v is computed as follows:

$$p_k(v|u) = \frac{\exp(-g_k(v, u))}{Z_k(u)},$$

where $Z_k(u)$ is a normalization factor for node u in layer k, which is defined as follows:

$$Z_k(u) = \sum_{(v,u) \in \mathcal{E}_k} \exp(-g_k(v, u)).$$

If the walk decides to walk to another layer, the probabilities to layer $k + 1$ and layer $k - 1$ are calculated as follows:

$$p_k\left(u^{(k)}, u^{(k+1)}\right) = \frac{w\left(u^{(k)}, u^{(k+1)}\right)}{w\left(u^{(k)}, u^{(k+1)}\right) + w\left(u^{(k)}, u^{(k-1)}\right)}$$
$$p_k\left(u^{(k)}, u^{(k-1)}\right) = 1 - p_k\left(u^{(k)}, u^{(k+1)}\right).$$

We can use this biased random walk to generate the set of random walks where we can extract the co-occurrence relations between nodes. Note that the co-occurrence relations are only extracted between different nodes but not between the same node from different layers. In other words, the co-occurrence relations are only generated when the random walk takes steps with the same layer. These co-occurrence relations can serve as the information to be reconstructed from the embedding domain as DeepWalk.

4.2.3 Preserving Node Status

The global status of nodes, such as their centrality scores introduced in Subsection 2.3.3, is important information in graphs. In Ma et al. (2017), a graph embedding method was proposed to jointly preserve node co-occurrence information and node global status. The method mainly consists of two components: (1) a component to preserve the co-occurrence information and (2) a component to keep the global status. The component to preserve the co-occurrence information is the same as in DeepWalk, introduced in Subsection 4.2.1. Hence, in this section, we focus on the component to preserve the global status information. Instead of preserving global status scores for nodes in the graph, the proposed method aims to preserve their global status ranking. Hence, the extractor calculates the global status scores and then ranks the nodes according to their scores. The reconstructor is utilized to restore the ranking information. Next, we detail the extractor and the reconstructor.

Extractor

The extractor first calculates the global status scores and then obtains the global rank of the nodes. Any of the centrality measurements introduced in Subsection 2.3.3 can be utilized to calculate the global status scores. After obtaining the global status scores, the nodes can be rearranged in descending order according to the scores. We denote the rearranged nodes as $(v_{(1)}, \ldots, v_{(N)})$ where the subscript indicates the rank of the node.

Reconstructor

The reconstructor is to recover the ranking information extracted by the extractor from the node embeddings. To reconstruct the global ranking, the reconstructor in Ma et al. (2017) aims to preserve the relative ranking of all pairs of nodes in $(v_{(1)}, \ldots, v_{(N)})$. Assume that the order between a pair of nodes is independent of other pairs in $(v_{(1)}, \ldots, v_{(N)})$; then the probability that the global ranking is preserved can be modeled using the node embedding as

$$p_{global} = \prod_{1 \le i < j \le N} p(v_{(i)}, v_{(j)}),$$

where $p(v_{(i)}, v_{(j)})$ is the probability that node $v_{(i)}$ is ranked before $v_{(j)}$ based on their node embeddings. In detail, it is modeled as

$$p\left(v_{(i)}, v_{(j)}\right) = \sigma\left(\mathbf{w}^T(\mathbf{u}_{(i)} - \mathbf{u}_{(j)})\right),$$

where $\mathbf{u}_{(i)}$ and $\mathbf{u}_{(j)}$ are the node embeddings for nodes $v_{(i)}$ and $v_{(j)}$, respectively (or outputs of the mapping function for $v_{(i)}$ and $v_{(j)}$), and $\mathbf{w}$ is a vector of parameters to be learned. To preserve the order information, we expect that any ordered pair $(v_{(i)}, v_{(j)})$ should have a high probability to be constructed from the embedding. This can be achieved by minimizing the following objective function:

$$\mathcal{L}_{global} = -\log p_{global}.$$

Note that this objective $\mathcal{L}_{global}$ can be combined with the objective to preserve the co-occurrence information such that the learned embeddings can preserve both the co-occurrence information and the global status.

4.2.4 Preserving Community Structure

Community structure is one of the most prominent features in graphs (Newman, 2006) and has motivated the development of embedding methods to preserve such critical information (Wang et al., 2017c; Li et al., 2018d). A matrix factorization–based method is proposed to preserve both node-oriented structure, such as connections and co-occurrence, and community structure (Wang et al., 2017c). Next, we use the general framework to describe its component to preserve node-oriented structure information and then introduce the component to preserve the community structure information with modularity maximization and discuss its overall objective.

Preserving Node-oriented Structure

Two types of node-oriented structure information are preserved (Wang et al., 2017c): pairwise connectivity information and similarity between the neighborhoods of nodes. Both types of information can be extracted from the given graph and represented in the form of matrices.

Extractor

The pairwise connection information can be extracted from the graph and represented as the adjacency matrix $\mathbf{A}$. The goal of the reconstrcutor is to reconstruct the pairwise connection information (or the adjacency matrix) of the graph. The neighborhood similarity measures how similar the neighborhoods of two nodes are. For nodes v_i and v_j, their pairwise neighborhood similarity is computed as follows:

$$s_{i,j} = \frac{\mathbf{A}_i \mathbf{A}_j{}^\top}{\|\mathbf{A}_i\| \|\mathbf{A}_j\|},$$

where $\mathbf{A}_i$ is the ith row of the adjacency matrix, which denotes the neighborhood information of node v_i. $s_{i,j}$ is larger when nodes v_i and v_j share more common neighbors and it is 0 if v_i and v_j do not share any neighbors. Intuitively, if v_i and v_j share many common neighbors – i.e., $s_{i,j}$ is large – they are likely to co-occur in the random walks described in DeepWalk. Hence, this information has an implicit connection with the co-occurrence. These pairwise neighborhood similarity relations can be summarized in a matrix $\mathbf{S}$, where the i, jth element is $s_{i,j}$. In summary, the extracted information can be denoted by two matrices $\mathbf{A}$ and $\mathbf{S}$.

Reconstructor and Objective

The reconstructor aims to recover these two types of extracted information in the form of $\mathbf{A}$ and $\mathbf{S}$. To reconstruct them simultaneously, it first linearly combines them as follows:

$$\mathbf{P} = \mathbf{A} + \eta \cdot \mathbf{S},$$

where $\eta > 0$ controls the importance of the neighborhood similarity. Then, the matrix $\mathbf{P}$ is reconstructed from the embedding domain as $\mathbf{W}_{con}\mathbf{W}_{cen}^T$, where $\mathbf{W}_{con}$ and $\mathbf{W}_{cen}$ are the parameters of two mapping functions f_{con} and f_{cen}. They have the same design as in DeepWalk. The objective can be formulated as follows:

$$\mathcal{L}(\mathbf{W}_{con}, \mathbf{W}_{cen}) = \|\mathbf{P} - \mathbf{W}_{con}\mathbf{W}_{cen}^T\|_F^2,$$

where $\|\cdot\|_F$ denotes the Frobenius norm of a matrix.

Preserving the Community Structure

In a graph, a community consists of a set of nodes that are densely connected. There often exist multiple communities in a graph. The task of community detection is to assign nodes in a graph into different communities. One popular community detection method is based on modularity maximization (Newman, 2006). Specifically, assuming that we are given a graph with two communities with known node–community assignment, the modularity can be defined as

$$Q = \frac{1}{2 \cdot \text{vol}(\mathcal{G})} \sum_{ij} (\mathbf{A}_{i,j} - \frac{d(v_i)d(v_j)}{\text{vol}(\mathcal{G})}) h_i h_j,$$

where $d(v_i)$ is the degree of node v_i, and $h_i = 1$ if node v_i belongs to the first community; otherwise, $h_i = -1$ and $\text{vol}(\mathcal{G}) = \sum_{v_i \in \mathcal{V}} d(v_i)$. In fact, $\frac{d(v_i)d(v_j)}{\text{vol}(\mathcal{G})}$ approximates the expected number of edges between nodes v_i and v_j in a randomly generated graph. The randomly generated graph has the same set of nodes, the same node degree, and the same number of edges as $\mathcal{G}$; however, its edges are randomly placed between nodes. Hence, the modularity Q is defined based on the difference between the fraction of observed edges that fall within communities in the original graph and the corresponding expected fraction in the randomly generated graph. A positive modularity Q suggests the possible presence of a community structure and often a larger modularity Q indicates that better community structures are discovered (Newman, 2006). Hence, to detect good communities, we can maximize the modularity Q by finding the proper community assignments. Furthermore, the modularity Q can be written in matrix form as

$$Q = \frac{1}{2 \cdot \text{vol}(\mathcal{G})} \mathbf{h}^T \mathbf{B} \mathbf{h},$$

where $\mathbf{h} \in \{-1, 1\}^N$ is the community assignment vector with the ith element $\mathbf{h}[i] = h_i$ and $\mathbf{B} \in \mathbb{R}^{N \times N}$ is defined as

$$\mathbf{B}_{i,j} = \mathbf{A}_{i,j} - \frac{d(v_i)d(v_j)}{\text{vol}(\mathcal{G})}.$$

The definition of modularity can be extended to $m > 2$ communities. In detail, the community assignment vector $\mathbf{h}$ can be generalized as a matrix $\mathbf{H} \in \{0, 1\}^{N \times m}$ where each column of $\mathbf{H}$ represents a community. The ith row of matrix $\mathbf{H}$ is a one-hot vector indicating the community of node v_i, where only one element of this row is 1 and the others are 0. Therefore, we have $tr(\mathbf{H}^T \mathbf{H}) = N$, where $tr(\mathbf{X})$ denotes the trace of a matrix $\mathbf{X}$. After discarding some constants, the modularity for a graph with m communities can be defined as $Q = tr(\mathbf{H}^T \mathbf{B} \mathbf{H})$. The assignment matrix $\mathbf{H}$ can be learned by maximizing the modularity Q as

$$\max_{\mathbf{H}} Q = tr(\mathbf{H}^T \mathbf{B} \mathbf{H}), \quad s.t. \ tr(\mathbf{H}^T \mathbf{H}) = N.$$

Note that $\mathbf{H}$ is a discrete matrix that is often relaxed to be a continuous matrix during the optimization process.

The Overall Objective

To jointly preserve the node-oriented structure information and the community structure information, another matrix $\mathbf{C}$ is introduced to reconstruct the indicator matrix $\mathbf{H}$ together with $\mathbf{W}_{cen}$. As a result, the objective of the entire framework is

$$\min_{\mathbf{W}_{con}, \mathbf{W}_{cen}, \mathbf{H}, \mathbf{C}} \|\mathbf{P} - \mathbf{W}_{con} \mathbf{W}_{cen}^T\|_F^2 + \alpha \|\mathbf{H} - \mathbf{W}_{cen} \mathbf{C}^T\|_F^2 - \beta \cdot tr(\mathbf{H}^T \mathbf{B} \mathbf{H}),$$

$$s.t. \quad \mathbf{W}_{con} \geq 0, \mathbf{W}_{cen} \geq 0, \mathbf{C} \geq 0, tr(\mathbf{H}^T \mathbf{H}) = N,$$

where the term $\|\mathbf{H} - \mathbf{W}_{cen} \mathbf{C}^T\|_F^2$ connects the community structure information with the node representations, the nonnegative constraints are added as nonnegative matrix factorization as adopted by Wang et al. (2017c), and the hyperparameters α and β control the balance among three terms.

4.3 Graph Embedding on Complex Graphs

In previous sections, we have discussed graph embedding algorithms for simple graphs. However, as shown in Section 2.6, real-world graphs present much more complicated patterns, resulting in numerous types of complex graphs. In this section, we introduce embedding methods for these complex graphs.

4.3.1 Heterogeneous Graph Embedding

In heterogeneous graphs, there are different types of nodes. In Chang et al. (2015), a framework Heterogeneous Network Embedding (HNE) was proposed to project different types of nodes in the heterogeneous graph into a common embedding space. To achieve this goal, a distinct mapping function is adopted for each type. Nodes are assumed to be associated with node features that can have different forms (e.g., images or texts) and dimensions. Thus, different deep models are employed for each type of node to map the corresponding features into the common embedding space. For example, if the associated feature is in the form of images, CNNs are adopted as the mapping function. HNE aims to preserve the pairwise connections between nodes. Thus, the extractor in HNE extracts node pairs with edges as the information to be reconstructed, which can be naturally denoted by the adjacency matrix $\mathbf{A}$. Hence, the reconstructor is to recover the adjacency matrix $\mathbf{A}$ from the node embeddings. Specifically, given a pair of nodes (v_i, v_j) and their embeddings $\mathbf{u}_i, \mathbf{u}_j$ learned by the mapping functions, the probability of the reconstructed adjacency element $\tilde{\mathbf{A}}_{i,j} = 1$ is computed as follows:

$$p(\tilde{\mathbf{A}}_{i,j} = 1) = \sigma(\mathbf{u}_i^\top \mathbf{u}_j),$$

where σ is the sigmoid function. Correspondingly,

$$p(\tilde{\mathbf{A}}_{i,j} = 0) = 1 - \sigma(\mathbf{u}_i^\top \mathbf{u}_j).$$

The goal is to maximize the probability such that the reconstructed adjacency matrix $\tilde{\mathbf{A}}$ is close to the original adjacency matrix $\mathbf{A}$. Therefore, the objective is modeled by the cross-entropy as follows:

$$-\sum_{i,j=1}^{N} \left(\mathbf{A}_{i,j} \log p(\tilde{\mathbf{A}}_{i,j} = 1) + (1 - \mathbf{A}_{i,j}) \log p(\tilde{\mathbf{A}}_{i,j} = 0) \right). \tag{4.10}$$

The mapping functions can be learned by minimizing the objective in Eq. (4.10) where the embeddings can be obtained. In heterogeneous graphs, different types of nodes and edges carry different semantic meanings. Thus, for heterogeneous network embedding, we should care about not only the structural correlations between nodes but also their semantic correlations. metapath2vec (Dong et al., 2017) is proposed to capture both correlations between nodes. Next, we detail the metapath2vec (Dong et al., 2017) algorithm including its extractor, reconstructor, and objective. Note that the mapping function in metapath2vec is the same as that in DeepWalk.

Meta-Path-Based Information Extractor

To capture both the structural and semantic correlations, meta-path-based random walks are introduced to extract the co-occurrence information. Specifically, metapaths are employed to constrain the decision of random walks. Next, we first introduce the concept of metapaths and then describe how to design the meta-path-based random walk.

Definition 4.5 (Metapath Schema) *Given a heterogeneous graph $\mathcal{G}$ as defined in Definition 2.35, a metapath schema ψ is a meta-template in $\mathcal{G}$ denoted as $A_1 \xrightarrow{R_1} A_2 \xrightarrow{R2} \cdots \xrightarrow{R_l} A_{l+1}$, where $A_i \in \mathcal{T}_n$ and $R_i \in \mathcal{T}_e$ denote certain types of nodes and edges, respectively. The metapath schema defines a composite relation between nodes from type A_1 to type A_{l+1} where the relation can be denoted as $R = R_1 \circ R_2 \circ \cdots R_{l-1} \circ R_l$. An instance of a metapath schema ψ is a metapath, where each node and edge in the path follows the corresponding types in the schema.*

Metapath schema can be used to guide the random walks. A meta-path-based random walk is a randomly generated instance of a given metapath schema ψ. The formal definition of a meta-path-based random walk is given here.

Definition 4.6 *Given a metapath schema $\psi : A_1 \xrightarrow{R_1} A_2 \xrightarrow{R2} \cdots \xrightarrow{R_l} A_{l+1}$, the transition probability of a random walk guided by ψ can be computed as*

$$p(v^{(t+1)}|v^{(t)}, \psi) = \begin{cases} \frac{1}{\left|\mathcal{N}_{t+1}^{R_t}(v^{(t)})\right|}, & \text{if } v^{(t+1)} \in \mathcal{N}_{t+1}^{R_t}(v^{(t)}), \\ 0, & \text{otherwise,} \end{cases}$$

where $v^{(t)}$ is a node of type A_t, corresponding to the position of A_t in the metapath schema. $\mathcal{N}_{t+1}^{R_t}(v^{(t)})$ denotes the set of neighbors of $v^{(t)}$ that have node type A_{t+1} and connect to $v^{(t)}$ through edge type R_t. It can be formally defined as:

$$\mathcal{N}_{t+1}^{R_t}(v^{(t)}) = \{v_j \mid v_j \in \mathcal{N}(v^{(t)}) \text{ and } \phi_n(v_j) = A_{t+1} \text{ and } \phi_e(v^{(t)}, v_j) = R_t\},$$

where $\phi_n(v_j)$ is a function to retrieve the type of node v_j and $\phi_e(v^{(t)}, v_j)$ is a function to retrieve the type of edge $(v^{(t)}, v_j)$ as introduced in Definition 2.35.

Then, we can generate random walks under the guidance of various meta-path schemas from which co-occurrence pairs can be extracted in the same way as in Subsection 4.2.1. Likewise, we denote tuples extracted from the random walks in the form of (v_{con}, v_{cen}) as $\mathcal{I}$.

Reconstructor

Two types of reconstructors were proposed in Dong et al. (2017). The first is the same as that for DeepWalk (or Eq. (4.2)) in Subsection 4.2.1. The other reconstructor is to define a multinomial distribution for each type of nodes instead of a single distribution over all nodes as in Eq. (4.2). For a node v_j with type nt, the probability of observing v_j given v_i can be computed as follows:

$$p(v_j|v_i) = \frac{exp(f_{con}(v_j)^\top f_{cen}(v_i))}{\sum\limits_{v \in \mathcal{V}_{nt}} exp(f_{con}(v)f_{cen}^\top(v_i))},$$

where $\mathcal{V}_{nt}$ is a set consisting of all nodes with type $nt \in \mathcal{T}_n$. We can adopt either of the two reconstructors and then construct the objective in the same way as that of DeepWalk in Subsection 4.2.1.

4.3.2 Bipartite Graph Embedding

As defined in Definition 2.36, in bipartite graphs there are two disjoint sets of nodes $\mathcal{V}_1$ and $\mathcal{V}_2$, and no edges exist within these two sets. For convenience, we use $\mathcal{U}$ and $\mathcal{V}$ to denote these two disjoint sets. In Gao et al. (2018b), a bipartite graph embedding framework BiNE was proposed to capture the relations between the two sets and the relations within each set. In particular two types of information are extracted: (1) the set of edges $\mathcal{E}$, which connect the nodes from the two sets, and (2) the co-occurrence information of nodes within each set. The same mapping function as in DeepWalk is adopted to map the nodes in the two sets to the node embeddings. We use $\mathbf{u}_i$ and $\mathbf{v}_i$ to denote the embeddings for nodes $u_i \in \mathcal{U}$ and $v_i \in \mathcal{V}$, respectively. Next, we introduce the information extractor, reconstructor, and objective for BiNE.

Information Extractor

Two types of information are extracted from the bipartite graph. One is the edges between the nodes from the two node sets, denoted as $\mathcal{E}$. Each edge $e \in \mathcal{E}$ can be represented as $(u_{(e)}, v_{(e)})$ with $u_{(e)} \in \mathcal{U}$ and $v_{(e)} \in \mathcal{V}$. The other is the co-occurrence information within each node set. To extract the co-occurrence information in each node set, two homogeneous graphs with

$\mathcal{U}$ and $\mathcal{V}$ as node sets are induced from the bipartite graph. Specifically, if two nodes are 2-hop neighbors in the original graph, they are connected in the induced graphs. We use $\mathcal{G}_{\mathcal{U}}$ and $\mathcal{G}_{\mathcal{V}}$ to denote the graphs induced for node sets $\mathcal{V}$ and $\mathcal{U}$, respectively. Then, the co-occurrence information can be extracted from the two graphs in the same way as in DeepWalk. We denote the extracted co-occurrence information as $\mathcal{I}_{\mathcal{U}}$ and $\mathcal{I}_{\mathcal{V}}$, respectively. Therefore, the information to be reconstructed includes the set of edges $\mathcal{E}$ and the co-occurrence information for $\mathcal{U}$ and $\mathcal{V}$.

Reconstructor and Objective

The reconstructor to recover the co-occurrence information in $\mathcal{U}$ and $\mathcal{V}$ from the embeddings is the same as that for DeepWalk. We denote the two objectives for reconstructing $\mathcal{I}_{\mathcal{U}}$ and $\mathcal{I}_{\mathcal{V}}$ as $\mathcal{L}_{\mathcal{U}}$ and $\mathcal{L}_{\mathcal{V}}$, respectively. To recover the set of edges $\mathcal{E}$, we model the probability of observing the edges based on the embeddings. Specifically, given a node pair (u_i, v_j) with $u_i \in \mathcal{U}$ and $v_j \in \mathcal{V}$, we define the probability that there is an edge between the two nodes in the original bipartite graph as

$$p(u_i, u_j) = \sigma(\mathbf{u}_i^\top \mathbf{v}_j),$$

where σ is the sigmoid function. The goal is to learn the embeddings such that the probability for the node pairs of edges in $\mathcal{E}$ can be maximized. Thus, the objective is defined as

$$\mathcal{L}_{\mathcal{E}} = - \sum_{(u_i, v_j) \in \mathcal{E}} \log p(u_i, v_j).$$

The final objective of BiNE is as follows:

$$\mathcal{L} = \mathcal{L}_{\mathcal{E}} + \eta_1 \mathcal{L}_{\mathcal{U}} + \eta_2 \mathcal{L}_{\mathcal{V}},$$

where η_1 and η_2 are the hyperparameters to balance the contributions for different types of information.

4.3.3 Multidimensional Graph Embedding

In a multidimensional graph, all dimensions share the same set of nodes while having their own graph structures. For each node, we aim to learn (1) a general node representation that captures the information from all dimensions and (2) a dimension-specific representation for each dimension, which focuses more on the corresponding dimension (Ma et al., 2018d). The general representations can be utilized to perform general tasks such as node classification, which requires node information from all dimensions. The dimension-specific representation can be utilized to perform dimension-specific tasks such as link prediction for a certain dimension. Intuitively, for each node, the general representation and the dimension-specific representation are not independent. Therefore, it is important to model their dependence. To achieve this goal, for each dimension d, we model the dimension-specific representation $\mathbf{u}_{d,i}$ for a given node v_i as

$$\mathbf{u}_{d,i} = \mathbf{u}_i + \mathbf{r}_{d,i}, \qquad (4.11)$$

where $\mathbf{u}_i$ is the general representation and $\mathbf{r}_{d,i}$ is the representation capturing information only in dimension d without considering the dependence. To learn these representations, we aim to reconstruct the co-occurrence relations in different dimensions. Specifically, we optimize mapping functions for $\mathbf{u}_i$ and $\mathbf{r}_{d,i}$ by reconstructing the co-occurrence relations extracted from different dimensions. Next, we introduce the mapping functions, the extractor, the reconstructor, and the objective for multidimensional graph embedding.

The mapping functions

The mapping function for the general representation is denoted as $f()$, and the mapping function for a specific dimension d is $f_d()$. Note that all of the mapping functions are similar to that in DeepWalk. They are implemented as lookup tables as follows:

$$\mathbf{u}_i = f(v_i) = e_i^{\top} \mathbf{W},$$
$$\mathbf{r}_{d,i} = f_d(v_i) = e_i^{\top} \mathbf{W}_d, d = 1 \ldots, D,$$

where D is the number of dimensions in the multidimensional graph.

Information Extractor

We extract co-occurrence relations for each dimension d as $\mathcal{I}_d$ using the co-occurrence extractor introduced in Subsection 4.2.1. The co-occurrence information of all dimensions is the union of that for each dimension as follows:

$$\mathcal{I} = \cup_{d=1}^{D} \mathcal{I}_d.$$

The Reconstructor and Objective

We aim to learn the mapping functions such that the probability of the co-occurrence $\mathcal{I}$ can be well reconstructed. The reconstructor is similar to that in DeepWalk. The only difference is that the reconstructor is now applied to the extracted relations from different dimensions. Correspondingly, the objective can be stated as follows:

$$\min_{\mathbf{W},\mathbf{W}_1,\dots,\mathbf{W}_D} -\sum_{d=1}^{D} \sum_{(v_{con},v_{cen})\in \mathcal{I}_d} \#(v_{con},v_{cen}) \cdot \log p(v_{con}|v_{cen}), \qquad (4.12)$$

where $\mathbf{W},\mathbf{W}_1,\dots,\mathbf{W}_D$ are the parameters of the mapping functions to be learned. Note that in Ma et al. (2018d), for a given node, the same representation is used for both the center and context representations.

4.3.4 Signed Graph Embedding

In signed graphs, there are both positive and negative edges between nodes, as introduced in Definition 2.38. Structural balance theory is one of the most important social theories for signed graphs. A signed graph embedding algorithm SiNE based on structural balance theory was proposed Wang et al. (2017b). As suggested by balance theory (Cygan et al., 2012), nodes should be closer to their "friends" (or nodes with positive edges) than their "foes" (or nodes with negative edges). For example, in Figure 4.4, v_j and v_k can be regarded as the friend and foe of v_i, respectively. SiNE aims to map friends closer than foes in the embedding domain; i.e., mapping v_j closer than v_k to v_i. Hence, the information to preserve by SiNE are the relative relations between friends and foes. Note that the mapping function in SiNE is the same as that in DeepWalk. Next, we describe the information extractor and then introduce the reconstructor.

Information Extractor
The information to preserve can be represented as a triplet (v_i, v_j, v_k) as shown in Figure 4.4, where nodes v_i and v_j are connected by a positive edge and nodes v_i and v_k connected by a negative edge. Let $\mathcal{I}_1$ denote a set of these triplets in a signed graph, which can be formally defined as

$$\mathcal{I}_1 = \left\{ (v_i, v_j, v_k) \,|\, \mathbf{A}_{i,j} = 1, \; \mathbf{A}_{i,k} = -1, \; v_i, v_j, v_k \in \mathcal{V} \right\},$$

where $\mathbf{A}$ is the adjacency matrix of the signed graph as defined in Definition 2.38. In the triplet (v_i, v_j, v_k), the node v_j is supposed to be more similar to v_i than the node v_k according to balance theory. For a given node v, we define its 2-hop subgraph as the subgraph formed by node v, nodes that are within 2-hops of v, and all edges between these nodes. In fact, the extracted information $\mathcal{I}_1$ does not contain any information for a node v whose 2-hop subgraph has only positive or negative edges. In this case, all triplets involving v contain edges

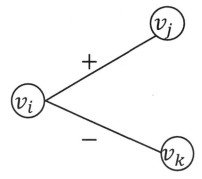

Figure 4.4 A triplet consists of a positive edge and a negative edge.

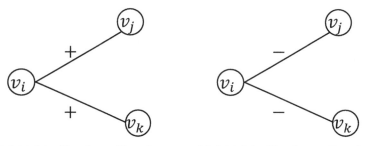

(a) A triplet with only positive edges   (b) A triplet with only negative edges

Figure 4.5 Triplets with edges of the same sign.

with the same sign as illustrated in Figure 4.5. Thus, we need to specify the information to preserve for these nodes in order to learn their representations.

It is evident that the cost of forming negative edges is higher than that of forming positive edges (Tang et al., 2014b). Therefore, in social networks, many nodes have only positive edges in their 2-hop subgraphs, whereas very few have only negative edges in their 2-hop subgraphs. Hence, we only consider handling nodes whose 2-hop subgraphs have only positive edges; a similar strategy can be applied to deal with the other type of nodes. To effectively capture the information for these nodes, we introduce a virtual node v_0 and then create negative edges between the virtual node v_0 and each of these nodes. In this way, a triplet (v_i, v_j, v_k) as shown in Figure 4.5a can be split into two triplets (v_i, v_j, v_0) and (v_i, v_k, v_0) as shown in Figure 4.6. Let $\mathcal{I}_0$ denote all of the edges involving the virtual node v_0. The information we extract can be denoted as $\mathcal{I} = \mathcal{I}_1 \cup \mathcal{I}_0$.

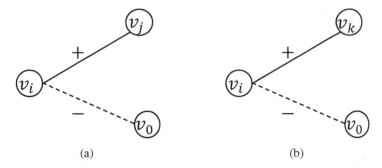

Figure 4.6 Expanding triplet in Figure 4.5a with a virtual node.

Reconstructor

To reconstruct the information of a given triplet, we aim to infer the relative relations of the triplet based on the node embeddings. For a triplet (v_i, v_j, v_k), the relative relation between v_i, v_j, and v_k can be mathematically reconstructed using their embeddings as follows:

$$s\left(f(v_i), f(v_j)\right) - (s(f(v_i), f(v_k)) + \delta)), \tag{4.13}$$

where $f()$ is the same mapping function as that in Eq. (4.1). The function $s(\cdot, \cdot)$ measures the similarity between two given node representations, which is modeled with feedforward neural networks. A positive value of Eq. (4.13) suggests that v_i is more similar to v_j than v_k, i.e, $s(f\left(v_i, v_j\right) > s(f(v_i, v_k))$. More specifically, $s(f\left(v_i, v_j\right) > s(f(v_i, v_k)) + \delta$, when the value of Eq. (4.13) is larger than 0. The parameter δ is a threshold to regulate the difference between the two similarities. To make the value of Eq. (4.13) be larger than 0, $s(f\left(v_i, v_j\right) - s(f(v_i, v_k))$ should be at least larger than δ. Hence, a larger δ requires the similarity between v_i and v_j to be much larger than the similarity between v_i and v_k to make the value of Eq. (4.13) remain positive. For any triplet (v_i, v_j, v_k) in $\mathcal{I}$, to be larger than 0 we expect the value of Eq. (4.13) such that the relative information can be preserved; i.e., v_i and v_j connected with a positive edge are more similar than v_i and v_k connected with a negative edge.

The Objective

To ensure that the information in $\mathcal{I}$ can be preserved by node representations, we need to optimize the mapping function such that the value of Eq. (4.13) can be larger than 0 for all triplets in $\mathcal{I}$. Hence, the objective function can be defined as follows:

$$\min_{\mathbf{W},\Theta} \frac{1}{|\mathcal{I}_0| + |\mathcal{I}_1|} [\sum_{(v_i,v_j,v_k)\in\mathcal{I}_1} \max\left(0, s(f(v_i), f(v_k)) + \delta - s(f(v_i), f(v_j))\right)$$

$$+ \sum_{(v_i,v_j,v_0)\in\mathcal{I}_0} \max\left((0, s(f(v_i), f(v_0)) + \delta_0 - s(f(v_i), f(v_j))\right)$$

$$+ \alpha(R(\Theta) + \|\mathbf{W}\|_F^2)],$$

where $\mathbf{W}$ are the parameters of the mapping function, Θ denotes the parameters of $s(\cdot, \cdot)$, and $R(\Theta)$ is the regularizer on the parameters. Note that we use different parameters δ and δ_0 for $\mathcal{I}_1$ and $\mathcal{I}_0$ to flexibly distinguish the triplets from the two sources.

4.3.5 Hypergraph Embedding

In a hypergraph, a hyperedge captures relations between a set of nodes, as introduced in Subsection 2.6.5. In Tu et al. (2018), a method Deep Hyper-Network Embedding (DHNE) was proposed to learn node representations for hypergraphs by utilizing the relations encoded in hyperedges. Specifically, two types of information are extracted from hyperedges that are reconstructed by the embeddings. One is the proximity described directly by hyperedges and the other is the co-occurrence of nodes in hyperedges. Next, we introduce the extractor, the mapping function, the reconstructor, and the objective of DHNE.

Information Extractor

Two types of information are extracted from the hypergraph. One is the hyperedges. The set of hyperedges denoted as $\mathcal{E}$ directly describes the relations between nodes. The other type is the hyperedge co-occurrence information. For a pair of nodes v_i and v_j, the frequency with which they co-occur in hyperedges indicates how strong their relation is. The hyperedge co-occurrence between any pair of nodes can be extracted from the incidence matrix $\mathbf{H}$ as follows:

$$\mathbf{A} = \mathbf{H}\mathbf{H}^\top - \mathbf{D}_v,$$

where $\mathbf{H}$ is the incidence matrix and $\mathbf{D}_v$ is the diagonal node degree matrix as introduced in Definition 2.39. The i, jth element $\mathbf{A}_{i,j}$ indicates the number of times that nodes v_i and v_j co-occurr in hyperedges. For a node v_i, the ith row of $\mathbf{A}$ describes its co-occurrence information with all nodes in the graph (or the global information of node v_i). In summary, the extracted information includes the set of hyperedges $\mathcal{E}$ and the global co-occurrence information $\mathbf{A}$.

The Mapping Function

The mapping function is modeled with multilayer feedforward networks with the global co-occurrence information as the input. Specifically, for node v_i, the process can be stated as

$$\mathbf{u}_i = f(\mathbf{A}_i; \mathbf{\Theta}),$$

where f denotes the feedforward networks with $\mathbf{\Theta}$ as its parameters.

Reconstructor and Objective

There are two reconstructors to recover the two types of extracted information. We first describe the reconstructor to recover the set of hyperedges $\mathcal{E}$ and then introduce the reconstructor for the co-occurrence information $\mathbf{A}$. To recover the hyperedge information from the embeddings, we model the probability of a hyperedge existing between any given set of nodes $\{v_{(1)}, \ldots, v_{(k)}\}$ and then aim to maximize the probability for those hyperedges in $\mathcal{E}$. For convenience, in Tu et al. (2018), all hyperedges are assumed to have a set of k nodes. The probability that a hyperedge exists in a given set of nodes $\mathcal{V}^i = \{v_{(1)}^i, \ldots, v_{(k)}^i\}$ is defined as

$$p(1|\mathcal{V}^i) = \sigma\left(g([\mathbf{u}_{(1)}^i, \ldots, \mathbf{u}_{(k)}^i])\right),$$

where $g()$ is a feedforward network that maps the concatenation of the node embeddings to a single scalar and $\sigma()$ is the sigmoid function that transforms the scalar to the probability. Let R^i denote the variable to indicate whether there is a hyperedge between the nodes in $\mathcal{V}^i$ in the hypergraph, where $R^i = 1$ denotes that there is a hyperedge and $R^i = 0$ means there is no hyperedge. Then the objective is modeled based on cross-entropy as

$$\mathcal{L}_1 = -\sum_{\mathcal{V}^i \in \mathcal{E} \cup \mathcal{E}'} R^i \log p(1|\mathcal{V}^i) + (1 - R^i) \log(1 - p(1|\mathcal{V}^i)),$$

where $\mathcal{E}'$ is a set of negative "hyperedges" that are randomly generated to serve as negative samples. Each of the negative hyperedges $\mathcal{V}^i \in \mathcal{E}'$ consists of a set of k randomly sampled nodes.

To recover the global co-occurrence information $\mathbf{A}_i$ for node v_i, a feedforward network, which takes the embedding $\mathbf{u}_i$ as input, is adopted as

$$\tilde{\mathbf{A}}_i = f_{re}(\mathbf{u}_i; \mathbf{\Theta}_{re}),$$

where $f_{re}()$ is the feedforward network to reconstruct the co-occurrence information with $\mathbf{\Theta}_{re}$ as its parameters. The objective is then defined with least squares as

$$\mathcal{L}_2 = \sum_{v_i \in \mathcal{V}} \|\mathbf{A}_i - \tilde{\mathbf{A}}_i\|_2^2.$$

The two objectives are then combined to form the objective for the entire network embdding framework as

$$\mathcal{L} = \mathcal{L}_1 + \eta \mathcal{L}_2,$$

where η is a hyperparameter to balance the two objectives.

4.3.6 Dynamic Graph Embedding

In dynamic graphs, edges are associated with timestamps that indicate their emergence time, as introduced in Subsection 2.6.6. It is vital to capture the temporal information when learning the node representations. In Nguyen et al. (2018), a temporal random walk was proposed to generate random walks that capture temporal information in the graph. The generated temporal random walks are then employed to extract the co-occurrence information to be reconstructed. Because its mapping function, reconstructor, and objective are the same as those in DeepWalk, we mainly introduce the temporal random walk and the corresponding information extractor.

Information Extractor

The temporal random walk was introduced in Nguyen et al. (2018) to capture both the temporal and graph structural information. A valid temporal random walk consists of a sequence of nodes connected by edges with nondecreasing timestamps. To formally introduce temporal random walks, we first define the set of temporal neighbors for a node v_i at a given time t as follows.

Definition 4.7 (Temporal Neighbors) *For a node $v_i \in \mathcal{V}$ in a dynamic graph $\mathcal{G}$, its temporal neighbors at time t are those nodes connected with v_i after time t. Formally, it can be expressed as follows:*

$$\mathcal{N}_{(t)}(v_i) = \{v_j | (v_i, v_j) \in \mathcal{E} \text{ and } \phi_e((v_i, v_j)) \geq t\},$$

where $\phi_e((v_i, v_j))$ is the temporal mapping function. It maps a given edge to its associated time as defined in Definition 2.40.

The temporal random walks can then be stated as follows.

Definition 4.8 (Temporal Random Walks) *Let $\mathcal{G} = \{\mathcal{V}, \mathcal{E}, \phi_e\}$ be a dynamic graph where ϕ_e is the temporal mapping function for edges. We consider a temporal random walk starting from a node $v^{(0)}$ with $(v^{(0)}, v^{(1)})$ as its first edge.*

Assume that at the kth step, it just proceeds from node $v^{(k-1)}$ to node $v^{(k)}$ and now we choose the next node from the temporal neighbors $\mathcal{N}_{(\phi_e((v^{(k-1)},v^{(k)})))}(v^{(k)})$ of node $v^{(k)}$ with the following probability:

$$p(v^{(k+1)}|v^{(k)}) = \begin{cases} pre(v^{(k+1)}) & if\ v^{(k+1)} \in \mathcal{N}_{(\phi_e((v^{(k-1)},v^{(k)})))}(v^{(k)}) \\ 0, & otherwise, \end{cases}$$

where $pre(v^{(k+1)})$ is defined below where nodes with smaller time gaps to the current time are chosen with higher probability:

$$pre(v^{(k+1)}) = \frac{\exp\left[\phi_e((v^{(k-1)}, v^{(k)})) - \phi_e((v^{(k)}, v^{(k+1)}))\right]}{\sum\limits_{v^{(j)}\in\mathcal{N}_{(\phi_e((v^{(k-1)},v^{(k)})))}(v^{(k)})} \exp\left[\phi_e((v^{(k-1)}, v^{(k)})) - \phi_e((v^{(k)}, v^{(j)}))\right]}.$$

A temporal random walk naturally terminates itself if there are no temporal neighbors to proceed. Hence, instead of generating random walks of fixed length as in DeepWalk, we generate temporal random walks with length between window size w for co-occurrence extraction and a predefined length T. These random walks are leveraged to generate the co-occurrence pairs, which are reconstructed with the same reconstructor as in DeepWalk.

4.4 Conclusion

In this chapter, we introduce a general framework and a new perspective to understand graph embedding methods in a unified way. It mainly consists of four components, including: (1) a mapping function, which maps nodes in a given graph to their embeddings in the embedding domain; (2) an information extractor, which extracts information from the graphs; (3) a reconstructor, which utilizes the node embeddings to reconstruct the extracted information; and (4) an objective, which often measures the difference between the extracted and reconstructed information. The embeddings can be learned by optimizing the objective. Following the general framework, we categorize graph embedding methods according to the information they aim to preserve, including co-occurrence-based, structural role–based, global status–based, and community-based methods, and then detail representative algorithms in each group. In addition, under the general framework, we introduce representative embedding methods for complex graphs, including heterogeneous graphs, bipartite graphs, multidimensional graphs, signed graphs, hypergraphs, and dynamic graphs.

4.5 Further Reading

There are embedding algorithms that preserve information beyond what we have discussed above. In Rossi et al. (2018), motifs are extracted and preserved in node representations. A network embedding algorithm to preserve asymmetric transitivity information was proposed in Ou et al. (2016) for directed graphs. In Bourigault et al. (2014), node representations are learned to model and predict information diffusion. For complex graphs, we only introduce the most representative algorithms. However, there are more algorithms for each type of complex graph, including heterogeneous graphs (Chen and Sun, 2017; Shi et al., 2018a; Chen et al., 2019b), bipartite graphs (Wang et al., 2019j; He et al., 2019), multidimensional graphs (Shi et al., 2018b), signed graphs (Yuan et al., 2017; Wang et al., 2017a), hypergraphs (Baytas et al., 2018), and dynamic graphs (Li et al., 2017a; Zhou et al., 2018b). There are also quite a few surveys on graph embedding (Hamilton et al., 2017b; Goyal and Ferrara, 2018; Cai et al., 2018; Cui et al., 2018).

5

Graph Neural Networks

5.1 Introduction

Graph neural networks (GNNs) are a set of methods that aim to apply deep neural networks to graph-structured data. The classical deep neural networks cannot be easily generalized to graph-structured data because the graph structure is not a regular grid. The investigation of GNNs dates back to the early 21st century, when the first GNN model (Scarselli et al., 2005, 2008) was proposed for both node- and graph-focused tasks. When deep learning techniques gained enormous popularity in many areas, such as computer vision and natural language processing, researchers started to dedicate more efforts to this research area.

Graph neural networks can be viewed as a process of representation learning on graphs. For node-focused tasks, GNNs target learning good features for each node such that node-focused tasks can be facilitated. For graph-focused tasks, they aim to learn representative features for the entire graph where learning node features is typically an intermediate step. The process of learning node features usually leverages both the input node features and the graph structure. More specifically, this process can be summarized as follows:

$$\mathbf{F}^{(\text{of})} = h(\mathbf{A}, \mathbf{F}^{(\text{if})}), \tag{5.1}$$

where $\mathbf{A} \in \mathbb{R}^{N \times N}$ denotes the adjacency matrix of the graph with N nodes (i.e., the graph structure) and $\mathbf{F}^{(\text{if})} \in \mathbb{R}^{N \times d_{\text{if}}}$ and $\mathbf{F}^{(\text{of})} \in \mathbb{R}^{N \times d_{\text{of}}}$ denote the input and output feature matrices where d_{if} and d_{of} are their dimensions, respectively. In this book, we generally refer to the process that takes node features and graph structure as input and outputs a new set of node features as *graph filtering* operation. The superscripts (or subscripts) "if" and "of" in Eq. (5.1) denote *the input of filtering* and *the output of filtering*, respectively. Correspondingly, the operator $h(\cdot, \cdot)$ is called as a *graph filter*. Figure 5.1 illustrates a typical

107

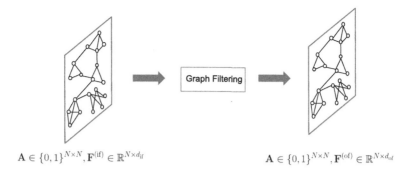

$$\mathbf{A} \in \{0,1\}^{N \times N}, \mathbf{F}^{(\text{if})} \in \mathbb{R}^{N \times d_{\text{if}}} \qquad\qquad \mathbf{A} \in \{0,1\}^{N \times N}, \mathbf{F}^{(\text{of})} \in \mathbb{R}^{N \times d_{\text{of}}}$$

Figure 5.1 Graph filtering operation.

graph filtering process where the filtering operation does not change the graph structure but only refines the node features.

For node-focused tasks, the graph filtering operation is sufficient, and multiple graph filtering operations are usually stacked consecutively to generate final node features. However, other operations are necessary for graph-focused tasks to generate the features for the entire graph from the node features. Similar to the classical convolutional neural networks (CNNs), pooling operations are proposed to summarize node features to generate graph-level features. The classical CNNs are applied to data residing on regular grids. However, the graph structure is irregular, which calls for dedicated pooling operations in GNNs. Intuitively, pooling operations on graphs should utilize the graph structure information to guide the pooling process. In fact, pooling operations often take a graph as input and then produce a coarsened graph with fewer nodes. Thus, the key to pooling operations is to generate the graph structure (or the adjacency matrix) and the node features for the coarsened graph. In general, as shown in Figure 5.2, a graph pooling operation can be described as follows:

$$\mathbf{A}^{(\text{op})}, \mathbf{F}^{(\text{op})} = \text{pool}(\mathbf{A}^{(\text{ip})}, \mathbf{F}^{(\text{ip})}), \qquad\qquad (5.2)$$

where $\mathbf{A}^{(\text{ip})} \in \mathbb{R}^{N_{\text{ip}} \times N_{\text{ip}}}$, $\mathbf{F}^{(\text{ip})} \in \mathbb{R}^{N_{\text{ip}} \times d_{\text{ip}}}$ and $\mathbf{A}^{(\text{op})} \in \mathbb{R}^{N_{\text{op}} \times N_{\text{op}}}$, $\mathbf{F}^{(\text{op})} \in \mathbb{R}^{N_{\text{op}} \times d_{\text{op}}}$ are the adjacency matrices and feature matrices before and after the pooling operation, respectively. Similarly, the superscripts (or subscripts) "ip" and "op" are used to indicate *the input of pooling* and *the output of pooling*, respectively. Note that N_{op} denotes the number of nodes in the coarsened graph and $N_{\text{op}} < N_{\text{ip}}$.

The architecture of a typical GNN model consists of graph filtering and/or graph pooling operations. For node-focused tasks, GNNs only utilize graph filtering operations. They are often composed with multiple consecutive graph

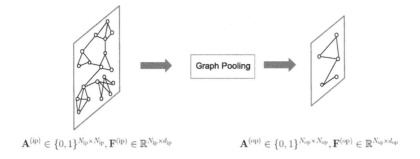

Figure 5.2 Graph pooling operation.

filtering layers where the output of the previous layer is the input for the following consecutive layer. For graph-focused tasks, GNNs require both graph filtering and graph pooling operations. Pooling layers usually separate the graph filtering layers into blocks. In this chapter, we first briefly introduce general architectures for GNNs and then provide the details of representative graph filtering and graph pooling operations.

5.2 The General GNN Frameworks

In this section, we introduce the general frameworks of GNNs for both node-focused and graph-focused tasks. We first introduce some notations that we use through the following sections. We denote a graph as $\mathcal{G} = \{\mathcal{V}, \mathcal{E}\}$. The adjacency matrix of the graph with N nodes is denoted as $\mathbf{A}$. The associated features are represented as $\mathbf{F} \in \mathbb{R}^{N \times d}$. Each row of $\mathbf{F}$ corresponds to a node, and d is the dimension of the features.

5.2.1 A General Framework for Node-Focused Tasks

A general framework for node-focused tasks can be regarded as a composition of graph filtering and nonlinear activation layers. A GNN framework with L graph filtering layers and $L-1$ activation layers (see Subsection 3.2.2 for representative activation functions) is shown in Figure 5.3, where $h_i()$ and $\alpha_i()$ denote the ith graph filtering layer and activation layer, respectively. We use $\mathbf{F}^{(i)}$ to denote the output of the ith graph filtering layer. Specifically, $\mathbf{F}^{(0)}$ is initialized to be the associated features $\mathbf{F}$. Furthermore, we use d_i to indicate the dimension of the output of the ith graph filtering layer. Because the graph

Graph Neural Networks

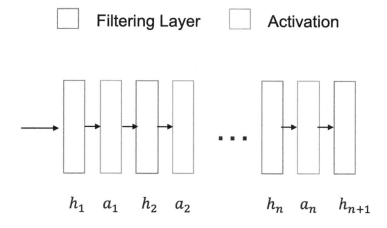

Figure 5.3 A general GNN architecture for node-focused tasks.

structure is unchanged, we have $\mathbf{F}^{(i)} \in \mathbb{R}^{N \times d_i}$. The ith graph filtering layer can be described as

$$\mathbf{F}^{(i)} = h_i \left(\mathbf{A}, \alpha_{i-1} \left(\mathbf{F}^{(i-1)} \right) \right),$$

where $\alpha_{i-1}()$ is the element-wise activation function following the $(i - 1)$st graph filtering layer. Note that we abuse the notation a little to use α_0 to denote the identity function because we do not apply the activation on the input features. The final output $\mathbf{F}^{(L)}$ is leveraged as the input to some specific layers according to the downstream node-focused tasks.

5.2.2 A General Framework for Graph-Focused Tasks

A general GNN framework for graph-focused tasks consists of three types of layers; i.e., the graph filtering layer, the activation layer, and the graph pooling layer. The graph filtering layer and the activation layer in the framework have functionalities similar to those in the node-focused framework. They are used to generate better node features. The graph pooling layer is utilized to summarize the node features and generate higher-level features that can capture the information of the entire graph. Typically, a graph pooling layer follows a series of graph filtering and activation layers. A coarsened graph with more abstract and higher-level node features is generated after the graph pooling layer. These layers can be organized into a *block* as shown in Figure 5.4, where h_i, α_i, and p denote the ith filtering layer, the ith activation layer, and the pooling layer in this block. The input of the block is the

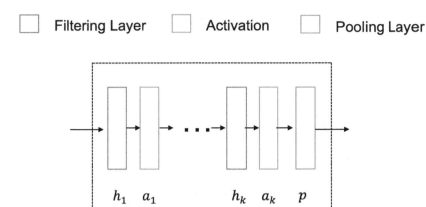

Figure 5.4 A block in GNNs for graph-focused tasks.

adjacency matrix $\mathbf{A}^{(\text{ib})}$ and the features $\mathbf{F}^{(\text{ib})}$ of a graph $\mathcal{G}_{ib} = \{\mathcal{V}_{ib}, \mathcal{E}_{ib}\}$ and the output are the newly generated adjacency matrix $\mathbf{A}^{(ob)}$ and the features $\mathbf{F}^{(ob)}$ for the coarsened graph $\mathcal{G}_{ob} = \{\mathcal{V}_{ob}, \mathcal{E}_{ob}\}$. The computation procedure of a block is formally stated as follows:

$$\mathbf{F}^{(i)} = h_i(\mathbf{A}^{(\text{ib})}, \alpha_{i-1}(\mathbf{F}^{(i-1)})) \quad \text{for} \quad i = 1, \dots k,$$
$$\mathbf{A}^{(ob)}, \mathbf{F}^{(ob)} = p(\mathbf{A}^{(\text{ib})}, \mathbf{F}^{(k)}), \tag{5.3}$$

where α_i is the activation function for $i \neq 0$ where α_0 is the identity function and $\mathbf{F}^{(0)} = \mathbf{F}^{ib}$. We can summarize the above computation process of a block as follows:

$$\mathbf{A}^{(ob)}, \mathbf{F}^{(ob)} = B(\mathbf{A}^{(\text{ib})}, \mathbf{F}^{(\text{ib})}).$$

The entire GNN framework can consist of one or more of these *blocks* as shown in Figure 5.5. The computation process of the GNN framework with L blocks can be formally defined as follows:

$$\mathbf{A}^{(j)}, \mathbf{F}^{(j)} = B^{(j)}(\mathbf{A}^{(j-1)}, \mathbf{F}^{(j-1)}) \quad \text{for} \quad j = 1, \dots, L, \tag{5.4}$$

where $\mathbf{F}^{(0)} = \mathbf{F}$ and $\mathbf{A}^{(0)} = \mathbf{A}$ are the initial node features and the adjacency matrix of the original graph, respectively. Note that the output of one block is utilized as the input for the consecutively following block as shown in Eq. (5.4). When there is only one block (or $L = 1$), the GNN framework can be regarded as *flat* because it directly generates graph-level features from the original graph. The GNN framework with pooling layers can be viewed

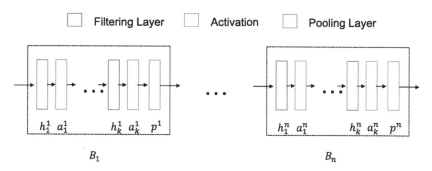

Figure 5.5 Architectures of GNNs for graph-focused tasks.

as a hierarchical process when $L > 1$, where the node features are gradually summarized to form the graph features by subsequently generating more and more coarsened graphs.

5.3 Graph Filters

There are various perspectives to design graph filters, which can be roughly split into two categories: (1) spatial-based graph filters and (2) spectral-based graph filters. The spatial-based graph filters explicitly leverage the graph structure (i.e., the connections between the nodes) to perform the feature refining process in the graph domain. In contrast, the spectral-based graph filters utilize spectral graph theory to design the filtering operation in the spectral domain. These two categories of graph filters are closely related. In particular, some of the spectral-based graph filters can be regarded as spatial-based filters. In this section, we introduce spectral-based graph filters and explain how some of the spectral-based graph filters can be viewed from a spatial perspective. We then discuss more spatial-based graph filters.

5.3.1 Spectral-Based Graph Filters

The spectral-based graph filters are designed in the spectral domain of graph signals. We first introduce the graph spectral filtering and then describe how it can be adopted to design spectral-based graph filters.

Graph Spectral Filtering
As shown in Figure 5.6, the idea of the graph spectral filtering is to modulate the frequencies of a graph signal such that some of its frequency components

are kept/amplified while others are removed/diminished. Hence, given a graph signal $\mathbf{f} \in \mathbb{R}^N$, we need first to apply graph Fourier transform to obtain its graph Fourier coefficients and then modulate these coefficients before reconstructing the signal in the spatial domain.

As introduced in Chapter 2, for a signal $\mathbf{f} \in \mathbb{R}^N$ defined on a graph $\mathcal{G}$, its graph Fourier transform is defined as follows:

$$\hat{\mathbf{f}} = \mathbf{U}^\top \mathbf{f},$$

where $\mathbf{U}$ consists of eigenvectors of the Laplacian matrix of $\mathcal{G}$ and $\hat{\mathbf{f}}$ are the obtained graph Fourier coefficients for the signal $\mathbf{f}$. These graph Fourier coefficients describe how each graph Fourier component contributes to the graph signal $\mathbf{f}$. Specifically, the ith element of $\hat{\mathbf{f}}$ corresponds to the ith graph Fourier component $\mathbf{u}_i$ with the frequency λ_i. Note that λ_i is the eigenvalue corresponding to $\mathbf{u}_i$. To modulate the frequencies of the signal $\mathbf{f}$, we filter the graph Fourier coefficients as follows:

$$\hat{\mathbf{f}}'[i] = \hat{\mathbf{f}}[i] \cdot \gamma(\lambda_i), \text{ for } \quad i = 1, \ldots, N,$$

where $\gamma(\lambda_i)$ is a function with the frequency λ_i as input, which determines how the corresponding frequency component should be modulated. This process can be expressed in matrix form as follows:

$$\hat{\mathbf{f}}' = \gamma(\mathbf{\Lambda}) \cdot \hat{\mathbf{f}} = \gamma(\mathbf{\Lambda}) \cdot \mathbf{U}^\top \mathbf{f},$$

where $\mathbf{\Lambda}$ is a diagonal matrix consisting of the frequencies (eigenvalues of the Laplacian matrix) and $\gamma(\mathbf{\Lambda})$ is applying the function $\gamma()$ to each element in the diagonal of $\mathbf{\Lambda}$. Formally, $\mathbf{\Lambda}$ and $\gamma(\mathbf{\Lambda})$ can be represented as follows:

$$\mathbf{\Lambda} = \begin{pmatrix} \lambda_1 & & 0 \\ & \ddots & \\ 0 & & \lambda_N \end{pmatrix}; \quad \gamma(\mathbf{\Lambda}) = \begin{pmatrix} \gamma(\lambda_1) & & 0 \\ & \ddots & \\ 0 & & \gamma(\lambda_N) \end{pmatrix}.$$

With the filtered coefficients, we can now reconstruct the signal to the graph domain using the inverse graph Fourier transform as follows:

$$\mathbf{f}' = \mathbf{U}\hat{\mathbf{f}}' = \mathbf{U} \cdot \gamma(\mathbf{\Lambda}) \cdot \mathbf{U}^\top \mathbf{f}, \tag{5.5}$$

where $\mathbf{f}'$ is the obtained filtered graph signal. The filtering process can be regarded as applying the operator $\mathbf{U} \cdot \gamma(\mathbf{\Lambda}) \cdot \mathbf{U}^\top$ to the input graph signal. For convenience, we sometimes refer to the function $\gamma(\mathbf{\Lambda})$ as the filter because it controls how each frequency component of the graph signal $\mathbf{f}$ is filtered. For example, in the extreme case, if $\gamma(\lambda_i)$ equals 0, then $\hat{\mathbf{f}}'[i] = 0$ and the frequency component $\mathbf{u}_i$ is removed from the graph signal $\mathbf{f}$.

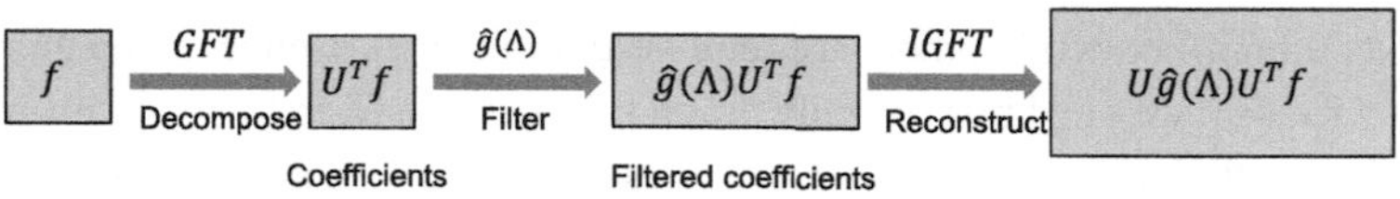

Figure 5.6 The process of spectral filtering.

Example 5.1   (Shuman et al., 2013) Suppose that we are given a noisy graph signal $\mathbf{y} = \mathbf{f}_0 + \eta$ defined on a graph $\mathcal{G}$, where η is uncorrelated additive Gaussian noise, and we wish to recover the original signal $\mathbf{f}_0$. The original signal $\mathbf{f}_0$ is assumed to be smooth with respect to the underlying graph $\mathcal{G}$. To enforce this prior information of the smoothness of the clean signal $\mathbf{f}_0$, a regularization term of the form $\mathbf{f}^\top \mathbf{L} \mathbf{f}$ is included in the optimization problem as follows:

$$\arg\min_{\mathbf{f}} \ \|\mathbf{f} - \mathbf{y}\|^2 + c\mathbf{f}^\top \mathbf{L} \mathbf{f}, \tag{5.6}$$

where $c > 0$ is a constant to control the smoothness. The objective is convex; hence, the optimal solution $\mathbf{f}'$ can be obtained by setting its derivative to 0 as follows:

$$2(\mathbf{f} - \mathbf{y}) + 2c\mathbf{L}\mathbf{f} = 0$$
$$\Rightarrow (I + c\mathbf{L})\mathbf{f} = \mathbf{y}$$
$$\Rightarrow (\mathbf{U}\mathbf{U}^\top + c\mathbf{U}\mathbf{\Lambda}\mathbf{U}^\top)\mathbf{f} = \mathbf{y}$$
$$\Rightarrow \mathbf{U}(\mathbf{I} + c\mathbf{\Lambda})\mathbf{U}^\top\mathbf{f} = \mathbf{y}$$
$$\Rightarrow \mathbf{f}' = \mathbf{U}(\mathbf{I} + c\mathbf{\Lambda})^{-1}\mathbf{U}^\top\mathbf{y}. \tag{5.7}$$

Comparing Eq. (5.7) with Eq. (5.5), we can find that the cleaner signal is obtained by filtering the noisy signal $\mathbf{y}$ with the filter $\gamma(\mathbf{\Lambda}) = (\mathbf{I} + c\mathbf{\Lambda})^{-1}$. For a specific frequency λ_l, the filter can be expressed as follows:

$$\gamma(\lambda_l) = \frac{1}{1 + c\lambda_l}, \tag{5.8}$$

which clearly indicates that $\gamma(\lambda_l)$ is a low-pass filter because $\gamma(\lambda_l)$ is large when λ_l is small and it is small when λ_l is large. Hence, solving the optimization problem in Eq. (5.6) is equivalent to applying the low-pass filter in Eq. (5.8) to the noisy signal $\mathbf{y}$.

Spectral-Based Graph Filters
We have introduced the graph spectral filtering operator, that can be used to filter certain frequencies in the input signal. For example, if we want to get

a smooth signal after filtering, we can design a low-pass filter where $\gamma(\lambda)$ is large when λ is small and small when λ is large. In this way, the obtained filtered signal is smooth because it mostly contains the low-frequency part of the input signal. An example of the low-pass filter is shown in Example 5.1. If we know how we want to modulate the frequencies in the input signal, we can design the function $\gamma(\lambda)$ in a corresponding way. However, when utilizing the spectral-based filter as a graph filter in GNNs, we often do not know which frequencies are more important. Hence, just like the classical neural networks, the graph filters can be learned in a data-driven way. Specifically, we can model $\gamma(\Lambda)$ with certain functions and then learn the parameters with the supervision from data.

A natural attempt is to give full freedom when designing $\gamma()$ (or a non-parametric model). In detail, the function $\gamma()$ is defined as follows (Bruna et al., 2013):

$$\gamma(\lambda_l) = \theta_l,$$

where θ_l is a parameter to be learned from the data. It can also be represented in matrix form as follows:

$$\gamma(\Lambda) = \begin{pmatrix} \theta_1 & & 0 \\ & \ddots & \\ 0 & & \theta_N \end{pmatrix}.$$

However, there are some limitations with this kind of filter. First, the number of parameters to be learned is equal to the number of nodes N, which can be extremely large in real-world graphs. Hence, it requires lots of memory to store these parameters and also abundant data to fit them. Second, the filter $\mathbf{U} \cdot \gamma(\Lambda) \cdot \mathbf{U}^\top$ is likely to be a dense matrix. Therefore, the calculation of the ith element of the output signal $\mathbf{f}'$ could relate to all nodes in the graph. In other words, the operator is not spatially localized. Furthermore, the computational cost for this operator is quite expensive due to the eigendecomposition of the Laplacian matrix and the matrix multiplication between dense matrices when calculating $\mathbf{U} \cdot \gamma(\Lambda) \cdot \mathbf{U}^\top$.

To address these issues, a polynomial filter operator, which we denote as Poly-Filter, was proposed in Defferrard et al. (2016). The function $\gamma()$ can be modeled with a K-order truncated polynomial as follows:

$$\gamma(\lambda_l) = \sum_{k=0}^{K} \theta_k \lambda_l^k. \tag{5.9}$$

In terms of the matrix form, it can be rewritten as

$$\gamma(\mathbf{\Lambda}) = \sum_{k=0}^{K} \theta_k \mathbf{\Lambda}^k. \tag{5.10}$$

Clearly, the number of parameters in Eq. (5.9) and Eq. (5.10) is $K+1$, which is not dependent on the number of nodes in the graph. Furthermore, we can show that $\mathbf{U} \cdot \gamma(\mathbf{\Lambda}) \cdot \mathbf{U}^\top$ can be simplified to be a polynomial of the Laplacian matrix. This means that (1) no eigendecomposition is needed and (2) the polynomial parameterized filtering operator is spatially localized; i.e., the calculation of each element of the output $\mathbf{f}'$ only involves a small number of nodes in the graph. Next, we first show that the Poly-Filter operator can be formulated as a polynomial of the Laplacian matrix and then understand it from a spatial perspective.

By applying this Poly-Filter operator on $\mathbf{f}$, according to Eq. (5.5), we can get the output $\mathbf{f}'$ as follows:

$$\mathbf{f}' = \mathbf{U} \cdot \gamma(\mathbf{\Lambda}) \cdot \mathbf{U}^\top \mathbf{f}$$

$$= \mathbf{U} \cdot \sum_{k=0}^{K} \theta_k \mathbf{\Lambda}^k \cdot \mathbf{U}^\top \mathbf{f}$$

$$= \sum_{k=0}^{K} \theta_k \mathbf{U} \cdot \mathbf{\Lambda}^k \cdot \mathbf{U}^\top \mathbf{f}. \tag{5.11}$$

To further simplify Eq. (5.11), we first show that $\mathbf{U} \cdot \mathbf{\Lambda}^k \cdot \mathbf{U}^\top = \mathbf{L}^k$ as follows:

$$\mathbf{U} \cdot \mathbf{\Lambda}^k \cdot \mathbf{U}^\top = \mathbf{U} \cdot (\mathbf{\Lambda} \mathbf{U}^\top \mathbf{U})^k \mathbf{U}^\top$$

$$= \underbrace{(\mathbf{U} \cdot \mathbf{\Lambda} \cdot \mathbf{U}^\top) \cdots (\mathbf{U} \cdot \mathbf{\Lambda} \cdot \mathbf{U}^\top)}_{k}$$

$$= \mathbf{L}^k. \tag{5.12}$$

With Eq. (5.12), we can now simplify Eq. (5.11) as follows:

$$\mathbf{f}' = \sum_{k=0}^{K} \theta_k \mathbf{U} \cdot \mathbf{\Lambda}^k \cdot \mathbf{U}^\top \mathbf{f}$$

$$= \sum_{k=0}^{K} \theta_k \mathbf{L}^k \mathbf{f}.$$

The polynomials of the Laplacian matrix are all sparse. In addition, the i,jth $(i \neq j)$ element of $\mathbf{L}^k$ is nonzero only when the length of the shortest path between node v_i and node v_j – i.e., $\text{dis}(v_i, v_j)$ – is less than or equal to k as described in the following lemma.

Lemma 5.2 *Let $\mathcal{G}$ be a graph and $\mathbf{L}$ be its Laplacian matrix. Then, the i, jth element of the kth power of the Laplacian matrix $\mathbf{L}_{i,j}^k = 0$ if $dis(v_i, v_j) > k$.*

Proof We prove this lemma by induction. When $k = 1$, by the definition of the Laplacian matrix $\mathbf{L}$ we naturally have that $\mathbf{L}_{i,j} = 0$ if $dis(v_i, v_j) > 1$. Assume for $k = n$ we have that $\mathbf{L}_{i,j}^n = 0$ if $dis(v_i, v_j) > n$. We proceed to prove that for $k = n + 1$ we have $\mathbf{L}_{i,j}^{n+1} = 0$ if $dis(v_i, v_j) > n + 1$. Specifically, the element $\mathbf{L}_{i,j}^{n+1}$ can be represented using $\mathbf{L}^n$ and $\mathbf{L}$ as

$$\mathbf{L}_{i,j}^{n+1} = \sum_{h=1}^{N} \mathbf{L}_{i,h}^n \mathbf{L}_{h,j}.$$

We next show that $\mathbf{L}_{i,h}^n \mathbf{L}_{h,j} = 0$ for $h = 1, \ldots, N$, which indicates that $\mathbf{L}_{i,j}^{n+1} = 0$.

If $\mathbf{L}_{h,j} \neq 0$, then $dis(v_h, v_j) \leq 1$; i.e., either $h = j$ or there is an edge between node v_i and node v_j. If we have $d(v_i, v_h) \leq n$, then, with $dis(v_i, v_j) \leq 1$, we have $dis(v_i, v_j) \leq n + 1$, which contradicts the assumption. Hence, $dis(v_i, v_h) > n$ must hold. Thus, we have $\mathbf{L}_{i,h}^n = 0$, which means $\mathbf{L}_{i,h}^n \mathbf{L}_{h,j} = 0$.

If $\mathbf{L}_{h,j} = 0$, then $\mathbf{L}_{i,h}^n \mathbf{L}_{h,j} = 0$ also holds. Therefore, $\mathbf{L}_{i,j}^{n+1} = 0$ if $dis(v_i, v_j) > n + 1$, which completes the proof. □

We now focus on a single element of the output signal $\mathbf{f}'$ to observe how the calculation is related to other nodes in the graph. More specifically, the value of the output signal at the node v_i can be calculated as

$$\mathbf{f}'[i] = \sum_{v_j \in \mathcal{V}} \left(\sum_{k=0}^{K} \theta_k \mathbf{L}_{i,j}^k \right) \mathbf{f}[j], \qquad (5.13)$$

which can be regarded as a linear combination of the original signal on all nodes according to the weight $\sum_{k=0}^{K} \theta_k \mathbf{L}_{i,j}^k$. According to Lemma 5.2, $\mathbf{L}_{i,j}^k = 0$ when $dis(v_i, v_j) > k$. Hence, not all nodes are involved in this calculation; rather, only those nodes that are within K-hop of the node v_i are involved. We can reorganize Eq. (5.13) with only those nodes that are within K-hop neighborhood of node v_i as

$$\mathbf{f}'[i] = b_{i,i}\mathbf{f}[i] + \sum_{v_j \in \mathcal{N}^K(v_i)} b_{i,j}\mathbf{f}[j], \qquad (5.14)$$

where $\mathcal{N}^K(v_i)$ denotes all of the nodes that are within K-hop neighborhood of node v_i and the parameter $b_{i,j}$ is defined as

$$b_{i,j} = \sum_{k=dis(v_i,v_j)}^{K} \theta_k \mathbf{L}_{i,j}^k,$$

where $\text{dis}(v_i, v_j)$ denotes the length of the shortest path between node v_i and node v_j. We can clearly observe that the Poly-Filter is localized in the spatial domain because it only involves K-hop neighborhoods when calculating the output signal value for a specific node. Furthermore, the Poly-Filter can be regarded as a spatial-based graph filter because the filtering process can be described based on the spatial graph structure as shown in Eq. (5.14). A similar graph filter operation was proposed in Atwood and Towsley (2016). Instead of using the powers of the Laplacian matrix, it linearly combines information aggregated from multi-hop neighbors of the center node with powers of the adjacency matrix.

Though the Poly-Filter enjoys various advantages, there are still some limitations. One major issue is that the basis of the polynomial (i.e., $1, x, x^2, \dots$) is not an orthogonal basis. Hence, the coefficients are dependent on each other, making them unstable under perturbation during the learning process. In other words, an update in one coefficient may lead to changes in other coefficients. To address this issue, the Chebyshev polynomial, which has a set of orthogonal basis, is utilized to model the filter (Defferrard et al., 2016). Next, we briefly discuss the Chebyshev polynomial and then detail the Cheby-Filter based on the Chebyshev polynomial.

Chebyshev Polynomial and Cheby-Filter

The Chebyshev polynomials $T_k(y)$ can be generated by the following recurrence relation:

$$T_k(y) = 2yT_{k-1}(y) - T_{k-2}(y), \tag{5.15}$$

with $T_0(y) = 1$ and $T_1(y) = y$, respectively. For $y \in [-1, 1]$, these Chebyshev polynomials can be represented in trigonometric expression as

$$T_k(y) = \cos(k \arccos(y)),$$

which means that each $T_k(y)$ is bounded in $[-1, 1]$. Furthermore, these Chebyshev polynomials satisfy the following relation:

$$\int_{-1}^{1} \frac{T_l(y)T_m(y)}{\sqrt{1 - y^2}} dy = \begin{cases} \delta_{l,m}\pi/2 & \text{if } m, l > 0, \\ \pi & \text{if } m = l = 0, \end{cases} \tag{5.16}$$

where $\delta_{l,m} = 1$ only when $l = m$; otherwise, $\delta_{l,m} = 0$. Equation (5.16) indicates that the Chebyshev polynomials are orthogonal to each other. Thus, the Chebyshev polynomials form an orthogonal basis for the Hilbert space of square integrable functions with respect to the measure $dy/\sqrt{1 - y^2}$, which is denoted as $L^2([-1, 1], dy/\sqrt{1 - y^2})$.

Because the domain for the Chebyshev polynomials is $[-1, 1]$, to approximate the filter with the Chebyshev polynomials, we rescale and shift the eigenvalues of the Laplacian matrix as follows:

$$\tilde{\lambda}_l = \frac{2 \cdot \lambda_l}{\lambda_{max}} - 1,$$

where $\lambda_{max} = \lambda_N$ is the largest eigenvalue of the Laplacian matrix. Clearly, all eigenvalues are transformed to the range $[-1, 1]$ by this operation. Correspondingly, in matrix form, the rescaled and shifted diagonal eigenvalue matrix is denoted as

$$\tilde{\mathbf{\Lambda}} = \frac{2\mathbf{\Lambda}}{\lambda_{max}} - \mathbf{I},$$

where $\mathbf{I}$ is the identity matrix. The Cheby-Filter, which is parameterized with the truncated Chebyshev polynomials, can be formulated as follows:

$$\gamma(\mathbf{\Lambda}) = \sum_{k=0}^{K} \theta_k T_k(\tilde{\mathbf{\Lambda}}).$$

The process of applying the Cheby-Filter on a graph signal $\mathbf{f}$ can be defined as

$$\mathbf{f}' = \mathbf{U} \cdot \sum_{k=0}^{K} \theta_k T_k(\tilde{\mathbf{\Lambda}})\mathbf{U}^{\top}\mathbf{f}$$

$$= \sum_{k=0}^{K} \theta_k \mathbf{U} T_k(\tilde{\mathbf{\Lambda}})\mathbf{U}^{\top}\mathbf{f}. \tag{5.17}$$

Next, we show that $\mathbf{U}T_k(\tilde{\mathbf{\Lambda}})\mathbf{U}^{\top} = T_k(\tilde{\mathbf{L}})$ with $\tilde{\mathbf{L}} = \frac{2\mathbf{L}}{\lambda_{max}} - \mathbf{I}$ in the following theorem.

Theorem 5.3 *For a graph $\mathcal{G}$ with Laplacian matrix $\mathbf{L}$, the following equation holds for $k \geq 0$:*

$$\mathbf{U}T_k(\tilde{\mathbf{\Lambda}})\mathbf{U}^{\top} = T_k(\tilde{\mathbf{L}}),$$

where

$$\tilde{\mathbf{L}} = \frac{2\mathbf{L}}{\lambda_{max}} - \mathbf{I}.$$

Proof For $k = 0$, the equation holds as $\mathbf{U}T_0(\tilde{\mathbf{\Lambda}})\mathbf{U}^{\top} = \mathbf{I} = T_0(\tilde{\mathbf{L}})$.

For $k = 1$,

$$\mathbf{U}T_1(\tilde{\mathbf{\Lambda}})\mathbf{U}^\top = \mathbf{U}\tilde{\mathbf{\Lambda}}\mathbf{U}^\top$$

$$= \mathbf{U}\left(\frac{2\mathbf{\Lambda}}{\mathbf{\Lambda}_{max}} - \mathbf{I}\right)\mathbf{U}^\top$$

$$= \frac{2\mathbf{L}}{\lambda_{max}} - \mathbf{I}$$

$$= T_1(\tilde{\mathbf{L}}).$$

Hence, the equation also holds for $k = 1$.

Assume that the equation holds for $k = n - 2$ and $k = n - 1$ with $n \geq 2$; then we show that the equation also holds for $k = n$ using the recursive relation in Eq. (5.15) as

$$\mathbf{U}T_n(\tilde{\mathbf{\Lambda}})\mathbf{U}^\top = \mathbf{U}\left[2\tilde{\mathbf{\Lambda}}T_{n-1}(\tilde{\mathbf{\Lambda}}) - T_{n-2}(\tilde{\mathbf{\Lambda}})\right]\mathbf{U}^\top$$

$$= 2\mathbf{U}\tilde{\mathbf{\Lambda}}T_{n-1}(\tilde{\mathbf{\Lambda}})\mathbf{U}^\top - \mathbf{U}T_{n-2}(\tilde{\mathbf{\Lambda}})\mathbf{U}^\top$$

$$= 2\mathbf{U}\tilde{\mathbf{\Lambda}}\mathbf{U}\mathbf{U}^\top T_{n-1}(\tilde{\mathbf{\Lambda}})\mathbf{U}^\top - T_{n-2}(\tilde{\mathbf{L}})$$

$$= 2\tilde{\mathbf{L}}T_{n-1}(\tilde{\mathbf{L}}) - T_{n-2}(\tilde{\mathbf{L}})$$

$$= T_n(\tilde{\mathbf{L}}),$$

which completes the proof.   □

With Theorem 5.3, we can further simplify Eq. (5.17) as

$$\mathbf{f}' = \sum_{k=0}^{K} \theta_k \mathbf{U}T_k(\tilde{\mathbf{\Lambda}})\mathbf{U}^\top \mathbf{f}$$

$$= \sum_{k=0}^{K} \theta_k T_k(\tilde{\mathbf{L}})\mathbf{f}.$$

Hence, the Cheby-Filter still enjoys the advantages of Poly-Filter but is more stable under perturbations.

GCN-Filter: Simplified Cheby-Filter Involving 1-Hop Neighbors

The Cheby-Filter involves a K-hop neighborhood of a node when calculating the new features for the node. In Kipf and Welling (2016a), a simplified Cheby-Filter named GCN-Filter is proposed. It is simplified from the Cheby-Filter by setting the order of Chebyshev polynomials to $K = 1$ and approximating $\lambda_{max} \approx 2$. Under this simplification and approximation, the Cheby-Filter with $K = 1$ can be simplified as follows:

$$\gamma(\mathbf{\Lambda}) = \theta_0 T_0(\tilde{\mathbf{\Lambda}}) + \theta_1 T_1(\tilde{\mathbf{\Lambda}})$$
$$= \theta_0 \mathbf{I} + \theta_1 \tilde{\mathbf{\Lambda}}$$
$$= \theta_0 \mathbf{I} + \theta_1 (\mathbf{\Lambda} - \mathbf{I}).$$

Correspondingly, applying the GCN-Filter to a graph signal $\mathbf{f}$, we can get the output signal $\mathbf{f}'$ as follows:

$$\mathbf{f}' = \mathbf{U}\gamma(\mathbf{\Lambda})\mathbf{U}^\top \mathbf{f}$$
$$= \theta_0 \mathbf{U}\mathbf{I}\mathbf{U}^\top \mathbf{f} + \theta_1 \mathbf{U}(\mathbf{\Lambda} - \mathbf{I})\mathbf{U}^\top \mathbf{f}$$
$$= \theta_0 \mathbf{f} - \theta_1 (\mathbf{L} - \mathbf{I})\mathbf{f}$$
$$= \theta_0 \mathbf{f} - \theta_1 (\mathbf{D}^{-\frac{1}{2}}\mathbf{A}\mathbf{D}^{\frac{1}{2}})\mathbf{f}. \tag{5.18}$$

Note that Eq. (5.18) holds because the normalized Laplacian matrix as defined in Definition 2.29 is adopted; i.e. $\mathbf{L} = \mathbf{I} - \mathbf{D}^{-\frac{1}{2}}\mathbf{A}\mathbf{D}^{-\frac{1}{2}}$. A further simplification is applied to Eq. (5.18) by setting $\theta = \theta_0 = -\theta_1$, which leads to

$$\mathbf{f}' = \theta_0 \mathbf{f} - \theta_1 (\mathbf{D}^{-\frac{1}{2}}\mathbf{A}\mathbf{D}^{\frac{1}{2}})\mathbf{f}$$
$$= \theta(\mathbf{I} + \mathbf{D}^{-\frac{1}{2}}\mathbf{A}\mathbf{D}^{-\frac{1}{2}})\mathbf{f}. \tag{5.19}$$

Note that the matrix $\mathbf{I} + \mathbf{D}^{-\frac{1}{2}}\mathbf{A}\mathbf{D}^{-\frac{1}{2}}$ has eigenvalues in the range $[0, 2]$, which may lead to numerical instabilities when this operator is repeatedly applied to a specific signal $\mathbf{f}$. Hence, a renormalization trick is proposed to alleviate this problem, which uses $\tilde{\mathbf{D}}^{-\frac{1}{2}}\tilde{\mathbf{A}}\tilde{\mathbf{D}}^{-\frac{1}{2}}$ to replace the matrix $\mathbf{I} + \mathbf{D}^{-\frac{1}{2}}\mathbf{A}\mathbf{D}$ in Eq. (5.19), where $\tilde{\mathbf{A}} = \mathbf{A} + \mathbf{I}$ and $\tilde{\mathbf{D}}_{ii} = \sum_j \tilde{\mathbf{A}}_{i,j}$. The final GCN-Filter after these simplifications is defined as

$$\mathbf{f}' = \theta\tilde{\mathbf{D}}^{-\frac{1}{2}}\tilde{\mathbf{A}}\tilde{\mathbf{D}}^{-\frac{1}{2}}\mathbf{f}. \tag{5.20}$$

The i, jth element of $\tilde{\mathbf{D}}^{-\frac{1}{2}}\tilde{\mathbf{A}}\tilde{\mathbf{D}}^{-\frac{1}{2}}$ is nonzero only when nodes v_i and v_j are connected. For a single node, this process can be viewed as aggregating information from its 1-hop neighbors where the node itself is also regarded as its 1-hop neighbor. Thus, the GCN-Filter can also be viewed as a spatial-based filter, which only involves directly connected neighbors when updating node features.

Graph Filters for Multichannel Graph Signals

We have introduced the graph filters for 1-channel graph signals, where each node is associated with a single scalar value. However, in practice, graph signals are typically multichannel, where each node has a vector of features.

A multichannel graph signal with d_{in} dimensions can be denoted as $\mathbf{F} \in \mathbb{R}^{N \times d_{in}}$. To extend the graph filters to the multichannel signals, we utilize the signals from all input channels to generate the output signal as follows:

$$\mathbf{f}_{out} = \sum_{d=1}^{d_{in}} \mathbf{U} \cdot \gamma_d(\mathbf{\Lambda}) \cdot \mathbf{U}^\top \mathbf{F}_{:,d},$$

where $\mathbf{f}_{out} \in \mathbb{R}^N$ is the 1-channel output signal of the filter and $\mathbf{F}_{:,d} \in \mathbb{R}^N$ denotes the dth channel of the input signal. Thus, the process can be viewed as applying the graph filter in each input channel and then calculating the summation of their results. Just as in classical CNNs, in most cases multiple filters are used to filter the input channels and the output is also a multichannel signal. Suppose that we use d_{out} filters; then the process to generate the d_{out}-channel output signal is defined as

$$\mathbf{F}'_{:,j} = \sum_{d=1}^{d_{in}} \mathbf{U} \cdot \gamma_{j,d}(\mathbf{\Lambda}) \cdot \mathbf{U}^\top \mathbf{F}_{:,d} \quad \text{for } j = 1, \ldots, d_{out}.$$

Specifically, in the case of the GCN-Filter in Eq. (5.20), this process for multi-channel input and output can be simply represented as

$$\mathbf{F}'_{:,j} = \sum_{d=1}^{d_{in}} \theta_{j,d} \tilde{\mathbf{D}}^{-\frac{1}{2}} \tilde{\mathbf{A}} \tilde{\mathbf{D}}^{-\frac{1}{2}} \mathbf{F}_{:,d} \quad \text{for } j = 1, \ldots, d_{out},$$

which can be further rewritten in matrix form as

$$\mathbf{F}' = \tilde{\mathbf{D}}^{-\frac{1}{2}} \tilde{\mathbf{A}} \tilde{\mathbf{D}}^{-\frac{1}{2}} \mathbf{F} \mathbf{\Theta}, \tag{5.21}$$

where $\mathbf{\Theta} \in \mathbb{R}^{d_{in} \times d_{out}}$ and $\mathbf{\Theta}_{d,j} = \theta_{j,d}$ is the parameter corresponding to the jth output channel and dth input channel. Specifically, for a single node v_i, the filtering process in Eq. (5.21) can also be formulated in the following form:

$$\mathbf{F}'_i = \sum_{v_j \in \mathcal{N}(v_i) \cup \{v_i\}} \left(\tilde{\mathbf{D}}^{-\frac{1}{2}} \tilde{\mathbf{A}} \tilde{\mathbf{D}}^{-\frac{1}{2}} \right)_{i,j} \mathbf{F}_j \mathbf{\Theta} = \sum_{v_j \in \mathcal{N}(v_i) \cup \{v_i\}} \frac{1}{\sqrt{\tilde{d}_i \tilde{d}_j}} \mathbf{F}_j \mathbf{\Theta}, \tag{5.22}$$

where $\tilde{d}_i = \tilde{\mathbf{D}}_{i,i}$ and we use $\mathbf{F}_i \in \mathbb{R}^{1 \times d_{out}}$ to denote the ith row of $\mathbf{F}$; i.e., the features for node v_i. The process in Eq. (5.22) can be regarded as aggregating information from 1-hop neighbors of node v_i.

5.3.2 Spatial-Based Graph Filters

As shown in Eq. (5.22), for a node v_i, the GCN-Filter performs a spatial information aggregation involving 1-hop neighbors and the matrix $\mathbf{\Theta}$ consisting of parameters for the filters can be regarded as a linear transformation applying to the input node features. In fact, spatial-based filters in GNNs were proposed even before deep learning became popular (Scarselli et al., 2005). More recently, A variety of spatial-based filters have been designed for GNNs. In this section, we review the very first spatial filter (Scarselli et al., 2005, 2008) and then more advanced spatial-based filters.

The Filter in the Very First GNN

The concept of GNNs was first proposed in Scarselli et al. (2008). This GNN model iteratively updates features of one node by utilizing features of its neighbors. Next, we briefly introduce the design of the filter in the very first GNN model. Specifically, the model is proposed to deal with graph data where each node is associated with an input label. For node v_i, its corresponding label can be denoted as l_i. For the filtering process, the input graph feature is denoted as $\mathbf{F}$, where $\mathbf{F}_i$ – i.e., the ith row of $\mathbf{F}$ – is the associated feature for node v_i. The output features of the filter are represented as $\mathbf{F}'$. The filtering operation for node v_i can be described as

$$\mathbf{F}'_i = \sum_{v_j \in \mathcal{N}(v_i)} g(l_i, \mathbf{F}_j, l_j),$$

where $g()$ is a parametric function called the *local transition function*, which is spatially localized. The filtering process for node v_i only involves its 1-hop neighbors. Typically $g()$ can be modeled by feedforward neural networks. The function $g()$ is shared by all nodes in the graph when performing the filtering process. Note that the node label information l_i can be viewed as the initial input information, which is fixed and utilized in the filtering process.

GraphSAGE-Filter

The GraphSAGE model proposed in Hamilton et al. (2017a) introduced a spatial-based filter that is also based on aggregating information from neighboring nodes. For a single node v_i, the process to generate its new features can be formulated as follows:

$$\mathcal{N}_S(v_i) = \text{SAMPLE}(\mathcal{N}(v_i), S) \tag{5.23}$$

$$\mathbf{f}'_{\mathcal{N}_S(v_i)} = \text{AGGREGATE}(\{\mathbf{F}_j, \forall v_j \in \mathcal{N}_S(v_i)\}) \tag{5.24}$$

$$\mathbf{F}'_i = \sigma\left([\mathbf{F}_i, \mathbf{f}'_{\mathcal{N}_S(v_i)}]\mathbf{\Theta}\right), \tag{5.25}$$

where SAMPLE() is a function that takes a set as input and randomly samples S elements from the input as output, AGGREGATE() is a function to combine the information from the neighboring nodes where $\mathbf{f}'_{\mathcal{N}_S(v_i)}$ denotes the output of the AGGREGATE() function, and $[\cdot, \cdot]$ is the concatenation operation. Hence, for a single node v_i, the filter in GraphSAGE first samples S nodes from its neighboring nodes $\mathcal{N}(v_i)$ as shown in Eq. (5.23). Then, the AGGREGATE() function aggregates the information from these sampled nodes and generates the feature $\mathbf{f}'_{\mathcal{N}_S(v_i)}$ as shown in Eq. (5.24). Finally, the generated neighborhood information and the old features of node v_i are combined to generate the new features for node v_i as shown in Eq. (5.25). Various AGGREGATE() functions were introduced in Hamilton et al. (2017a) as described below.

- **Mean aggregator.** The mean aggregator is to simply take the element-wise mean of the vectors in $\{\mathbf{F}_j, \forall v_j \in \mathcal{N}_S(v_i)\}$. The mean aggregator here is very similar to the filter in a GCN. When dealing with a node v_i, both of them take the (weighted) average of the neighboring nodes as its new representation. The difference is how the input representation $\mathbf{F}_j$ of node v_i gets involved in the calculation. It is clear that in GraphSAGE, $\mathbf{F}_i$ is concatenated to the aggregated neighboring information $\mathbf{f}'_{\mathcal{N}_S(v_i)}$. However, in the GCN-Filter, node v_i is treated in the same way as its neighbors and $\mathbf{F}_i$ is a part of the weighted average process.

- **LSTM aggregator.** The LSTM aggregator is to treat the set of the sampled neighboring nodes $\mathcal{N}_S(v_i)$ of node v_i as a sequence and utilize the LSTM architecture to process the sequence. The output of the last unit of the LSTM serves as the result $\mathbf{f}'_{\mathcal{N}_S(v_i)}$. However, there is no natural order among the neighbors; hence, a random ordering was adopted in Hamilton et al. (2017a).

- **Pooling operator.** The pooling operator adopts the max pooling operation to summarize the information from the neighboring nodes. Before summarizing the results, input features at each node are first transformed with a layer of a neural network. The process can be described as follows:

$$\mathbf{f}'_{\mathcal{N}_S(v_i)} = \max(\{\alpha(\mathbf{F}_j \boldsymbol{\Theta}_{\text{pool}}), \forall v_j \in \mathcal{N}_S(v_i)\}),$$

where max() denotes the element-wise max operator, $\boldsymbol{\Theta}_{\text{pool}}$ denotes a transformation matrix, and $\alpha()$ is a nonlinear activation function.

The GraphSAGE-Filter is spatially localized because it only involves 1-hop neighbors no matter which aggregator is used. The aggregator is also shared among all nodes.

GAT-Filter

A self-attention mechanism (Vaswani et al., 2017) is introduced to build spatial graph filters in graph attention networks (GATs; Veličković et al., 2017). For convenience, we call the graph filter in GAT a GAT-Filter. The

GAT-Filter is similar to the GCN-Filter because it also performs information aggregation from neighboring nodes when generating new features for each node. The aggregation in GCN-Filter is solely based on the graph structure, whereas the GAT-Filter tries to differentiate the importance of the neighbors when performing the aggregation. More specifically, when generating the new features for a node v_i, it attends to all of its neighbors to generate an importance score for each neighbor. These importance scores are then adopted as linear coefficients during the aggregation process. Next, we detail the GAT-Filter.

The importance score of node $v_j \in \mathcal{N}(v_i) \cup \{v_i\}$ to node v_i can be calculated as follows:

$$e_{ij} = a(\mathbf{F}_i\mathbf{\Theta}, \mathbf{F}_j\mathbf{\Theta}), \tag{5.26}$$

where $\mathbf{\Theta}$ is a shared parameter matrix. $a()$ is a shared attention function, which is a single-layer feedforward network in Veličković et al. (2017) as

$$a(\mathbf{F}_i\mathbf{\Theta}, \mathbf{F}_j\mathbf{\Theta}) = \text{LeakyReLU}(\mathbf{a}^\top[\mathbf{F}_i\mathbf{\Theta}, \mathbf{F}_j\mathbf{\Theta}]),$$

where $[\cdot, \cdot]$ denotes the concatenation operation, $\mathbf{a}$ is a parameterized vector, and LeakyReLU is the nonlinear activation function introduced in Subsection 3.2.2. The scores calculated by Eq. (5.26) are then normalized before being utilized because the weights in the aggregation process keep the output representation in a reasonable scale. The normalization over all neighbors of v_i is performed through a softmax layer as

$$\alpha_{ij} = \frac{\exp(e_{ij})}{\sum_{v_k \in \mathcal{N}(v_i) \cup \{v_i\}} \exp(e_{ik})},$$

where α_{ij} is the normalized importance score indicating the importance of node v_j to node v_i. With the normalized importance scores, the new representation $\mathbf{F}'_i$ of node v_i can be computed as

$$\mathbf{F}'_i = \sum_{v_j \in \mathcal{N}(v_i) \cup \{v_i\}} \alpha_{ij}\mathbf{F}_j\mathbf{\Theta}, \tag{5.27}$$

where $\mathbf{\Theta}$ is the same transforming matrix as in Eq. (5.26). To stabilize the learning process of self-attention, multihead attention (Vaswani et al., 2017) is adopted. Specifically, M independent attention mechanisms in the form of Eq. (5.27) with different $\mathbf{\Theta}^m$ and α_{ij}^m are performed in parallel. Their outputs are then concatenated to generate the final representation of node v_i as

$$\mathbf{F}'_i = \|_{m=1}^{M} \sum_{v_j \in \mathcal{N}(v_i) \cup \{v_i\}} \alpha_{ij}^m\mathbf{F}_j\mathbf{\Theta}^m, \tag{5.28}$$

where we use $\|$ to denote the concatenation operator. Note that the GAT-Filter is spatially localized, because for each node only its 1-hop neighbors are utilized in the filtering process to generate the new features. In the original model (Veličković et al., 2017), activation functions are applied to the output of each attention head before the concatenation. The formulation in Eq. (5.28) did not include activation functions for convenience.

EC-Filter

When there is edge information available in the graph, it can be utilized for designing the graph filters. Specifically, in Simonovsky and Komodakis (2017), an edge-conditioned graph filter (EC-Filter) was designed for edges of various types (the number of types is finite). For a given edge (v_i, v_j), we use $tp(v_i, v_j)$ to denote its type. Then the EC-Filter is defined as

$$\mathbf{F}'_i = \frac{1}{|\mathcal{N}(v_i)|} \sum_{v_j \in \mathcal{N}(v_i)} \mathbf{F}_j \mathbf{\Theta}_{tp(v_i,v_j)},$$

where $\mathbf{\Theta}_{tp(v_i,v_j)}$ is the parameter matrix shared by the edges with type $tp(v_i, v_j)$.

GGNN-Filter

The GGNN-Filter (Li et al., 2015) adapts the original GNN-Filter in Scarselli et al. (2008) with gated recurrent unit (GRU; see Section 3.4 for details on GRU). The GGNN-Filter is designed for graphs where the edges are directed and also have different types. Specifically, for an edge $(v_i, v_j) \in \mathcal{E}$, we use $tp(v_i, v_j)$ to denote its type. Note that because the edges are directed, the types of edges (v_i, v_j) and (v_j, v_i) can be different; i.e., $tp(v_i, v_j) \neq tp(v_j, v_i)$. The filtering process of the GGNN-Filter for a specific node v_i can be formulated as follows:

$$\mathbf{m}_i = \sum_{(v_j,v_i)\in\mathcal{E}} \mathbf{F}_j \mathbf{\Theta}^e_{tp(v_j,v_i)} \tag{5.29}$$

$$\mathbf{z}_i = \sigma(\mathbf{m}_i\mathbf{\Theta}^z + \mathbf{F}_i\mathbf{U}^z) \tag{5.30}$$

$$\mathbf{r}_i = \sigma(\mathbf{m}_i\mathbf{\Theta}^r + \mathbf{F}_i\mathbf{U}^r) \tag{5.31}$$

$$\widetilde{\mathbf{F}}_i = \tanh(\mathbf{m}_i\mathbf{\Theta} + (\mathbf{r}_i \odot \mathbf{F}_i)\mathbf{U}) \tag{5.32}$$

$$\mathbf{F}'_i = (1 - \mathbf{z}_i) \odot \mathbf{F}_i + \mathbf{z}_i \odot \widetilde{\mathbf{F}}_i, \tag{5.33}$$

where $\mathbf{\Theta}^e_{tp(v_j,v_i)}, \mathbf{\Theta}^z, \mathbf{\Theta}^r$, and $\mathbf{\Theta}$ are parameters to be learned. The first step as in Eq. (5.29) is to aggregate information from both the in-neighbors and out-neighbors of node v_i. During this aggregation, the transform matrix $\mathbf{\Theta}^e_{tp(v_j,v_i)}$ is shared by all nodes connected to v_i via the edge type $tp(v_j, v_i)$. The remaining equations (or Eqs. (5.30)–(5.33)) are GRU steps to update the hidden representations with the aggregated information $\mathbf{m}_i$. $\mathbf{z}_i$ and $\mathbf{r}_i$ are the update and reset gates, $\sigma(\cdot)$ is the sigmoid function, and $\odot$ denotes the Hadamand operation. Hence, the GGNN-Filter can also be written as

$$\mathbf{m}_i = \sum_{(v_j,v_i)\in\mathcal{E}} \mathbf{F}_j \mathbf{\Theta}^e_{tp(v_j,v_i)} \tag{5.34}$$

$$\mathbf{F}'_i = \text{GRU}(\mathbf{m}_i, \mathbf{F}_i), \tag{5.35}$$

where Eq. (5.35) summarizes Eqs. (5.30) to (5.33).

Mo-Filter

In Monti et al. (2017), a general framework – i.e., mixture model networks (MoNet) – is introduced to perform convolution operations on non-Euclidean data such as graphs and manifolds. Next, we introduce the graph filtering operation in Monti et al. (2017), which we name the Mo-Filter. We take node v_i as an example to illustrate its process. For each neighbor $v_j \in \mathcal{N}(v_i)$, a pseudo-coordinate is introduced to denote the relevant relation between nodes v_j and v_i. Specifically, for the center node v_i and its neighbor v_j, the pseudo-coordinate is defined with their degrees as

$$c(v_i, v_j) = \left(\frac{1}{\sqrt{d_i}}, \frac{1}{\sqrt{d_j}} \right)^\top, \tag{5.36}$$

where d_i and d_j denote the degrees of nodes v_i and v_j, respectively. Then a Gaussian kernel is applied on the pseudo-coordinate to measure the relation between the two nodes as

$$\alpha_{i,j} = \exp\left(-\frac{1}{2}(c(v_i, v_j) - \mu)^\top \Sigma^{-1}(c(v_i, v_j) - \mu) \right), \tag{5.37}$$

where μ and Σ are the mean vector and the covariance matrix of the Gaussian kernel to be learned. Note that instead of using the original pseudo-coordinate, we can also utilize a feedforward network to first transform $c(v_i, v_j)$. The aggregation process is

$$\mathbf{F}'_i = \sum_{v_j\in\mathcal{N}(v_i)} \alpha_{i,j} \mathbf{F}_j. \tag{5.38}$$

In Eq. (5.38), a single Gaussian kernel is used. However, typically, a set of K kernels with different means and covariances is adopted, which results in the following process:

$$\mathbf{F}'_i = \sum_{k=1}^{K} \sum_{v_j\in\mathcal{N}(v_i)} \alpha^{(k)}_{i,j} \mathbf{F}_j,$$

where $\alpha^{(k)}_{i,j}$ is from the kth Gaussian kernel.

MPNN: A General Framework for Spatial-Based Graph Filters

A message passing neural network (MPNN) is a general GNN framework. Many spatial-based graph filters including GCN-Filter, GraphSAGE-Filter, and GAT-Filter are special cases of MPNNs (Gilmer et al., 2017). For a node v_i, the MPNN-Filter updates its features as follows:

$$\mathbf{m}_i = \sum_{v_j \in \mathcal{N}(v_i)} M(\mathbf{F}_i, \mathbf{F}_j, \mathbf{e}_{(v_i, v_j)}), \tag{5.39}$$

$$\mathbf{F}'_i = U(\mathbf{F}_i, \mathbf{m}_i), \tag{5.40}$$

where $M()$ is the message function, $U()$ is the update function, and $\mathbf{e}_{(v_i, v_j)}$ is the edge feature, if available. The message function $M()$ generates the messages to pass to node v_i from its neighbors. The update function $U()$ then updates the features of node v_i by combining the original features and the aggregated message from its neighbors. The framework can be even more general if we replace the summation operation in Eq. (5.39) with other aggregation operations.

5.4 Graph Pooling

The graph filters refine the node features without changing the graph structure. After the graph filter operation, each node in the graph has a new feature representation. Typically, the graph filter operations are sufficient for node-focused tasks that take advantage of the node representations. However, for graph-focused tasks, a representation of the entire graph is desired. To obtain such representation, we need to summarize the information from the nodes. There are two main kinds of information that are important for generating the graph representation: the node features and the graph structure. The graph representation is expected to preserve both the node feature information and the graph structure information. Similar to the classical CNNs, graph pooling layers are proposed to generate graph-level representations. The early designs of graph pooling layers are usually flat. In other words, they generate the graph-level representation directly from the node representations in a single step. For example, the average pooling layers and max pooling layers can be adapted to GNNs by applying them to each feature channel. Hierarchical graph pooling designs have been developed to summarize the graph information by coarsening the original graph step by step. In the hierarchical graph pooling design, there are often several graph pooling layers, each of which follows a stack of several filters, as shown in Figure 5.5. Typically, a single graph pooling layer (both in the flat and the hierarchical cases) takes a graph as input and outputs a coarsened graph. Recall that the process has been summarized by Eq. (5.2) as

$$\mathbf{A}^{(\text{op})}, \mathbf{F}^{(\text{op})} = \text{pool}(\mathbf{A}^{(\text{ip})}, \mathbf{F}^{(\text{ip})}). \tag{5.41}$$

Next, we first describe representative flat pooling layers and then introduce hierarchical pooling layers.

5.4.1 Flat Graph Pooling

A flat pooling layer directly generates a graph-level representation from the node representations. In flat pooling layers, there is no new graph but a single node is generated. Thus, instead of Eq. (5.41), the pooling process in flat pooling layers can be summarized as

$$\mathbf{f}_{\mathcal{G}} = \text{pool}(\mathbf{A}^{(\text{ip})}, \mathbf{F}^{(\text{ip})}),$$

where $\mathbf{f}_{\mathcal{G}} \in \mathbb{R}^{1 \times d_{\text{op}}}$ is the graph representation. Next, we introduce some representative flat pooling layers. The max pooling and average pooling operations in classical CNNs can be adapted to GNNs. Specifically, the operation of the graph max-pooling layer can be expressed as

$$\mathbf{f}_{\mathcal{G}} = \max(\mathbf{F}^{(\text{ip})}),$$

where the max operation is applied to each channel as follows:

$$\mathbf{f}_{\mathcal{G}}[i] = \max(\mathbf{F}^{(\text{ip})}_{:,i}),$$

where $\mathbf{F}^{(\text{ip})}_{:,i}$ denotes the ith channel of $\mathbf{F}^{(\text{ip})}$. Similarly, graph average pooling operation applies the average pooling operation channel-wise as

$$\mathbf{f}_{\mathcal{G}} = ave(\mathbf{F}^{(\text{ip})}).$$

In Li et al. (2015), an attention-based flat pooling operation, which is called gated global pooling, was proposed. An attention score measuring the importance of each node is utilized to summarize the node representations for generating the graph representation. Specifically, the attention score for node v_i is computed as

$$s_i = \frac{\exp\left(h\left(\mathbf{F}^{(\text{ip})}_i\right)\right)}{\sum\limits_{v_j \in \mathcal{V}} \exp\left(h\left(\mathbf{F}^{(\text{ip})}_j\right)\right)},$$

where $h()$ is a feedforward network to map $\mathbf{F}_i^{(ip)}$ to a scalar, which is then normalized through softmax. With the learned attention scores, the graph representation can be summarized from the node representations as

$$\mathbf{f}_{\mathcal{G}} = \sum_{v_i \in \mathcal{V}} s_i \cdot \tanh\left(\mathbf{F}_i^{(ip)} \mathbf{\Theta}_{ip}\right),$$

where $\mathbf{\Theta}_{ip}$ are parameters to be learned and the activation function $\tanh()$ can also be replaced with the identity function.

Some flat graph pooling operations are embedded in the design of the filtering layer. A "fake" node is added to the graph that is connected to all of the nodes (Li et al., 2015). The representation of this fake node can be learned during the filtering process. Its representation captures the information of the entire graph because it is connected to all nodes in the graph. Hence, the representation of the fake node can be leveraged as the graph representation for downstream tasks.

5.4.2 Hierarchical Graph Pooling

Flat pooling layers usually ignore the hierarchical graph structure information when summarizing the node representations for the graph representation. Hierarchical graph pooling layers aim to preserve the hierarchical graph structural information by coarsening the graph step by step until the graph representation is achieved. Hierarchical pooling layers can be roughly grouped according to the ways they coarsen the graph. One type of hierarchical pooling layer coarsens the graph by subsampling; i.e., selecting the most important nodes as the nodes for the coarsened graph. A different kind of hierarchical pooling layer combines nodes in the input graph to form supernodes that serve as the nodes for the coarsened graph. The main difference between these two types of coarsening methods is that the sub-sampling-based methods keep nodes from the original graph, whereas the super-node-based methods generate new nodes for the coarsened graph. Next, we describe some representative techniques in these two categories. Specifically, we elaborate on the process of hierarchical pooling layers in Eq. (5.41) by explaining how the coarsened graph $\mathbf{A}^{(op)}$ and node features $\mathbf{F}^{(op)}$ are generated.

Downsampling-Based Pooling

To coarsen the input graph, a set of N_{op} nodes is selected according to some importance measures and then graph structure and node features for the coarsened graph are formed upon these nodes. There are three key components in a downsampling-based graph pooling layer: (1) developing the measure for down-sampling; (2) generating a graph structure for the coarsened graph; and (3) generating node features for the coarsened graph. Different downsampling-based pooling layers usually have distinct designs in these components. Next, we introduce representative downsampling-based graph pooling layers.

The gPool layer (Gao and Ji, 2019) was the first to adopt the downsampling strategy to perform graph coarsening for graph pooling. In gPool, the importance measure for nodes is learned from the input node features $\mathbf{F}^{(ip)}$ as

$$\mathbf{y} = \frac{\mathbf{F}^{(ip)}\mathbf{p}}{\|\mathbf{p}\|}, \tag{5.42}$$

where $\mathbf{F}^{(ip)} \in \mathbb{R}^{N_{ip} \times d_{ip}}$ is the matrix denoting the input node features and $\mathbf{p} \in \mathbb{R}^{d_{ip}}$ is a vector to be learned to project the input features into importance scores. After obtaining the importance scores $\mathbf{y}$, we can rank all of the nodes and select the N_{op} most important ones as

$$\text{idx} = \text{rank}(\mathbf{y}, N_{op}),$$

where N_{op} is the number of nodes in the coarsened graph and idx denotes the indices of the selected top N_{op} nodes. With the selected nodes represented with their indices idx, we proceed to generate the graph structure and node features for the coarsened graph. Specifically, the graph structure for the coarsened graph can be induced from the graph structure of the input graph as

$$\mathbf{A}^{(op)} = \mathbf{A}^{(ip)}(\text{idx}, \text{idx}),$$

where $\mathbf{A}^{(ip)}(\text{idx}, \text{idx})$ performs row and column extraction from $\mathbf{A}^{(ip)}$ with the selected indices idx. Similarly, the node features can also be extracted from the input node features. In Gao and Ji (2019), a gating system was adopted to control the information flow from the input features to the new features. Specifically, the selected nodes with higher importance scores can have more information being preserved and flowing to the coarsened graph, which can be modeled as

$$\tilde{\mathbf{y}} = \sigma(\mathbf{y}(\text{idx}))$$
$$\tilde{\mathbf{F}} = \mathbf{F}^{(ip)}(\text{idx}, :)$$
$$\mathbf{F}_p = \tilde{\mathbf{F}} \odot (\tilde{\mathbf{y}}\mathbf{1}_{d_{ip}}^{\top}),$$

where $\sigma()$ is the sigmoid function mapping the importance score to $(0, 1)$ and $\mathbf{1}_{d_{ip}} \in \mathbb{R}^{d_{ip}}$ is an all-ones vector. Note that $\mathbf{y}(\text{idx})$ extracts the corresponding elements from $\mathbf{y}$ according to the indices in idx and $\mathbf{F}^{(ip)}(\text{idx})$ retrieves the corresponding rows according to idx.

In gPool, the importance score is learned solely based on the input features, as shown in Eq. (5.42). It ignores the graph structure information. To incorporate the graph structure information when learning the importance score, the GCN-Filter is utilized to learn the importance score (Lee et al., 2019). Specifically, the importance score can be obtained as follows:

$$\mathbf{y} = \alpha \left(\text{GCN-Filter}(\mathbf{A}^{(ip)}, \mathbf{F}^{(ip)}) \right). \tag{5.43}$$

where α is an activation function such as tanh. Note that $\mathbf{y}$ is a vector instead of a matrix. In other words, the number of the output channel of the GCN-Filter is set to 1. This graph pooling operation is named SAGPool.

Super-Node-Based Hierarchical Graph Pooling

The downsampling-based hierarchical graph pooling layers try to coarsen the input graph by selecting a subset of nodes according to some importance measures. During the process, the information about the unselected nodes is lost as these nodes are discarded. Super-node-based pooling methods aim to coarsen the input graph by generating supernodes. Specifically, they try to learn to assign the nodes in the input graph into different clusters, where these clusters are treated as supernodes. These supernodes are regarded as the nodes in the coarsened graph. The edges between the supernodes and the features of these supernodes are then generated to form the coarsened graph. There are three key components in a super-node-based graph pooling layer: (1) generating super-nodes as the nodes for the coarsened graph; (2) generating a graph structure for the coarsened graph; and (3) generating node features for the coarsened graph. Next, we describe some representative supernode based graph pooling layers.

diffpool

The diffpool algorithm generates the supernodes in a differentiable way. In detail, a soft assignment matrix from the nodes in the input graph to the supernodes is learned using a GCN-Filter as

$$\mathbf{S} = \text{softmax} \left(\text{GCN-Filter}(\mathbf{A}^{(ip)}, \mathbf{F}^{(ip)}) \right), \tag{5.44}$$

where $\mathbf{S} \in \mathbb{R}^{N_{ip} \times N_{op}}$ is the assignment matrix to be learned. Note that as shown in Eq. (5.3), $\mathbf{F}^{(ip)}$ is usually the output of the latest graph filtering layer. However, in Ying et al. (2018c), the input of the pooling layer is the output of the previous pooling layer; i.e., the input of a learning block $\mathbf{F}^{(ib)}$ (see details on *block* in Subsection 5.2.2). Furthermore, several GCN-Filters can be stacked to learn the assignment matrix, though only a single filter is utilized in Eq. (5.44).

Each column of the assignment matrix can be regarded as a supernode. The softmax function is applied row-wise; hence, each row is normalized to have a summation of 1. The jth element in the ith row indicates the probability of assigning the ith node to the jth supernode. With the assignment matrix $\mathbf{S}$, we can proceed to generate the graph structure and node features for the coarsened graph. Specifically, the graph structure for the coarsened graph can be generated from the input graph by leveraging the soft assignment matrix $\mathbf{S}$ as

$$\mathbf{A}^{(\text{op})} = \mathbf{S}^{\top}\mathbf{A}^{(\text{ip})}\mathbf{S} \in \mathbb{R}^{N_{\text{op}} \times N_{\text{op}}}.$$

Similarly, the node features for the supernodes can be obtained by linearly combining the node features of the input graph according to the assignment matrix $\mathbf{S}$ as

$$\mathbf{F}^{(\text{op})} = \mathbf{S}^{\top}\mathbf{F}^{(\text{inter})} \in \mathbb{R}^{N_{\text{op}} \times d_{\text{op}}},$$

where $\mathbf{F}^{(\text{inter})} \in \mathbb{R}^{N_{\text{ip}} \times d_{\text{op}}}$ are the intermediate features learned through GCN-Filters as follows:

$$\mathbf{F}^{(\text{inter})} = \text{GCN-Filter}(\mathbf{A}^{(\text{ip})}, \mathbf{F}^{(\text{ip})}). \tag{5.45}$$

Multiple GCN-Filters can be stacked, though only one is shown in Eq. (5.45). The process of diffpool can be summarized as

$$\mathbf{A}^{(\text{op})}, \mathbf{F}^{(\text{op})} = \text{diffpool}(\mathbf{A}^{(\text{ip})}, \mathbf{F}^{(\text{ip})}).$$

EigenPooling

EigenPooling (Ma et al., 2019b) generates the supernodes using spectral clustering methods and focuses on forming graph structure and node features for the coarsened graph. After applying the spectral clustering algorithm, a set of nonoverlapping clusters is obtained, which are also regarded as the supernodes for the coarsened graph. The assignment matrix between the nodes of the input graph and the supernodes can be denoted as $\mathbf{S} \in \{0, 1\}^{N_{\text{ip}} \times N_{\text{op}}}$, where only a single element in each row is 1 and all others are 0. More specifically, $\mathbf{S}_{i,j} = 1$ only when the ith node is assigned to the jth supernode. For the kth super-node, we use $\mathbf{A}^{(k)} \in \mathbb{R}^{N^{(k)} \times N^{(k)}}$ to describe the graph structure in its corresponding cluster, where $N^{(k)}$ is the number of nodes in this cluster. We define a sampling operator $\mathbf{C}^{(k)} \in \{0, 1\}^{N_{\text{ip}} \times N^{(k)}}$ as

$$\mathbf{C}^{(k)}_{i,j} = 1 \quad \text{if and only if} \quad \Gamma^{(k)}(j) = v_i,$$

where $\Gamma^{(k)}$ denotes the list of nodes in the kth cluster and $\Gamma^{(k)}(j) = v_i$ means that node v_i corresponds to the jth node in this cluster. With this sampling operator, the adjacency matrix for the kth cluster can be formally defined as

$$\mathbf{A}^{(k)} = (\mathbf{C}^{(k)})^{\top}\mathbf{A}^{(\text{ip})}\mathbf{C}^{(k)}.$$

Next, we discuss the process of generating graph structure and node features for the coarsened graph. To form the graph structure between the supernodes, only the connections across the clusters in the original graph are considered. To achieve the goal, we first generate the intracluster adjacency matrix for the input graph, which only consists of the edges within each cluster, as

$$\mathbf{A}_{int} = \sum_{k=1}^{N_{op}} \mathbf{C}^{(k)}\mathbf{A}^{(k)}(\mathbf{C}^{(k)})^{\top}.$$

Then, the intercluster adjacency matrix, which only consists of the edges across the clusters, can be represented as $\mathbf{A}_{ext} = \mathbf{A} - \mathbf{A}_{int}$. The adjacency matrix for the coarsened graph can be obtained as

$$\mathbf{A}^{op} = \mathbf{S}^{\top}\mathbf{A}_{ext}\mathbf{S}.$$

Graph Fourier transform is adopted to generate node features. Specifically, graph structure and node features of each subgraph (or cluster) are utilized to generate the node features for the corresponding supernode. Next, we take the kth cluster as an illustrative example to demonstrate the process. Let $\mathbf{L}^{(k)}$ denote the Laplacian matrix for this subgraph and $\mathbf{u}_1^{(k)}, \ldots, \mathbf{u}_{n^{(k)}}^{(k)}$ are its corresponding eigenvectors. The features of the nodes in this subgraph can be extracted from $\mathbf{F}^{(ip)}$ by using the sampling operator $\mathbf{C}^{(k)}$ as follows:

$$\mathbf{F}_{ip}^{(k)} = (\mathbf{C}^{(k)})^{\top}\mathbf{F}^{(ip)},$$

where $\mathbf{F}_{ip}^{(k)} \in \mathbb{R}^{N^{(k)} \times d_{ip}}$ are the input features for nodes in the kth cluster.

Then, we apply graph Fourier transform to generate the graph Fourier coefficients for all channels of $\mathbf{F}_{ip}^{(k)}$ as

$$\mathbf{f}_i^{(k)} = (\mathbf{u}_i^{(k)})^{\top}\mathbf{F}_{ip}^{(k)} \quad \text{for} \quad i = 1, \ldots, N^{(k)},$$

where $\mathbf{f}_i^{(k)} \in \mathbb{R}^{1 \times d_{ip}}$ consists of the ith graph Fourier coefficients for all feature channels. The node features for the kth supernode can be formed by concatenating these coefficients as

$$\mathbf{f}^{(k)} = [\mathbf{f}_1^{(k)}, \ldots, \mathbf{f}_{N^{(k)}}^{(k)}].$$

We usually only utilize the first few coefficients to generate features of supernodes for two reasons. First, different subgraphs may have varied numbers of nodes; hence, to ensure the same dimension of features, some of the coefficients need to be discarded. Second, the first few coefficients typically capture most of the important information because in reality the majority of the graph signals are smooth.

5.5 Parameter Learning for Graph Neural Networks

In this section, we use node classification and graph classification as examples of downstream tasks to illustrate how to learn parameters of GNNs. Note that we have formally defined the tasks of node classification and graph classification in Definition 2.42 and Definition 2.46, respectively.

5.5.1 Parameter Learning for Node Classification

As introduced in Definition 2.42, the node set of a graph $\mathcal{V}$ can be divided in to two disjoint sets, $\mathcal{V}_l$ with labels and $\mathcal{V}_u$ without labels. The goal of node classification is to learn a model based on the labeled nodes $\mathcal{V}_l$ to predict the labels of the unlabeled nodes in $\mathcal{V}_u$. The GNN model usually takes the entire graph as input to generate node representations, which are then utilized to train a node classifier. Specifically, let $GNN_{\text{node}}(,)$ denote a GNN model with several graph filtering layers stacked as introduced in Subsection 5.2.1. The $GNN_{\text{node}}(,)$ function takes the graph structure and the node features as input and outputs the refined node features as follows:

$$\mathbf{F}^{(\text{out})} = GNN_{\text{node}}(\mathbf{A}, \mathbf{F}; \Theta_1), \tag{5.46}$$

where Θ_1 denotes the model parameters, $\mathbf{A} \in \mathbb{R}^{N \times N}$ is the adjacency matrix, $\mathbf{F} \in \mathbb{R}^{N \times d_{\text{in}}}$ are the input features of the original graph, and $\mathbf{F}^{(\text{out})} \in \mathbb{R}^{N \times d_{\text{out}}}$ are the produced output features. Then, the output node features are utilized to perform node classification as

$$\mathbf{Z} = \text{softmax}(\mathbf{F}^{(\text{out})} \Theta_2), \tag{5.47}$$

where $\mathbf{Z} \in \mathbb{R}^{N \times C}$ are the output logits for all nodes and $\Theta_2 \in \mathbb{R}^{d_{\text{out}} \times C}$ is the parameter matrix to transform the features $\mathbf{F}_{out}$ into the dimension of the number of classes C. The ith row of $\mathbf{Z}$ indicates the predicted class distribution of node v_i and the predicted label is usually the one with the largest probability. The entire process can be summarized as

$$\mathbf{Z} = f_{GNN}(\mathbf{A}, \mathbf{F}; \Theta), \tag{5.48}$$

where the function f_{GNN} consists of the processes in Eq. (5.46) and Eq. (5.47) and Θ includes the parameters Θ_1 and Θ_2. The parameters Θ in Eq. (5.48) can be learned by minimizing the following objective:

$$\mathcal{L}_{train} = \sum_{v_i \in \mathcal{V}_l} \ell(f_{GNN}(\mathbf{A}, \mathbf{F}; \Theta)_i, y_i), \tag{5.49}$$

where $f_{GNN}(\mathbf{A}, \mathbf{F}; \mathbf{\Theta})_i$ denotes the ith row of the output – i.e., the logits for node $v_i - y_i$ is the associated label, and $\ell(\cdot, \cdot)$ is a loss function such as cross-entropy loss.

5.5.2 Parameter Learning for Graph Classification

As introduced in Definition 2.46, in the task of graph classification, each graph is treated as a sample with an associated label. The training set can be denoted as $\mathcal{D} = \{\mathcal{G}_i, y_i\}$, where y_i is the corresponding label for graph $\mathcal{G}_i$. The task of graph classification is to train a model on the training set $\mathcal{D}$ such that it can perform good predictions on unlabeled graphs. The GNN model is usually utilized as a feature encoder, which maps an input graph into a feature representation as follows:

$$\mathbf{f}_\mathcal{G} = GNN_{\text{graph}}(\mathcal{G}; \mathbf{\Theta}_1), \qquad (5.50)$$

where GNN_{graph} is the GNN model to learn graph-level representations. It often consists of graph filtering and graph pooling layers. $\mathbf{f}_\mathcal{G} \in \mathbb{R}^{1 \times d_{out}}$ is the produced graph-level representation. This graph-level representation is then utilized to perform the graph classification as

$$\mathbf{z}_\mathcal{G} = \text{softmax}(\mathbf{f}_\mathcal{G} \mathbf{\Theta}_2), \qquad (5.51)$$

where $\mathbf{\Theta}_2 \in \mathbb{R}^{d_{out} \times C}$ transforms the graph representation to the dimension of the number of classes C and $\mathbf{z}_\mathcal{G} \in \mathbb{R}^{1 \times C}$ denotes the predicted logits for the input graph $\mathcal{G}$. The graph $\mathcal{G}$ is typically assigned to the label with the largest logit. The entire process of graph classification can be summarized as follows:

$$\mathbf{z}_\mathcal{G} = f_{GNN}(\mathcal{G}; \mathbf{\Theta}), \qquad (5.52)$$

where f_{GNN} is a function includes Eq. (5.50) and Eq. (5.51) as its building components. The parameter $\mathbf{\Theta}$ can be learned by minimizing the following objective:

$$\mathcal{L}_{train} = \sum_{\mathcal{G}_i \in \mathcal{D}} \ell(f_{GNN}(\mathcal{G}_i, \mathbf{\Theta}), y_i),$$

where y_i is the associated label of $\mathcal{G}_i$ and $\ell(\cdot, \cdot)$ is a loss function.

5.6 Conclusion

In this chapter, we introduce GNN frameworks for both node-focused and graph-focused tasks. Specifically, we introduce two major components: (1) the graph filtering layer, which refines the node features, and (2) the graph pooling layer, which aims to coarsen the graph and finally generate the graph-level representation. We categorize graph filters as spectral-based and spatial-based filters and then review representative algorithms for each category and discuss the connections between these two categories. We group graph pooling as flat graph pooling and hierarchical graph pooling and introduce representative methods for each group. Finally, we present how to learn GNN parameters via downstream tasks including node classification and graph classification.

5.7 Further Reading

In addition to the GNN models introduced in this chapter, there are some other attempts to learn graph-level representations for graph classification utilizing neural networks (Yanardag and Vishwanathan, 2015; Niepert et al., 2016; Lee et al., 2018). In addition to representative graph filtering and pooling operations introduced above, there are more graph filtering and pooling methods (Li et al., 2018c; Gao et al., 2018a; Zhang et al., 2018a; Liu et al., 2019b; Velickovic et al., 2019; Morris et al., 2019; Gao et al., 2020; Yuan and Ji, 2019). In addition, several surveys introduce and summarize the GNN models from different perspectives (Zhou et al., 2018a; Wu et al., 2020; Zhang et al., 2018c). As GNN research has gained increasing attention, multiple handy libraries have been designed to ease the development of GNN models. These packages include *PyTorch Geometric* (Fey and Lenssen, 2019), which was developed based on PyTorch, and *Deep Graph Library* (Wang et al., 2019e), which has various deep learning frameworks including PyTorch and TensorFlow as its backend.

6

Robust Graph Neural Networks

6.1 Introduction

As the generalization of traditional deep neural networks (DNNs) to graphs, graph neural networks (GNNs) inherit both advantages and disadvantages of traditional DNNs. Like traditional DNNs, GNNs have been shown to be effective in many graph-related tasks such as node-focused and graph-focused tasks. Traditional DNNs have been demonstrated to be vulnerable to dedicated designed adversarial attacks (Goodfellow et al., 2014b; Xu et al., 2019b). Under adversarial attacks, the victimized samples are perturbed in such a way that they are not easily noticeable, but they can lead to wrong results. It is increasingly evident that GNNs also inherit this drawback. The adversary can generate graph adversarial perturbations by manipulating the graph structure or node features to fool the GNN models. This limitation of GNNs has raised immense concerns on adopting them in safety-critical applications such as financial systems and risk management. For example, in a credit scoring system, fraudsters can fake connections with several high-credit customers to evade the fraudster detection models, and spammers can easily create fake followers to increase the chance of fake news being recommended and spread. Therefore, we have witnessed more and more research attention to graph adversarial attacks and their countermeasures. In this chapter, we first introduce concepts and definitions of graph adversarial attacks and detail some representative adversarial attack methods on graphs. Then, we discuss representative defense techniques against these adversarial attacks.

6.2 Graph Adversarial Attacks

In graph-structured data, the adversarial attacks are usually conducted by modifying the graph structure and/or node features in an unnoticeable way

138

such that the prediction performance of models can be impaired. Specifically, we denote a graph adversarial attacker as $\mathcal{T}$. Given a targeted model $f_{GNN}(; \Theta))$ (for either node classification or graph classification), the attacker $\mathcal{T}$ tries to modify a given graph $\mathcal{G}$ and generate an attacked graph $\mathcal{G}'$ as

$$\mathcal{G}' = \mathcal{T}(\mathcal{G}; f_{GNN}(; \Theta)) = \mathcal{T}(\{\mathbf{A}, \mathbf{F}\}; f_{GNN}(; \Theta)),$$

where $\mathcal{G} = \{\mathbf{A}, \mathbf{F}\}$ is the input graph with $\mathbf{A}$ and $\mathbf{F}$ denoting its adjacency matrix and feature matrix and $\mathcal{G}' = \{\mathbf{A}', \mathbf{F}'\}$ is the produced attacked graph. Note that in this chapter, without specific mention, both the graph structure and the input features are assumed to be discrete; i.e., $\mathbf{A} \in \{0, 1\}^{N \times N}$ and $\mathbf{F} \in \{0, 1\}^{N \times d}$, respectively. The attacker is usually constrained to make unnoticeable modifications on the input graph, which can be represented as

$$\mathcal{G}' \in \Phi(\mathcal{G}),$$

where $\Phi(\mathcal{G})$ denotes a constraint space that consists of graphs that are "close" to the graph $\mathcal{G}$. There are various ways to define the space $\Phi(\mathcal{G})$, which we will introduce when describing the attack methods. A typical and most commonly adopted constraint space is defined as

$$\Phi(\mathcal{G}) = \{\mathcal{G}' = \{\mathbf{A}', \mathbf{F}'\}; \|\mathbf{A}' - \mathbf{A}\|_0 + \|\mathbf{F}' - \mathbf{F}\|_0 \le \Delta\}, \qquad (6.1)$$

which means that the constraint space $\Phi(\mathcal{G})$ contains all of the graphs that are within a given perturbation budget Δ away from the input graph $\mathcal{G}$. The goal of the attacker $\mathcal{T}$ is that the prediction results on the attacked graph $\mathcal{G}'$ are different from the original input graph. For the node classification task, we focus on the prediction performance of a subset of nodes, called the victimized nodes and denoted as $\mathcal{V}_t \subseteq \mathcal{V}_u$, where $\mathcal{V}_u$ is the set of unlabeled nodes in $\mathcal{G}$. For the graph classification task, we concentrate on the prediction performance on a test set of graphs.

6.2.1 Taxonomy of Graph Adversarial Attacks

We can categorize graph adversarial attack algorithms differently according to the capacity, available resources, goals, and accessible knowledge of attackers.

Attacker's Capacity

Adversaries can perform attacks during both the model training and the model test stages. We can roughly divide attacks in to evasion and poisoning attacks based on the attacker's capacity to insert adversarial perturbations:

- **Evasion Attack.** The attack is conducted on the trained GNN model or in the test stage. Under the evasion attack setting, the adversaries cannot change the model parameters or structures.
- **Poisoning Attack.** An attack occurs before the GNN model is trained. Thus, the attackers can insert "poisons" into the training data such that the GNN models trained on these data have malfunctions.

Perturbation Type

In addition to node features, graph-structured data provide rich structural information. Thus, the attacker can perturb graph-structured data from different perspectives such as modifying node features, adding/deleting edges, and adding fake nodes:

- **Modifying Node Features.** Attackers can slightly modify the node features while keeping the graph structure.
- **Adding or deleting edges:** Attackers can add or delete edges.
- **Injecting Nodes.** Attackers can inject fake nodes to the graph and link them with some benign nodes in the graph.

Attacker's Goal

According to the attacker's goal, we can divide the attacks into two groups:

- **Targeted Attack.** Given a small set of test nodes (or targeted nodes), the attackers target making the model misclassify these test samples. Targeted attacks can be further grouped into (1) direct attacks where the attacker directly perturbs the targeted nodes and (2) influencer attacks where the attacker can only manipulate other nodes to influence the targeted nodes.
- **Untargeted Attack.** The attacker aims to perturb the graph to reduce the model's overall performance.

Attacker's Knowledge

The attacks can be categorized into three classes according to the level of accessible knowledge of the GNN model $f_{GNN}(; \Theta)$ as follows:

- **White-box attack.** In this setting, the attackers are allowed to access full information of the attacked model $f_{GNN}(; \Theta)$ (or the victim model) such as its architecture, parameters, and training data.
- **Gray-box attack.** In this setting, the attackers cannot access the architecture and the parameters of the victim model but they can access the data utilized to train the model.

- **Black-box attack.** In this setting, the attackers can access to minimal information of the victim model. The attackers cannot access the architecture, model parameters, and the training data. The attackers are only allowed to query from the victim model to obtain the predictions.

In the following sections, we present some representative attack methods from each category based on attacker's knowledge; i.e., white-box, gray-box, and black-box attacks.

6.2.2 White-Box Attack

In the white-box attack setting, the attacker is allowed to access full information of the victim model. In reality, this setting is not practical because complete information is often unavailable. However, it can still provide some information about the model's robustness against adversarial attacks. Most existing methods in this category utilize the gradient information to guide the attacker. There are two main ways to use the gradient information: (1) formulating the attack problem as an optimization problem that is addressed by the gradient-based method and (2) using the gradient information to measure the effectiveness of modifying graph structure and features. Next, we present representative white-box attacks from these two ways.

Projected Gradient Descent Topology Attack

In Xu et al. (2019c), the attacker is only allowed to modify the graph structure but not the node features. The goal of the attacker is to reduce the node classification performance on a set of victimized nodes $\mathcal{V}_t$. A symmetric Boolean matrix $\mathbf{S} \in \{0, 1\}^{N \times N}$ is introduced to encode the modification made by the attacker $\mathcal{T}$. Specifically, the edge between node v_i and node v_j is modified (added or removed) only when $\mathbf{S}_{i,j} = 1$; otherwise, the edge is not modified. Given the adjacency matrix of a graph $\mathcal{G}$, its supplement can be represented as $\bar{\mathbf{A}} = \mathbf{1}\mathbf{1}^\top - \mathbf{I} - \mathbf{A}$, where $\mathbf{1} \in \mathbb{R}^N$ is a vector with all elements as 1. Applying the attacker $\mathcal{T}$ on the graph $\mathcal{G}$ can be represented as

$$\mathbf{A}' = \mathcal{T}(\mathbf{A}) = \mathbf{A} + (\bar{\mathbf{A}} - \mathbf{A}) \odot \mathbf{S}, \tag{6.2}$$

where $\odot$ denotes the Hadamand product. The matrix $\bar{\mathbf{A}} - \mathbf{A}$ indicates whether an edge exists in the original graph or not. Specifically, when $(\bar{\mathbf{A}} - \mathbf{A})_{i,j} = 1$, there is no edge existing between node v_i and node v_j; thus, the edge can be added by the attacker. When $(\bar{\mathbf{A}} - \mathbf{A})_{i,j} = -1$, there is an edge between nodes v_i and v_j, and it can be removed by the attacker.

The goal of the attacker $\mathcal{T}$ is to find $\mathbf{S}$ that can lead to bad prediction performance. For a certain node v_i, given its true label y_i, the prediction performance can be measured by the following Carlini–Wagner-type loss adapted from Carlini–Wagner attacks in the image domain (Carlini and Wagner, 2017):

$$\ell(f_{GNN}(\mathcal{G}'; \Theta)_i, y_i) = \max\left\{ \mathbf{Z}'_{i,y_i} - \max_{c \neq y_i} \mathbf{Z}'_{i,c}, -\kappa \right\}, \tag{6.3}$$

where $\mathcal{G}' = \{\mathbf{A}', \mathbf{F}\}$ is the attacked graph, $f_{GNN}(\mathcal{G}'; \Theta)_i$ is utilized to denote the ith row of $f_{GNN}(\mathcal{G}'; \Theta)$, and $\mathbf{Z}' = f_{GNN}(\mathcal{G}'; \Theta)$ are the logits calculated with Eq. (5.48) on the attacked graph $\mathcal{G}'$. Note that we use the class labels y_i and c as the indices to retrieve the predicted probabilities of the corresponding classes. Specifically, $\mathbf{Z}'_{i,y_i}$ is the y_ith element of the ith row of $\mathbf{Z}'$, which indicates the probability of node v_i predicted as class y_i. The term $\mathbf{Z}'_{i,y_i} - \max_{c \neq y_i} \mathbf{Z}'_{i,c}$ in Eq. (6.3) measures the difference of the predicted probability between the true label y_i and the largest logit among all other classes. It is smaller than 0 when the prediction is wrong. Hence, for the goal of the attacker, we include a penalty when its value is larger than 0. Furthermore, in Eq. (6.3), $\kappa > 0$ is included as a confidence level for making wrong predictions. It means that a penalty is given when the difference between the logit of the true label y_i and the largest logit among all other classes is larger than $-\kappa$. A larger κ means that the prediction needs to be strongly wrong to avoid a penalty.

The attacker $\mathcal{T}$ is to find $\mathbf{S}$ in Eq. (6.2) such that it can minimize the Carlini–Wagner loss in Eq. (6.3) for all nodes in the victimized node set $\mathcal{V}_t$ given a limited budget. Specifically, this can be represented as the following optimization problem:

$$\min_{\mathbf{s}} \mathcal{L}(\mathbf{s}) = \sum_{v_i \in \mathcal{V}_t} \ell(f_{GNN}(\mathcal{G}'; \Theta)_i, y_i)$$

$$\text{subject to} \quad \|\mathbf{s}\|_0 \leq \Delta, \mathbf{s} \in \{0, 1\}^{N(N-1)/2}, \tag{6.4}$$

where Δ is the budget to modify the graph and $\mathbf{s} \in \{0, 1\}^{N(N-1)/2}$ is the vectorized $\mathbf{S}$ consisting of its independent perturbation variables. Note that $\mathbf{S}$ contains $N(N-1)/2$ independent perturbation variables, because $\mathbf{S}$ is a symmetric matrix with diagonal elements fixed to 0. The constraint term can be regarded as limiting the attacked graph $\mathcal{G}'$ in the space $\Phi(\mathcal{G})$ defined by the constraint on $\mathbf{s}$. The problem in Eq. (6.4) is a combinatorial optimization problem. For ease of optimization, the constraint $\mathbf{s} \in \{0, 1\}^{N(N-1)/2}$ is relaxed to its convex hull $\mathbf{s} \in [0, 1]^{N(N-1)/2}$. Specifically, we denote the constraint space as $\mathcal{S} = \{\mathbf{s}; \|\mathbf{s}\|_0 \leq \Delta, \mathbf{s} \in [0, 1]^{N(N-1)/2}\}$. Then the problem in Eq. (6.4) is transformed to a continuous optimization problem. It can be solved by the projected gradient descent (PGD) method as

$$\mathbf{s}^{(t)} = \mathcal{P}_{\mathcal{S}}[\mathbf{s}^{(t-1)} - \eta_t \nabla \mathcal{L}(\mathbf{s}^{(t-1)})],$$

where $\mathcal{P}_S(\mathbf{x}) := \arg\min_{\mathbf{s} \in S} \|\mathbf{s} - \mathbf{x}\|_2^2$ is the projection operator to project $\mathbf{x}$ into the continuous space S. After obtaining the continuous $\mathbf{s}$ using the PGD method, the discrete $\mathbf{s}$ can be randomly sampled from it. Specifically, each element in the obtained $\mathbf{s}$ is regarded as the probability to sample 1 for the corresponding element of the discrete $\mathbf{s}$.

Integrated Gradient Guided Attack

The gradient information is utilized as scores to guide the attack (Wu et al., 2019). The attacker is allowed to modify both the graph structure and the features. The attacker's goal is to impair the node classification performance of a single victimized node v_i. When modifying the structure, the attacker $\mathcal{T}$ is allowed to remove/add edges. The node features are assumed to be discrete features such as word occurrence or categorical features with binary values. Hence, the modification on both the graph structure and node features is limited to changing from either 0 to 1 or 1 to 0. This process can be guided by the gradient information of the objective function (Wu et al., 2019).

Inspired by fast gradient sign method (Goodfellow et al., 2014b), one way to find the adversarial attack is to maximize the loss function used to train the neural network with respective to the input sample. For the victimized node v_i with label y_i, this loss can be denoted as

$$\mathcal{L}_i = \ell(f_{GNN}(\mathbf{A}, \mathbf{F}; \mathbf{\Theta})_i, y_i).$$

In the fast gradient sign method, a one-step gradient ascent method is utilized to maximize the loss and consequently find the adversarial sample. However, in the graph setting, both the graph structure and node features are discrete, which cannot be derived by gradient-based methods. Instead, the gradient information corresponding to each element in $\mathbf{A}$ and $\mathbf{F}$ is used to measure how their changes affect the value of loss function. Thus, it can be used to guide the attacker to perform the adversarial perturbation. However, because the attacker is only allowed to perform modification from either 0 to 1 or 1 to 0, the gradient information may not help too much for the following reason: Given that the GNN model is nonlinear, the gradient on a single point cannot reflect the effect of a large change such as from 0 to 1 or from 1 to 0. Hence, inspired by the integrated gradients (Sundararajan et al., 2017), discrete integrated gradients are utilized to design the scores, which are called the integrated gradient (IG) scores. Specifically, the IG score discretely accumulates the gradient information of changing from 0 to 1 or from 1 to 0 as

$$IG_{\mathbf{H}}(i, j) = \frac{\mathbf{H}_{i,j}}{m} \sum_{k=1}^{m} \frac{\partial \mathcal{L}_i(\frac{k}{m}(\mathbf{H}_{i,j} - 0))}{\partial \mathbf{H}_{i,j}}; \quad 1 \to 0, \text{ when } \mathbf{H}_{i,j} = 1;$$

$$IG_{\mathbf{H}}(i, j) = \frac{1 - \mathbf{H}_{i,j}}{m} \sum_{k=1}^{m} \frac{\partial \mathcal{L}_i(0 + \frac{k}{m}(1 - \mathbf{H}_{i,j}))}{\partial \mathbf{H}_{i,j}}; \quad 0 \to 1, \text{ when } \mathbf{H}_{i,j} = 0,$$

where $\mathbf{H}$ could be either $\mathbf{A}$ or $\mathbf{F}$, and m is a hyperparameter indicating the number of discrete steps. We denote the IG scores for the candidate changes in $\mathbf{A}$ and $\mathbf{F}$ as $IG_{\mathbf{A}}$ and $IG_{\mathbf{F}}$, respectively, which measure how the corresponding change in each element of $\mathbf{A}$ and $\mathbf{F}$ affects the loss $\mathcal{L}_i$. Then, the attacker $\mathcal{T}$ can make the modification by selecting the action with the largest IG score among $IG_{\mathbf{A}}$ and $IG_{\mathbf{F}}$. The attacker repeats this process as long as the resulting graph $\mathcal{G}' \in \Phi(\mathcal{G})$, where $\Phi(\mathcal{G})$ is defined as in Eq. (6.1).

6.2.3 Gray-Box Attack

In the gray-box attack setting, the attacker is not allowed to access the architecture and parameters of the victim model but can access the data utilized to train the model. Hence, instead of directly attacking the given model, a gray-box attack often first trains a surrogate model with the provided training data and then attacks the surrogate model on a given graph. They assume that these attacks on the graph via the surrogate model can also damage the performance of the victim model. In this section, we introduce representative gray-box attack methods.

Nettack

The Nettack model (Zügner et al., 2018) targets generating adversarial graphs for the node classification task. A single node v_i is selected as the victim node to be attacked and the goal is to modify the structure and/or the features of this node or its nearby nodes to change the prediction on this victim node. Let us denote the label of the victim node v_i as y_i, where y_i could be either the ground truth or the label predicted by the victim model $f_{GNN}(\mathbf{A}, \mathbf{F}; \Theta)$ on the original clean graph $\mathcal{G}$. The goal of the attacker is to modify the graph $\mathcal{G}$ to $\mathcal{G}' = \{\mathbf{A}', \mathbf{F}'\}$ such that the model trained on the attacked graph $\mathcal{G}'$ classifies the node v_i as a new class c. In general, the attacking problem can be described as the following optimization problem:

$$\arg\max_{\mathcal{G}' \in \Phi(\mathcal{G})} \left(\max_{c \neq y_i} \ln \mathbf{Z}'_{i,c} - \ln \mathbf{Z}'_{i,y_i} \right), \tag{6.5}$$

where $\mathbf{Z}' = f_{GNN}(\mathbf{A}', \mathbf{F}'; \boldsymbol{\Theta}')$ with the parameters $\boldsymbol{\Theta}'$ learned by minimizing Eq. (5.49) on the attacked graph $\mathcal{G}'$. Here, the space $\Phi(\mathcal{G})$ is defined based on the limited budget constraint as Eq. (6.1) and two more constraints on the perturbations. These two constraints are (1) the degree distribution of the attacked graph should be close to that of the original graph and (2) the distribution of the feature occurrences (for the discrete features) of the attacked graph should be close to that of the original graph. Solving the problem in Eq. (6.5) directly is very challenging because the problem involves two dependent stages. The discrete structure of the graph data further increases the difficulty. To address these difficulties, we first train a *surrogate model* on the original clean graph data $\mathcal{G}$ and then generate the adversarial graph by attacking the surrogate model. The adversarial graph is treated as the attacked graph. When attacking a GNN model built upon GCN-Filters (see Subsection 5.3.2 for details on GCN-Filter) for node classification, the following surrogate model with two GCN-Filters and no activation layers is adopted:

$$\mathbf{Z}^{sur} = \text{softmax}(\tilde{\mathbf{A}}\tilde{\mathbf{A}}\mathbf{F}\boldsymbol{\Theta}_1\boldsymbol{\Theta}_2) = \text{softmax}(\tilde{\mathbf{A}}^2\mathbf{F}\boldsymbol{\Theta}), \qquad (6.6)$$

where the parameters $\boldsymbol{\Theta}_1$ and $\boldsymbol{\Theta}_2$ are absorbed in $\boldsymbol{\Theta}$. The parameters $\boldsymbol{\Theta}$ are learned from the original clean graph $\mathcal{G}$ with the provided training data. To perform the adversarial attack based on the surrogate model, as in Eq. (6.5), we aim to find these attacks that maximize the difference; i.e., $\max_{c\neq y_i} ln\mathbf{Z}^{sur}_{i,c} - ln\mathbf{Z}^{sur}_{i,y_i}$. To further simplify the problem, the instance-independent softmax normalization is removed, which results in the following surrogate loss:

$$\mathcal{L}_{sur}(\mathbf{A}, \mathbf{F}; \boldsymbol{\Theta}, v_i) = \max_{c\neq y_i} \left([\tilde{\mathbf{A}}^2\mathbf{F}\boldsymbol{\Theta}]_{i,c} - [\tilde{\mathbf{A}}^2\mathbf{F}\boldsymbol{\Theta}]_{i,y_i}\right).$$

Correspondingly, the optimization problem can be expressed as

$$\text{argmax}_{\mathcal{G}'\in\Phi(\mathcal{G})}\mathcal{L}_{sur}(\mathbf{A}', \mathbf{F}'; \boldsymbol{\Theta}, v_i). \qquad (6.7)$$

Though much simpler, this problem is still intractable to be solved exactly. Hence, a greedy algorithm is adopted, where we measure the scores of all of the possible steps (adding/deleting edges and flipping features) as follows:

$$s_{str}(e; \mathcal{G}^{(t)}, v_i) := \mathcal{L}_{sur}(\mathbf{A}^{(t+1)}, \mathbf{F}^{(t)}; \boldsymbol{\Theta}, v_i)$$
$$s_{feat}(f; \mathcal{G}^{(t)}, v_i) := \mathcal{L}_{sur}(\mathbf{A}^{(t)}, \mathbf{F}^{(t+1)}; \boldsymbol{\Theta}, v_i),$$

where $\mathcal{G}^{(t)} = \{\mathbf{A}^{(t)}, \mathbf{F}^{(t)}\}$ is the intermediate result of the algorithm at step t, $\mathbf{A}^{(t+1)}$ is one-step change from $\mathbf{A}^{(t)}$ by adding/deleting edge e, and $\mathbf{F}^{(t+1)}$ is one step change away from $\mathbf{F}^{(t)}$ by flipping the feature f. The score $s_{str}(e; \mathcal{G}^{(t)}, v_i)$ measures the impact of changing edge e on the loss function, and $s_{feat}(f; \mathcal{G}^{(t)}, v_i)$ indicates how changing the feature f affects the loss function.

In each step, the greedy algorithm chooses the edge or the feature with the largest score to perform the corresponding modification (i.e., adding/deleting edges or flipping features). The process is repeated as long as the resulting graph is still in the space of $\Phi(\mathcal{G})$.

Metattack

The metattack method in Zügner and Günnemann (2019) tries to modify the graph to reduce the overall node classification performance on the test set; i.e., the victim node set $\mathcal{V}_t = \mathcal{V}_u$. The attacker in metattack is limited to modify the graph structure. The constraint space $\Phi(\mathcal{G})$ is adopted from nettack where the limited budget constraint and the degree-preserving constraint are used to define the constraint space. The metattack is a poisoning attack. Thus, after generating the adversarial attacked graph, we need to retrain the victim model on the attacked graph. The goal of the attacker is to find such an adversarial attacked graph that the performance of the retrained victim GNN model is impaired. Hence, the attacker can be mathematically formulated as a bilevel optimization problem as

$$\min_{\mathcal{G}' \in \Phi(\mathcal{G})} \mathcal{L}_{atk}(f_{GNN}(\mathcal{G}'; \Theta^*)) \quad s.t. \quad \Theta^* = \arg\min_{\Theta} \mathcal{L}_{tr}(f_{GNN}(\mathcal{G}'; \Theta)), \quad (6.8)$$

where $f_{GNN}()$ is the victim model and $\mathcal{L}_{tr}$ denotes the loss function used to train the model as defined in Eq. (5.49) over the training set $\mathcal{V}_l$. The loss function $\mathcal{L}_{atk}$ is to be optimized to generate the adversarial attack. In particular, the lower-level optimization problem with respect to Θ is to find the best model parameters Θ^* given the attacked graph $\mathcal{G}'$, and the higher-level optimization problem is to minimize $\mathcal{L}_{atk}$ to generate the attacked graph $\mathcal{G}'$. Because the goal of the attacker is to impair the performance on the unlabeled nodes, ideally, $\mathcal{L}_{atk}$ should be defined based on $\mathcal{V}_u$. However, we cannot directly calculate the loss based on $\mathcal{V}_u$ without the labels. Instead, one approach, which is based on the argument that the model cannot generalize well if it has high training error, is to define $\mathcal{L}_{atk}$ as the negative of the $\mathcal{L}_{tr}$; i.e., $\mathcal{L}_{atk} = -\mathcal{L}_{tr}$. Another way to formulate $\mathcal{L}_{atk}$ is to first predict labels for the unlabeled nodes using a well-trained surrogate model on the original graph $\mathcal{G}$ and then use the predictions as the "labels." More specifically, let C'_u denote the labels of unlabeled nodes $\mathcal{V}_u$ predicted by the surrogate model. The loss function $\mathcal{L}_{self} = \mathcal{L}(f_{GNN}(\mathcal{G}'; \Theta^*), C'_u)$ measures the disagreement between the labels C'_u and the predictions from $f_{GNN}(\mathcal{G}'; \Theta^*)$ as in Eq. (5.49) over the set $\mathcal{V}_u$. The second option of $\mathcal{L}_{atk}$ can be defined as $\mathcal{L}_{atk} = -\mathcal{L}_{self}$. Finally, $\mathcal{L}_{atk}$ is defined as a combination of the two loss functions as

$$\mathcal{L}_{atk} = -\mathcal{L}_{tr} - \beta \cdot \mathcal{L}_{self},$$

where β is a parameter controlling the importance of $\mathcal{L}_{self}$.

To solve the bilevel optimization problem in Eq. (6.8), the metagradients, which have traditionally been used in metalearning, are adopted. Metagradients can be viewed as the gradients with respect to the hyperparameters. In this specific problem, the graph structure (or the adjacency matrix $\mathbf{A}$) is treated as the hyperparameters. The goal is to find the "optimal" structure such that the loss function $\mathcal{L}_{atk}$ is minimized. The metagradient with respect to the graph $\mathcal{G}$ can be defined as

$$\nabla_{\mathcal{G}}^{meta} := \nabla_{\mathcal{G}} \mathcal{L}_{atk}(f_{GNN}(\mathcal{G}; \Theta^*)) \quad s.t. \quad \Theta^* = \arg\min_{\Theta} \mathcal{L}_{tr}(f_{GNN}(\mathcal{G}; \Theta)). \quad (6.9)$$

Note that the metagradient is related to the parameter Θ^* as Θ^* is a function of the graph $\mathcal{G}$ according to the second part of Eq. (6.9). The metagradient indicates how a small change in the graph $\mathcal{G}$ affects the attacker loss $\mathcal{L}_{atk}$, which can guide us to modify the graph.

The inner problem of Eq. (6.8) (the second part of Eq. (6.9)) typically does not have an analytic solution. Instead, a differentiable optimization procedure such as vanilla gradient descent or stochastic gradient descent is adopted to obtain Θ^*. This optimization procedure can be represented as $\Theta^* = \mathrm{opt}_{\Theta} \mathcal{L}_{tr}(f_{GNN}(\mathcal{G}; \Theta))$. Thus, the metagradient can be reformulated as

$$\nabla_{\mathcal{G}}^{meta} := \nabla_{\mathcal{G}} \mathcal{L}_{atk}(f_{GNN}(\mathcal{G}; \Theta^*)) \quad s.t. \quad \Theta^* = \mathrm{opt}_{\Theta} \mathcal{L}_{tr}(f_{GNN}(\mathcal{G}; \Theta)). \quad (6.10)$$

As an illustration, the opt_{Θ} with vanilla gradient descent can be formalized as

$$\Theta_{t+1} = \Theta_t - \eta \cdot \nabla_{\Theta_t} \mathcal{L}_{tr}(f_{GNN}(\mathcal{G}; \Theta)) \quad \text{for } t = 0, \ldots, T - 1,$$

where η is the learning rate, Θ_0 denotes the initialization of the parameters, T is the total number of steps of the gradient descent procedure, and $\Theta^* = \Theta_T$. The metagradient can now be expressed by unrolling the training procedure as follows:

$$\nabla_{\mathcal{G}}^{meta} = \nabla_{\mathcal{G}} \mathcal{L}_{atk}(f_{GNN}(\mathcal{G}; \Theta_T))$$
$$= \nabla_{f_{GNN}} \mathcal{L}_{atk}(f_{GNN}(\mathcal{G}; \Theta_T)) \cdot [\nabla_{\mathcal{G}} f_{GNN}(\mathcal{G}; \Theta_T) + \nabla_{\Theta_T} f_{GNN}(\mathcal{G}; \Theta_T) \cdot \nabla_{\mathcal{G}} \Theta_T],$$

where

$$\nabla_{\mathcal{G}} \Theta_{t+1} = \nabla_{\mathcal{G}} \Theta_t - \eta \nabla_{\mathcal{G}} \nabla_{\Theta_t} \mathcal{L}_{tr}(f_{GNN}(\mathcal{G}; \Theta_t)).$$

Note that the parameter Θ_t is dependent on the graph $\mathcal{G}$; thus, the derivative with respect to the graph $\mathcal{G}$ has to chain back all the way to the initial parameter Θ_0. After obtaining the metagradient, we can now use it to update the graph as

$$\mathcal{G}^{(k+1)} = \mathcal{G}^{(k)} - \gamma \nabla_{\mathcal{G}^{(k)}} \mathcal{L}_{atk}(f_{GNN}(\mathcal{G}; \Theta_T)). \qquad (6.11)$$

The gradients are dense; thus, the operation in Eq. (6.11) results in a dense graph, which is not desired. Furthermore, because the structure and the parameters of the model are unknown in the gray-box setting, the metagradients cannot be obtained. To solve these two issues, a greedy algorithm utilizing the meta-gradient calculated on a surrogate model as guidance to choose the action was proposed in Zügner and Günnemann (2019). We next introduce the meta-gradient-based greedy algorithm. The same surrogate model as in Eq. (6.6) is utilized to replace $f_{GNN}(\mathcal{G}; \Theta)$ in Eq. (6.8). A score to measure how a small change in the i, jth element of the adjacency matrix $\mathbf{A}$ affects the loss function $\mathcal{L}_{atk}$ is defined by using the metagradient as

$$s(i, j) = \nabla_{\mathbf{A}_{i,j}}^{meta} \cdot (-2 \cdot \mathbf{A}_{i,j} + 1),$$

where the term $(-2 \cdot \mathbf{A}_{i,j} + 1)$ is used to flip the sign of the metagradients when $\mathbf{A}_{i,j} = 1$; i.e., the edge between nodes v_i and v_j exists and can only be removed. After calculating the score for each possible action based on the metagradients, the attacker takes the action with the largest score. For a chosen node pair (v_i, v_j), the attacker adds an edge between them if $\mathbf{A}_{i,j} = 0$ while removing the edge between them if $\mathbf{A}_{i,j} = 1$. The process is repeated as long as the resulting graph is in the space $\Phi(\mathcal{G})$.

6.2.4 Black-Box Attack

In the black-box attack setting, the victim model's information is not accessible to the attacker. The attacker can only query the prediction results from the victim model. Most methods in this category adopt reinforcement learning to learn the strategies of the attacker. They treat the victim model as a black-box query machine and use the query results to design the reward for reinforcement learning.

RL-S2V

The RL-S2V method is a black-box attack model using reinforcement learning (Dai et al., 2018). In this setting, a target classifier $f_{GNN}(\mathcal{G}; \Theta)$ is given with the parameters Θ learned and fixed. The attacker is asked to modify the graph such that the classification performance is impaired. The RL-S2V attacker can be used to attack both the node classification task and the graph classification task. The RL-S2V attacker only modifies the graph structure and leaves the graph features untouched. To modify the graph structure, the RL-S2V attacker is allowed to add or delete edges from the original graph $\mathcal{G}$. The constraint space for RL-S2V can be defined as

$$\Phi(\mathcal{G}) = \{\mathcal{G}'; |(\mathcal{E} - \mathcal{E}') \cup (\mathcal{E}' - \mathcal{E})| \leq \Delta\} \tag{6.12}$$
$$\text{with } \mathcal{E}' \subset \mathcal{N}(\mathcal{G}, b),$$

where $\mathcal{E}$ and $\mathcal{E}'$ denote the edge sets of the original graph $\mathcal{G}$ and the attacked graph $\mathcal{G}'$, respectively. Δ is the budget limit to remove and add edges. Furthermore, $\mathcal{N}(\mathcal{G}, b)$ is defined as

$$\mathcal{N}(\mathcal{G}, b) = \{(v_i, v_j) : v_i, v_j \in \mathcal{V}, \text{dis}^{(\mathcal{G})}(v_i, v_j) \leq b\},$$

where $\text{dis}^{(\mathcal{G})}(v_i, v_j)$ denotes the shortest path distance between node v_i and node v_j in the original graph $\mathcal{G}$. $\mathcal{N}(\mathcal{G}, b)$ includes all edges connecting nodes at most b-hop away in the original graph. The attacking procedure of RL-S2V is modeled as a finite Markov decision process (MDP), which can be defined as follows:

- **Action:** As mentioned before, there are two types of actions: adding and deleting edges. Furthermore, only those actions that lead to a graph in the constraint space $\Phi(\mathcal{G})$ are considered as valid actions.
- **State:** The state s_t at time step t is the intermediate graph $\mathcal{G}_t$, which is obtained by modifying the intermediate graph $\mathcal{G}_{t-1}$ by a single action.
- **Reward:** The purpose of the attacker is to modify the graph such that the targeted classifier would be fooled. A reward is only granted when the attacking process (MDP) has been terminated. More specifically, a positive reward $r(s_t, a_t) = 1$ is granted if the targeted model makes a different prediction from the original one; otherwise, a negative reward of $r(s_t, a_t) = -1$ is granted. For all intermediate steps, the reward is set to $r(s_t, a_t) = 0$.
- **Terminal:** The MDP has a total budget of Δ to perform the actions. The MDP is terminated once the agent reaches the budget Δ; i.e., the attacker has modified Δ edges.

Deep Q-learning is adopted to learn the MDP (Dai et al., 2018). Specifically, Q-learning (Watkins and Dayan, 1992) is to fit the following Bellman optimal equation:

$$Q^*(s_t, a_t) = r(s_t, a_t) + \gamma \max_{a'} Q^*(s_{t+1}, a').$$

In particular, $Q^*()$ is a parameterized function to approximate the optimal expected future value (or the expected total reward of all future steps) given a state action pair and γ is the discount factor. Once the $Q^*()$ function is learned during training, it implicitly indicates a greedy policy:

$$\pi(a_t|s_t; Q^*) = \arg \max_{a_t} Q^*(s_t, a_t).$$

With the above policy, at state s_t, the action a_t that can maximize the $Q^*()$ function is chosen. The $Q^*()$ function can be parameterized with GNN models for learning the graph-level representation, because the state s_t is a graph.

Note that an action a_t involves two nodes, which means that the search space for an action is $O(N^2)$. This might be too expensive for large graphs. Hence, in Dai et al. (2018), a decomposition of the action a_t was proposed as

$$a_t = (a_t^{(1)}, a_t^{(2)}),$$

where $a_t^{(1)}$ is the subaction to choose the first node and $a_t^{(2)}$ is the subaction to choose the second node. A hierarchical $Q^*()$ function is designed to learn the policies for the decomposed actions.

ReWatt

ReWatt (Ma et al., 2020a) is a black-box attacker that targets the graph classification task. In this setting, the graph classification model $f_{GNN}(\mathcal{G}; \Theta)$ as defined in Subsection 5.5.2 is given and fixed. The attacker cannot access any information about the model except querying prediction results for graph samples. It is argued in Ma et al. (2020a) that the operations such as deleting/adding edges are not unnoticeable enough. Hence, a less noticeable operation–i.e., the rewiring operation–is proposed to attack graphs. A rewiring operation rewires an existing edge from one node to another node, which can be formally defined as follows.

Definition 6.1 (Rewiring Operation)   *A rewiring operation* $a = (v_{fir}, v_{sec}, v_{thi})$ *involves three nodes, where* $v_{sec} \in \mathcal{N}(v_{fir})$ *and* $v_{thi} \in \mathcal{N}^2(v_{fir})/\mathcal{N}(v_{fir})$ *with* $\mathcal{N}^2(v_{fir})$ *denoting the 2-hop neighbors of node* v_i. *The rewiring operation* a *deletes the existing edge between nodes* v_{fir} *and* v_{sec} *and adds a new edge between nodes* v_{fir} *and* v_{thi}.

The rewiring operation is theoretically and empirically shown to be less noticeable than other operations such as deleting/adding edges (Ma et al., 2020a). The constraint space of the ReWatt attack is defined based on the rewiring operation as:

$$\Phi(\mathcal{G}) = \{\mathcal{G}' | \text{if } \mathcal{G}' \text{ can be obtained by applying at most } \Delta \text{ rewiring operations to } \mathcal{G}\},$$

where the budget Δ is usually defined based on the size of the graph as $p \cdot |\mathcal{E}|$ with $p \in (0, 1)$. The attack procedure is modeled as a finite MDP, which is defined as follows:

- **Action:** The action space consists of all of the valid rewiring operations as defined in Definition 6.1.
- **State:** State s_t at time step t is the intermediate graph $\mathcal{G}_t$, which is obtained by applying one rewiring operation on the intermediate graph $\mathcal{G}_{t-1}$.
- **State Transition Dynamics:** Given an action $a_t = (v_{\text{fir}}, v_{\text{sec}}, v_{\text{thi}})$, the state is transited from state s_t to state s_{t+1} by deleting an edge between v_{fir} and v_{sec} and adding an edge to connect v_{fir} with v_{thi} in state s_t.
- **Reward Design:** The goal of the attacker is to modify the graph such that the predicted label is different from the one predicted for the original graph (or the initial state s_1). Furthermore, the attacker is encouraged to take few actions to achieve the goal so that the modifications to the graph structure are minimal. Hence, a positive reward is granted if the action leads to a change of the label; otherwise, a negative reward is assigned. Specifically, the reward $R(s_t, a_t)$ can be defined as follows:

$$R(s_t, a_t) = \begin{cases} 1 & \text{if } f_{GNN}(s_t; \mathbf{\Theta}) \neq f_{GNN}(s_1; \mathbf{\Theta}); \\ n_r & \text{if } f_{GNN}(s_t; \mathbf{\Theta}) = f_{GNN}(s_1; \mathbf{\Theta}), \end{cases}$$

where n_r is the negative reward, which is adaptive dependent on the size of graph as $n_r = -\frac{1}{p \cdot |\mathcal{E}|}$. Note that we abuse the definition $f_{GNN}(\mathcal{G}; \mathbf{\Theta})$ a little to have the predicted label as its output.

- **Termination:** The attacker stops the attacking process either when the predicted label has been changed or when the resulting graph is not in the constraint space $\Phi(\mathcal{G})$.

Various reinforcement learning techniques can be adopted to learn this MDP. Specifically, in Ma et al. (2020a), GNNs based policy networks are designed to choose the rewiring actions according to the state and the policy gradient algorithm (Sutton et al., 2000) is employed to train the policy networks.

6.3 Graph Adversarial Defenses

To defend against adversarial attacks on graph-structured data, various defense techniques have been proposed. These defense techniques can be majorly classified to four different categories: (1) graph adversarial training, which incorporates adversarial samples into the training procedure to improve the robustness of the models; (2) graph purification, which tries to detect the adversarial attacks and remove them from the attacked graph to generate a clean graph; (3) graph attention, which identifies the adversarial attacks during the training stage and gives them less attention while training the model; and (4) graph structure learning, which aims to learn a clean graph from the attacked graph while jointly training the GNN model. Next, we introduce some representative methods in each category.

6.3.1 Graph Adversarial Training

The idea of adversarial training (Goodfellow et al., 2014b) is to incorporate the adversarial examples into the training stage of the model; hence, the robustness of the model can be improved. It has demonstrated its effectiveness in training robust deep models in the image domain (Goodfellow et al., 2014b). There are usually two stages in adversarial training: (1) generating adversarial attacks and (2) training the model with these attacks. In the graph domain, the adversarial attackers are allowed to modify the graph structure and/or node features. Hence, the graph adversarial training techniques can be categorized according to the adversarial attacks they incorporate: (1) only attacks on graph structure $\mathbf{A}$; (2) only attacks on node features $\mathbf{F}$; and (3) attacks on both graph structure $\mathbf{A}$ and node features $\mathbf{F}$. Next, we introduce representative graph adversarial training techniques.

Graph Adversarial Training on Graph Structure

An intuitive and simple graph adversarial training method was proposed in Dai et al. (2018). During the training stage, edges are randomly dropped from the input graph to generate the "adversarial attacked graphs." Though simple and not very effective in improving the robustness, this is the first technique to explore the adversarial training on graph-structured data. Later, a graph adversarial training technique based on the PGD topology attack is proposed. In detail, this adversarial training procedure can be formulated as the following min–max optimization problem:

$$\min_{\Theta} \max_{\mathbf{s} \in S} -\mathcal{L}(\mathbf{s}; \Theta), \qquad (6.13)$$

where the objective $\mathcal{L}(\mathbf{s}; \Theta)$ is defined as similar to Eq. (6.4) over the entire training set $\mathcal{V}_l$ as

$$\mathcal{L}(\mathbf{s}; \Theta) = \sum_{v_i \in \mathcal{V}_l} \ell(f_{GNN}(\mathcal{G}'; \Theta)_i, y_i)$$

$$\text{subject to} \quad \|\mathbf{s}\|_0 \leq \Delta, \mathbf{s} \in \{0, 1\}^{N \times (N-1)/2}.$$

Solving the min–max problem in Eq. (6.13) is to minimize the training loss under the perturbation in graph structure generated by the PGD topology attack algorithm. The minimization problem and the maximization problem are processed in an alternative way. In particular, the maximization problem can be solved using the PGD algorithm, as introduced in Subsection 6.2.2. It results in a continuous solution of **s**. The nonbinary adjacency matrix **A** is generated according to the continuous **s**. It serves as the adversarial graph for the minimization problem to learn the parameters Θ for the classification model.

Graph Adversarial Training on Node Features

GraphAT (Feng et al., 2019a) incorporates node features–based adversarial samples into the training procedure of the classification model. The adversarial samples are generated by perturbing the node features of the clean node samples such that the neighboring nodes are likely to be assigned to different labels. One important assumption in GNN models is that neighboring nodes tend to be similar with each other. Thus, the adversarial attacks on the node features make the model likely to make mistakes. These generated adversarial samples are then utilized in the training procedure in the form of a regularization term. Specifically, the graph adversarial training procedure can be expressed as the following min–max optimization problem:

$$\min_{\Theta} \mathcal{L}_{train} + \beta \sum_{v_i \in \mathcal{V}} \sum_{v_j \in \mathcal{N}(v_i)} d(f_{GNN}(\mathbf{A}, \mathbf{F} \star \mathbf{r}_i^g; \Theta)_i, f_{GNN}(\mathbf{A}, \mathbf{F}; \Theta)_j);$$

$$\mathbf{r}_i^g = \arg \max_{\mathbf{r}_i, \|\mathbf{r}_i\| \le \epsilon} \sum_{v_j \in \mathcal{N}(v_i)} d(f_{GNN}(\mathbf{A}, \mathbf{F} \star \mathbf{r}_i; \Theta)_i, f_{GNN}(\mathbf{A}, \mathbf{F}; \Theta)_j), \quad (6.14)$$

where the maximization problem generates the adversarial node features for the nodes, which break the smoothness between the connected nodes. The minimization problem learns the parameters Θ, which not only enforce a small training error but also encourage the smoothness between the adversarial samples and their neighbors via the additional regularization term. In Eq. (6.14), $\mathcal{L}_{train}$ is the loss defined in Eq. (5.49), $\mathbf{r}_i \in \mathbb{R}^{1 \times d}$ is a row-wise adversarial vector, and the operation $\mathbf{F} \star \mathbf{r}_i$ means to add $\mathbf{r}_i$ into the ith row of $\mathbf{F}$; i.e., adding adversarial noise to node v_i's features. $f_{GNN}(\mathbf{A}, \mathbf{F} \star \mathbf{r}_i^g; \Theta)_i$ denotes the ith row of $f_{GNN}(\mathbf{A}, \mathbf{F} \star \mathbf{r}_i^g; \Theta)$, which are the predicted logits for node v_i. The function $d(\cdot, \cdot)$ is the Kullback–Leibler divergence (Joyce, 2011), which measures the distance between the predicted logits. The minimization problem and the maximization problem are processed in an alternative way.

Graph Adversarial Training on Graph Structures and Node Features

Given the challenges from the discrete nature of the graph structure **A** and the node features **F**, a graph adversarial training technique proposes to modify the continuous output of the first graph filtering layer $\mathbf{F}^{(1)}$ (Jin and Zhang, n.d.).

The method generates adversarial attacks for the first hidden representation $\mathbf{F}^{(1)}$ and incorporates them into the model training stage. Specifically, it can be modeled as the following min–max optimization problem:

$$\min_{\Theta} \max_{\zeta \in D} \mathcal{L}_{train}\left(\mathbf{A}, \mathbf{F}^{(1)} + \zeta; \Theta\right), \tag{6.15}$$

where the maximization problem generates a small adversarial perturbation on the first layer hidden representation $\mathbf{F}^{(1)}$, which indirectly represents the perturbation in the graph structure $\mathbf{A}$ and the node features $\mathbf{F}$. The minimization problem learns the parameters of the model while incorporating the generated perturbation into the learning procedure. ζ is the adversarial noise to be learned and D denotes the constraint domain of the noise, which is defined as follows:

$$D = \{\zeta; \|\zeta_i\|_2 \leq \Delta\},$$

where ζ_i denotes the ith row of ζ and Δ is a predefined budget. Note that in Eq. (6.15), $\mathcal{L}_{train}\left(\mathbf{A}, \mathbf{F}^{(1)} + \zeta; \Theta\right)$ is overloaded to denote a similar loss as Eq. (5.49) except that it is based on the perturbed hidden representation $\mathbf{F}^{(1)} + \zeta$. Similar to other adversarial training techniques, the minimization problem and the maximization problem are processed in an alternative way.

6.3.2 Graph Purification

Graph purification–based defense techniques have been developed to defend against the adversarial attacks on graph structure. Specifically, these methods try to identify adversarial attacks in a given graph and remove them before using the graph for model training. Hence, most graph purification methods can be viewed as performing preprocessing on graphs. Next, we introduce two defense techniques based on graph purification.

Removing Edges with Low Feature Similarity

Empirical explorations show that many adversarial attack methods (e.g., nettack and IG-fast gradient sign method) tend to add edges to connect nodes with significantly different node features (Wu et al., 2019; Jin et al., 2020a). Similarly, when removing edges, these attack methods tend to remove the edges between nodes with similar features. Hence, based on these observations, a simple and efficient approach was proposed in Wu et al. (2019) that tries to remove the edges between nodes with very different features. More specifically, a scoring function is proposed to measure the similarity between the node features. For example, for binary features, the Jaccard similarity (Tan et al., 2016) is adopted as the scoring function. The edges with scores that are smaller than a threshold are then removed from the graph. The preprocessed graph is then employed to train the GNN models.

Low-Rank Approximation of Adjacency Matrix

Empirical studies have been carried out to analyze the adversarial perturbations generated by nettack (Entezari et al., 2020; Jin et al., 2020a). It turns out that netttack tends to perturb the graph structure to increase the adjacency matrix's rank. It is argued that the number of low-value singular values of the adjacency matrix is increased. Hence, a singular value decomposition–based preprocessing method was proposed in Entezari et al. (2020) to remove the adversarial perturbation added into the graph structure. Specifically, given an adjacency matrix $\mathbf{A}$ of a graph, singular value decomposition is used to decompose it, and then only the top-k singular values are kept to reconstruct (approximate) the adjacency matrix. The reconstructed adjacency matrix is then treated as the purified graph structure and utilized to train the graph neural network models.

6.3.3 Graph Attention

Instead of removing the adversarial attacks from the graph as with graph purification-based methods, graph attention-based methods aim to learn to focus less on the nodes/edges affected by the adversarial attacks in the graph. Graph attention-based defense techniques are usually end-to-end. In other words, they include the graph attention mechanism as a building component in the GNN models. Next, we introduce two attention-based defense techniques.

Robust Graph Convolutional Networks (RGCN): Modeling Hidden Representations with a Gaussian Distribution

To improve the robustness of GNN models, instead of plain vectors, a multivariate Gaussian distribution was adopted to model the hidden representations in Zhu et al. (2019a). The adversarial attacks generate perturbations on the graph structure, which, in turn, cause abnormal effects on the node representations. Though plain vector-based hidden representations cannot adapt themselves to the adversarial impacts, the Gaussian distribution–based hidden representations can absorb the effects caused by the adversarial attacks and thus can lead to more robust hidden representations. Furthermore, a variance-based attention mechanism is introduced to prevent the adversarial effects from propagation across the graph. Specifically, the nodes affected by adversarial attacks typically have large variances because the attacks tend to connect nodes with very different features and/or from different communities. Hence, when performing neighbor information aggregation to update node features, less attention is assigned to those neighbors with large variances to prevent the adversarial effects from propagation. Next, we describe the details of the RGCN Filter; i.e., the graph filter built upon the intuitions above.

The RGCN-Filter is built upon the GCN-Filter as described in Eq. (5.22). For ease of description, we recall Eq. (5.22) as follows:

$$\mathbf{F}'_i = \sum_{v_j \in \mathcal{N}(v_i) \cup \{v_i\}} \frac{1}{\sqrt{\tilde{\mathbf{d}}_i \tilde{\mathbf{d}}_j}} \mathbf{F}_j \Theta,$$

where $\tilde{d}_i = \tilde{\mathbf{D}}_{i,i}$. Instead of plain vectors, the RGCN-Filter utilizes Gaussian distributions to model the node representations. For node v_i, its representation is denoted as

$$\mathbf{F}_i \sim \mathcal{N}(\mu_i, \mathrm{diag}(\sigma_i)),$$

where $\mu_i \in \mathbb{R}^d$ is the mean of the representations and $diag(\sigma_i) \in \mathbb{R}^{d \times d}$ is the diagonal variance matrix of the representations. When updating the node representations, it has two aggregation processes on the mean and variance of the representations. In addition, an attention mechanism based on the variance of representations is introduced to prevent the adversarial effects from propagating across the graph. Specifically, for nodes with larger variances, smaller attention scores are assigned. The attention score for node v_i is modeled through a smooth exponential function as

$$a_i = \exp(-\gamma \sigma_i),$$

where γ is a hyperparameter. With the definition of the Gaussian-based representations and the attention scores, the update process for the representation of node v_i can be stated as

$$\mathbf{F}'_i \sim \mathcal{N}(\mu'_i, \mathrm{diag}(\sigma'_i)),$$

where

$$\mu'_i = \alpha \left(\sum_{v_j \in \mathcal{N}(v_i) \cup \{v_i\}} \frac{1}{\sqrt{\tilde{\mathbf{d}}_i \tilde{\mathbf{d}}_j}} (\mu_j \odot a_j) \Theta_\mu \right);$$

$$\sigma'_i = \alpha \left(\sum_{v_j \in \mathcal{N}(v_i) \cup \{v_i\}} \frac{1}{\tilde{\mathbf{d}}_i \tilde{\mathbf{d}}_j} (\sigma_j \odot a_j \odot a_j) \Theta_\sigma \right).$$

Here α denotes nonlinear activation functions, $\odot$ is the Hadamard multiplication operator, and Θ_μ and Θ_σ are learnable parameters to transform the aggregated information of mean and variance, respectively.

Penalized Aggregation Graph Neural Networks (PA-GNN): Transferring Robustness from Clean Graphs

Instead of penalizing the affected nodes as with a RGCN, a PA-GNN (Tang et al., 2019) aims to penalize the adversarial edges for preventing the adversarial effects from propagating through the graph. Specifically, it aims to learn an attention mechanism that can assign low attention scores to adversarial edges. However, typically, we do not have knowledge about the adversarial edges. Hence, PA-GNN aims to transfer this knowledge from clean graphs where adversarial attacks can be generated to serve as supervision signals to learn the desired attention scores.

The PA-GNN model is built upon the graph attention network as described in Eq. (5.27), which can be written as

$$\mathbf{F}'_i = \sum_{v_j \in \mathcal{N}(v_i) \cup \{v_i\}} a_{ij} \mathbf{F}_j \mathbf{\Theta}, \qquad (6.16)$$

where a_{ij} denotes the attention score for aggregating information from node v_j to node v_i through edge e_{ij}. Intuitively, we desire the attention scores of the adversarial edges to be small so that the adversarial effects can be prevented from propagating. Assume that we know a set of adversarial edges, which is denoted as $\mathcal{E}_{ad}$, and the set of the remaining "clean" edges can be denoted as $\mathcal{E}/\mathcal{E}_{ad}$. To ensure that the attention scores for the adversarial edges are small, the following term can be added to the training loss to penalize the adversarial edges:

$$\mathcal{L}_{\text{dist}} = -\min\left(\eta, \underset{\substack{e_{ij} \in \mathcal{E}/\mathcal{E}_{ad} \\ 1 \le l \le L}}{\mathbb{E}} a_{ij}^{(l)} - \underset{\substack{e_{ij} \in \mathcal{E}_{ad} \\ 1 \le l \le L}}{\mathbb{E}} a_{ij}^{(l)}\right),$$

where $a_{ij}^{(l)}$ is the attention score assigned to edge e_{ij} in the lth graph filtering layer, L is the total number of graph filtering layers in the model, and η is a hyperparameter controlling the margin between the two expectations. The expectations of the attention coefficients are estimated by their empirical means as

$$\underset{\substack{e_{ij} \in \mathcal{E}\setminus\mathcal{E}_{ad} \\ 1 \le l \le L}}{\mathbb{E}} a_{ij}^{(l)} = \frac{1}{L|\mathcal{E}\setminus\mathcal{E}_{ad}|} \sum_{l=1}^{L} \sum_{e_{ij} \in \mathcal{E}\setminus\mathcal{E}_{ad}} a_{ij}^{(l)}$$

$$\underset{\substack{e_{ij} \in \mathcal{E}_{ad} \\ 1 \le l \le L}}{\mathbb{E}} a_{ij}^{(l)} = \frac{1}{L|\mathcal{E}_{ad}|} \sum_{l=1}^{L} \sum_{e_{ij} \in \mathcal{E}_{ad}} a_{ij}^{(l)},$$

where $|\cdot|$ denotes the cardinality of a set. To train the classification model while assigning lower attention scores to the adversarial edges, we combine the loss $\mathcal{L}_{dist}$ with the semi-supervised node classification loss $\mathcal{L}_{train}$ in Eq. (5.49) as

$$\min_{\Theta} \mathcal{L} = \min_{\Theta} \left(\mathcal{L}_{train} + \lambda \mathcal{L}_{dist} \right), \tag{6.17}$$

where λ is a hyperparameter balancing the importance between the two types of loss. So far, the set of adversarial edges $\mathcal{E}_{ad}$ is assumed to be known, which is impractical. Hence, instead of directly formulating and optimizing Eq. (6.17), we try to transfer the ability of assigning low attention scores to adversarial edges from those graphs with known adversarial edges. To obtain the graphs with known adversarial edges, we collect clean graphs from similar domains as the given graph and apply existing adversarial attacks such as *metattack* to generate attacked graphs. Then, we can learn the ability from these attacked graphs and transfer it to the given graph. Next, we first briefly discuss the overall framework of PA-GNN and then detail the process of learning the attention mechanism and transferring its ability to the target graph. As shown in Figure 6.1, given a set of K clean graphs denoted as $\{\mathcal{G}_1, \cdots, \mathcal{G}_K\}$, we use existing attacking methods such as metattack to generate a set of adversarial edges $\mathcal{E}_{ad}^i$ for each graph. Furthermore, the node set $\mathcal{V}^i$ in each graph is split into the training set $\mathcal{V}_l^i$ and the test set $\mathcal{V}_u^i$. Then, we try to optimize the loss function in Eq. (6.17) for each graph. Specifically, for the graph $\mathcal{G}_i$, we denote its corresponding loss as $\mathcal{L}_i$. As inspired by the meta-optimization algorithm Model-Agnostic Meta-Learning (MAML) (Finn et al., 2017), all graphs share the same initialization Θ and the goal is to learn these parameters Θ that can be easily adapted to learning the task on each graph, separately. As shown in Figure 6.1, the ideal shared initialization parameters Θ are learned through meta-optimization, which we will detail later in this section. These shared parameters Θ are considered to carry the ability to assign lower attention scores to the adversarial edges. To transfer this ability to the given graph $\mathcal{G}$, we use the shared parameters Θ as the initialization parameters to train the GNN model on graph $\mathcal{G}$ and the obtained fine-tuned parameters are denoted as $\Theta_{\mathcal{G}}$. Next, we describe the meta-optimization algorithm adopted from MAML to learn the optimal shared parameters Θ.

The optimization process first adapts (fine-tunes) the parameters Θ to each graph $\mathcal{G}_i$ by using the gradient descent method as

$$\Theta_i' = \Theta - \alpha \nabla_{\Theta} \mathcal{L}_i^{tr}(\Theta),$$

where Θ_i' are the specific parameters for the learning task on the graph $\mathcal{G}_i$ and $\mathcal{L}_i^{tr}$ denotes the loss in Eq. (6.17) evaluated on the corresponding training set $\mathcal{V}_l^i$. The test sets of all graphs $\{\mathcal{V}_u^1, \ldots, \mathcal{V}_u^K\}$ are then used to update the shared parameters Θ such that each of the learned classifiers can work well for each graph. Hence, the objective of the meta-optimization can be summarized as

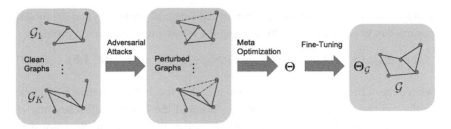

Figure 6.1 The overall framework of PA-GNN.

$$\min_{\Theta} \sum_{i=1}^{K} \mathcal{L}_i^{te}\left(\Theta_i'\right) = \min_{\Theta} \sum_{i=1}^{K} \mathcal{L}_i^{te}\left(\theta - \alpha \nabla_\Theta \mathcal{L}_i^{tr}(\Theta)\right),$$

where $\mathcal{L}_i^{te}\left(\Theta_i'\right)$ denotes the loss in Eq. (6.17) evaluated on the corresponding test set $\mathcal{V}_u^i$. The shared parameters Θ can be updated using stochastic gradient descent as

$$\Theta \leftarrow \Theta - \beta \nabla_\Theta \sum_{i=1}^{K} \mathcal{L}_i^{te}\left(\Theta_i'\right).$$

Once the shared parameters Θ are learned, they can be used as the initialization for the learning task on the given graph $\mathcal{G}$.

6.3.4 Graph Structure Learning

In Subsection 6.3.2, we introduced the graph purification-based defense techniques. They often first identify the adversarial attacks and then remove them from the attacked graph before training the GNN models. Those methods typically consist of two stages; i.e., the purification stage and the model training stage. With such a two-stage strategy, the purified graphs might be suboptimal to learn the model parameters for downstream tasks. In Jin et al. (2020b), an end-to-end method, which jointly purifies the graph structure and learns the model parameters, was proposed to train robust GNN models. As described in Subsection 6.3.2, the adversarial attacks usually tend to add edges to connect nodes with different node features and increase the rank of the adjacency matrix. Hence, to reduce the effects of the adversarial attacks, Pro-GNN (Jin et al., 2020b) aims to learn a new adjacency matrix $\mathbf{S}$ that is close to the original adjacency matrix $\mathbf{A}$ while being low-rank and also ensuring feature smoothing. Specifically, the purified adjacency matrix $\mathbf{S}$ and the model parameters Θ can be learned by solving the following optimization problem:

$$\min_{\Theta,\mathbf{S}} \mathcal{L}_{train}(\mathbf{S},\mathbf{F};\Theta) + \|\mathbf{A} - \mathbf{S}\|_F^2 + \beta_1\|\mathbf{S}\|_1 + \beta_2\|\mathbf{S}\|_* + \beta_3 \cdot tr(\mathbf{F}^T\mathbf{L}\mathbf{F}), \quad (6.18)$$

where the term $\|\mathbf{A} - \mathbf{S}\|_F^2$ is to make sure that the learned matrix $\mathbf{S}$ is close to the original adjacency matrix; the L_1 norm of the learned adjacency matrix $\|\mathbf{S}\|_1$ ensures the learned matrix $\mathbf{S}$ to be sparse; $\|\mathbf{S}\|_*$ is the nuclear norm to ensure that the learned matrix $\mathbf{S}$ is low-rank; and the term $tr(\mathbf{F}^T\mathbf{L}\mathbf{F})$ is to force the feature smoothness. Note that the feature matrix $\mathbf{F}$ is fixed, and the term $tr(\mathbf{F}^T\mathbf{L}\mathbf{F})$ forces the Laplacian matrix $\mathbf{L}$, built upon $\mathbf{S}$, to ensure that the features are smooth. The hyperparameters β_1, β_2, and β_3 control the balance between these terms. The matrix $\mathbf{S}$ and the model parameters Θ can be optimized alternatively as follows:

- **Update Θ:** We fix the matrix $\mathbf{S}$ and remove the terms that are irrelevant to $\mathbf{S}$ in Eq. (6.18). The optimization problem is then reformulated as

$$\min_{\Theta} \mathcal{L}_{train}(\mathbf{S},\mathbf{F};\Theta).$$

- **Update $\mathbf{S}$:** We fix the model parameters Θ and optimize the matrix $\mathbf{S}$ by solving the following optimization problem:

$$\min_{\mathbf{S}} \mathcal{L}_{train}(\mathbf{S},\mathbf{F};\Theta) + \|\mathbf{A} - \mathbf{S}\|_F^2 + \alpha\|\mathbf{S}\|_1 + \beta\|\mathbf{S}\|_* + \lambda \cdot tr(\mathbf{F}^T\mathbf{L}\mathbf{F}).$$

6.4 Conclusion

In this chapter, we focus on the robustness of GNNs, which is critical for applying GNN models to real-world applications. Specifically, we first describe various adversarial attack methods designed for graph-structured data, including white-box, gray-box, and black-box attacks. They demonstrate that GNN models are vulnerable to deliberately designed unnoticeable perturbations on graph structures and/or node features. Then, we introduced a variety of defense techniques to improve the robustness of GNN models including graph adversarial training, graph purification, graph attention, and graph structure learning.

6.5 Further Reading

The research area of robust GNNs is still fast evolving. Thus, a comprehensive repository for graph adversarial attacks and defenses has been built

(Li et al., 2020a). The repository enables systematical experiments on existing algorithms and efficient new algorithm development. An empirical study has been conducted based on the repository (Jin et al., 2020a). It provides deep insights about graph adversarial attacks and defenses that can deepen our knowledge and foster this research field. In addition to the graph domain, there are adversarial attacks and defenses in other domains such as images (Yuan et al., 2019; Xu et al., 2019b; Ren et al., 2020) and texts (Xu et al., 2019b; Zhang et al., 2020).

7

Scalable Graph Neural Networks

7.1 Introduction

Graph neural networks suffer from severe scalability issues, which prevents them from being adapted to large-scale graphs. Take the GCN-Filter–based model for the node classification task as an example, where we adopt gradient-based methods to minimize the following loss function (the same as Eq. (5.49)):

$$\mathcal{L}_{train} = \sum_{v_i \in \mathcal{V}_l} l(f_{GCN}(\mathbf{A}, \mathbf{F}^{(in)}; \Theta)_i, y_i), \qquad (7.1)$$

where $f_{GCN}(\mathbf{A}, \mathbf{F}^{(in)}; \Theta)$ consists of L GCN-Filter layers as described in Eq. (5.21) as:

$$\mathbf{F}^{(l)} = \hat{\mathbf{A}} \mathbf{F}^{(l-1)} \Theta^{(l-1)}, \quad l = 1, \ldots, L, \qquad (7.2)$$

where $\hat{\mathbf{A}}$ is used to denote $\tilde{\mathbf{D}}^{-\frac{1}{2}} \tilde{\mathbf{A}} \tilde{\mathbf{D}}^{-\frac{1}{2}}$. For convenience of analysis, the node representations in all layers are assumed to have the same dimension d. Note that, in this formulation, we ignore the activation layer that can be added between the graph filtering layers. The parameters Θ in Eq. (7.1) include $\Theta^{(l)}$, $l = 1, \ldots, L$ and the parameters Θ_2 to perform the prediction as in Eq. (5.47). One step of the gradient descent algorithm to minimize the loss can be described as

$$\Theta \leftarrow \Theta + \eta \cdot \nabla_\Theta \mathcal{L}_{train}, \qquad (7.3)$$

where η is the learning rate and the gradient $\nabla_\Theta \mathcal{L}_{train}$ needs to be evaluated over the entire training set $\mathcal{V}_l$. Furthermore, due to the design of the GCN-Filter layers as shown in Eq. (7.2), when evaluating $\mathcal{L}_{train}$ in the forward pass, all nodes in $\mathcal{V}$ are involved in the calculation because all node representations are computed in each layer. Hence, in the forward pass of each training epoch,

162

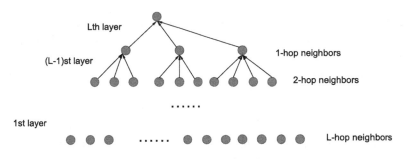

Figure 7.1 The aggregation process.

the representations for all nodes and the parameters in each graph filtering layer need to be stored in the memory, which becomes prohibitively large when the scale of the graph grows. Specifically, we can calculate the required memory explicitly as follows. During the forward pass, the normalized adjacency matrix $\hat{\mathbf{A}}$, the node representations in all layers $\mathbf{F}^{(l)}$, and the parameters in all layers $\mathbf{\Theta}^{(l)}$ need to be stored in the memory, which requires $O(|\mathcal{E}|)$, $O(L \cdot |\mathcal{V}| \cdot d)$, and $O(L \cdot d^2)$, respectively. Thus, in total, the required memory is $O(|\mathcal{E}| + L \cdot |\mathcal{V}| \cdot d + L \cdot d^2)$. When the size of the graph is large–i.e., $|\mathcal{V}|$ and/or $|\mathcal{E}|$ are large–it becomes impossible to fit them into the memory. Furthermore, the calculation in the form of Eq. (7.2) is not efficient because the final representations (or the representations after the Lth layer) for the unlabeled nodes in $\mathcal{V}_u$ are also calculated, although they are not required for evaluating Eq. (7.1). In detail, $O(L \cdot (|\mathcal{E}| \cdot d + |\mathcal{V}| \cdot d^2)) = O(L \cdot |\mathcal{V}| \cdot d^2)$ operations are required to perform the full epoch of the forward process. As in a traditional deep learning scenario, a natural idea to reduce the memory requirement during training is to adopt stochastic gradient descent (SGD). Instead of using all of the training samples, it utilizes a single training sample (or a subset of training samples) to estimate the gradient. However, adopting SGD in graph-structured data is not as convenient as that in the traditional scenario because the training samples in Eq. (7.1) are connected to other labeled/unlabeled samples in the graph. To calculate the loss $l(f_{GCN}(\mathbf{A}, \mathbf{F}_{in}; \mathbf{\Theta})_i, y_i)$ for node v_i, the node representations of many other nodes (or even the entire graph as indicated by the adjacency matrix $\hat{\mathbf{A}}$) are also involved due to the graph filtering operations as described in Eq. (7.2). To perceive the calculation more clearly, we analyze Eq. (7.2) from a local view for a node v_i as

$$\mathbf{F}_i^{(l)} = \sum_{v_j \in \tilde{\mathcal{N}}(v_i)} \hat{\mathbf{A}}_{i,j} \mathbf{F}_j^{(l-1)} \mathbf{\Theta}^{(l-1)}, \quad l = 1, \dots, L, \tag{7.4}$$

which takes the form of aggregating information from neighboring nodes. Note that we use $\mathbf{F}_i$ to denote the node representation for node v_i; $\hat{\mathbf{A}}_{i,j}$ to indicate the i, jth element of $\hat{\mathbf{A}}$ and $\tilde{N}(v_i) = N(v_i) \cup \{v_i\}$ to denote the set of neighbors of node v_i including itself. Hence, clearly, to calculate the representation of node v_i in the lth graph filtering layer, only the representations of its neighbors (including itself) in the $(l-1)$st layer are required. To calculate the $(l-1)$ layer representation for a node $v_j \in \tilde{N}(v_i)$, all of the $(l-2)$ layer representations of its neighbors are required. The neighbors of all nodes in $\tilde{N}(v_i)$ are the "neighbors of neighbors" of node v_i; i.e., the 2-hop neighbors of node v_i. Following this procedure, we can obtain the nodes involved in the process to compute the loss term for node v_i. As shown in Figure 7.1, from a top-down perspective, its l-hop neighbors are required in the $(L - l + 1)$st graph filtering layer; thus, its L-hop neighbors are required for the entire process of calculation. We rewrite the loss for the node v_i as

$$l(f_{GCN}(\mathbf{A}, \mathbf{F}_{in}; \mathbf{\Theta})_i, y_i) = l(f_{GCN}(\mathbf{A}\{N^L(v_i)\}, \mathbf{F}^{(in)}\{N^L(v_i)\}; \mathbf{\Theta}), y_i), \qquad (7.5)$$

where $N^L(v_i)$ is the set of all nodes within L-hop away from node v_i–i.e., all nodes shown in Figure 7.1–$\mathbf{A}\{N_L(v_i)\}$ denotes the induced structure on $N_L(v_i)$, (i.e., the rows and columns in the adjacent matrix corresponding to nodes in $N_L(v_i)$ are retrieved) and $\mathbf{F}^{(in)}\{N^L(v_i)\}$ are the input features for nodes in $N^L(v_i)$. Typically, the mini-batch SGD algorithm, where a mini-batch of training instances is sampled from V_l to estimate the gradient, is used for parameter updates. The batch-wise loss function can be expressed as

$$\mathcal{L}_\mathcal{B} = \sum_{v_i \in \mathcal{B}} l(f_{GCN}(\mathbf{A}\{N^L(v_i)\}, \mathbf{F}^{(in)}\{N^L(v_i)\}; \mathbf{\Theta}), y_i), \qquad (7.6)$$

where $\mathcal{B} \subset V_l$ is the sampled mini-batch. However, even if SGD is adopted for optimization, the memory requirement can be still high. The major issue is that, as shown in Figure 7.1, the node set $N^L(v_i)$ expands exponentially as the number of graph filtering layers L increases. Specifically, the number of nodes in $N^L(v_i)$ is on the order of deg^L, where deg denotes the average degree of the nodes in the graph. Furthermore, in practice, we need to prepare the memory that is sufficient for the "worst" batch that requires the "most" memory instead of the average one. This could lead to quite a lot of memory when there is a node with a large degree in the batch, because many other nodes are involved due to the inclusion of this large degree node. Thus, to perform SGD optimization, $O(deg^L \cdot d)$ memory is required to store the node representations. This issue of exponentially growing neighborhood is usually referred as "neighborhood expansion" or "neighborhood explosion" (Chen et al., 2018a,b; Huang et al., 2018). When L is larger than the diameter of the graph, we have $\mathcal{N}^L(v_i) = \mathcal{V}$. This means that the entire node set is required for calculation, which demonstrates an extreme case of neighborhood explosion. Furthermore, the neighborhood explosion issue affects the time efficiency of the SGD algorithm. Specifically, the time complexity to calculate the final representation $\mathbf{F}_i^{(L)}$ for the node v_i is $O(deg^L \cdot (deg \cdot d + d^2))$, which is $O(deg^L \cdot d^2)$ because deg is usually much smaller than d. Then, the time complexity to run an epoch over the entire training set $\mathcal{V}_l$ is $O(|\mathcal{V}_l| \cdot deg^L \cdot d^2)$ when we assume that each batch only contains a single training sample. Because some of the involved nodes may exist in $\mathcal{N}^L(v_i)$ for several samples v_i in batch $\mathcal{B}$ and their representations can be shared during the calculation, the time complexity can be lower when the batch size $|\mathcal{B}| > 1$. Compared to the full gradient algorithm, which takes $O(L \cdot |\mathcal{V}| \cdot d^2)$ to run a full epoch, the time complexity for SGD can be even higher when L is large, although no extra final representations for unlabeled nodes are calculated.

Although we introduce the neighborhood explosion issue for the graph neural network (GNN) models with GCN-Filters, this issue exists in GNN models with other graph filters as long as they follow a neighborhood aggregation process as in Eq. (7.4). In this chapter, without loss of generality, the discussion and analysis are based on the GCN-Filters. To solve the neighborhood explosion issue and correspondingly improve the scalability of GNN models, various neighborhood sampling methods have been proposed. The main idea of sampling methods is to reduce the number of nodes involved in the calculation of Eq. (7.6) and hence lower the required time and memory to perform the calculation. There are three main types of sampling methods:

- **Node-wise sampling methods.** To calculate the node representation for a node v_i with Eq. (7.4), a set of nodes in each layer is sampled from its neighbors. Then, instead of aggregating information from its entire neighborhood, the node representation will only be calculated based on these sampled nodes.
- **Layer-wise sampling methods.** A set of nodes is sampled for the node representation calculation of the entire layer. In other words, to calculate $\mathbf{F}_i^{(l)}$ and $\mathbf{F}_j^{(l)}$ for nodes v_i and v_j, the same set of sampled nodes is utilized to perform the calculation.
- **Subgraph-wise sampling methods.** A subgraph is sampled from the original graph. Then, the node representation learning is based on the sampled subgraph.

In this chapter, we detail and analyze representative algorithms from each group of sampling methods.

7.2 Node-wise Sampling Methods

The node-wise aggregation process in Eq. (7.4) can be rewritten as:

$$\mathbf{F}_i^{(l)} = |\tilde{\mathcal{N}}(v_i)| \sum_{v_j \in \tilde{\mathcal{N}}(v_i)} \frac{1}{|\tilde{\mathcal{N}}(v_i)|} \hat{\mathbf{A}}_{i,j} \mathbf{F}_j^{(l-1)} \mathbf{\Theta}^{(l-1)}, \tag{7.7}$$

which can be regarded as the following expectation form:

$$\mathbf{F}_i^{(l)} = |\tilde{\mathcal{N}}(v_i)| \cdot \mathbb{E}[\mathscr{F}_{v_i}], \tag{7.8}$$

where $\mathscr{F}_{v_i}$ is a discrete random variable as defined below:

$$p\left(\mathscr{F}_{v_i} = \hat{\mathbf{A}}_{i,j}\mathbf{F}_j^{(l-1)}\mathbf{\Theta}^{(l-1)}\right) = \begin{cases} \frac{1}{\tilde{\mathcal{N}}(v_i)}, & \text{if } v_j \in \tilde{\mathcal{N}}(v_i), \\ 0, & \text{otherwise.} \end{cases} \tag{7.9}$$

A natural idea to speed up the computation while reducing the memory need for Eq. (7.8) is to approximate the expectation by Monte Carlo sampling. Specifically, the expectation $\mathbb{E}[\mathscr{F}_{v_i}]$ can be estimated as

$$\mathbb{E}[\mathscr{F}_{v_i}] \approx \hat{\mathscr{F}}_{v_i} = \frac{1}{|n^l(v_i)|} \sum_{v_j \in n^l(v_i)} \hat{\mathbf{A}}_{i,j}\mathbf{F}_j^{(l-1)}\mathbf{\Theta}^{(l-1)}, \tag{7.10}$$

where $n^l(v_i) \subset \tilde{\mathcal{N}}(v_i)$ is a set of nodes sampled from $\mathcal{V}$ for the lth layer according to the following probability distribution:

$$p\left(v_j|v_i\right) = \begin{cases} \frac{1}{\tilde{\mathcal{N}}(v_i)}, & \text{if } v_j \in \tilde{\mathcal{N}}(v_i), \\ 0, & \text{otherwise.} \end{cases} \tag{7.11}$$

The estimator in Eq. (7.10) is unbiased as shown below:

$$\begin{aligned}
\mathbb{E}[\hat{\mathscr{F}}_{v_i}] &= \mathbb{E}\left[\frac{1}{|n^l(v_i)|}\sum_{v_j \in n^l(v_i)} \hat{\mathbf{A}}_{i,j}\mathbf{F}_j^{(l-1)}\mathbf{\Theta}^{(l-1)}\mathbf{1}\{v_j \in n^l(v_i)\}\right] \\
&= \mathbb{E}\left[\frac{1}{|n^l(v_i)|}\sum_{v_j \in \mathcal{V}} \hat{\mathbf{A}}_{i,j}\mathbf{F}_j^{(l-1)}\mathbf{\Theta}^{(l-1)}\mathbf{1}\{v_j \in n^l(v_i)\}\right] \\
&= \frac{1}{|n^l(v_i)|}\sum_{v_j \in \mathcal{V}} \hat{\mathbf{A}}_{i,j}\mathbf{F}_j^{(l-1)}\mathbf{\Theta}^{(l-1)}\mathbb{E}\left[\mathbf{1}\{v_j \in n^l(v_i)\}\right] \\
&= \frac{1}{|n^l(v_i)|}\sum_{v_j \in \mathcal{V}} \hat{\mathbf{A}}_{i,j}\mathbf{F}_j^{(l-1)}\mathbf{\Theta}^{(l-1)}\frac{|n^l(v_i)|}{|\tilde{\mathcal{N}}(v_i)|} \\
&= \frac{1}{|\tilde{\mathcal{N}}(v_i)|}\sum_{v_j \in \mathcal{V}} \hat{\mathbf{A}}_{i,j}\mathbf{F}_j^{(l-1)}\mathbf{\Theta}^{(l-1)} \\
&= \mathbb{E}[\mathscr{F}_{v_i}],
\end{aligned} \tag{7.12}$$

where $\mathbf{1}\{v_j \in n^l(v_i)\}$ is an indicator random variable, which takes a value of 1 if $v_j \in n^l(v_i)$ and 0 otherwise.

With Eq. (7.10), the node-wise aggregation process can be expressed as:

$$\mathbf{F}_i^{(l)} = \frac{|\tilde{\mathcal{N}}(v_i)|}{|n^l(v_i)|} \sum_{v_j \in n^l(v_i)} \hat{\mathbf{A}}_{i,j} \mathbf{F}_j^{(l-1)} \mathbf{\Theta}^{(l-1)}. \tag{7.13}$$

The sampling process utilized in Eq. (7.13) is called *node-wise sampling*, because the node set $n^l(v_i)$ is sampled only for the node v_i and is not shared with other nodes. Specifically, the GraphSAGE-Filter can be viewed as a node-wise sampling method due to the neighbor sampling process. Typically, for a specific graph filtering layer, the sampling size $|n^l(v_i)|$ is set to a fixed value $|n^l(v_i)| = m$ for all nodes. Though different graph filtering layers can have different sampling sizes, for convenience, we assume that they all have the same sampling size m in this chapter.

Although node-wise sampling methods can help control the size of the number of involved nodes in each layer to a fixed size m, they still suffer from the neighborhood explosion issue when m is large. In detail, following the same top-down perspective in Figure 7.1, the number of nodes involved to calculate the final representation $\mathbf{F}_i^{(L)}$ for node v_i is on the order of m^L, which increases exponentially as the number of layer L grows. The space and time complexity are $O(m^L \cdot d^2)$ and $O(|\mathcal{V}_l| \cdot m^L \cdot d^2)$, respectively. One way to alleviate this issue is to control the sampling size m to be a small number. However, a small m leads to a large variance in the estimation in Eq. (7.10), which is not desired.

A sampling method that utilizes an extremely small sampling size m (as small as 2) while maintaining a reasonable variance was proposed in Chen et al. (2018a). The idea is to keep a historical representation $\bar{\mathbf{F}}_i^{(l-1)}$ for each $\mathbf{F}_i^{(l-1)}$ for $l = 2, \ldots, L$, and then use these historical representations during the calculation in Eq. (7.4). Each time $\mathbf{F}_i^{(l)}$ is calculated, we update its corresponding historical representation $\bar{\mathbf{F}}_i^{(l)}$ with $\mathbf{F}_i^{(l)}$. The historical representations are expected to be similar to the real representations if the model parameters do not change too fast during the training process. We still use Monte Carlo sampling to estimate Eq. (7.4). However, for those nodes that are not sampled to $n^l(v_i)$, we include their historical representations in the calculation. Formally, Eq. (7.4) can be decomposed into two terms as

$$\mathbf{F}_i^{(l)} = \sum_{v_j \in \tilde{\mathcal{N}}(v_i)} \hat{\mathbf{A}}_{i,j} \Delta \mathbf{F}_j^{(l-1)} \mathbf{\Theta}^{(l-1)} + \sum_{v_j \in \tilde{\mathcal{N}}(v_i)} \hat{\mathbf{A}}_{i,j} \bar{\mathbf{F}}_j^{(l-1)} \mathbf{\Theta}^{(l-1)}, \tag{7.14}$$

where

$$\Delta \mathbf{F}_j^{(l-1)} = \mathbf{F}_j^{(l-1)} - \bar{\mathbf{F}}_j^{(l-1)}. \tag{7.15}$$

The term $\Delta\mathbf{F}_j^{(l-1)}$ denotes the difference between the real up-to-date representation and the historical representation. Instead of using Monte Carlo sampling to estimate the entire term in Eq. (7.4), only the difference is estimated as

$$\sum_{v_j \in \tilde{\mathcal{N}}(v_i)} \hat{\mathbf{A}}_{i,j}\Delta\mathbf{F}_j^{(l-1)}\mathbf{\Theta}^{(l-1)} \approx \frac{|\tilde{\mathcal{N}}(v_i)|}{|n^l(v_i)|}\sum_{v_j \in n^l(v_i)} \hat{\mathbf{A}}_{i,j}\Delta\mathbf{F}_j^{(l-1)}\mathbf{\Theta}^{(l-1)}. \tag{7.16}$$

With Eq. (7.16), the aggregation process in Eq. (7.14) can be estimated as

$$\mathbf{F}_i^{(l)} \approx \frac{|\tilde{\mathcal{N}}(v_i)|}{|n^l(v_i)|}\sum_{v_j \in n^l(v_i)} \hat{\mathbf{A}}_{i,j}\Delta\mathbf{F}_j^{(l-1)}\mathbf{\Theta}^{(l-1)} + \sum_{v_j \in \tilde{\mathcal{N}}(v_i)} \hat{\mathbf{A}}_{i,j}\bar{\mathbf{F}}_j^{(l-1)}\mathbf{\Theta}^{(l-1)}, \tag{7.17}$$

which is named the control variate (CV) estimator and is used to update the node representations. Note that the second term on the right-hand side of Eq. (7.17) is calculated from stored historical node representations, which does not require the recursive calculation process and thus is computationally efficient. The CV estimator is unbiased because the estimation in Eq. (7.16) is unbiased. The variance of Eq. (7.17) is smaller than that of Eq. (7.13) because $\Delta\mathbf{F}_i^{(l-1)}$ is much smaller than $\mathbf{F}_i^{(l-1)}$. However, the reduced variance does not come free. Though the time complexity of this process remains $O(m^L \cdot d^2)$ (m can be much smaller in the CV estimator) as in the aggregation process described in Eq. (7.13), much more memory is required. In fact, to store the historical representations for all nodes involved in the process, $O(deg^L \cdot d)$ memory is required. It is the same as the SGD process without the node-wise sampling. Note that the space complexity is not dependent on the sampling size m; hence, a smaller m cannot ensure a lower space complexity.

7.3 Layer-wise Sampling Methods

In node-wise sampling methods, to calculate the final representation $\mathbf{F}_i^{(L)}$ for node v_i, the node set $n^L(v_i)$ is sampled from $\tilde{\mathcal{N}}(v_i)$ and $\mathbf{F}_j^{(L-1)}$ for $v_j \in n^l(v_i)$ is used during the calculation. Furthermore, to calculate $\mathbf{F}_j^{(L-1)}$ for each $v_j \in n^L(v_i)$, a node set $n^{(L-1)}(v_j)$ needs to be sampled. Specifically, let N^l denote all of the nodes sampled for the calculation of the lth layer, then N^l can be recursively defined from the top down as

$$N^{l-1} = \cup_{v_j \in N^l} n^{l-1}(v_j), \quad \text{with } N^L = n^L(v_i). \quad l = L, \ldots, 2, 1. \tag{7.18}$$

When the mini-batch SGD is adopted and the final representations of a batch $\mathcal{B}$ of nodes need to be calculated, N^L can be defined as $N^L = \cup_{v_i \in \mathcal{B}} n^L(v_i)$. This recursive process in Eq. (7.18) makes N^l grow exponentially; thus, the node-wise sampling methods still suffer from the neighborhood explosion issue. One way to solve the issue is to utilize the same set of sampled nodes to calculate all node representations in a specific layer. In other words, we allow $n^{l-1}(v_j) = n^{l-1}(v_k)$ for $\forall v_j, v_k \in N^l$; thus, the size of N^l remains constant as L increases. Then, we only need to sample once for each layer, and this strategy is called as *layer-wise sampling*. However, it is impractical to make $n^{l-1}(v_j) = n^{l-1}(v_k)$ because they are sampled according to different node-specific distributions as described in Eq. (7.11). In detail, the set $n^{l-1}(v_j)$ is sampled from the neighborhood of, and node v_j, and $n^{l-1}(v_k)$ is sampled from the neighborhood of node v_k.

Importance sampling was adopted by Chen et al. (2018b) and Huang et al. (2018) to design the layer-wise sampling methods. For the lth layer, instead of using the node-specific distributions to sample the nodes, a shared distribution that is defined over the entire node set $\mathcal{V}$ is utilized to sample a shared set of nodes. Then all of the output node representations for this layer are calculated only based on these shared sampled nodes. Next, we introduce the details of two representative layer-wise sampling methods (Chen et al., 2018b; Huang et al., 2018). Because these two methods follow the same design, we focus on introducing the method in Huang et al. (2018) and then briefly describe the one in Chen et al. (2018b).

To be consistent with the original paper (Huang et al., 2018), we first reformulate the process from Eq. (7.7) to Eq. (7.11). The node-wise aggregation process in Eq. (7.4) can be rewritten as

$$\mathbf{F}_i^{(l)} = D(v_i) \sum_{v_j \in \mathcal{N}(v_i)} \frac{\hat{\mathbf{A}}_{i,j}}{D(v_i)} \mathbf{F}_j^{(l-1)} \mathbf{\Theta}^{(l-1)}, \qquad (7.19)$$

where $D(v_i) = \sum_{v_j \in \tilde{\mathcal{N}}(v_i)} \hat{\mathbf{A}}_{i,j}$. Eq. (7.19) can be regarded as the following expectation form:

$$\mathbf{F}_i^{(l)} = D(v_i) \cdot \mathbb{E}[\mathscr{F}_{v_i}], \qquad (7.20)$$

where $\mathscr{F}_{v_i}$ is a discrete random variable as defined below:

$$p\left(\mathscr{F}_{v_i} = \mathbf{F}_j^{(l-1)} \mathbf{\Theta}^{(l-1)}\right) = \begin{cases} \frac{\hat{\mathbf{A}}_{i,j}}{D(v_i)}, & \text{if } v_j \in \tilde{\mathcal{N}}(v_i), \\ 0, & \text{otherwise.} \end{cases} \qquad (7.21)$$

Assume that $q^l(v_j)$ is a known distribution defined on the entire node set $\mathcal{V}$ and $q^l(v_j) > 0, \forall v_j \in \mathcal{V}$. Instead of using Monte Carlo sampling to estimate $\mathbb{E}[\mathscr{F}_{v_i}]$, we use importance sampling based on $q^l(v_j)$ as

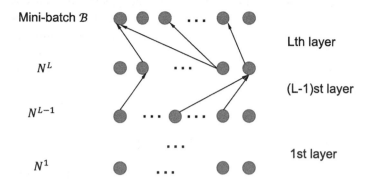

Figure 7.2 Layer-wise sampling.

$$\mathbb{E}[\mathscr{F}_{v_i}] \approx \hat{\mathscr{F}}_{v_i} = \frac{1}{|N^l|} \sum_{v_j \in N^l} \frac{p(v_j|v_i)}{q^l(v_j)} \mathbf{F}_j^{(l-1)} \mathbf{\Theta}^{(l-1)}, v_j \sim q^l(v_j) \ \forall v_j \in N^l, \quad (7.22)$$

where N^l denotes a set of nodes sampled according to the distribution $q^l(v_j)$ and $p(v_j|v_i) = \frac{\hat{\mathbf{A}}_{i,j}}{D(v_i)}$ if $v_j \in \tilde{N}(v_i)$; otherwise, $p(v_j|v_i) = 0$. The superscript l in $q^l(v_j)$ indicates that the distribution is utilized in the lth layer to sample the node set N^l and different layers may use different sampling distributions. The set of nodes N^l is shared by all nodes (e.g., v_i) that need to calculate the representations (e.g., $\mathbf{F}_i^{(l)}$) in the lth layer. With the importance sampling estimation for $\mathbb{E}[\mathscr{F}_{v_i}]$ in Eq. (7.22), the node-wise aggregation process (as described in Eq. (7.20)) with the layer-wise sampling strategy can then be described as

$$\mathbf{F}_i^{(l)} = D(v_i) \cdot \frac{1}{|N^l|} \sum_{v_j \in N^l} \frac{p(v_j|v_i)}{q(v_j)} \mathbf{F}_j^{(l-1)} \mathbf{\Theta}^{(l-1)} \quad (7.23)$$

$$= \frac{1}{|N^l|} \sum_{v_j \in N^l} \frac{\hat{\mathbf{A}}_{i,j}}{q^l(v_j)} \mathbf{F}_j^{(l-1)} \mathbf{\Theta}^{(l-1)}, \quad (7.24)$$

where nodes in N^l are sampled from $q^l(v_j)$. Before describing how to design the sampling distribution $q^l(v_j)$ appropriately, we first introduce the process to sample nodes and build the computational graph to calculate the final representations for all nodes in a sampled batch $\mathcal{B}$. As shown in Figure 7.2, from a top-down perspective, to calculate $\mathbf{F}_i^{(L)}$ for each node $v_i \in \mathcal{B}$, a set of nodes N^L is sampled according to $q^L(v_j)$. The representations $\mathbf{F}_j^{(L-1)}$ of $v_j \in N^L$ are used to calculate $\mathbf{F}_i^{(L)}$ for each node $v_i \in \mathcal{B}$ according to Eq. (7.24). To calculate $\mathbf{F}_j^{(L-1)}$ of $v_j \in N^L$, we need to sample N^{L-1} and aggregate information from them. This process goes to the bottom layer where N^1 is sampled and the input features $\mathbf{F}_j^{(0)}$ for $v_j \in N^1$ are used for the calculation. The memory required to compute the final representation $\mathbf{F}_i^{(L)}$ for each node $v_i \in \mathcal{B}$ according to Eq. (7.24), assuming $|N^l| = m$ for all layers, is $O(L \cdot m \cdot d)$. It is much smaller than that required by node-wise sampling–based methods. Correspondingly, the time efficiency for each epoch is improved because fewer node representations are required to be computed during this process.

The importance sampling–based estimator in Eq. (7.22) is unbiased and we want to find a distribution $q(v_j)$ such that the variance of Eq. (7.22) can be minimized. According to the derivations of importance sampling in Owen (2013), we conclude the following.

Proposition 7.1 *(Huang et al., 2018) The variance of the estimator $\hat{\mathscr{F}}_{v_i}$ in Eq. (7.22) is given by*

$$Var_q(\hat{\mathscr{F}}_{v_i}) = \frac{1}{|N^l|} \left[\frac{(p(v_j|v_i) \cdot |\mathbf{F}_j^{(l-1)}\mathbf{\Theta}^{(l-1)}| - \mathbb{E}[\mathscr{F}_{v_i}] \cdot q(u_j))^2}{q^2(v_j)} \right]. \quad (7.25)$$

The optimal sampling distribution $q(v_j)$, which minimizes the above variance, is given by

$$q^l(v_j) = \frac{p(v_j|v_i) \cdot |\mathbf{F}_j^{(l-1)}\mathbf{\Theta}^{(l-1)}|}{\sum\limits_{v_k \in \mathcal{V}} p(v_k|v_i) \cdot |\mathbf{F}_k^{(l-1)}\mathbf{\Theta}^{(l-1)}|}. \quad (7.26)$$

However, the optimal sampling distribution in Eq. (7.26) is not feasible because it is dependent on all node representations in the $(l-1)$st layer $\mathbf{F}^{(l-1)}$ but we are trying to use the sampling distribution to decide which of them to calculate. Note that in Chen et al. (2018b), the variance to be minimized is based on all of the nodes in the same layer instead of a single node v_i as in Proposition 7.1 and the optimal distribution takes a slightly different form but is still dependent on $\mathbf{F}^{(l-1)}$.

Hence, two different approaches are proposed in Chen et al. (2018b) and Huang et al. (2018). In Chen et al. (2018b), the dependence on $\mathbf{F}^{(l-1)}$ is directly discarded and a sampling distribution designed according to the optimal probability distribution is adopted as $q(v_j)$:

$$q(v_j) = \frac{\|\hat{\mathbf{A}}_{:,j}\|^2}{\sum\limits_{v_k \in \mathcal{V}} \|\hat{\mathbf{A}}_{:,k}\|^2}. \tag{7.27}$$

Note that the same $p(v_j)$ as described in Eq. (7.27) is used for all layers. Hence, the superscript l is removed from $q^l(v_j)$. In Huang et al. (2018), $\mathbf{F}_j^{(l-1)}\mathbf{\Theta}^{(l-1)}$ is replaced by $\mathbf{F}_j^{(0)}\mathbf{\Theta}_{in}$, where $\mathbf{F}_j^{(0)}$ denotes the input features of node v_j and $\mathbf{\Theta}_{in}$ is a linear projection to be learned. Furthermore, the sampling distribution in Eq. (7.26) is optimal for a specific node v_i but is not ready for layer-wise sampling. To make the distribution applicable to layer-wise sampling, the following distribution, which summarizes computations over all nodes in $\mathcal{N}^{l+1}$, is proposed in Huang et al. (2018):

$$q^l(v_j) = \frac{\sum\limits_{v_i \in N^{l+1}} p(v_j|v_i) \cdot |\mathbf{F}_j^{(0)}\mathbf{\Theta}_{in}|}{\sum\limits_{v_k \in \mathcal{V}} \sum\limits_{v_i \in N^{l+1}} p(v_k|v_i) \cdot |\mathbf{F}_k^{(0)}\mathbf{\Theta}_{in}|}. \tag{7.28}$$

Note that N^{l+1} denotes the nodes involved in the $(l+1)$st layer, which is on the top of the lth layer. Hence, the distribution $q^l(v_j)$ is dependent on the nodes in its top layer. Furthermore, the distribution changes in an adaptive way during training because the parameters $\mathbf{\Theta}_{in}$ are kept updated. With these modifications to the optimal distribution in Eq. (7.26), the distribution in Eq. (7.28) is not guaranteed to lead to minimal variance. Therefore, the variance terms are directly included in the loss function to be explicitly minimized during the training process (Huang et al., 2018).

7.4 Subgraph-wise Sampling Methods

The layer-wise sampling–based methods largely reduce the number of nodes involved in calculating final node representations and resolve the neighborhood explosion issue. However, the nature of layer-wise sampling methods is likely to cause another issue in the aggregation process from layer to layer. Specifically, it can be observed from Eq. (7.24) that the aggregation process to generate $\mathbf{F}_i^{(l)}$ is dependent on the term $\hat{\mathbf{A}}_{i,j}$ in each sampled node to be aggregated. This observation indicates that not all nodes in N^l are used to generate $\mathbf{F}_i^{(l)}$ but rather that only those that have connections to node v_i are utilized. Then, if the connections between node v_i and the sampled nodes in N^l are too sparse, the representation $\mathbf{F}_i^{(l)}$ of node v_i may not be well learned. In an extreme case where there are no nodes in N^l connected to node v_i, the representation of node v_i is rendered to 0 according to Eq. (7.24). Hence, to improve the stability of the training process, we need to sample N^l with a reasonable number of connections to node v_i. In other words, we need to ensure that the connectivity between the sampled nodes in N^l and N^{l-1} is dense so that all nodes are likely to have some nodes to aggregate information from. Note that the layer-wise sampling methods described in Section 7.3 do not take this into consideration when designing the layer-wise sampling distribution. In fact, to improve the connections between sampled nodes in consecutive layers, the sampling distributions for consecutive layers must be designed in a dependent way, which introduces significant difficulty. One way to ease the design is to use the same set of sampled nodes for all layers; i.e., $N^l = N^{l-1}$ for $l = L \ldots, 1$. Then, only one sample distribution needs to be designed such that more connections between the sampled nodes are encouraged. Furthermore, if the same set of nodes, denoted as $\mathcal{V}_s$, is adopted for all layers, the layer-wise aggregation in Eq. (7.24) is actually running the full neighborhood aggregations on the graph $\mathcal{G}_s$ that is induced on the sampled node sets $\mathcal{V}_s$. The induced graph $\mathcal{G}_s$ is a subgraph of the original graph $\mathcal{G}$ as $\mathcal{V}_s \subset \mathcal{V}$ and $\mathcal{E}_s \subset \mathcal{E}$. Instead of sampling $\mathcal{V}_s$, for each batch we can directly sample a subgraph $\mathcal{G}_s$ from $\mathcal{G}$ and perform model training on the subgraph. The strategy to sample subgraphs for node representation and model training is called *subgraph-wise sampling*. There exist various subgraph-wise sampling–based methods (Chiang et al., 2019; Zeng et al., 2019) with different focuses on the sampled graph $\mathcal{G}_s$.

In Chiang et al. (2019), graph clustering methods such as Metis (Karypis and Kumar, 1998) and Graclus (Dhillon et al., 2007) are adopted to partition the graph $\mathcal{G}$ into a set of subgraphs (clusters) $\{\mathcal{G}_s\}$ such that the number of links within each cluster is much more than that between clusters. To perform SGD, a subgraph is sampled from $\{\mathcal{G}_s\}$ each time and the gradient is estimated based on the following loss function:

$$\mathcal{L}_{\mathcal{G}_s} = \sum_{v_i \in \mathcal{V}_i \cup \mathcal{V}_s} l(f_{GNN}(\mathbf{A}_s, \mathbf{F}^{(in)}; \mathbf{\Theta})_i, y_i), \tag{7.29}$$

where $\mathbf{A}_s$ denotes the adjacency matrix for the sampled subgraph $\mathcal{G}_s$. The memory required to perform one step of SGD based on the sampled subgraph $\mathcal{G}_s$ is $O(|\mathcal{E}_s| + L \cdot |\mathcal{V}_s| \cdot d + L \cdot d^2)$.

In Zeng et al. (2019), various node samplers are designed to sample a set of nodes $\mathcal{V}_s$ that induces the subgraph $\mathcal{G}_s$. Specifically, an edge-based node sampler is designed to sample nodes pair-wise that have a large influence on each other and a random walk–based sampler is designed to improve the connectivity between the sampled nodes. We briefly describe these two samplers.

- **Edge-based Sampler:** Given a budget m, m edges are randomly sampled according to the following distribution:

$$p((u, v)) = \frac{\left(\frac{1}{deg(u)+deg(v)}\right)}{\sum\limits_{(u',v')\in\mathcal{E}}\left(\frac{1}{deg(u')+deg(v')}\right)}, \tag{7.30}$$

where $deg(v)$ denotes the degree of node v. The end nodes of the m sampled edges consist of the sampled nodes $\mathcal{V}_s$, which is used to induce the subgraph $\mathcal{G}_s$.

- **RW-based Sampler:** A set of r root nodes is uniformly sampled (with replacement) from the $\mathcal{V}$. Then starting from each sampled node, a random walk is generated. The nodes in the random walk consist of the final sampled node set $\mathcal{V}_s$, which is used to induce the subgraph $\mathcal{G}_s$.

Some normalization tricks are introduced in the aggregation process to make it less biased:

$$\mathbf{F}_i^{(l)} = \sum_{v_j\in\mathcal{V}_s} \frac{\hat{\mathbf{A}}_{i,j}}{\alpha_{i,j}} \mathbf{F}_j^{(l-1)} \mathbf{\Theta}^{(l-1)}, \tag{7.31}$$

where $\alpha_{i,j}$ can be estimated from the sampled subgraphs. In detail, a set of M subgraphs is sampled from the samplers and C_i and $C_{i,j}$ count the frequency with which node v_i and edge (v_i, v_j) appear in the sampled M graphs. Then, $\alpha_{i,j}$ is estimated by $C_{i,j}/C_i$. Furthermore, the loss function for a mini-batch based on the sampled subgraph $\mathcal{G}_s$ is normalized as

$$\mathcal{L}_{\mathcal{G}_s} = \sum_{v_i\in\mathcal{V}_l\cup\mathcal{V}_s} \frac{1}{\lambda_i} l(f_{GNN}(\mathbf{A}_s, \mathbf{F}^{(in)}; \mathbf{\Theta})_i, y_i), \tag{7.32}$$

where λ_i can be estimated as C_i/M. This normalization also makes the loss function less biased.

7.5 Conclusion

In this chapter, we discuss various sampling based methods to improve the scalability of GNN models. We first introduce the neighborhood explosion issue, which makes the SGD methods impractical in training GNN models. Then, we present three types of sampling methods, including node-wise, layer-wise, and subgraph-wise sampling. The aim is to reduce the number of involved nodes during the forward pass of mini-batch SGD and correspondingly improve the scalability. For each group, we discuss their advantages and disadvantages and introduce representative algorithms.

7.6 Further Reading

In this chapter, we mainly discuss sampling-based methods to improve the scalability of the GNNs. Some of the introduced sampling techniques have been successfully applied to real-world applications. For example, the node-wise sampling-based method GraphSage is adapted and applied to large scale graph-based recommendation (Ying et al., 2018a); and the layer-wise sampling-based method FastGCN (Chen et al., 2018b) is adopted to antimoney laundering in large scale bitcoin transaction network (Weber et al., 2019). Other efforts have been made to develop distributed frameworks for GNNs (Ma et al., 2018a; Wang et al., 2019e; Zhu et al., 2019c; Ma et al., 2019a). These distributed architectures for GNNs can handle large graphs with distributed data storage and parallel computation.

8
Graph Neural Networks for Complex Graphs

8.1 Introduction

In the earlier chapters, we have discussed graph neural network (GNN) models with the focus on simple graphs where the graphs are static and have only one type of node and one type of edge. However, graphs in many real-world applications are much more complex. They typically have multiple types of nodes and often are dynamic. As a consequence, these complex graphs present more complicated patterns that are beyond the capacity of the aforementioned GNN models for simple graphs. Thus, dedicated efforts are desired to design GNN models for complex graphs. These efforts can greatly affect the successful adoption and use of GNNs in a broader range of applications. In this chapter, using complex graphs introduced in Section 2.6 as examples, we discuss how to extend the GNN models to capture more sophisticated patterns. More specifically, we describe more advanced graph filters designed for complex graphs to capture their specific properties.

8.2 Heterogeneous Graph Neural Networks

Heterogeneous graphs, which consist of multiple types of nodes and edges as defined in Definition 2.35, are widely observed in real-world applications. For example, the multiple relations between papers, authors, and venues can be described by a heterogeneous graph as discussed in Subsection 2.6.1. GNN models have been adapted to heterogeneous graphs (Zhang et al., 2018b; Wang et al., 2019i; Chen et al., 2019b). Metapaths (see the definition of metapath schema and metapaths in Definition 4.5), which capture various relations between nodes with different semantics, are adopted to deal with the heterogeneity in heterogeneous graphs. In Zhang et al. (2018a) and Chen et al.

(2019b), metapaths are utilized to split a heterogeneous graph into several homogeneous graphs. Specifically, metapaths are treated as edges between nodes, and those metapaths with the same metapath schema are treated as the same type of edge. Each metapath schema defines a simple homogeneous graph with metapath instances following this schema as the edges. Graph filtering operations in Chapter 5 are applied to these homogeneous simple graphs to generate node representations capturing different local semantic information, which are then combined to generate the final node representations. Similarly, metapaths are used to define metapath-based neighbors, which are treated differently during the graph filtering process in Wang et al. (2019i). Specifically, given a metapath schema ψ, a node v_j is defined as a ψ-neighbor for another node v_i, if node v_j can be reached by node v_i through a metapath following the schema ψ. The information aggregated from different types of meta-path-based neighbors is combined through the attention mechanism to generate the updated node representations (Wang et al., 2019i). Next, we first formally define the meta-path-based neighbors and then describe the graph filters designed for heterogeneous graphs.

Definition 8.1 (Meta-path-based neighbors) *Given a node v_i and a metapath schema ψ in a heterogeneous graph, the ψ-neighbors of node v_i, which can be denoted as $N_\psi(v_i)$, consist of those nodes that connect with node v_i through a metapath following schema ψ.*

The graph filters for heterogeneous graphs are designed in two steps: (1) aggregating information from ψ-based neighbors for each $\psi \in \Psi$, where Ψ denotes the set of metapath schemes adopted in the task, and (2) combining the information aggregated from each type of neighbor to generate the node representations. Specifically, for a node v_i, the graph filtering operation (for the lth layer) updates its representation as

$$\mathbf{z}_{\psi,i}^{(l)} = \sum_{v_j \in N_\psi(v_i)} \alpha_{\psi,ij}^{(l-1)} \mathbf{F}_j^{(l-1)} \mathbf{\Theta}_\psi \qquad (8.1)$$

$$\mathbf{F}_i^{(l)} = \sum_{\psi \in \Psi} \beta_\psi^{(l)} \mathbf{z}_{\psi,i}^{(l)}, \qquad (8.2)$$

where $\mathbf{z}_{\psi,i}^{(l)}$ is the information aggregated from ψ-neighbors of node v_i, $\mathbf{\Theta}_\psi$ are parameters specific to metapath ψ-based neighbors, and $\alpha_{\psi,ij}^{(l-1)}$ and $\beta_\psi^{(l)}$ are attention scores, which can be learned similar to the GAT-Filter introduced in Subsection 5.3.2. Specifically, $\alpha_{\psi,ij}^{(l-1)}$ is used to update node representations of v_i that indicate the contribution from the metapath ψ-based neighbor v_j in the aggregation. It is formally defined as

$$\alpha_{\psi,ij}^{(l-1)} = \frac{\exp\left(\sigma\left(\mathbf{a}_{\psi}^{\mathrm{T}} \cdot \left[\mathbf{F}_i^{(l-1)}\mathbf{\Theta}_{\psi} \| \mathbf{F}_j^{(l-1)}\mathbf{\Theta}_{\psi}\right]\right)\right)}{\sum_{v_k \in \mathcal{N}_{\psi}(v_i)} \exp\left(\sigma\left(\mathbf{a}_{\psi}^{\mathrm{T}} \cdot \left[\mathbf{F}_i^{(l-1)}\mathbf{\Theta}_{\psi} \| \mathbf{F}_k^{(l-1)}\mathbf{\Theta}_{\psi}\right]\right)\right)}, \tag{8.3}$$

where $\mathbf{a}_{\psi}$ is a vector of parameters to be learned. The attention score $\beta_{\psi}^{(l)}$ to combine information from different meta-based neighbors is not specific for each node but is shared by all nodes. $\beta_{\psi}^{(l)}$ indicates the contribution from ψ-neighbors of node v_i. It is formally defined as

$$\beta_{\psi}^{(l)} = \frac{\exp\left(\frac{1}{|\mathcal{V}|} \sum_{i \in \mathcal{V}} \mathbf{q}^{\mathrm{T}} \cdot \tanh\left(\mathbf{z}_{\psi,i}^{(l)}\mathbf{\Theta}_{\beta} + \mathbf{b}\right)\right)}{\sum_{\psi \in \Psi} \exp\left(\frac{1}{|\mathcal{V}|} \sum_{i \in \mathcal{V}} \mathbf{q}^{\mathrm{T}} \cdot \tanh\left(\mathbf{z}_{\psi,i}^{(l)}\mathbf{\Theta}_{\beta} + \mathbf{b}\right)\right)}, \tag{8.4}$$

where $\mathbf{q}$, $\mathbf{\Theta}_{\beta}$, and $\mathbf{b}$ are the parameters.

8.3 Bipartite Graph Neural Networks

Bipartite graphs are widely observed in real-world applications such as recommendations where users and items are the two disjoint sets of nodes and their interactions are the edges. In this section, we briefly introduce some general graph filters designed for bipartite graphs because we will present the advanced filters in Subsection 12.2.2, when we discuss the applications of GNNs in recommendations.

As introduced in Definition 2.36, there are two disjoint sets of nodes $\mathcal{U}$ and $\mathcal{V}$, which can be of different types. There are only edges across the two sets, and no edges exist within each set. To design the spatial-based graph filters, the key idea is to aggregate information from neighboring nodes. In bipartite graphs, for any node $u_i \in \mathcal{U}$, its neighbors are a subset of $\mathcal{V}$; i.e., $\mathcal{N}(u_i) \subset \mathcal{V}$. Similarly, for a node $v_j \in \mathcal{V}$, its neighbors are from $\mathcal{U}$. Hence, two graph filtering operations are needed for these two sets of nodes, which can be described as

$$\mathbf{F}_{u_i}^{(l)} = \frac{1}{|\mathcal{N}(u_i)|} \sum_{v_j \in \mathcal{N}(u_i)} \mathbf{F}_{v_j}^{(l-1)}\mathbf{\Theta}_v \tag{8.5}$$

$$\mathbf{F}_{v_i}^{(l)} = \frac{1}{|\mathcal{N}(v_i)|} \sum_{u_j \in \mathcal{N}(v_i)} \mathbf{F}_{u_j}^{(l-1)}\mathbf{\Theta}_u, \tag{8.6}$$

where we use $\mathbf{F}_{u_i}^{(l)}$ to denote the node representation of node u_i after the lth layer, and $\mathbf{\Theta}_v$ and $\mathbf{\Theta}_u$ are parameters to transform embedding from the node space $\mathcal{V}$ to $\mathcal{U}$ and $\mathcal{U}$ to $\mathcal{V}$, respectively.

8.4 Multidimensional Graph Neural Networks

In many real-world graphs, multiple relations can simultaneously exist between a pair of nodes. These graphs with multiple types of relations can be modeled as multidimensional graphs as introduced in Subsection 2.6.3. In multidimensional graphs, the same set of nodes is shared by all dimensions and each dimension has its own structure. Hence, when designing graph filters for multidimensional graphs, it is necessary to consider interactions both within and across dimensions. Specifically, the within-dimension interactions are through the connections between the nodes in the same dimension and the across-dimension interactions are between the "copies" of the same node in different dimensions. In Ma et al. (2019c), a graph filter that captures information both within and across dimensions is proposed. In detail, during the graph filtering process, for each node v_i, a set of representations of node v_i in all dimensions is first learned and then combined to generate an overall representation for node v_i. To update the representation of node v_i in dimension d, we need to aggregate information from its neighbors from the same dimension and also information about v_i from the other dimensions. Hence, we define two types of neighbors in multidimensional graphs: the within-dimension neighbors and the across-dimension neighbors. For a given node v_i in dimension d, the within-dimension neighbors are those nodes that directly connect to node v_i in dimension d and the across-dimension neighbors consist of the copies of node v_i in other dimensions. The set of within-dimension neighbors of node v_i in dimension d is denoted as $\mathcal{N}_d(v_i)$. For example, in the multidimensional graph shown in Figure 8.1, for node 4, its within-dimension neighbors in the "red" dimension include nodes $1, 2$, and 5. Furthermore, the same node 4 is shared by all dimensions, which can be viewed as copies of the same node in different dimensions. These copies of node 4 implicitly connect to each other, and we call them the across-dimension neighbors for node 4. As shown in Figure 8.1, the across-dimension neighbors for node 4 in the red dimension are the copies of node 4 in the "blue" and "green" dimensions. With these two types of neighbors, we can now describe the graph filtering operation (for node v_i in the lth layer) designed for the multidimensional graph in Ma et al. (2019c) as

$$\mathbf{F}_{d,j}^{(l-1)} = \sigma\left(\mathbf{F}_j^{(l-1)}\mathbf{\Theta}_d^{(l-1)}\right) \quad \text{for } v_j \in \mathcal{N}_d(v_i) \qquad (8.7)$$

$$\mathbf{F}_{g,i}^{(l-1)} = \sigma\left(\mathbf{F}_i^{(l-1)}\mathbf{\Theta}_g^{(l-1)}\right) \quad \text{for } g = 1, \dots D \qquad (8.8)$$

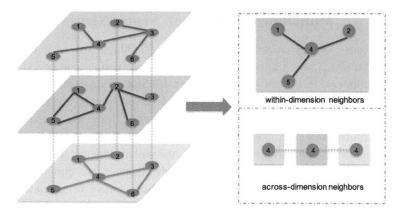

Figure 8.1 An illustrative example of two types of neighbors in the multi-dimensional graph.

$$\mathbf{F}^{(l)}_{w,d,i} = \sum_{v_j \in \mathcal{N}_d(v_i)} \mathbf{F}^{(l-1)}_{d,j} \qquad (8.9)$$

$$\mathbf{F}^{(l)}_{a,d,i} = \sum_{g=1}^{D} \beta^{(l-1)}_{g,d} \mathbf{F}^{(l-1)}_{g,i} \qquad (8.10)$$

$$\mathbf{F}^{(l)}_{i} = \alpha \mathbf{F}^{(l)}_{w,d,i} + (1 - \alpha)\mathbf{F}^{(l)}_{a,d,i}. \qquad (8.11)$$

We next explain the steps of graph filters as described from Eq. (8.7) to Eq. (8.11). In Eq. (8.7), the representations of within-dimension neighbors of node v_i from the previous layer (the $(l-1)$st layer) are mapped to dimension d by $\Theta^{(l-1)}_d$ and $\sigma()$ is a nonlinear activation function. Similarly, the representation of node v_i from the previous layer is projected to different dimensions where D is the total number of dimensions in the multidimension graph. The within-dimension aggregation is performed in Eq. (8.9), which generates the within-dimension representation for node v_i in the lth layer. The across-dimension information aggregation is performed in Eq. (8.10), where $\beta^{(l-1)}_{g,d}$ is the attention score modeling the impact of dimension g on dimension d, which is calculated as

$$\beta_{g,d} = \frac{tr(\Theta_g^T \mathbf{W}^{(l-1)}\Theta_d^{(l-1)})}{\sum_{g=1}^{D} tr(\Theta_g^T \mathbf{W}^{(l-1)}\Theta_d^{(l-1)})}, \qquad (8.12)$$

where $\mathbf{W}^{(l-1)}$ is a parameter matrix to be learned. Finally, the within-dimension representation and the across-dimension representation of node v_i are combined in Eq. (8.11) to generate the updated representation of node v_i $\mathbf{F}_i^{(l)}$ after the lth layer.

8.5 Signed Graph Neural Networks

In many real-world systems, relations can be both positive and negative. For instance, social media users not only have positive links such as friends (e.g., Facebook and Slashdot), followers (e.g., Twitter), and trust (e.g., Epinions) but also can establish negative links such as foes (e.g., Slashdot), distrust (e.g., Epinions), and blocked and unfriended users (e.g., Facebook and Twitter). These relations can be represented as graphs with both positive and negative edges. Signed graphs have become increasingly ubiquitous with the growing popularity of online social networks. A formal definition of signed graphs can be found in Subsection 2.6.4. The graph filters designed for simple graphs in Chapter 5 cannot be directly applied to signed graphs because of the existence of the negative edges. The negative edges carry very different or even opposite relations compared with the positive edges. Hence, to design graph filters for signed graphs, dedicated efforts are desired to handling the negative edges properly. A naive approach to handling the negative edges is to split a signed graph into two separate unsigned graphs, each of which consists of only positive or negative edges. Then the graph filters in Section 5.3 can be separately applied to these two graphs and the final node representations can be obtained by combining the representations from these two graphs. However, this approach totally ignores the complex interactions between the positive and negative links suggested by social balance theories (Heider, 1946; Cartwright and Harary, 1956; Leskovec et al., 2010b), which can provide fruitful results if extracted properly (Kunegis et al., 2009; Leskovec et al., 2010a; Tang et al., 2016b). In Derr et al. (2018), balance theory is facilitated to model the relations between the positive and negative edges, based on which a specific graph filter is designed for signed graphs. Specifically, balanced and unbalanced paths are proposed based on balance theory, which are then utilized to guide the aggregation process when designing the graph filters for signed graphs. Two representations for each node are maintained; i.e., one capturing the information aggregated from balanced paths and the other capturing information aggregated from unbalanced paths. Next, we introduce the balanced and unbalanced paths and the graph filters designed for signed

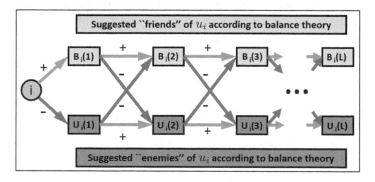

Figure 8.2 Balanced and unbalanced neighbors.

graphs. In general, balance theory (Heider, 1946; Cartwright and Harary, 1956) suggests that "the friend of my friend is my friend" and "the enemy of my friend is my enemy." Based on this, the cycles in the graphs are classified as *balanced* or *unbalanced*. Specifically, a cycle with an even number of negative edges is considered balanced. It is evident from numerous empirical studies that the majority of circles in real-world signed graphs are balanced (Tang et al., 2016b). Inspired by the definition of balanced cycles, we define a path consisting of an even number of negative edges as a *balanced path*, whereas an *unbalanced path* consists of an odd number of negative edges. Given the definition of the balanced path, we can see that a balanced path between node v_i and node v_j indicates a positive relation between them because a balanced cycle is expected according to balance theory and empirical studies. Similarly, an unbalanced path between nodes v_i and v_j indicates a negative relation between them. Given the definition of balanced and unbalanced paths, we then define the balanced and unbalanced multi-hop neighbors. Nodes that can be reached by a balanced path with length $l - 1$ from node v_i are defined as the $(l - 1)$-hop balanced neighbors of node v_i, denoted as $B^{(l-1)}(v_i)$. Similarly the set of unbalanced $(l - 1)$-hop neighbors can be defined and denoted as $U^{l-1}(v_i)$. Given the $(l - 1)$-hop balanced and unbalanced neighbors, we can conveniently introduce the l-hop balanced and unbalanced neighbors. As shown in Figure 8.2, adding a positive edge to a balanced path of length $l-1$ or adding a negative edge to an unbalanced path of length $l-1$ will lead to positive paths of length l. Unbalanced paths of length l can be similarly defined. Formally, we can define the balanced neighbors and unbalanced neighbors of different hops iteratively as follows:

$$B^{l-1}(v_i) = \{v_j | v_k \in B^{(l-1)}(v_i) \text{ and } v_j \in \mathcal{N}^+(v_k)\}$$
$$\cup \{v_j | v_k \in U^{(l-1)}(v_i) \text{ and } v_j \in \mathcal{N}^-(v_k)\}$$
$$U^{l-1}(v_i) = \{v_j | v_k \in U^{(l-1)}(v_i) \text{ and } v_j \in \mathcal{N}^+(v_k)\} \qquad (8.13)$$
$$\cup \{v_j | v_k \in B^{(l-1)}(v_i) \text{ and } v_j \in \mathcal{N}^-(v_k)\},$$

where $\mathcal{N}^+(v_i)$ and $\mathcal{N}^-(v_i)$ denote 1-hop positive and 1-hop negative neighbors of node v_i. Hence, we have $B^1(v_i) = \mathcal{N}^+(v_i)$ and $U^1(v_i) = \mathcal{N}^-(v_i)$.

When designing the graph filters for signed graphs, the information from balanced neighbors and unbalanced neighbors should be separately maintained, because they could carry very different information. In particular, the balanced neighbors can be regarded as potential "friends," whereas the unbalanced neighbors can be viewed as potential "foes." Hence, two types of representations are maintained to keep information aggregated from balanced and unbalanced neighbors. For a node v_i, $\mathbf{F}_i^{(B,l)}$ and $\mathbf{F}_i^{(U,l)}$ are used to denote the representations of node v_i containing information aggregated from balanced and unbalanced neighbors, respectively, after l graph filtering layers. Specifically, the process of the graph filters in the lth layer can be described as

$$\mathbf{F}_i^{(B,l)} = \sigma\left(\left[\sum_{v_j \in \mathcal{N}^+(v_i)} \frac{\mathbf{F}_j^{(B,l-1)}}{|\mathcal{N}^+(v_i)|}, \sum_{v_k \in \mathcal{N}^-(v_i)} \frac{\mathbf{F}_k^{(U,l-1)}}{|\mathcal{N}^-(v_i)|}, \mathbf{F}_i^{(B,l-1)}\right]\Theta^{(B,l)}\right)$$
$$\mathbf{F}_i^{(U,l)} = \sigma\left(\left[\sum_{v_j \in \mathcal{N}^+(v_i)} \frac{\mathbf{F}_j^{(U,l-1)}}{|\mathcal{N}^+(v_i)|}, \sum_{v_k \in \mathcal{N}^-(v_i)} \frac{\mathbf{F}_k^{(B,l-1)}}{|\mathcal{N}^-(v_i)|}, \mathbf{F}_i^{(U,l-1)}\right]\Theta^{(U,l)}\right). \qquad (8.14)$$

In Eq. (8.14), the balanced representations are aggregated from node v_i's positive neighbors and the unbalanced representations are aggregated from its negative neighbors. As shown in Figure 8.2 and the definitions of balanced and unbalanced neighbors, both sources of information are aggregated through balanced paths for node v_i. In particular, $\mathbf{F}_i^{(B,l)}$ is the concatenation of three types of information: (1) the aggregation of balanced representations from the friends of the $l-1$ balanced neighbors—i.e., $\sum_{v_j \in \mathcal{N}^+(v_i)} \frac{\mathbf{F}_j^{(B,l-1)}}{|\mathcal{N}^+(v_i)|}$; (2) the aggregation of unbalanced representations from the enemies of the $(l-1)$ unbalanced neighbors—i.e., $\sum_{v_k \in \mathcal{N}^-(v_i)} \frac{\mathbf{F}_k^{(U,l-1)}}{|\mathcal{N}^-(v_i)|}$; and (3) the balanced representation of v_i in the $(l-1)$st layer. Similarly, $\mathbf{F}_i^{(U,l)}$ is generated by aggregating information from unbalanced paths. After L graph filtering layers, the balanced and unbalanced representations for node v_i are combined to form the final representation for v_i, which can be utilized for downstream tasks, as

$$\mathbf{z}_i = [\mathbf{F}_i^{(B,L)}, \mathbf{F}_i^{(U,L)}], \qquad (8.15)$$

where $\mathbf{z}_i$ denotes the generated final representation for node v_i. In Li et al. (2020b), an attention mechanism is adopted to differentiate the importance of nodes when performing the aggregation in Eq. (8.14). In detail, GAT-Filter is used to perform aggregation from the balanced/unbalanced neighbors in Eq. (8.14).

8.6 Hypergraph Neural Networks

In many real-world problems, relations go beyond pairwise associations. For example, in a graph describing the relations between the papers, a specific author may connect with more than two papers that are authored by him or her. Here the "author" can be viewed as a "hyperedge" connecting with multiple "papers" (nodes). Compared with edges in simple graphs, hyperedges can encode higher-order relations. The graphs with the hyperedges are called hypergraphs. A formal definition of hypergraphs can be found in Subsection 2.6.5. The key to building graph filters for hypergraphs is to facilitate the high-order relations encoded by hyperedges. Specifically, pairwise relations are extracted from these hyperedges, which render the hypergraphs into a simple graph and graph filters designed for simple graphs as introduced in Section 5.3 can thus be applied (Feng et al., 2019b; Yadati et al., 2019). Next, we introduce some representative ways to extract the pairwise relations from the hyperedges. In Feng et al. (2019b), pairwise relations between node pairs are estimated through the hyperedges. Two nodes are considered to be related if they appear together in at least one hyperedge. If they appear in several hyperedges, the impact from these hyperedges is combined. An "adjacency matrix" describing the pairwise node relations can be formulated as

$$\tilde{\mathbf{A}}_{hy} = \mathbf{D}_v^{-1/2}\mathbf{H}\mathbf{W}\mathbf{D}_e^{-1}\mathbf{H}^\top\mathbf{D}_v^{-1/2}, \tag{8.16}$$

where the matrices $\mathbf{D}_v, \mathbf{H}, \mathbf{W}, \mathbf{D}_e$ are defined in Definition 2.39. In detail, $\mathbf{H}$ is the indication matrix describing relations between nodes and hyperedges, $\mathbf{W}$ is a diagonal matrix describing the weights on the hyperedges, and $\mathbf{D}_v$ and $\mathbf{D}_e$ are the node and hyperedge degree matrices, respectively. Graph filters can then be applied to the simple graph defined by the matrix $\tilde{\mathbf{A}}_{hy}$. In Feng et al. (2019b), the GCN-Filter is adopted, which can be described as:

$$\mathbf{F}^{(l)} = \sigma(\tilde{\mathbf{A}}_{hy}\mathbf{F}^{(l-1)}\mathbf{\Theta}^{(l-1)}), \tag{8.17}$$

where $\sigma()$ is a nonlinear activation function.

In Yadati et al. (2019), the method proposed in Chan et al. (2018) is adopted to convert the hyperedges to pairwise relations. For each hyperedge e, two nodes are chosen to be used to generate a simple edge as

$$(v_i, v_j) := \arg\max_{v_i, v_j \in e} \|\mathbf{h}(v_i) - \mathbf{h}(v_j)\|_2^2, \tag{8.18}$$

where $\mathbf{h}(v_i)$ can be regarded as some attributes (or some features) that are associated with node v_i. Specifically, in the setting of GNNs, for the lth layer, the hidden representations learned from the previous layer $\mathbf{F}^{(l-1)}$ are the features to measure the relations. A weighted graph can then be constructed by adding all of these extracted pairwise relations to the graph, and the weights for these edges are determined by their corresponding hyperedges. We then use $\mathbf{A}^{(l-1)}$ to denote the adjacency matrix describing these relations. The graph filter for the lth layer can then be expressed as

$$\mathbf{F}^{(l)} = \sigma(\tilde{\mathbf{A}}^{(l-1)} \mathbf{F}^{(l-1)} \Theta^{(l-1)}), \tag{8.19}$$

where $\tilde{\mathbf{A}}^{(l-1)}$ is a renormalized version of $\mathbf{A}^{l-1}$ with the trick introduced in the GCN-Filter in Subsection 5.3.2. Note that the adjacency matrix $\mathbf{A}^{(l-1)}$ for the graph filter is not fixed but is adapted according to the hidden representations from the previous layer.

One major shortcoming for this definition is that only two nodes of each hyperedge are connected, which is likely to result in information loss for other nodes in the hyperedge. Furthermore, this might lead to a very sparse graph. Hence, an improved way to generate the adjacency matrix was proposed in Chan and Liang (2019), where the two chosen nodes of each hyperedge are also connected to all of the remaining nodes in their corresponding hyperedges. Hence, each hyperedge results in $2|e| + 3$ edges where $|e|$ denotes the number of nodes in hyperedge e. The weight of each extracted edge is also assigned as $1/(2|e| + 3)$. The adjacency matrix $\mathbf{A}^{(l-1)}$ is then built upon these edges, which can be utilized in the graph filtering process in Eq. (8.19).

8.7 Dynamic Graph Neural Networks

Dynamic graphs are constantly evolving; thus, the existing GNN models are inapplicable because they are not able to capture the temporal information. In Pareja et al. (2019), a GNN model that has evolving weights across graph snapshots over time, named EolveGCN, was proposed to deal with discrete dynamic graphs (see the definition of discrete dynamic graphs in Subsection 2.6.6). For a discrete dynamic graph consisting of T snapshots, T GNN models with the same structure are learned. The model parameters for the first GNN

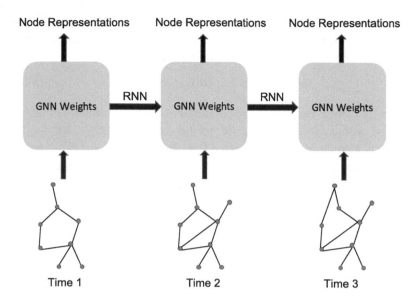

Figure 8.3 An illustration of EvolveGCN.

model are randomly initialized and learned during training, and the model parameters for the tth GNN model evolve from the model parameters for the $(t-1)$st model. As shown in Figure 8.3, the recurrent neural network (RNN) architecture is adopted to update the model parameters. Both the long short-term memory and gated recurrent unit (GRU) variants of RNN as introduced in Subsection 3.4.2 can be used to update the model parameters. We take GRU as an example to illustrate the lth graph filtering layer for the tth graph snapshot as

$$\Theta^{(l-1,t)} = \text{GRU}(\mathbf{F}^{(l-1,t)}, \Theta^{(l-1,t-1)}), \tag{8.20}$$

$$\mathbf{F}^{(l,t)} = \text{GNN-Filter}(\mathbf{A}^{(t)}, \mathbf{F}^{(l-1,t)}, \Theta^{(l-1,t)}), \tag{8.21}$$

where $\Theta^{(l-1,t)}$ and $\mathbf{F}^{(l,t)}$ denote the parameters and the output for the lth graph filtering layer of the tth GNN model, respectively. The matrix $\mathbf{A}^{(t)}$ is the adjacency matrix of the tth graph snapshot. Note that the parameters $\Theta^{(l-1,t)}$ of the l-th layer for the t-th GNN model in Eq. (8.21) are evolved from $\Theta^{(l-1,t-1)}$ with GRU as shown in Eq. (8.20). The detailed architecture of a GRU can be found in Subsection 3.4.3. General GNN-Filters can be adopted in Eq. (8.21), and the GCN-Filter is adopted in Pareja et al. (2019).

8.8 Conclusion

In this chapter, we describe how GNN models can be extended to complex graphs such as heterogeneous graphs, bipartite graphs, multidimensional graphs, signed graphs, hypergraphs, and dynamic graphs. For each type of complex graph we introduce representative graph filters that have been specifically designed to capture the properties in these complex graphs.

8.9 Further Reading

Though we have introduced some GNNs for these complicated graphs, more works continue to emerge. In Zhang et al. (2019a), a random walk is utilized to sample heterogeneous neighbors to GNNs for heterogeneous graphs. In Sankar et al. (2018), a self-attention mechanism is utilized for discrete dynamic graphs. Attention mechanisms are introduced for modelling hypergraph neural networks in Bai et al. (2019). Graph neural networks have been designed for dynamic hypergraphs in Jiang et al. (2019).

9
Beyond GNNs
More Deep Models on Graphs

9.1 Introduction

There are many traditional deep models, such as convolutional neural networks (CNNs), recurrent neural networks (RNNs), deep autoencoders, and generative adversarial networks (GANs). These models have been designed for different types of data. For example, CNNs can process regular grid-like data such as images, and RNNs can deal with sequential data such as text. They have also been designed in different settings. For instance, a large number of labeled data is needed to train good CNNs and RNNs (or the supervised setting), whereas autoencoders and GANs can extract complex patterns with only unlabeled data (or the unsupervised setting). These different architectures enable deep learning techniques to apply to many fields such as computer vision, natural language processing, data mining, and information retrieval. We have introduced various graph neural networks (GNNs) for simple and complex graphs in previous chapters. However, these models have been developed only to certain graph tasks such as node classification and graph classification, and they often require labeled data for training. Thus, efforts have been made to adopt more deep architectures to graph-structured data. Autoencoders have been extended to graph-structured data for node representation learning (Wang et al., 2016; Kipf and Welling, 2016b; Pan et al., 2018). Deep generative models, such as variational autoencoder and generative adversarial networks, have also been adapted to graph-structured data for node representation learning (Kipf and Welling, 2016b; Pan et al., 2018; Wang et al., 2018a) and graph generation (Simonovsky and Komodakis, 2018; De Cao and Kipf, 2018). These deep graph models have facilitated a broader range of graph tasks under different settings beyond the capacity of GNNs and have greatly advanced deep learning techniques on graphs. This chapter aims to cover more deep models on graphs, including deep autoencoders, variational autoencoders, recurrent neural networks, and generative adversarial networks.

9.2 Autoencoders on Graphs

Autoencoders, which were introduced in Section 3.5, can be regarded as unsupervised learning models to obtain compressed low-dimensional representations for input data samples. Autoencoders have been adopted to learn low-dimensional node representations (Wang et al., 2016; Kipf and Welling, 2016b; Pan et al., 2018). In Wang et al. (2016), the neighborhood information of each node is utilized as the input to be reconstructed; hence, the learned low-dimensional representation can preserve the structural information of the nodes. Both the encoder and decoder are modeled with feedforward neural networks as introduced in Section 3.5. In Kipf and Welling (2016b) and Pan et al. (2018), the GNN model, which utilizes both the input node features and graph structure, was adopted as the encoder to encode nodes into low-dimensional representations. These encoded node representations are then employed to reconstruct the graph structural information. Next, we briefly introduce these two types of graph autoencoders for learning low-dimensional node representations.

In Wang et al. (2016), for each node $v_i \in \mathcal{V}$, its corresponding row in the adjacency matrix of the graph $\mathbf{a}_i = \mathbf{A}_i$ is served as the input of the encoder to obtain its low-dimensional representation as

$$\mathbf{z}_i = f_{enc}(\mathbf{a}_i; \mathbf{\Theta}_{enc}),$$

where f_{enc} is the encoder, which is modeled with a feedworward neural network parameterized by $\mathbf{\Theta}_{enc}$. Then $\mathbf{z}_i$ is utilized as the input to the decoder, which aims to reconstruct $\mathbf{a}_i$ as

$$\tilde{\mathbf{a}}_i = f_{dec}(\mathbf{z}_i; \mathbf{\Theta}_{dec}),$$

where f_{dec} is the decoder and $\mathbf{\Theta}_{dec}$ denotes its parameters. The reconstruction loss can thus be built by constraining $\tilde{\mathbf{a}}_i$ to be similar to $\mathbf{a}_i$ for all nodes in $\mathcal{V}$ as

$$\mathcal{L}_{enc} = \sum_{v_i \in \mathcal{V}} \|\mathbf{a}_i - \tilde{\mathbf{a}}_i\|_2^2.$$

Minimizing the above reconstruction loss can "compress" the neighborhood information into the low-dimensional representation $\mathbf{z}_i$. The pairwise similarity between the neighborhood of nodes (i.e., the similarity between the input) is not explicitly captured. However, because the autoencoder (the parameters) is shared by all of the nodes, the encoder is expected to map those nodes that have similar inputs to similar node representations, which implicitly preserves the similarity. The above reconstruction loss might be problematic due to the inherent sparsity of the adjacency matrix $\mathbf{A}$. A large portion of the elements in $\mathbf{a}_i$ is 0, which might lead the optimization process to easily overfit to reconstructing the 0 elements. To solve this issue, a greater penalty is imposed to the reconstruction error of the nonzero elements by modifying the reconstruction loss as

$$\mathcal{L}_{enc} = \sum_{v_i \in \mathcal{V}} \| (\mathbf{a}_i - \tilde{\mathbf{a}}_i) \odot \mathbf{b}_i \|_2^2,$$

where $\odot$ denotes the Hadamard product, $\mathbf{b}_i = \{b_{i,j}\}_{j=1}^{|\mathcal{V}|}$, with $b_{i,j} = 1$ when $A_{i,j} = 0$ and $b_{i,j} = \beta > 1$ when $A_{i,j} \neq 0$. β is a hyperparameter to be tuned. Furthermore, to directly enforce connected nodes to have similar low-dimensional representations, a regularization loss is introduced as

$$\mathcal{L}_{con} = \sum_{v_i, v_j \in \mathcal{V}} \mathbf{A}_{i,j} \cdot \|\mathbf{z}_i - \mathbf{z}_j\|_2^2.$$

Finally, regularization loss on the parameters of encoder and decoder is also included in the objective, which leads to the following loss to be minimized:

$$\mathcal{L} = \mathcal{L}_{enc} + \lambda \cdot \mathcal{L}_{con} + \eta \cdot \mathcal{L}_{reg},$$

where $\mathcal{L}_{reg}$ denotes the regularization on the parameters, which can be expressed as

$$\mathcal{L}_{reg} = \|\mathbf{\Theta}_{enc}\|_2^2 + \|\mathbf{\Theta}_{dec}\|_2^2. \tag{9.1}$$

The graph autoencoder model introduced above can only utilize the graph structure but is not able to incorporate node features when they are available. In Kipf and Welling (2016b), the GNN model is adopted as the encoder, which utilizes both the graph structural information and node features. Specifically, the encoder is modeled as

$$\mathbf{Z} = f_{GNN}(\mathbf{A}, \mathbf{X}; \mathbf{\Theta}_{GNN}),$$

where f_{GNN} is the encoder. In Kipf and Welling (2016b), the GCN-Filter is adopted to build the encoder. The decoder is to reconstruct the graph, which includes the adjacency matrix $\mathbf{A}$ and the attribute matrix $\mathbf{X}$. In Kipf and Welling (2016b), only the adjacency matrix $\mathbf{A}$ is used as the target for reconstruction.

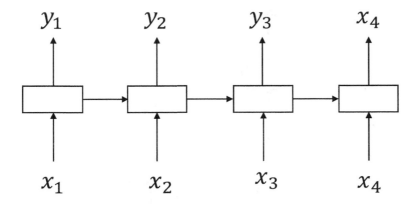

Figure 9.1 An illustrative sequence.

Specifically, the adjacency matrix can be reconstructed from the encoded representations $\mathbf{Z}$ as

$$\hat{\mathbf{A}} = \sigma(\mathbf{Z}\mathbf{Z}^T),$$

where $\sigma(\cdot)$ is the sigmoid function. The low-dimensional representations $\mathbf{Z}$ can be learned by minimizing the reconstruction error between $\hat{\mathbf{A}}$ and $\mathbf{A}$. The objective can be modeled as

$$-\sum_{v_i, v_j \in \mathcal{V}} \left(\mathbf{A}_{i,j} \log \hat{\mathbf{A}}_{i,j} + \left(1 - \mathbf{A}_{i,j}\right) \log \left(1 - \hat{\mathbf{A}}_{i,j}\right) \right),$$

which can be viewed as the cross-entropy loss between $\mathbf{A}$ and $\hat{\mathbf{A}}$.

9.3 Recurrent Neural Networks on Graphs

Recurrent neural networks (Section 3.4) were originally designed to deal with sequential data and have been generalized to learning representations for graph-structured data in recent years. In Tai et al. (2015), Tree-LSTM was introduced to generalize the LSTM model to tree-structured data. A tree can be regarded as a special graph that does not have any loops. In Liang et al. (2016), Graph-LSTM was proposed to further extend the Tree-LSTM to generic graphs. In this section, we first introduce the Tree-LSTM and then discuss Graph-LSTM.

As shown in Figure 9.1, a sequence can be regarded as a specific tree where each node (except for the first one) has only a single child; i.e., its previous

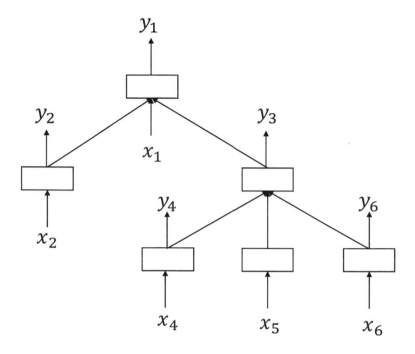

Figure 9.2 An illustrative tree.

node. The information flows from the first node to the last node in the sequence. Hence, as introduced in Subsection 3.4.2 and illustrated in Figure 3.13, the LSTM model composes the hidden state of a given node in a sequence by using the input at this node and also the hidden state from its previous node. However, in comparison, as shown in Figure 9.2, in a tree, a node can have an arbitrary number of child nodes. In a tree, the information is assumed to always flow from the child nodes to the parent node. Hence, when composing the hidden state for a node, we need to utilize its input and the hidden states of its child nodes. Based on this intuition, the Tree-LSTM model is proposed to deal with tree-structured data. To introduce the Tree-LSTM model, we follow the same notations as those in Subsection 3.4.2. Specifically, for node v_k in the tree, we use $\mathbf{x}^{(k)}$ as its input, $\mathbf{h}^{(k)}$ as its hidden state, $\mathbf{C}^{(k)}$ as its cell memory, and $\mathcal{N}_c(v_k)$ as the set of its child nodes. Given a tree, the Tree-LSTM model composes the hidden state of node v_k as

$$\tilde{\mathbf{h}}^{(k)} = \sum_{v_j \in \mathcal{N}_c(v_k)} \mathbf{h}^{(j)} \tag{9.2}$$

$$\mathbf{f}_{kj} = \sigma(\mathbf{W}_f \cdot \mathbf{x}^{(k)} + \mathbf{U}_f \cdot \mathbf{h}^{(j)} + \mathbf{b}_f) \quad \text{for } v_j \in \mathcal{N}_c(v_k) \tag{9.3}$$

$$\mathbf{i}_k = \sigma(\mathbf{W}_i \cdot \mathbf{x}^{(k)} + \mathbf{U}_i \cdot \tilde{\mathbf{h}}^{(k)} + \mathbf{b}_i) \tag{9.4}$$

$$\mathbf{o}_k = \sigma(\mathbf{W}_o \cdot \mathbf{x}^{(k)} + \mathbf{U}_o \cdot \tilde{\mathbf{h}}^{(k)} + \mathbf{b}_o) \tag{9.5}$$

$$\tilde{\mathbf{C}}^{(k)} = tanh(\mathbf{W}_c \cdot \mathbf{x}^{(k)} + \mathbf{U}_c \cdot \tilde{\mathbf{h}}^{(k)} + \mathbf{b}_c) \tag{9.6}$$

$$\mathbf{C}^{(k)} = \mathbf{i}_t \odot \tilde{\mathbf{C}}^{(k)} + \sum_{v_j \in \mathcal{N}_c(v_k)} \mathbf{f}_{kj} \odot \mathbf{C}^{(j)} \tag{9.7}$$

$$\mathbf{h}^{(k)} = \mathbf{o}_t \odot tanh(\mathbf{C}^{(k)}). \tag{9.8}$$

We next briefly describe the operation procedure of the Tree-LSTM model. The hidden states of the child nodes of v_k are aggregated to generate $\tilde{\mathbf{h}}^{(k)}$ as shown in Eq. (9.2). The aggregated hidden state $\tilde{\mathbf{h}}^{(k)}$ is utilized to generate the input gate, output gate, and candidate cell memory in Eq. (9.4), Eq. (9.5), and Eq. (9.6), respectively. In Eq. (9.3), for each child $v_j \in \mathcal{N}_c(v_k)$, a corresponding forget gate is generated to control the information flow from this child node to v_k when updating the memory cell for v_k in Eq. (9.7). Finally, in Eq. (9.8), the hidden state for node v_k is updated.

Unlike trees, there are often loops in generic graphs. Hence, there is no natural ordering for nodes in the generic graphs as that in trees. Breadth-first search and depth-first search are the possible ways to define an ordering for the nodes as proposed in Liang et al. (2016). Furthermore, the ordering of nodes can be defined according to the specific application at hand. After obtaining an ordering for the nodes, we can use similar operations, as shown from Eq. (9.2) to Eq. (9.8), to update the hidden state and cells for these nodes following the obtained ordering. The major difference is that in undirected graphs, Eq. (9.2) aggregates hidden states from all neighbors $\mathcal{N}(v_k)$ of node v_k, while Tree-LSTM in Eq. (9.2) only aggregates information from the child nodes of v_k. Furthermore, the hidden states of some nodes in neighbors $\mathcal{N}(v_k)$ may not have been updated. In this case, the pre-updated hidden states are utilized in the aggregation process.

9.4 Variational Autoencoders on Graphs

A variational autoencoder is a kind of generative model that aims to model the probability distribution of a given data set $\mathcal{X} = \{\mathbf{x}_1, \dots, \mathbf{x}_N\}$. It is also a latent variable model that generates samples from latent variables. Given a latent variable $\mathbf{z}$ sampled from a standard normal distribution $p(\mathbf{z})$, we want to learn a latent model that can generate similar samples as in the given data with the following probability:

$$p(\mathbf{x}|\mathbf{z}; \Theta) = \mathcal{N}(\mathbf{x}|f(\mathbf{z}; \Theta), \sigma^2 \cdot \mathbf{I}), \tag{9.9}$$

where $\mathcal{N}(|f(\mathbf{z}; \Theta), \sigma^2 \cdot \mathbf{I})$ denotes a Gaussian distribution with $f(\mathbf{z}; \Theta)$, $\sigma^2 \cdot \mathbf{I}$ as the mean and covariance matrix, respectively; Θ is the parameter to be learned; and $\mathbf{x}$ is a generated sample in the same domain as the given data. For example, if the input data samples are images, we want to generate images as well. $f(\mathbf{z}; \Theta)$ is a deterministic function that maps the latent variable $\mathbf{z}$ to the mean of the probability of the generative model in Eq. (9.9). Note that, in practice, the probability distribution of the generated samples is not necessarily Gaussian but can be other distributions according to specific applications. Here, for convenience, we use a Gaussian distribution as an example, which is adopted when generating images in computer vision tasks. To ensure that the generative model in Eq. (9.9) is representative of the given data $\mathcal{X}$, we need to maximize the following log-likelihood for each sample $\mathbf{x}_i$ in $\mathcal{X}$:

$$\log p(\mathbf{x}_i) = \log \int p(\mathbf{x}_i|\mathbf{z}; \Theta)p(\mathbf{z})d\mathbf{z} \text{ for } \mathbf{x}_i \in \mathcal{X}. \tag{9.10}$$

However, the integral in Eq. (9.10) is intractable. Furthermore, the true posterior $p(\mathbf{z}|\mathbf{x}; \Theta)$ is also intractable, which hinders the possibility of using the EM algorithm. To remedy this issue, an inference model $q(\mathbf{z}|\mathbf{x}; \Phi)$ parameterized with Φ, which is an approximation of the intractable true posterior $p(\mathbf{z}|\mathbf{x}; \Theta)$, is introduced (Kingma and Welling, 2013). Usually, $q(\mathbf{z}|\mathbf{x}; \Phi)$ is modeled as a Gaussian distribution $q(\mathbf{z}|\mathbf{x}; \Phi) = \mathcal{N}(\mu(\mathbf{x}; \Phi), \Sigma(\mathbf{x}; \Phi))$, where the mean and covariance matrix are learned through some deterministic function parameterized with Φ. Then, the log-likelihood in Eq. (9.10) can be rewritten as

$$\log p(\mathbf{x}_i) = D_{KL}(q(\mathbf{z}|\mathbf{x}; \Phi)\|p(\mathbf{z}|\mathbf{x}; \Theta)) + \mathcal{L}(\Theta, \Phi; \mathbf{x}_i),$$

where $\mathcal{L}(\Theta, \Phi; \mathbf{x}_i)$ is called the variational lower bound of the log-likelihood of $\mathbf{x}_i$ because the Kullback–Leibler divergence of the approximate and the true posterior (the first term on the righthand side) is nonnegative. Specifically, the variational lower bound can be written as

$$\mathcal{L}(\Theta, \Phi; \mathbf{x}_i) = \underbrace{\mathbb{E}_{q(\mathbf{z}|\mathbf{x}_i; \Phi)}\left[\log p(\mathbf{x}_i|\mathbf{z}; \Theta)\right]}_{reconstruction} - \underbrace{D_{KL}(q(\mathbf{z}|\mathbf{x}_i; \Phi)\|p(\mathbf{z}))}_{regularization}. \tag{9.11}$$

Instead of maximizing the log-likelihood in Eq. (9.10) for samples in $\mathcal{X}$, we aim to differentiate and maximize the variational lower bound in Eq. (9.11) with respect to both Θ and Φ. Note that minimizing the negation of the variational lower bound $-\mathcal{L}(\Theta, \Phi; x_i)$ resembles the process of the classic autoencoder as introduced in Section 3.5, which gives the name "variational autoencoder" to the model. Specifically, the first term on the right-hand side of Eq. (9.11) can be regarded as the reconstruction process, where $q(\mathbf{z}|\mathbf{x_i}; \Phi)$ is the encoder (the inference model) and $p(\mathbf{x}_i|\mathbf{z}; \Theta)$ is the decoder (the generative model). Different from the classical autoencoder, where the encoder maps a given input to a representation, this encoder $q(\mathbf{z}|\mathbf{x_i}; \Phi)$ maps an input $\mathbf{x}_i$ into a latent Gaussian distribution. Maximizing the first term on the right-hand side of Eq. (9.11) can be viewed as minimizing the distance between the input $\mathbf{x}_i$ and the decoded mean $f(\mathbf{z}; \Theta)$ of $p(\mathbf{x}_i|\mathbf{z}; \Theta)$. The second term on the right-hand side of Eq. (9.11) can be regarded as a regularization term, which enforces the approximated posterior $q(\mathbf{z}|\mathbf{x_i}; \Phi)$ to be close to the prior distribution $p(\mathbf{z})$. After training, the generative model $p(\mathbf{x}_i|\mathbf{z}; \Theta)$ can be utilized to generate samples that are similar to the ones in the given data and the latent variable can be sampled from the standard Gaussian distribution $p(\mathbf{z})$.

9.4.1 Variational Autoencoders for Node Representation Learning

In Kipf and Welling (2016b), the variational autoencoder was adopted to learn node representations on graphs. The inference model is to encode each node into a multivariate Gaussian distribution and the joint distribution of all nodes as shown below:

$$q(\mathbf{Z}|\mathbf{X}, \mathbf{A}; \Phi) = \prod_{v_i \in \mathcal{V}} q(\mathbf{z}_i|\mathbf{X}, \mathbf{A}; \Phi)$$

$$\text{with } q(\mathbf{z}_i|\mathbf{X}, \mathbf{A}; \Phi) = \mathcal{N}\left(\mathbf{z}_i|\mu_i, \text{diag}\left(\sigma_i^2\right)\right), \tag{9.12}$$

where μ_i and σ_i are the mean and variance learned through deterministic GNN models as follows:

$$\mu = \text{GNN}(\mathbf{X}, \mathbf{A}; \Phi_\mu),$$
$$\log \sigma = \text{GNN}(\mathbf{X}, \mathbf{A}; \Phi_\sigma),$$

where μ and σ are matrices with μ_i and σ_i respectively indicating their ith rows. The parameters Φ_μ and Φ_σ can be summarized as Φ in Eq. (9.12). Specifically, in Kipf and Welling (2016b), the GCN-Filter was adopted as the GNN model to build the inference model. The generative model, which is to generate (reconstruct) the adjacent matrix of the graph, is modeled by the inner product between the latent variables $\mathbf{Z}$ as follows:

$$p(\mathbf{A}|\mathbf{Z}) = \prod_{i=1}^{N} \prod_{j=1}^{N} p\left(\mathbf{A}_{i,j}|\mathbf{z}_i, \mathbf{z}_j\right),$$

$$\text{with } p\left(\mathbf{A}_{i,j} = 1|\mathbf{z}_i, \mathbf{z}_j\right) = \sigma\left(\mathbf{z}_i^\top \mathbf{z}_j\right),$$

where $\mathbf{A}_{i,j}$ is the i, jth element of the adjacency matrix $\mathbf{A}$ and $\sigma(\cdot)$ is the sigmoid function. Note that there are no parameters in the generative model. The variational parameters in the inference model are learned by optimizing the variational lower bound as shown below:

$$\mathcal{L} = \mathbb{E}_{q(\mathbf{Z}|\mathbf{X}, \mathbf{A}; \Phi)}[\log p(\mathbf{A}|\mathbf{Z})] - \text{KL}[q(\mathbf{Z}|\mathbf{X}, \mathbf{A}; \Phi)\|p(\mathbf{Z})],$$

where $p(\mathbf{Z}) = \prod_i p(\mathbf{z_i}) = \prod_i \mathcal{N}(\mathbf{z}_i|0, \mathbf{I})$ is a Gaussian prior enforced to the latent variables $\mathbf{Z}$.

9.4.2 Variational Autoencoders for Graph Generation

In the task of graph generation, we are given a set of graph $\{\mathcal{G}_i\}$ and try to generate graphs that are similar to them. A variational autoencoder has been adopted to generate small graphs such as molecular graphs (Simonovsky and Komodakis, 2018). Specifically, given a graph $\mathcal{G}$, the inference model $q(\mathbf{z}|\mathcal{G}; \Phi)$ aims to map it to a latent distribution. In addition, the decoder can be represented by a generative model $p(\mathcal{G}|\mathbf{z}; \Theta)$. Both Φ and Θ are parameters that can be learned by optimizing the following variational lower bound of the log-likelihood $\log p(\mathcal{G}; \Theta)$) of $\mathcal{G}$:

$$\mathcal{L}(\Phi, \Theta; \mathcal{G}) = \mathbb{E}_{q(\mathbf{z}|\mathcal{G}; \Phi)}\left[\log p(\mathcal{G}|\mathbf{z}; \Theta)\right] - D_{\text{KL}}\left[q(\mathbf{z}|\mathcal{G}; \Phi)\|p(\mathbf{z})\right], \qquad (9.13)$$

where $p(\mathbf{z}) = \mathcal{N}(\mathbf{0}, \mathbf{I})$ is a Gaussian prior on $\mathbf{z}$. Next, we describe the details about the encoder (inference model) $q(\mathbf{z}|\mathcal{G}; \Phi)$ and the decoder (generative model) $p(\mathcal{G}|\mathbf{z}; \Theta)$ and discuss how to evaluate $\mathbb{E}_{q(\mathbf{z}|\mathcal{G}; \Phi)}\left[\log p(\mathcal{G}|\mathbf{z}; \Theta)\right]$.

Encoder: The Inference Model

In Simonovsky and Komodakis (2018), the goal is to generate small graphs with few nodes. For example, molecular graphs are usually quite small. Furthermore, these graphs are assumed to be associated with node and edge attributes. In the case of molecular graphs, the node and edge attributes indicate the type of nodes and edges, which are encoded as 1-hot vectors. Specifically, a graph $\mathcal{G} = \{\mathbf{A}, \mathbf{F}, \mathbf{E}\}$ can be represented by its adjacency matrix $\mathbf{A} \in \{0, 1\}^{N \times N}$, node attributes $\mathbf{F} \in \{0, 1\}^{N \times t_n}$, and edge attributes $\mathbf{E} \in \{0, 1\}^{N \times N \times t_e}$. Usually, in molecular graphs, the number of nodes N is on the order of tens. $\mathbf{F}$ is the matrix indicting the attribute (type) of each node, where t_n is the number of node types. Specifically, the ith row of $\mathbf{F}$ is a 1-hot vector indicating the type of ith node. Similarly, $\mathbf{E}$ is a tensor indicating the types of edges where t_e is the number of edge types. Note that the graph is typically not complete and thus we do not have $N \times N$ edges. Hence, in $\mathbf{E}$, the 1-hot vectors corresponding to the nonexisting edges are $\mathbf{0}$ vectors. To fully utilize the given graph information, the GNN model with pooling layers is utilized to model the encoder as

$$q(\mathbf{z}|\mathcal{G}; \mathbf{\Phi}) = \mathcal{N}(\mu, \sigma^2),$$
$$\mu = pool(\text{GNN}_\mu(\mathcal{G})); \quad \log \sigma = pool(\text{GNN}_\sigma(\mathcal{G})),$$

where the mean and variance are learned by GNN models. In detail, the EC-Filter as introduced in Subsection 5.3.2 is utilized to build the GNN model to learn the node representations and the gated global pooling introduced in Subsection 5.4.1 is adopted to pool the node representations to generate the graph representation.

Decoder: The Generative Model

The generative model aims to generate a graph $\mathcal{G}$ given a latent representation $\mathbf{z}$. In other words, it is to generate the three matrices $\mathbf{A}$, $\mathbf{E}$, and $\mathbf{F}$. In Simonovsky and Komodakis (2018), the size of the graphs to be generated is limited to a small number k. In detail, the generative model is asked to output a probabilistic fully connected graph with k nodes $\widetilde{\mathcal{G}} = \{\widetilde{\mathbf{A}}, \widetilde{\mathbf{E}}, \widetilde{\mathbf{F}}\}$. In this probabilistic graph, the nodes and edges are modeled as Bernoulli variables and the types of nodes and edges are modeled as multinomial variables. Specifically, the predicted fully connected adjacency matrix $\widetilde{\mathbf{A}} \in [0, 1]^{k \times k}$ contains both the node existence probabilities at the diagonal elements $\widetilde{\mathbf{A}}_{i,i}$ and the edge existence probabilities at the off-diagonal elements $\widetilde{\mathbf{A}}_{i,j}$. The edge type probabilities are contained in the tensor $\widetilde{\mathbf{E}} \in \mathbb{R}^{k \times k \times t_e}$. The node type probabilities are expressed in the matrix $\widetilde{\mathbf{F}} \in \mathbb{R}^{k \times t_n}$. Different architectures can be used for modeling the generative model. In Simonovsky and Komodakis (2018), a simple feedforward network model that takes the latent variable $\mathbf{z}$ as input and outputs three matrices in its last layer was adopted. A sigmoid function is applied to obtain $\widetilde{\mathbf{A}}$, which demonstrates the probability of the existence of nodes and edges. Edge-wise and node-wise softmax functions are applied to obtain $\widetilde{\mathbf{E}}$ and $\widetilde{\mathbf{F}}$, respectively. Note that the obtained probabilistic graph $\widetilde{\mathcal{G}}$ can be regarded as a generative model, which can be expressed as

$$p(\mathcal{G}|\mathbf{z}; \mathbf{\Theta}) = p(\mathcal{G}|\widetilde{\mathcal{G}}),$$

where

$$\widetilde{G} = \text{MLP}(\mathbf{z}; \mathbf{\Theta}).$$

MLP() denotes the feedforward network model.

Reconstruction Loss

To optimize Eq. (9.13), it remains to evaluate $\mathbb{E}_{q(\mathbf{z}|G;\Phi)} [\log p(G|\mathbf{z}; \mathbf{\Theta})]$, which can be regarded as evaluating how close the input graph G and the reconstructed probabilistic graph $\widetilde{G}$ are. Because there is no particular node ordering in graphs, comparing two graphs is difficult. In Simonovsky and Komodakis (2018), the max pooling matching algorithm (Cho et al., 2014b) was adopted to find correspondences $\mathbf{P} \in \{0, 1\}^{k \times N}$ between the input graph G and the probabilistic graph $\widetilde{G}$. It is based on the similarity between the nodes from the two graphs, where N denotes the number of nodes in G and k is the number of nodes in $\widetilde{G}$. Specifically, $\mathbf{P}_{i,j} = 1$ only when the ith node in $\widetilde{G}$ is aligned with the jth node in the original graph G; otherwise, $\mathbf{P}_{i,j} = 0$. Given the alignment matrix $\mathbf{P}$, the information in the two graphs can be aligned to be comparable. In particular, the input adjacency matrix can be mapped to the predicted graph as $\mathbf{A}' = \mathbf{PAP}^T$, and the predicted node types and edge types can be mapped to the input graph as $\widetilde{\mathbf{F}}' = \mathbf{P}^T\widetilde{\mathbf{F}}$ and $\widetilde{\mathbf{E}}'_{:,:,l} = \mathbf{P}^T\widetilde{\mathbf{E}}_{:,:,l}\mathbf{P}$. Then, $\mathbb{E}_{q(\mathbf{z}|G;\Phi)} [\log p(G|\mathbf{z}; \mathbf{\Theta})]$ is estimated with a single latent variable $\mathbf{z}$ sampled from $q(\mathbf{z}|G)$ as follows:

$$\mathbb{E}_{q(\mathbf{z}|G;\Phi)} [\log p(G|\mathbf{z}; \mathbf{\Theta})] \approx \log p(G|\mathbf{z}; \mathbf{\Theta}) = \log p\left(\mathbf{A}', \mathbf{E}, \mathbf{F}|\widetilde{\mathbf{A}}, \widetilde{\mathbf{E}}'\widetilde{\mathbf{F}}'\right),$$

where $p\left(\mathbf{A}', \mathbf{E}, \mathbf{F}|\widetilde{\mathbf{A}}, \widetilde{\mathbf{E}}'\widetilde{\mathbf{F}}'\right)$ can be modeled as

$$p\left(\mathbf{A}', \mathbf{E}, \mathbf{F}|\widetilde{\mathbf{A}}, \widetilde{\mathbf{E}}'\widetilde{\mathbf{F}}'\right)$$
$$= \lambda_A \log p(\mathbf{A}'|\widetilde{\mathbf{A}}) + \lambda_E \log p(\mathbf{E}|\widetilde{\mathbf{E}}') + \lambda_F \log p(\mathbf{F}|\widetilde{\mathbf{F}}'), \qquad (9.14)$$

where $\lambda_{\mathbf{A}}, \lambda_E$, and λ_F are hyperparameters. Specifically, the three terms in Eq. (9.14) are the log-likelihood of $\mathbf{A}'$, $\mathbf{E}$, and $\mathbf{F}$, respectively, which can be modeled as the negation of the cross-entropy between $\mathbf{A}'$ and $\widetilde{\mathbf{A}}$, $\mathbf{E}$ and $\widetilde{\mathbf{E}}'$, $\mathbf{E}$ and $\widetilde{\mathbf{E}}'$, respectively. In detail, they can be formally stated as

$$\log p(\mathbf{A}'|\widetilde{\mathbf{A}}) = \frac{1}{k} \sum_{i=1}^{k} \left[\mathbf{A}'_{i,i} \log \widetilde{\mathbf{A}}_{i,i} + (1 - \mathbf{A}'_{i,i}) \log(1 - \widetilde{\mathbf{A}}_{i,i}) \right]$$

$$+ \frac{1}{k(k-1)} \sum_{i \neq j}^{k} \left[\mathbf{A}'_{i,j} \log \widetilde{\mathbf{A}}_{i,j} + (1 - \mathbf{A}'_{i,j}) \log(1 - \widetilde{\mathbf{A}}_{i,j}) \right],$$

$$\log p(\mathbf{E}|\widetilde{\mathbf{E}}') = \frac{1}{\|\mathbf{A}\|_1 - N} \sum_{i \neq j}^{N} \log \left(\mathbf{E}_{i,j,:}^{\top} \widetilde{\mathbf{E}}_{i,j,:} \right),$$

$$\log p(\mathbf{F}|\widetilde{\mathbf{F}}') = \frac{1}{N} \sum_{i=1}^{N} \log \left(\mathbf{F}_{i,:}^{\top} \widetilde{\mathbf{F}}'_{i,:} \right).$$

9.5 Generative Adversarial Networks on Graphs

GANs are a framework to estimate the complex data distribution via an adversarial process where the generative model is pitted against an adversary: a discriminative model that learns to tell whether a sample is from the original data or generated by the generative model (Goodfellow et al., 2014a). In detail, the generative model $G(\mathbf{z}; \mathbf{\Theta})$ maps a noise variable $\mathbf{z}$ sampled from a prior noise distribution $p(\mathbf{z})$ to the data space with $\mathbf{\Theta}$ as its parameters. In contrast, the discriminative model $D(\mathbf{x}; \mathbf{\Phi})$ is modeled as a binary classifier with the parameters $\mathbf{\Phi}$, which tells whether a given data sample $\mathbf{x}$ is sampled from the data distribution $p_{data}(\mathbf{x})$ or generated by the generative model G. Specifically, $D(\mathbf{x}; \mathbf{\Phi})$ maps $\mathbf{x}$ to a scalar indicating the probability that $\mathbf{x}$ comes from the given data rather than being generated by the generative model. During the training procedure, the two models are competing against each other. The generative model tries to learn to generate fake samples that are good enough to fool the discriminator, and the discriminator tries to improve itself to identify the samples generated by the generative model as fake samples. The competition drives both models to improve themselves until the generated samples are indistinguishable from the real ones. This competition can be modeled as a two-player minimax game as

$$\min_{\mathbf{\Theta}} \max_{\mathbf{\Phi}} \mathbb{E}_{\mathbf{x} \sim p_{data}(\mathbf{x})} \left[\log D(\mathbf{x}; \mathbf{\Phi}) \right] + \mathbb{E}_{\mathbf{z} \sim p(\mathbf{z})} \left[\log(1 - D(G(\mathbf{z}; \mathbf{\Theta}))) \right].$$

The parameters of the generative model and the discriminative model are optimized alternatively. In this section, we will use node representation learning and graph generation tasks as examples to describe how the GAN frameworks can be applied to graph-structured data.

9.5.1 Generative Adversarial Networks for Node Representation Learning

In Wang et al. (2018a), the GAN framework was adapted for node representation learning. Given a node v_i, the generative model aims to approximate the distribution of its neighbors. It can be denoted as $p(v_j|v_i)$ that is defined over the entire set of nodes $\mathcal{V}$. The set of its real neighbors $\mathcal{N}(v_i)$ can be regarded as the observed samples drawn from $p(v_j|v_i)$. The generator, which is denoted as $G(v_j|v_i;\Theta)$, tries to generate (more precisely, select) the node that is most likely connected with node v_i from $\mathcal{V}$. $G(v_j|v_i;\Theta)$ can be regarded as the probability of sampling v_j as a fake neighbor of node v_i. The discriminator, which we denote as $D(v_j, v_i;\Phi)$, tries to tell whether a given pair of nodes (v_j, v_i) are connected or not in the graph. The output of the discriminator can be regarded as the probability of an edge existing between the two nodes v_j and v_i. The generator G and discriminator D compete against each other: The generator G tries to fit the underlying probability distribution $p_{true}(v_j|v_i)$ perfectly such that the generated (selected) node v_j is relevant enough to node v_i to fool the discriminator and the discriminator tries to differentiate the nodes generated by the generator from the real neighbors of node v_i. Formally, the two models are playing the following minimax game:

$$\min_{\Theta} \max_{\Phi} V(G, D) = \sum_{v_i \in \mathcal{V}} \left(\mathbb{E}_{v_j \sim p_{true}(v_j|v_i)} \left[\log D\left(v_j, v_i; \Phi\right) \right] \right. $$
$$\left. + \mathbb{E}_{v_j \sim G(v_j|v_i;\Theta)} \left[\log\left(1 - D\left(v_j, v_i; \Phi\right)\right) \right] \right)$$

The parameters of the generator G and the discriminator D can be optimized by alternatively maximizing and minimizing the objective function $V(G, D)$. Next, we describe the details of the design of the generator and the discriminator.

The Generator

A straightforward way to model the generator is to use a softmax function over all nodes $\mathcal{V}$ as

$$G(v_j|v_i;\Theta) = \frac{\exp\left(\theta_j^\top \theta_i\right)}{\sum\limits_{v_k \in \mathcal{V}} \exp\left(\theta_k^\top \theta_i\right)}, \tag{9.15}$$

where $\theta_i \in \mathbb{R}^d$ denotes the d-dimensional representation for the node v_i specific to the generator and Θ includes the representations for all nodes. (They are also the parameters of the generator.) Note that, in this formulation, the relevance between nodes is measured by the inner product of the representations of the two nodes. This idea is reasonable because we expect the low-dimensional representations to be closer if the two nodes are more relevant to each other.

Once the parameters Θ are learned, given a node v_i, the generator G can be used to sample nodes according to the distribution $G(v_j|v_i; \Theta)$. As we mentioned before, instead of generating fake nodes, the procedure of the generator should be more precisely described as selecting a node from the entire set $\mathcal{V}$.

Though the softmax function in Eq. (9.15) provides an intuitive way to model the probability distribution, it suffers from severe computational issues. Specifically, the computational cost of the denominator of Eq. (9.15) is prohibitively expensive due to the summation over all nodes in $\mathcal{V}$. To solve this issue, hierarchical softmax (Morin and Bengio, 2005; Mikolov et al., 2013), introduced in Subsection 4.2.1, can be adopted.

The Discriminator

The discriminator is modeled as a binary classifier that aims to tell whether a given pair of nodes (v_j, v_i) is connected with an edge in the graph or not. In detail, $D\left(v_j, v_i; \Phi\right)$ models the probability of the existence of an edge between nodes v_j and v_i as

$$D\left(v_j, v_i; \Phi\right) = \sigma\left(\phi_j^\top \phi_i\right) = \frac{1}{1 + \exp\left(-\phi_j^\top \phi_i\right)}, \tag{9.16}$$

where $\phi_i \in \mathbb{R}^d$ is the low-dimensional representation of node v_i specific to the discriminator. We use the notation Φ to denote the union of representations of all nodes, which are the parameters of the discriminator to be learned. After training, the node representations from both the generator and discriminator or their combination can be utilized for the downstream tasks.

9.5.2 Generative Adversarial Networks for Graph Generation

The framework of generative adversarial networks was adapted for graph generation in De Cao and Kipf (2018). Specifically, the GAN framework is adopted to generate molecular graphs. Similar to Subsection 9.4.2, a molecular graph $\mathcal{G}$ with N nodes is represented by two objects: (1) A matrix $\mathbf{F} \in \{0, 1\}^{N \times t_e}$, which indicates the type of all nodes. The ith row of the matrix $\mathbf{F}$ corresponds to the ith node and t_n is the number of node types (or different atoms). (2) A tensor $\mathbf{E} \in \{0, 1\}^{N \times N \times t_e}$ indicating the type of all edges where t_e is the number of edge types (or different bonds). The generator's goal is not only to generate molecular graphs similar to a given set of molecules but also to optimize some specific properties such as the solubility of these generated molecules. Hence, in addition to the generator and the discriminator in the GAN framework, there is also a judge. It measures how good a generated graph is in terms of the specific property (to assign a reward). The judge is a network pretrained on some external molecules with ground truth. It is only used to provide guidance for generating desirable graphs. During the training procedure, the generator and discriminator are trained by competing against each other. However, the judge network is fixed and serves as a black box. Specifically, the generator and the discriminator are playing the following two-player minimax game:

$$\min_{\Theta} \max_{\Phi} \mathbb{E}_{\mathcal{G} \sim p_{data}(\mathcal{G})} \left[\log D(\mathcal{G}; \Phi) \right] + \mathbb{E}_{\mathbf{z} \sim p(\mathbf{z})} \left[\log(1 - D(G(\mathbf{z}; \Theta))) - \lambda J(G(\mathbf{z}; \Theta)) \right],$$

where $p_{data}(\mathcal{G})$ denotes the true distribution of the given molecular graphs and $J()$ is the judge network. The judge network produces a scalar indicating some specific property of the input required to be maximized. Next, we describe the generator, the discriminator, and the judge network in the framework.

The Generator

The generator $G(\mathbf{z}; \Theta)$ is similar to the one we introduced in Subsection 9.4.2, where a fully connected probabilistic graph is generated given a latent representation $\mathbf{z}$ sampled from a noise distribution $p(\mathbf{z}) = \mathcal{N}(0, \mathbf{I})$. Specifically, the generator $G(\mathbf{z}; \Theta)$ maps a latent representation $\mathbf{z}$ to two continuous dense objects. They are used to describe the generated graph with k nodes–$\tilde{\mathbf{E}} \in \mathbb{R}^{k \times k \times t_e}$, which indicates the probability distributions of the type of edges, and $\tilde{\mathbf{F}} \in \mathbb{R}^{k \times t_n}$, which denotes the probability distribution of the types of nodes. To generate molecular graphs, discrete matrices of $\mathbf{E}$ and $\mathbf{F}$ are sampled from $\tilde{\mathbf{E}}$ and $\tilde{\mathbf{F}}$, respectively. During the training procedure, the continuous probabilistic graphs $\tilde{\mathbf{E}}$ and $\tilde{\mathbf{F}}$ can be utilized such that the gradient can be successfully obtained through backpropagation.

The Discriminator and the Judge Network

Both the discriminator and the judge network receive a graph $\mathcal{G} = \{\mathbf{E}, \mathbf{F}\}$ as input and output a scalar value. In De Cao and Kipf (2018), a GNN model is adopted to model these two components. In detail, the graph representation of the input graph $\mathcal{G}$ is obtained as

$$\mathbf{h}_{\mathcal{G}} = pool(\text{GNN}(\mathbf{E}, \mathbf{F})),$$

where GNN() denotes several stacked graph filtering layers and pool() indicates the graph pooling operation. Specifically, in De Cao and Kipf (2018), the gated global pooling operation introduced in Subsection 5.4.1 was adopted as the pooling operation to generate the graph representation $\mathbf{h}_{\mathcal{G}}$. The graph representation is then fed into a few fully connected layers to produce a scalar value. In particular, in the discriminator, the produced scalar value between 0 and 1 measures the probability that the generated graph is a "real" molecular graph from the given set of graphs. The judge network outputs a scalar value that indicates the specific property of the graph. The discriminator needs to be trained alternatively with the generator. However, the judge network is pretrained with the additional source of molecular graphs and then it is treated as a fixed black box during the training of the GAN framework.

9.6 Conclusion

This chapter introduces more deep learning techniques on graphs. They include deep autoencoders, variational autoencoders, RNNs, and GANs. Specifically, we introduce graph autoencoders and RNNs, which are utilized to learn node representations. We then introduce two deep generative models: variational autoencoder and generative adversarial networks. We use the tasks of node representation learning and graph generation to illustrate how to adapt them to graphs.

9.7 Further Reading

Deep graph models beyond GNNs have greatly enriched deep learning methods on graphs and tremendously extended its application areas. In this chapter, we only introduce representative algorithms in one or two application areas. There are more algorithms and applications. In Jin et al. (2018), a variational autoencoder is utilized with graph neural networks for molecular graph generation. In Ma et al. (2018b), additional constraints are introduced to variational graph autoencoders to generate semantically valid molecule graphs. In You et al. (2018a), the GAN framework is combined with reinforcement learning techniques for molecule generation, where GNNs are adopted to model the policy network. Furthermore, RNNs are utilized for graph generation (You et al., 2018b; Liao et al., 2019), where a sequence of nodes and the connections between these nodes is generated.

Part III

Applications

10

Graph Neural Networks in Natural Language Processing

10.1 Introduction

Graphs have been extensively utilized in natural language process (NLP) to represent linguistic structures. The constituency-based parse trees represent phrase structures for a given sentence. The syntactic dependency trees encode syntactic relations in terms of tree structures (Jurafsky and Martin, n.d.). Abstract meaning representation (AMR) denotes semantic meanings of sentences as rooted and labeled graphs that are easy for the program to traverse (Banarescu et al., 2013). These graph representations of natural languages carry rich semantic and/or syntactic information in an explicit structural way. Graph neural networks (GNNs) have been adopted by various NLP tasks where graphs are involved. These graphs include those mentioned above and also other graphs designed specifically for particular tasks. Specifically, GNNs have been utilized to enhance many NLP tasks, such as semantic role labeling (Marcheggiani and Titov, 2017), (multihop) question answering (QA; De Cao et al., 2019; Cao et al., 2019; Song et al., 2018a; Tu et al., 2019), relation extraction (Zhang et al., 2018c; Fu et al., 2019; Guo et al., 2019; Zhu et al., 2019b; Sahu et al., 2019; Sun et al., 2019a; Zhang et al., 2019d), neural machine translation (Marcheggiani et al., 2018; Beck et al., 2018), and graph to sequence learning (Cohen, 2019; Song et al., 2018b; Xu et al., 2018b). Furthermore, knowledge graphs, which encode multirelational information in terms of graphs, are widely adopted by NLP tasks. There are also many works (Hamaguchi et al., 2017; Schlichtkrull et al., 2018; Nathani et al., 2019; Shang et al., 2019a; Wang et al., 2019c; Xu et al., 2019a) generalizing GNN models to knowledge graphs. In this chapter, we take semantic role labeling, neural machine translation, relation extraction, question answering, and graph to sequence learning as examples to demonstrate how GNNs

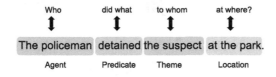

Figure 10.1 An illustrative sentence with semantic labels.

can be applied to NLP tasks. We also introduce the GNN models designed for knowledge graphs.

10.2 Semantic Role Labeling

In Marcheggiani and Titov (2017), GNNs were utilized on syntactic dependency trees to incorporate syntactic information to improve the performance of semantic role labeling (SRL). It is among the first to show that GNN models are effective on NLP tasks. In this section, we first describe the task of SRL and then introduce how GNNs can be leveraged for this task.

Semantic role labeling aims to discover the latent predicate-argument structure of a sentence, which can be informally regarded as the task of discovering "who did what to whom at where?" For example, a sentence with semantic labels is shown in Figure 10.1 where the word "detained" is the predicate and "the policeman" and "the suspect" are its two arguments with different labels. More formally, the task of SRL involves the following steps: (1) detecting the predicates such as "detained" in Figure 10.1 and (2) identifying the arguments and labeling them with semantic roles; i.e., "the policeman" is the agent and "the suspect" is the theme. In Marcheggiani and Titov (2017), the studied SRL problem (on CoNLL-2009 benchmark) is simplified slightly, where the predicate is given in the test time (e.g., we know that "detained" is the predicate in the example shown in Figure 10.1); hence, no predicate detection is needed. The remaining task is to identify the arguments of the given predicate and label them with semantic roles. It can be treated as a sequence labeling task. In detail, the SRL model is asked to label all of the arguments of the given predicate with their corresponding labels and label all non-argument elements "NULL."

To tackle this problem, a bidirectional long short-term memory (Bi-LSTM) encoder was adopted by Marcheggiani and Titov (2017) to learn context-aware word representations. These learned word representations are later utilized to label each of the elements in the sequence. We denote a sentence as $[w_0, \ldots, w_n]$, where each word w_i in the sequence is associated with an input representation $\mathbf{x}_i$. The input representation consists of four components: (1) a randomly initialized embedding; (2) a pretrained word embedding; (3) a randomly initialized embedding for its corresponding part-of-speech tag; and (4) a randomly initialized lemma embedding, which is active only when the word is a predicate. These four embeddings are concatenated to form the input representation $\mathbf{x}_i$ for each word w_i. Three of the embeddings except the pretrained embedding are updated during training. The sequence $[\mathbf{x}_0, \ldots, \mathbf{x}_n]$ is then utilized as the input for the Bi-LSTM (Goldberg, 2016). Specifically, the Bi-LSTM model consists of two LSTMs, with one dealing with the input sequence for the forward pass and the other handling the sequence for the backward pass. The operations of a single LSTM unit were introduced in Subsection 3.4.2. In the following, we abuse the notation to use LSTM() to denote the process of dealing with a sequence with LSTM. The process of the forward and backward LSTM can be denoted as

$$[\mathbf{x}_0^f, \ldots, \mathbf{x}_n^f] = \text{LSTM}^f([\mathbf{x}_0, \ldots, \mathbf{x}_n]),$$
$$[\mathbf{x}_0^b, \ldots, \mathbf{x}_n^b] = \text{LSTM}^b([\mathbf{x}_n, \ldots, \mathbf{x}_0]),$$

where LSTM^f denotes the forward LSTM, which captures the left context for each word, and LSTM^b denotes the backward LSTM, which captures the right context for each word. Note that $\mathbf{x}_i^b$ is the output representation from LSTM^b for the word w_{n-i}. The outputs of the two LSTMs are concatenated as the output of the Bi-LSTM, which captures the context information from both directions as

$$[\mathbf{x}_0^{\text{bi}}, \ldots, \mathbf{x}_n^{\text{bi}}] = \text{Bi-LSTM}([\mathbf{x}_0, \ldots, \mathbf{x}_n]),$$

where $\mathbf{x}_i^{\text{bi}}$ is the concatenation of $\mathbf{x}_i^f$ and $\mathbf{x}_{n-i}^b$. With the output of the Bi-LSTM, the labeling task is treated as a classification problem for each candidate word with the semantic labels and "NULL" as labels. Specifically, the input of the classifier is the concatenation of the output representations from the Bi-LSTM for the candidate word $\mathbf{x}_c^{\text{bi}}$ and for the predicate $\mathbf{x}_p^{\text{bi}}$.

To enhance the algorithm described above, syntactic structure information is incorporated by utilizing GNN models on syntactic dependency trees (Marcheggiani and Titov, 2017). In detail, the aggregation process in the GNN model is generalized to incorporate directed labeled edges such that it can be applied to syntactic dependency trees. To incorporate the sentence's syntactic information, the output of the Bi-LSTM layer is employed as the input of the GNN model. Then, the output of the GNN model is used as the input

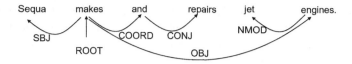

Figure 10.2 The dependency tree of the sentence "Sequa makes and repairs jet engines."

for the linear classifier described above. Next, we briefly introduce syntactic dependency trees and then describe how the GNN model is modified for syntactic dependency trees.

A syntactic dependency tree is a directed labeled tree encoding the syntactic dependencies in a given sentence. Specifically, the words in the sentence are treated as the nodes for the dependency tree and the directed edges describe the syntactic dependency between them. The edges are labeled with various dependency relations such as "Subject" (SBJ) and "Direct Object" (DOBJ). As an illustrative example, the dependency tree of the sentence "Sequa makes and repairs jet engines" is shown in Figure 10.2, where "Sequa" is the subject of the verb "makes" and "engines" is the objective of "makes." As the edges are directed and labeled in the dependency tree, to adopt a GNN model to incorporate the direction and label information in the edge, the following generalized graph filtering operator (for the lth layer) is proposed (Marcheggiani and Titov, 2017):

$$\mathbf{F}_i^{(l)} = \sigma\left(\sum_{v_j \in \mathcal{N}(v_i)} \mathbf{F}_j^{(l-1)} \Theta_{dir(i,j)}^{(l-1)} + \mathbf{b}_{lab(i,j)}\right), \qquad (10.1)$$

where $\mathcal{N}(v_i)$ consists of both in-going and out-going neighbors of node v_i, $dir(i, j) \in \{\text{in-going, out-going}\}$ denotes the direction of the edge (v_i, v_j) in terms of the center node v_i, $\Theta_{dir(i,j)}^{(l-1)}$ are the parameters shared by the edges that have the same direction as (v_i, v_j), and $\mathbf{b}_{lab(i,j)}$ is a bias term to incorporate the label information on the edge, with $lab(i, j)$ denoting the dependency relation of (v_i, v_j). The filter described in Eq. (10.1) is utilized to build a GNN model with L layers for the SRL task.

10.3 Neural Machine Translation

Machine translation is an essential task in NLP. With the development of deep learning, neural networks have been widely adopted for machine translation. These neural network–based models are called neural machine translation models, which usually take the form of encoder–decoder. The encoder takes a sequence of words in the source language as input and outputs a representation for each word in the sequence. Then the decoder, relying on the representations from the encoder, outputs a translation (or a sequence of words in the target language). Both the encoder and decoder are usually modeled with recurrent neural networks (RNNs) or their variants. For example, the Bi-LSTM introduced in Section 10.2 is a popular choice for the encoder and an RNN model equipped with the attention mechanism (Bahdanau et al., 2014) is a popular choice for the decoder. To incorporate the syntactic structure information in the sentence to enhance the performance of machine translation, the same strategy that is introduced in Section 10.2 was adopted in Marcheggiani et al. (2018) to design the encoder. The decoder is the same as in the traditional model; i.e., the attention-based RNN model. Next, we briefly describe the encoder, which was introduced in Section 10.2. Specifically, a Bi-LSTM model is first utilized for encoding the sequence. These representations from Bi-LSTM then serve as the input for a GNN model on the syntactic dependency tree. The formulation of a single graph filtering operation of the GNN model is shown in Eq. (10.1). The output of the GNN model is then leveraged as the input for the decoder (Bastings et al., 2017).

10.4 Relation Extraction

Graph neural networks have also been applied to the relation extraction (RE) task (Zhang et al., 2018c; Fu et al., 2019; Guo et al., 2019; Zhu et al., 2019b; Sahu et al., 2019; Sun et al., 2019a; Zhang et al., 2019d). Specifically, Zhang et al. (2018c), Fu et al. (2019), and Guo et al. (2019) adopt and/or modify the GNN model (i.e., Eq. (10.1)) in Marcheggiani and Titov (2017) to incorporate the syntactic information for the task of relation extraction. The first work applying GNNs to RE was introduced in Zhang et al. (2018c). In this section, we briefly describe the task of RE and then use the model in Zhang et al. (2018c) to demonstrate how GNNs can be adapted to RE.

The task of RE is to discern whether a relation exists between two entities (i.e., *subject* and *object*) in a sentence. More formally, it can be defined as follows. Let $\mathcal{W} = [w_1, \ldots, w_n]$ denote a sentence, where w_i is the ith token in the sentence. An entity is a span consisting of consecutive words in the sentence. Specifically, a subject entity, which consists of a series of consecutive words, can be represented as $\mathcal{W}_s = [w_{s1} : w_{s2}]$. Similarly, an object entity can be expressed as $\mathcal{W}_o = [w_{o1} : w_{o2}]$. The goal of relation extraction is to predict the relation for the subject entity $\mathcal{W}_s$ and the object entity $\mathcal{W}_o$ given the sentence $\mathcal{W}$, where $\mathcal{W}_s$ and $\mathcal{W}_o$ are assumed to be given. The relation is from a predefined set $\mathcal{R}$, which also includes a special relation "no relation" indicating that there is no relation between these two entities. The problem of RE is treated as a classification problem (Zhang et al., 2018c). The input is the concatenation of the representations of the sentence $\mathcal{W}$, the subject entity $\mathcal{W}_s$, and the object entity $\mathcal{W}_o$. The output labels are the relations in $\mathcal{R}$. Specifically, the relation prediction for a pair of entities is through a feedforward neural network (FFNN) with parameters Θ_{FFNN} as shown below:

$$\mathbf{p} = \text{softmax}([\mathbf{F}_{sent}, \mathbf{F}_s, \mathbf{F}_o]\Theta_{FFNN})),$$

where softmax() is the softmax function, $\mathbf{p}$ is the probability distribution over the relations in the set $\mathcal{R}$, and $\mathbf{F}_{sent}, \mathbf{F}_s, \mathbf{F}_o$ represent the vector representations of the sentence, the subject entity, and the object entity, respectively. To capture the context information of the sentence while also capturing the syntactic structure of the sentence, a procedure similar to that in Marcheggiani and Titov (2017; i.e., the model introduced in Section 10.2 for SRL) is adopted to learn the word representations, which are then utilized to learn the representations for the sentence, subject entity, and object entity. The major difference is that a self-loop is introduced to include the word itself during representation updating in Eq. (10.1). In other words, $\mathcal{N}(v_i)$ in Eq. (10.1) for RE consists of the node v_i and its in-going and out-going neighbors. They also empirically find that including the direction and edge label information does not help for the RE task.

Given the word representations from the model consisting of L graph filtering layers described above, the representations for sentence, subject entity, and object entity are obtained by max pooling as

$$\begin{aligned} \mathbf{F}_{sent} &= \max(\mathbf{F}^{(L)}), \\ \mathbf{F}_s &= \max(\mathbf{F}^{(L)}[s1 : s2]), \\ \mathbf{F}_o &= \max(\mathbf{F}^{(L)}[o1 : o2]), \end{aligned} \qquad (10.2)$$

where $\mathbf{F}^{(L)}$, $\mathbf{F}^{(L)}[s1 : s2]$, and $\mathbf{F}^{(L)}[o1 : o2]$ denote the sequence of word representations for the entire sentence, the subject entity, and the object entity, respectively. The max pooling operation takes the maximum of each dimension and thus results in a vector with the same dimension as the word representation.

10.5 Question Answering

Machine reading comprehension or QA aims to generate the correct answer for a given query/question by consuming and comprehending documents. It is an important but challenging task in NLP. GNNs have been widely adopted to facilitate the QA task, especially multihop QA (De Cao et al., 2019; Cao et al., 2019; Song et al., 2018a; Tu et al., 2019), where across-document reasoning is needed to answer a given query. This section introduces multihop QA and a representative work that utilizes GNNs for this task. We first introduce the setting of multihop QA based on the WIKIHOP data set (Welbl et al., 2018), which was created specifically for evaluating multihop QA models. We then describe the Entity-GCN proposed in De Cao et al. (2019) to tackle the multihop QA task.

10.5.1 The Multihop QA Task

In this subsection, we briefly discuss the setting of multihop QA based on the WIKIHOP data set. The WIKIHOP data set consists of a set of QA samples. Each sample can be denoted as a tuple $(q, S_q, C_q, a^\star)$, where q is a query/question, S_q is a set of supporting documents, C_q is a set of candidate answers to be chosen from (all of which are entities in the set of supporting documents S_q), and $a^\star \in C_q$ is the correct answer to the query. Instead of natural language, the query q is given in the form of a tuple $(s, r, ?)$, where s is the subject, r denotes the relation, and the object entity is unknown (marked as "?") and to be inferred from the support documents. A sample from the WIKIHOP data set is shown in Figure 10.3, where the goal is to choose the correct "country" for the Hanging Gardens of Mumbai from the candidate set C_q ={Iran, India, Pakistan, Somalia}. In this example, to find the correct answer for the query, multihop reasoning is required: (1) from the first document, it can be figured out that *Hanging Gardens* are located in *Mumbai* and (2) then, from the second document, it can be found that *Mumbai* is a city in *India*, which, together with the first evidence, can lead to the correct answer for the query. The goal of multihop QA is to learn a model that can identify the correct

---

The Hanging Gardens, in [Mumbai], also known as
Pherozeshah Mehta Gardens, are terraced gardens ... They
provide sunset views over the [Arabian Sea] ...

Mumbai (also known as Bombay, the official name until 1995)
is the capital city of the Indian state of Maharashtra. It is the
most populous city in India ...

The Arabian Sea is a region of the northern Indian Ocean
bounded on the north by Pakistan and Iran, on the west by
northeastern Somalia and the Arabian Peninsula, and on the
east by India ...

Q: {Hanging gardens of Mumbai, country, ?}

Options: {Iran, India, Pakistan, Somalia, ...}

Figure 10.3 A sample from the WIKIHOP data set.

answer $a^\star$ for a given query q from the candidate set C_q by consuming and comprehending the set of the support documents S_q.

10.5.2 Entity-GCN

To capture the relations between the entities within and across documents and consequently help the reasoning process across documents, each sample $(q, S_q, C_q, a^\star)$ of the multihop QA task is organized into a graph by connecting mentions of candidate answers within and across the supporting documents. A generalized GNN model (i.e., Entity-GCN) is then proposed to learn the node representations, which are later used to identify the correct answer from the candidate sets for the given query. Note that L graph filtering layers are applied to ensure that each mention (or node) can access rich information from a wide range of neighborhoods. Next, we first describe how the graph is built and then introduce the process of solving the QA task using the proposed Entity-GCN.

Entity Graph

For a given sample $(q, S_q, C_q, a^\star)$, to build a graph, the mentions of entities in $C_q \cup \{s\}$ are identified from the supporting document set S_q, and each mention is considered a node in the graph. These mentions include (1) entities in S_q that exactly match an element in $C_q \cup \{s\}$ and (2) entities that are in the same co-reference chain as an element in $C_q \cup \{s\}$. An end-to-end co-reference resolution technique (Lee et al., 2017) is used to discover the co-reference chains. Various types of edges are constructed to connect these mentions (or nodes) as follows: (1) "Match": two mentions (either within or across documents) are connected by a "Match" edge if they are identical; (2) "DOC-BASED": two mentions are connected via "DOC-BASED" if they co-occur in the same support document; and (3) "COREF": two mentions are connected by a "COREF" edge if they are in the same co-reference chain. These three types of edges describe three different types of relations between these mentions. In addition, to avoid disconnected components in the graph, a fourth type of edge is added between any pairs of nodes that are not connected. These edges are denoted as "COMPLEMENT" edges, which make the graph a complete graph.

Multistep Reasoning with Entity-GCN on Entity Graph
To approach multistep reasoning, a generalized GNN model Entity-GCN is proposed to transform and propagate the node representations through the built entity graph. Specifically, the graph filter (for the *l*th layer) in Entity-GCN can be regarded as instantiating the Message Passing Neural Network (MPNN) framework in Eq. (5.40) to deal with edges of different types as

$$\mathbf{m}_i^{(l-1)} = \mathbf{F}_i^{(l-1)}\mathbf{\Theta}_s^{(l-1)} + \frac{1}{|\mathcal{N}(v_i)|}\sum_{r \in \mathcal{R}}\sum_{v_j \in \mathcal{N}_r(v_i)}\mathbf{F}_j^{(l-1)}\mathbf{\Theta}_r^{(l-1)}, \qquad (10.3)$$

$$\mathbf{a}_i^{(l-1)} = \sigma\left(\left[\mathbf{m}_i^{(l)}, \mathbf{F}_i^{(l-1)}\right]\mathbf{\Theta}_a^{(l-1)}\right), \qquad (10.4)$$

$$\mathbf{h}_i^{(l)} = \rho\left(\mathbf{m}_i^{(l-1)}\right) \odot \mathbf{a}_i^{(l-1)} + \mathbf{F}_i^{(l-1)} \odot \left(1 - \mathbf{a}_i^{(l-1)}\right), \qquad (10.5)$$

where $\mathcal{R} = \{MATCH, DOC\text{-}BASED, COREF, COMPLEMENT\}$ denotes the set of types of edges, $\mathcal{N}_r(v_i)$ is the set of nodes connected to node v_i through edges of type r, $\mathbf{\Theta}_r^{(l-1)}$ indicates parameters shared by edges of type r, and $\mathbf{\Theta}_s^{(l-1)}$ and $\mathbf{\Theta}_a^{(l-1)}$ are shared by all nodes. The output in Eq. (10.4) serves as a gating system to control the information flow in the message update part of Eq. (10.5). The representation for each node v_i is initialized as

$$\mathbf{F}_i^{(0)} = f_x(\mathbf{q}, \mathbf{x}_i),$$

where $\mathbf{q}$ denotes the query representation from the pretrained model ELMo (Peters et al., 2018), $\mathbf{x}_i$ is the pretrained representation for node v_i from ELMo, and $f_x(,)$ is parameterized by an FFNN.

The final node representations $\mathbf{F}_i^{(L)}$ from the Entity-GCN with L graph filtering layers are used to select the answer for the given query from the candidate set. In detail, the probability of selecting a candidate $c \in C_q$ as the answer is modeled as

$$P\left(c|q, C_q, S_q\right) \propto \exp\left(\max_{v_i \in \mathcal{M}_c} f_o\left(\left[\mathbf{q}, \mathbf{F}_i^{(L)}\right]\right)\right),$$

where f_o is a parameterized transformation, $\mathcal{M}_c$ is the set of mentions corresponding to candidate c, and the max operator is to select the mention in $\mathcal{M}_c$ with the largest predicted probability for the candidate. In Song et al. (2018a), instead of selecting the mention with the largest probability in $\mathcal{M}_c$, all mentions of a candidate c are utilized to model $P\left(c|q, C_q, S_q\right)$. Specifically,

$$P\left(c|q, C_q, S_q\right) = \frac{\sum\limits_{v_i \in \mathcal{M}_c} \alpha_i}{\sum\limits_{v_i \in \mathcal{M}} \alpha_i},$$

where we use $\mathcal{M}$ to denote all mentions–i.e., all nodes in the entity graph–and α_i is modeled by the softmax function as

$$\alpha_i = \frac{\exp\left(f_o\left(\left[\mathbf{q}, \mathbf{F}_i^{(L)}\right]\right)\right)}{\sum\limits_{v_i \in \mathcal{M}} \exp\left(f_o\left(\left[\mathbf{q}, \mathbf{F}_i^{(L)}\right]\right)\right)}.$$

10.6 Graph to Sequence Learning

Sequence to sequence models have been broadly applied to natural language processing tasks such as neural machine translation (Bahdanau et al., 2014) and natural language generation (Song et al., 2017). Most of these proposed models can be viewed as encoder–decoder models. In an encoder–decoder model, an encoder takes a sequence of tokens as input and encodes it into a sequence of continuous vector representations. Then, a decoder takes the encoded vector representations as input and outputs a new target sequence. Usually, a recurrent neural network (RNN) and its variants serve as both the encoder and the decoder. Because natural languages can be represented in terms of graphs, graph to sequence models have emerged to tackle various tasks in NLP, such as neural machine translation (Marcheggiani et al., 2018; Beck et al. 2018; see Section 10.3 for details) and AMR to text (Cohen, 2019; Song et al., 2018b). These graph to sequence models usually utilize GNNs as the encoder (or a part of the encoder) while still adopting RNN and its variants as its decoder. Specifically, a GNN model described in Eq. (10.1) (Marcheggiani and Titov, 2017) is utilized as the encoder in Marcheggiani et al. (2018), Song et al. (2018b), and Cohen (2019) for neural machine translation and AMR-to-text tasks. A general encoder–decoder graph2seq framework for graph to sequence learning was proposed in Xu et al. (2018b). It utilizes the GNN model as the encoder and an attention mechanism–equipped RNN model as the decoder. We first describe the GNN-based encoder model and then briefly describe the decoder.

GNN-Based Encoder

Most graphs in NLP applications such as AMR and syntactic dependency trees are directed. Hence, the GNN-based encoder in graph2seq is designed to differentiate the incoming and outgoing neighbors while aggregating information. Specially, for a node v_i, its neighbors are split into two sets: the incoming neighbors $\mathcal{N}_{\text{in}}(v_i)$ and the outgoing neighbors $\mathcal{N}_{\text{out}}(v_i)$. The aggregation operation in GraphSAGE-Filter (see details on GraphSAGE-Filter in Subsection 5.3.2) is used to aggregate and update the node representations. Specifically, two node representations for each node are maintained; i.e., the in-representation and the out-representation. The updating process for node v_i in the lth layer can be expressed as

$$\mathbf{F}^{(l)}_{\mathcal{N}_{\text{in}}(v_i)} = \text{AGGREGATE}(\{\mathbf{F}^{(l-1)}_{\text{out}}(v_j), \forall v_j \in \mathcal{N}_{\text{in}}(v_i)\}),$$

$$\mathbf{F}^{(l)}_{\text{in}}(v_i) = \sigma\left([\mathbf{F}^{(l-1)}_{\text{in}}(v_i), \mathbf{F}^{(l)}_{\mathcal{N}_{\text{in}}(v_i)}]\mathbf{\Theta}^{(l-1)}_{\text{in}}\right),$$

$$\mathbf{F}^{(l)}_{\mathcal{N}_{\text{out}}(v_i)} = \text{AGGREGATE}(\{\mathbf{F}^{(l-1)}_{\text{in}}(v_j), \forall v_j \in \mathcal{N}_{\text{out}}(v_i)\}),$$

$$\mathbf{F}^{(l)}_{\text{out}}(v_i) = \sigma\left([\mathbf{F}^{(l-1)}_{\text{out}}(v_i), \mathbf{F}^{(l)}_{\mathcal{N}_{\text{out}}(v_i)}]\mathbf{\Theta}^{(l-1)}_{\text{out}}\right),$$

where $\mathbf{F}^{(l)}_{\text{in}}(v_i)$ and $\mathbf{F}^{(l)}_{\text{out}}(v_i)$ denote the in- and out-representations for node v_i after the lth layer. As introduced for the GraphSAGE-Filter in Subsection 5.3.2, various designs for AGGREGATE() functions can be adopted. The final in- and out-representations after L graph filtering layers are denoted as $\mathbf{F}^{(L)}_{\text{in}}(v_i)$ and $\mathbf{F}^{(L)}_{\text{out}}(v_i)$, respectively. These two types of representations are concatenated to generate the final representations containing information from both directions as

$$\mathbf{F}^{(L)}(v_i) = \left[\mathbf{F}^{(L)}_{\text{in}}(v_i), \mathbf{F}^{(L)}_{\text{out}}(v_i)\right].$$

After obtained the node representations, a graph representation is also generated by using pooling methods, which are used to initialize the decoder. The pooling process can be expressed as

$$\mathbf{F}_G = \text{Pool}\left(\{\mathbf{F}^{(L)}(v_i), \forall v_i \in \mathcal{V}\}\right).$$

Here, various flat pooling methods such as max pooling and average pooling can be adopted. The decoder is modeled by an attention-based RNN. It attends to all node representations when generating each token of the sequence. Note that the graph representation $\mathbf{F}_G$ is utilized as the initial state of the RNN decoder.

10.7 Graph Neural Networks on Knowledge Graphs

Formally, a knowledge graph $G = (\mathcal{V}, \mathcal{E}, \mathcal{R})$ consists a set of nodes $\mathcal{V}$, a set of relational edges $\mathcal{E}$, and a set of relations $\mathcal{R}$. The nodes are various types of entities and attributes, and the edges include different types of relations between the nodes. Specifically, an edge $e \in \mathcal{E}$ can be represented as a triplet (s, r, t) where $s, t \in \mathcal{V}$ are the source and target nodes of the edge, respectively, and $r \in \mathcal{R}$ denotes the relation between them. Graph neural networks have been extended to knowledge graphs to learn node representations and thus facilitate various downstream tasks, including knowledge graph completion (Hamaguchi et al., 2017; Schlichtkrull et al., 2018; Nathani et al., 2019; Shang et al., 2019a; Wang et al., 2019f), node importance estimation (Park et al., 2019), entity linking (Zhang et al., 2019b), and cross-language knowledge graph alignment (Wang et al., 2018c; Xu et al., 2019e). The major difference between knowledge graphs and simple graphs is the relational information, which is important to consider when designing GNNs for knowledge graphs. In this section, we describe how GNNs are generalized to knowledge graphs. In particular, there are two main ways to deal with the relational edges in knowledge graphs: (1) incorporating the relational information of the edges into the design of graph filters and (2) transforming the relational knowledge graph into a simple undirected graph by capturing the relational information. Then, we use the task of knowledge graph completion as an example to illustrate GNN-based applications on knowledge graphs.

10.7.1 Graph Filters for Knowledge Graphs

Various graph filters have been specifically designed for knowledge graphs. We describe representative ones next. The GCN-Filter described in Eq. (5.22) is adapted to knowledge graphs (Schlichtkrull et al., 2018) as

$$\mathbf{F}_i^{(l)} = \sum_{r \in \mathcal{R}} \sum_{v_j \in \mathcal{N}_r(v_i)} \frac{1}{|\mathcal{N}_r(v_i)|} \mathbf{F}_j^{(l-1)} \mathbf{\Theta}_r^{(l-1)} + \mathbf{F}_i^{(l-1)} \mathbf{\Theta}_0^{(l-1)}, \qquad (10.6)$$

where $\mathcal{N}_r(v_i)$ denotes the set of neighbors that connect to node v_i through the relation r. It can be defined as

$$\mathcal{N}(v_i) = \{v_j | (v_j, r, v_i) \in \mathcal{E}\}.$$

In Eq. (10.6), the parameters $\mathbf{\Theta}_r^{(l-1)}$ are shared by the edges with the same relation $r \in \mathcal{R}$. Similar ideas can be also found in Hamaguchi et al. (2017). Note that the Entity-GCN described in Subsection 10.5.2 is inspired by the graph filter in Eq. (10.6). In Shang et al. (2019a), instead of learning different transformation parameters for different relations, a scalar score is learned to capture the importance for each relation. It leads to the following graph filtering operation:

$$\mathbf{F}_i^{(l)} = \sum_{r \in \mathcal{R}} \sum_{v_j \in \mathcal{N}_r(v_i)} \frac{1}{|\mathcal{N}_r(v_i)|} \alpha_r^{(l)} \mathbf{F}_j^{(l-1)} \mathbf{\Theta}^{(l-1)} + \mathbf{F}_i^{(l-1)} \mathbf{\Theta}_0^{(l-1)}, \qquad (10.7)$$

where $\alpha_r^{(l)}$ is the importance score to be learned for the relation r.

To reduce the parameters involved in Eq. (10.6), relation embeddings are learned for different relations (Vashishth et al., 2019). Specifically, the relation embeddings for all relations in $\mathcal{R}$ after $l - 1$ layer can be denoted as $\mathbf{Z}^{(l-1)}$ with $\mathbf{Z}_r^{(l-1)}$ the embedding for relation r. The relation embeddings can be updated for the lth layer as

$$\mathbf{Z}^{(l)} = \mathbf{Z}^{(l-1)} \mathbf{\Theta}_{rel}^{(l-1)},$$

where $\mathbf{\Theta}_{rel}^{(l-1)}$ are the parameters to be learned. We use $\mathcal{N}(v_i)$ to denote the set of neighbors of node v_i that contains nodes that connect to v_i with different relations. Hence, we use (v_j, r) to indicate a neighbor of v_i in $\mathcal{N}(v_i)$, where v_j is the node connecting with v_i through the relation r. Furthermore, in Vashishth et al. (2019), the reverse edge of any edge in $\mathcal{E}$ is also treated as an edge. In other words, if $(v_i, r, v_j) \in \mathcal{E}$, $(v_j, \hat{r}, v_i)$ is also considered as an edge with $\hat{r}$ as the reverse relation of r. Note that, for convenience, we abuse the notation $\mathcal{E}$ and $\mathcal{R}$ a little to denote the augmented edge set and relation set. The relations now have directions and we use $dir(r)$ to denote the direction of a relation r. Specifically, $dir(r) = 1$ for all original relations, and $dir(\hat{r}) = -1$ for all reverse relations. The filtering operation is then designed as

$$\mathbf{F}_i^{(l)} = \sum_{(v_j, r) \in \mathcal{N}(v_i)} \phi(\mathbf{F}_j^{(l-1)}, \mathbf{Z}_r^{l-1}) \mathbf{\Theta}_{dir(r)}^{(l-1)}, \qquad (10.8)$$

where $\phi(,)$ denotes nonparameterized operations such as subtraction and multiplication and $\mathbf{\Theta}_{dir(r)}^{(l-1)}$ are parameters shared by all relations with the same direction.

10.7.2 Transforming Knowledge Graphs to Simple Graphs

In Wang et al. (2018c), instead of designing specific graph filtering operations for knowledge graphs, a simple graph was built to capture the directed relational information in knowledge graphs. Then, existing graph filtering operations can be naturally applied to the transformed simple graph.

Two scores are proposed to measure the influence of an entity to another entity through a specific type of relation r as

$$\text{fun}(r) = \frac{\#\text{Source\_with\_r}}{\#\text{Edges\_with\_r}},$$

$$\text{ifun}(r) = \frac{\#\text{Taget\_with\_r}}{\#\text{Edges\_with\_r}},$$

where #Edges_with_r is the total number of edges with the relation r, #Source_with_r denotes the number of unique source entities with relation r, and #Target_with_r indicates the number of unique target entities with relation r. Then, the overall influence of the entity v_i to the entity v_j is defined as

$$\mathbf{A}_{i,j} = \sum_{(v_i,r,v_j) \in \mathcal{E}} \text{ifun}(r) + \sum_{(v_j,r,v_i) \in \mathcal{E}} \text{fun}(r),$$

where $\mathbf{A}_{i,j}$ is the i,jth element for the adjacency matrix $\mathbf{A}$ of the generated simple graph.

10.7.3 Knowledge Graph Completion

Knowledge graph completion, which aims to predict the relation between a pair of disconnected entities, is an important task because knowledge graphs are usually incomplete or fast evolving, with new entities emerging. Specifically, the task is to predict whether a given triplet (s, r, t) is a real relation or not. To achieve this goal, we need to assign a score $f(s, r, t)$ to the triplet (s, r, t) to measure the probability of the triplet being a real relation. In particular, DistMult factorization (Yang et al., 2014) is adopted as the scoring function, which can be expressed as

$$f(s, r, t) = \mathbf{F}_s^{(L)\top} \mathbf{R}_r \mathbf{F}_t^{(L)},$$

where $\mathbf{F}_s^{(L)}$ and $\mathbf{F}_t^{(L)}$ are the representations of source node s and target node t, respectively. They are learned by GNNs after L filtering layers; $\mathbf{R}_r$ is a diagonal matrix corresponding to the relation r to be learned during training. The model can be trained using negative sampling with cross-entropy loss. In particular, for each observed edge sample $e \in \mathcal{E}$, k negative samples are generated by randomly replacing either its subject or object with another entity. With the observed samples and the negative samples, the cross-entropy loss to be optimized can be expressed as

$$\mathcal{L} = -\frac{1}{(1+k)|\mathcal{E}|} \sum_{(s,r,o,y) \in \mathcal{T}} y \log \sigma\left(f(s, r, o)\right) + (1 - y) \log\left(1 - \sigma\left(f(s, r, o)\right)\right),$$

where $\mathcal{T}$ denotes the set of positive samples observed in $\mathcal{E}$ and randomly generated negative samples and y is an indicator that is set to 1 for the observed samples and 0 for the negative samples.

10.8 Conclusion

In this chapter, we introduce how GNNs can be applied to NLP. We present representative tasks in natural language processing, including SRL, RE, QA, and graph to sequence learning, and describe how GNNs can be employed to advance their corresponding models' performance. We also discuss knowledge graphs, which are widely used in many NLP tasks, and present how GNNs can be generalized to knowledge graphs.

10.9 Further Reading

In addition to GNNs, the Graph-LSTM algorithms introduced in Section 9.3 have also been adopted to advance the relation extraction tasks (Miwa and Bansal, 2016; Song et al., 2018c). In addition, GNNs have been applied to many other NLP tasks such as abusive language detection (Mishra et al., 2019), neural summarization (Fernandes et al., 2018), and text classification (Yao et al., 2019). Transformer (Vaswani et al., 2017) has been widely adopted to deal with sequences in natural language processing. The pretrained model BERT (Devlin et al., 2018), which is built upon transformer, has advanced many tasks in NLP. When applied to a given sequence, the transformer can be regarded as a special GNN. It is applied to a graph induced from the input sequence. In detail, the sequence can be regarded as a fully connected graph, where elements in the sequence are treated as the nodes. Then a single self-attention layer in the transformer is equivalent to the GAT-Filter layer (see Subsection 5.3.2 for details of GAT-Filter).

11

Graph Neural Networks in Computer Vision

11.1 Introduction

Graph-structured data widely exist in numerous tasks in the area of computer vision. In the task of visual question answering, where a question is required to be answered based on content in a given image, graphs can be utilized to model the relations among the objects in the image. In the task of skeleton-based recognition, where the goal is to predict human action based on the skeleton dynamics, the skeletons can be represented as graphs. In image classification, different categories are related to each other through knowledge graphs or category co-occurrence graphs (Wang et al., 2018b; Chen et al., 2019c). Furthermore, point cloud, which is a type of irregular data structure representing shapes and objects, can also be denoted as graphs. Therefore, graph neural networks can be naturally utilized to extract patterns from these graphs to facilitate the corresponding computer vision tasks. This chapter demonstrates how graph neural networks (GNNs) can be adapted to the aforementioned computer vision tasks with representative algorithms.

11.2 Visual Question Answering

Given an image and a question described in natural language, the task of visual question answering (VQA) is to answer the question based on the information provided in the image. An illustrative example of the VQA task is shown in Figure 11.1, where the task is to figure out the color of the fruit at the left of the image. To perform the VQA task properly, it is necessary to understand the question and the image, which requires techniques from both natural language processing and computer vision. Typically, convolutional neural networks (CNNs) are adopted to learn the image representation. Then,

Question q: What is the color of fruit at the left?

Figure 11.1 An illustrative example of the VQA task.

it is combined with the representation of the question to perform the VQA task. As illustrated in Figure 11.1, the relations between objects in the image can also be important to answer the question correctly. Better capturing the semantic and spatial relations between the objects can potentially facilitate the VQA task. For example, to answer the question q in Figure 11.1 properly, the relative locations between the fruits are necessary. To denote the objects' interactions explicitly, graphs are adopted to model the connections between objects. GNNs are then adopted to learn the representations for these graphs generated from images (Teney et al., 2017; Norcliffe-Brown et al., 2018). Specifically, some works assume that the graph is given for each image (Teney et al., 2017), whereas others incorporate the graph generation process as a part of the proposed models (Norcliffe-Brown et al., 2018). In this section, we introduce the two models proposed in Teney et al. (2017) and Norcliffe-Brown et al. (2018) as examples to show how GNNs can be adopted in the VQA task.

The task of VQA is modeled as a classification problem, where each class corresponds to one of the most common answers in the training set. Formally, each sample of this classification problem can be denoted as (q, I), where q is the question and I is the image. To tackle this classification problem utilizing the information from the question and the image, their representations are learned and combined to serve as the input for the prediction layer based on a feedforward network. In Norcliffe-Brown et al. (2018), the image is transferred to a graph in an end-to-end manner while training the entire framework. In Teney et al. (2017), both the question q and the image I are preprocessed as graphs and dealt with a GNN model.

11.2.1 Images as Graphs

In Norcliffe-Brown et al. (2018), the question q is encoded to a representation $\mathbf{q}$ using a recurrent neural network with a gated recurrent unit (GRU). To learn the representation for the image I, a graph is generated from the image I dependent on the question q, and a GNN model is applied on the generated graph to learn its representation. Next, we first describe how the graph is generated given the image I and the question representation $\mathbf{q}$. Then, we introduce the GNN model to learn the graph representation $\mathbf{F}_I$. Finally, we briefly describe the prediction layer, which takes the representations for the question q and the image I as input.

For an image I and a set of n visual features bounded by boxes generated by an object detector, each bounding box serves as a node in the generated graph. An initial representation $\mathbf{x}_i$ is produced for each node v_i by taking the average of the corresponding convolutional feature maps in the bounding box. These nodes consist of the node set for the generated graph, denoted as $\mathcal{V}_I$. We then generate the set of edges $\mathcal{E}_I$ to describe the relations between these nodes. These edges are constructed based on the pair-wise similarity and the relevance to the given question q. To combine these two types of information, for each node, a question-dependent representation is generated as

$$\mathbf{e}_i = h([\mathbf{x}_i, \mathbf{q}]),$$

where $\mathbf{e}_i$ is the question-dependent node representation for node v_i and $h()$ is a nonlinear function to combine these two types of information. The question-dependent representations for all nodes can be summarized by a matrix $\mathbf{E}$ where the ith row corresponds to the ith node in the generated graph. Then the adjacency matrix of the graph is calculated as

$$\mathbf{A} = \mathbf{E}\mathbf{E}^T. \tag{11.1}$$

However, the adjacency matrix learned by Eq. (11.1) is fully connected, which is not optimal for both efficiency and the performance of the model. Hence, to generate a sparse adjacency matrix, only the stronger connections for each node are kept. Specifically, we only keep the top m values of each row and set other values to 0, where m is a hyperparameter. The graph generated for image I is denoted as $\mathcal{G}_I$.

After obtaining the question-dependent graph $\mathcal{G}_I$ for the objects detected in the image, the Mo-Filter introduced in Subsection 5.3.2 is adapted to generate the node representations. The operation for a node v_i can be formulated as

$$\mathbf{F}_i^{(l)} = \sum_{v_j \in \mathcal{N}(v_i)} w(\mathbf{u}(i, j))\mathbf{F}_j^{(l-1)}\alpha_{i,j}, \tag{11.2}$$

where $\mathcal{N}(v_i)$ denotes the set of neighbors for node v_i, $w(\cdot)$ is a learnable Gaussian kernel, $\alpha_{i,j} = \text{softmax}(\mathbf{A}_i)[j]$ indicates the strength of connectivity between nodes v_i and v_j, and $\mathbf{u}(i, j)$ is a pseudo-coordinate function. This pseudo-coordinate function $\mathbf{u}(i, j)$ returns a polar coordinate vector (ρ, θ), which describes the relative spatial positions of the centers of the bounding boxes corresponding to nodes v_i and v_j. After applying L consecutive graph filtering layers as described in Eq. (11.2), the final representation for each node v_i is obtained as $\mathbf{F}_i^{(L)}$. In Norcliffe-Brown et al. (2018), K different Gaussian kernels are used and the output representations of the K kernels are combined as

$$\mathbf{F}_i = \|_{k=1}^{K} \mathbf{F}_{i|k}^{(L)} \mathbf{\Theta}_k,$$

where $\mathbf{F}_{i|k}^{(L)}$ is the output from the kth kernel and $\mathbf{\Theta}_k$ is a learnable linear transformation. The final representations for all nodes in the graph can be summarized in a matrix $\mathbf{F}$ where each row corresponds to a node.

Once these final node representations are obtained, a max pooling layer is applied to generate the representation $\mathbf{F}_I$ for the graph $\mathcal{G}_I$. The graph representation $\mathbf{F}_I$ and the question representation $\mathbf{q}$ are combined through the element-wise product to generate the task representation, which is then input into the feedforward network–based prediction layer to perform the classification.

11.2.2 Images and Questions as Graphs

In Teney et al. (2017), both the question q and the image I are preprocessed as graphs. The question q is modeled as a syntactic dependency tree. In the tree, each word in the sentence is a node, and the dependency relations between words are edges. We denote the graph generated for a question q as $\mathcal{G}_q = \{\mathcal{V}_q, \mathcal{E}_q, \mathcal{R}_q\}$, where $\mathcal{R}_q$ is the set of possible dependency relations. Meanwhile, the image I is preprocessed as a fully connected graph. In the graph, the objects in the image I are extracted as nodes, and they are connected pair-wise. We denote the graph generated for the image I as $\mathcal{G}_I = \{\mathcal{V}_I, \mathcal{E}_I\}$. Each object (or node) $v_i \in \mathcal{V}_I$ is associated with its visual features $\mathbf{x}_i$ and each edge $(v_i, v_j) \in \mathcal{E}_I$ between nodes v_i and v_j is associated with a vector $\mathbf{x}_{ij}$ that encodes the relative spatial relations between v_i and v_j.

Both graphs are processed with GNNs to generate node representations, which are later combined to generate a representation for the pair (q, I). In Teney et al. (2017), a slightly modified version of GGNN-Filter as introduced in Subsection 5.3.2 was utilized to process these two graphs. The modified GGNN-Filter can be described as

$$\mathbf{m}_i = \sum_{v_j \in \mathcal{N}(v_i)} \mathbf{x}'_{ij} \odot \mathbf{x}'_j, \tag{11.3}$$

$$\mathbf{h}_i^{(t)} = \text{GRU}([\mathbf{m}_i, \mathbf{x}'_i], \mathbf{h}_i^{(t-1)}); t = 1, \ldots T, \tag{11.4}$$

where $\mathbf{x}'_j$ and $\mathbf{x}'_{ij}$ are the features for node v_j and edge (v_i, v_j), respectively. For the question graph $\mathcal{G}_q$, $\mathbf{x}'_j$ and $\mathbf{x}'_{ij}$ are randomly initialized. In detail, node features are word-specific; i.e., each word is initialized with a representation and edge features are relation specific; i.e., edges with the same relation $r \in \mathcal{R}_q$ share the same features. For the image graph $\mathcal{G}_I$, $\mathbf{x}'_i$ and $\mathbf{x}'_{ij}$ are transformed using feedforward networks from the associated features $\mathbf{x}_i$ and $\mathbf{x}_{ij}$, respectively. In Eq. (11.4), the GRU update unit (with $\mathbf{h}_0^{(0)} = \mathbf{0}$) runs T times and finally obtains the final representation $\mathbf{h}_i^{(T)}$ for node v_i. Note that in Teney et al. (2017), a single layer of graph filter as described in Eq. (11.3) and Eq. (11.4) was utilized to process the graphs. In other words, there are a single aggregation step and T GRU update steps. We denote the final node representations learned from the graph filtering as $\mathbf{h}_i^{(T,q)}$ and $\mathbf{h}_j^{(T,I)}$ for node $v_i \in \mathcal{V}_q$ in the question graph $\mathcal{G}_q$ and $v_j \in \mathcal{V}_I$ in the image graph $\mathcal{G}_I$, respectively. These node representations from the two graphs are combined as

$$\mathbf{h}_{i,j} = \alpha_{i,j} \cdot [\mathbf{h}_i^{(T,q)}, \mathbf{h}_j^{(T,I)}], i = 1, \ldots |\mathcal{V}_q|; j = 1, \ldots, |\mathcal{V}_I|, \tag{11.5}$$

$$\mathbf{h}'_i = f_1 \left(\sum_{j=1}^{|\mathcal{V}_I|} \mathbf{h}_{i,j} \right), \tag{11.6}$$

$$\mathbf{h}_{(q,I)} = f_2 \left(\sum_{i=1}^{|\mathcal{V}_q|} \mathbf{h}'_i \right), \tag{11.7}$$

where $\alpha_{i,j}$ in Eq. (11.5), which is learned using the raw features $\mathbf{x}'$, can be regarded as a relevance measure between a question node and an image node. Specifically, it can be modeled as

$$\alpha_{i,j} = \sigma \left(f_3 \left(\frac{\mathbf{x}_i'^Q}{\|\mathbf{x}_i'^Q\|} \odot \frac{\mathbf{x}_j'^I}{\|\mathbf{x}_j'^I\|} \right) \right),$$

where we use the superscripts Q and I to differentiate the features for nodes from the question graph and the image graph, respectively; $\odot$ is the Hadarmard product; $f_3()$ is modeled as a linear transformation; and $\sigma()$ is the sigmoid function. $\mathbf{h}_{i,j}$ is a mixed representation of a node from the question graph and a node from the image graph. These representations $\mathbf{h}_{i,j}$ are hierarchically aggregated to generate the representation $\mathbf{h}_{(q,I)}$ for the pair (q, I) in Eq. (11.6) and Eq. (11.7), where $f_1()$ and $f_2()$ are feedforward neural networks. The representation can be utilized to perform the classification on the candidate sets.

11.3 Skeleton-Based Action Recognition

Human action recognition is an active research area and plays a vital role in video understanding. Human body skeleton dynamics can capture important information about human actions, which have often been leveraged for action recognition. The skeleton dynamics can be naturally modeled as a time series of human joint locations and interactions between them. In particular, the spatial relations between the joints can be modeled as a graph with the joints as the nodes and the bones as edges connecting them. Then, the skeleton dynamics can be represented as a sequence of graphs that share the same spatial structure and the node attributes (or location coordinates of the joints) of the graph in the sequence are different. Graph neural networks have been adopted to learn better representations of the skeleton dynamics and thus improve the performance of skeleton-based action recognition (Yan et al., 2018; Li et al., 2018a; Shi et al., 2019a; Si et al., 2018; Wen et al., 2019; Li et al., 2019c; Si et al., 2019). In this section, we take the framework proposed in Yan et al. (2018) as one example to demonstrate how GNNs can be applied to the skeleton-based action recognition task. It is the first to explore GNNs for skeleton-based action recognition.

As shown in Figure 11.2, a sequence of skeletons is represented as a spatial–temporal graph $\mathcal{G} = \{\mathcal{V}, \mathcal{E}\}$, where $\mathcal{V}$ denotes the set of nodes and $\mathcal{E}$ is the set of edges, respectively. The node set $\mathcal{V}$ consists of all joints in the skeleton sequence; i.e., $\mathcal{V} = \{v_{ti}|t = 1, \ldots, T; i = 1, \ldots, N\}$, where N is the number of joints in a single skeleton graph and T is the number of skeletons in the sequence. The edge set $\mathcal{E}$ consists of two types of edges: (1) the intra-skeleton edges within the same skeleton, which are defined based on the bones between the joints, and (2) the inter- skeleton edges, which connect the same joints in consecutive skeletons in the sequence. For the illustrative example in Figure 11.2, the intra-skeleton edges are highlighted in green and the inter-skeleton edges are shown in blue. The skeleton-based action recognition task can then be converted into a graph classification task where the classes are the actions to predict, such as running. To perform this graph classification task, a graph filtering operation is proposed for the spatial–temporal graph to learn node representations. After the node representations are learned, the graph representation is obtained by applying a global pooling layer, such as max pooling. The graph representation is then utilized as the input to the

Figure 11.2 An illustrative example of a spatial–temporal skeleton graph.

feedforward network–based prediction layer. Next, we present the details of the proposed graph filter for the spatial–temporal graph.

The proposed graph filter is adapted from the GCN-Filter (see Subsection 5.3.2 for details of the GCN-Filter), which aggregates information from neighboring nodes in the spatial–temporal graph. Specifically, for a node v_{ti} in the tth skeleton, its spatial neighbors $\mathcal{N}(v_{ti})$ consist of its 1-hop neighbors in the tth skeleton graph and the node v_{ti} itself. Then its spatial–temporal neighbors $\mathcal{N}^T(v_{ti})$ on the spatial–temporal graph $\mathcal{G}$ can be defined as

$$\mathcal{N}^T(v_{ti}) = \{v_{\tau j} | v_{tj} \in \mathcal{N}(v_{ti}) \text{ and } |\tau - t| \leq \Gamma\}. \tag{11.8}$$

The constraint $|\tau - t| \leq \Gamma$ in Eq. (11.8) indicates that the temporal distance between these two skeleton graphs where the nodes $v_{\tau j}$ and v_{tj} are located should be smaller than Γ. Hence, the spatial temporal neighbors $\mathcal{N}^T(v_{ti})$ of node v_{ti} include not only its spatial neighbors from the same skeleton but also "temporal neighbors" from close skeletons in the sequence. Furthermore, instead of treating the neighbors equally, neighbors are split into different subsets and different transformation matrices are utilized for their transformation. In particular, the spatial neighbors $\mathcal{N}(v_{ti})$ of a node v_{ti} in a skeleton graph are divided in to three subsets as follows: (1) the root node itself (i.e., node v_{ti}); (2) the neighboring nodes that are closer to the gravity center of skeleton than the root node; and (3) all other nodes. The neighboring nodes of node v_{ti} in other skeleton graphs can be divided similarly; hence, the neighboring set $\mathcal{N}^T(v_{ti})$ can be divided into $3(2\Gamma + 1)$ sets. For convenience, we use $s(v_{\tau j})$ to indicate the subset that a given node $v_{\tau j} \in \mathcal{N}^T(v_{ti})$ belongs to. Then, the graph filtering process for a given node v_{ti} can be described as

$$\mathbf{F}_{ti}^{(l)} = \sum_{v_{\tau j} \in \mathcal{N}^T(v_{ti})} \frac{1}{\#s(v_{\tau j})} \cdot \mathbf{F}_{\tau j}^{(l-1)} \mathbf{\Theta}_{s(v_{\tau j})}^{(l-1)}, \qquad (11.9)$$

where $\mathbf{F}_{ti}^{(l)}$ denotes node representations of node v_{ti} after the lth layer, and $\mathbf{F}_{\tau j}^{(l-1)}$ denotes node representations of node $v_{\tau j}$ after the $(l-1)$st layer. $\#s(v_{\tau j})$ denotes the number of neighbors in subset $v_{\tau j}$ and the transformation parameter $\mathbf{\Theta}_{s(v_{\tau j})}^{(l-1)}$ is shared by all neighbors belonging to subset $s(v_{\tau j})$. The node representations are learned by stacking L graph filtering layers as in Eq. (11.9) with activation layers. Then, the graph representation is obtained by applying a global pooling layer to these node representations. Note that in the framework we introduced above, the relations between the joints in the skeleton are naturally defined through the bones. Hence, only spatially close joints are connected to each other. However, it is possible that some distant joints are also related, particularly when doing some specific actions. For example, two hands are highly related to each other when doing the action "clapping hands." Thus, it is important to also encode relations between distant joints. In Shi et al. (2019a,b) and Li et al. (2019c), the graphs between the joints are learned together with the parameters of the model.

11.4 Image Classification

Image classification aims to classify an image into certain categories. GNNs have been adopted to advance image classification, especially under zero-shot, few-shot, and multilabel settings. In this section, we discuss GNN-based image classification under these three settings with representative algorithms. As shown in Figure 3.11 in Subsection 3.3.5, a CNN-based image classifier usually consists of two parts: (1) feature extraction, which is built with convolutional and pooling layers, and (2) the classification component, which is typically modeled as a fully connected layer. Specifically, this fully connected layer (without considering the softmax layer) can be represented as a matrix $\mathbf{W} \in \mathbb{R}^{d \times c}$, where d is the dimension of the extracted features, and c is the number of categories in the task. The ith row of $\mathbf{W}$ denoted as $\mathbf{w}_i$ is corresponding to the ith category. In this section, we loosely call $\mathbf{w}_i$ the "classifier" of the ith category.

11.4.1 Zero-Shot Image Classification

In the traditional setting of the image classification task in computer vision, abundant images of each category are assumed to be available for training the classifiers for these categories. These learned classifiers can only recognize the images from the categories they are trained with. To recognize images from a new category, thousands of images of this category are required, and their corresponding classifiers must be retrained together with newly collected images. The task of zero-shot image classification is to learn a classifier for a new category without any training images but only based on information about the category, such as its description or its relations with other categories. GNNs were adopted in Wang et al. (2018b) to learn classifiers for categories without any training images by propagating information from other categories through a knowledge graph describing the relations between categories. Next, we first formally describe the setting of the zero-shot image classification task and then present how GNNs are adopted to tackle this problem.

In the zero-shot image classification setting, we are given a set of n categories, among which the first m have sufficient training images and the remaining $n - m$ categories have no images. Each category c_i is associated with a short description, which can be projected to a semantic embedding $\mathbf{x}_i$. Furthermore, there is a knowledge graph (e.g., WordNet; Miller, 1998) $\mathcal{G} = \{\mathcal{V}, \mathcal{E}\}$ describing the relations between these categories, where the categories are the nodes. In the introduction of this section, we use $\mathbf{w}_i$ to loosely denote a classifier of a category c_i. For a linear classifier such as logistic regression for a given category c_i, it can be also represented by its parameters $\mathbf{w}_i \in \mathbb{R}^d$, where d is the dimension of the features of the input image. Given an image, its features can be extracted using some pretrained CNNs. For those m categories with sufficient training samples, their corresponding classifier can be learned from these training samples. The goal of the zero-shot image classification task is to learn classifiers for those $n - m$ categories without any images by leveraging their semantic embeddings and/or the given knowledge graph $\mathcal{G}$.

A straightforward way to predict the classifiers is to adopt a neural network that takes the semantic embedding of a category as input and produces its corresponding classifier as output. However, in practice, the number of categories with sufficient training samples is generally too small (e.g., on the order of hundreds) to train the neural network. Hence, instead of deep neural networks, a GNN model is adopted to predict the classifiers. The GNN model is applied to the knowledge graph with the semantic embeddings of categories as input, and its output is the corresponding classifiers of these categories. In Wang et al. (2018b), a GCN-Filter was adopted as the graph filtering operation, and L graph filtering layers were stacked to refine the features (with the semantic embeddings as the initial features) before finally obtaining the classifiers. Specifically, the task can be modeled as a regression problem, where the classifiers $\{\mathbf{w}_1, \ldots, \mathbf{w}_m\}$ for the first m categories are served as the ground truth. In Wang et al. (2018b), the number of layers L is set to a relatively large number (e.g., six) such that distant information can be propagated through the knowledge graph. However, it is empirically shown that increasing the number of layers of GNNs may hurt the performance (Kampffmeyer et al., 2019). Hence, to propagate distant information without reducing the performance, a dense graph is constructed from the given knowledge graph. Any given node is connected to all of its ancestors in the knowledge graph. Two graph filtering layers are applied based on the constructed dense graph. In the first layer, information is only aggregated from descendants to ancestors, and in the second layer, information flows from ancestors to descendants.

11.4.2 Few-Shot Image Classification

In zero-shot learning, we aim to learn classifiers for unseen categories without any training samples. In the setting of few-shot learning image classification, we are given a set of n categories, among which the first m categories have sufficient training images and the remaining $n - m$ categories are with only k labeled images, where k is usually a very small number such as 3. Specifically, when $k = 0$, it can be treated as the the zero-shot image classification task. In this section, we specifically focus on the case where $k > 0$.

In few-shot image classification, because all categories have labeled images (either sufficient or not), classifiers can be learned for all categories. We denote the classifier learned for the ith category as $\mathbf{w}_i$. The classifiers $\{\mathbf{w}_1, \ldots, \mathbf{w}_m\}$ learned for those m categories with sufficient labeled training images are good and can be employed to perform predictions on unseen samples. However, the classifiers $\{\mathbf{w}_{m+1}, \ldots, \mathbf{w}_n\}$ for the $n - m$ categories with only k images may not be sufficient to perform reasonable predictions. Hence, the goal is to learn better classifiers for these $n - m$ categories.

An approach similar to that introduced in Subsection 11.4.1 can be used to refine the classifiers $\{\mathbf{w}_{m+1}, \ldots, \mathbf{w}_n\}$. Specifically, these learned classifiers $\{\mathbf{w}_{m+1}, \ldots, \mathbf{w}_n\}$ can be used as the input of a GNN model to produce the refined classifiers. The GNN model can be trained on those categories with sufficient labels (Gidaris and Komodakis, 2019). In particular, to mimic the process of refining less well-trained classifiers to generate well-trained classifiers, for each of the categories with sufficient training samples, we can sample k training samples to form a "fake" training set, which simulates the setting of those categories with only k labeled samples. Then, a set of classifiers $\{\hat{\mathbf{w}}_1, \ldots, \hat{\mathbf{w}}_m\}$ can be learned from the fake training sets. These fake classifiers $\{\hat{\mathbf{w}}_1, \ldots, \hat{\mathbf{w}}_m\}$ and the ones learned with sufficient training samples $\{\mathbf{w}_1, \ldots, \mathbf{w}_m\}$ can be used as training data to train the GNN model. Specifically, the GNN model is similar to the one introduced in Subsection 11.4.1, where the difference is that, instead of using word embedding as input, the model now takes the fake classifiers as input. After training, the GNN model can be utilized to refine the classifiers $\{\mathbf{w}_{m+1}, \ldots, \mathbf{w}_n\}$ for those categories with k training samples. As mentioned in Subsection 11.4.1, knowledge graphs describing the relations between the categories can be used as the graphs, to which the GNN model is applied. In Gidaris and Komodakis (2019), the graph between the categories is built upon the similarity between the classifiers before refining.

11.4.3 Multilabel Image Classification

Given an image, the task of multilabel image classification is to predict a set of objects that are presented in the given image. A simple way is to treat this problem as a set of binary classification problems. Each binary classifier predicts whether a certain object is presented in the image or not. However, in the physical world, certain objects frequently occur together. For example, *tennis ball* and *tennis racket* frequently co-occur. Capturing the dependencies between the objects is key to the success of multilabel image classification model. In Chen et al. (2019c), a graph describing the relations between the objects is learned from the training set, and a GNN model is applied to this graph to learn interdependent classifiers. These classifiers predict whether objects are presented in a given image or not. As described in Subsection 11.4.1, the classifiers are denoted by vectors $\mathbf{w}_i$.

Given an image I, the goal of multilabel image classification is to predict which objects from a candidate set $C = \{c_1, \ldots, c_K\}$ are presented in the given image. Hence, a set of K binary classifiers needs to be learned to perform the task, which can be denoted as $\{\mathbf{w}_1, \ldots, \mathbf{w}_K\}$, with $\mathbf{w}_i \in \mathbb{R}^d$. The dimension d of the classifiers is defined by the image representation $\mathbf{x}_I \in \mathbb{R}^d$, which can be extracted by some pretrained convolutional neural networks. To learn the object classifiers, which can capture the interdependencies between the objects, a GNN model is applied to a graph $\mathcal{G}$ that describes the relations between the objects. In Chen et al. (2019c), the graph $\mathcal{G}$ consists of the objects as nodes and the connections between them are built according to their co-occurrence in the training data. Specifically, we first count the co-occurrence (i.e., appearing in the same image) of any pair of objects in the training set and get a matrix $\mathbf{M} \in \mathbb{R}^{K \times K}$, where $\mathbf{M}_{i,j}$ denotes the count of co-occurrence of the ith and jth objects. Then, each row of this matrix is normalized as

$$\mathbf{P}_i = \mathbf{M}_i / N_i,$$

where $\mathbf{P}_i$, $\mathbf{M}_i$ denote the ith row of matrices $\mathbf{P}$, $\mathbf{M}$, respectively, and N_i is the occurrence of the ith object. To sparsify the matrix $\mathbf{P}$, we further use a threshold τ to filter the noisy edges as

$$A_{i,j} = \begin{cases} 0, & \text{if } P_{i,j} < \tau; \\ 1, & \text{if } P_{i,j} \geq \tau. \end{cases}$$

The matrix $\mathbf{A}$ can be regarded as the adjacency matrix of the built graph. Once the graph is constructed, the GNN model can be applied to learn the classifiers for different objects. Specifically, the classifiers for the objects are the output of the GNN model, where the input is the word embeddings for these objects. After obtaining the classifiers $\{\mathbf{w}_1, \ldots, \mathbf{w}_K\}$, the classification can be done by mapping the image representation $\mathbf{x}_I$ to a score $\mathbf{w}_i^T \mathbf{x}_I$ that can be utilized for binary classification for each object c_i. Note that the entire process is end to end with the image as input and the prediction as output.

11.5 Point Cloud Learning

Point clouds provide flexible geometric representations for 3D shapes and objects. More formally, a point cloud consists of a set of points $\{v_1, \ldots, v_n\}$ where each point contains 3D geometric coordinates $v_i = (x_i, y_i, z_i)$ representing geometric locations. A point cloud can usually represent a 3D object or shape. Like graphs, the point clouds are irregular because the points in the set are not ordered or well structured. Hence, it is not straightforward to apply classical deep learning techniques such as CNNs for point cloud learning. The topological information in the cloud points is implicitly represented by the distance between the points. To capture the local topology in a cloud point, a graph is built based on the distance between the set of points in the point cloud (Wang et al., 2019k). Specifically, k-nearest neighbors of each point v_i are considered as its neighbors in the built graph. Then, graph filtering operations are utilized to learn the representations for the points, which can be utilized for downstream tasks. Similar to graphs, there are two types of tasks on point clouds: point-focused tasks such as segmentation, which aims to assign a label for each point, and cloud-focused tasks such as classification, which is to assign a label for the entire point cloud. For the cloud-focused task, pooling methods are required to learn a representation from the point representations for the entire point cloud. Next, we describe the graph filtering operation introduced in Wang et al. (2019k). For a single point v_i, the process can be expressed as

$$\mathbf{F}_i^{(l)} = \text{AGGREGATE}\left(\left\{h_{\Theta^{(l-1)}}(\mathbf{F}_i^{(l-1)}, \mathbf{F}_j^{(l-1)}) \mid v_j \in \mathcal{N}^{(l-1)}(v_i)\right\}\right), \quad (11.10)$$

where AGGREGATE() is an aggregation function such as summation or a maximum as introduced in the GraphSAGE-Filter (see Subsection 5.3.2 for details of GraphSAGE-Filter), the function $h_{\Theta^{(l-1)}}()$ parameterized by $\Theta^{(l)}$ is to calculate the edge information to be aggregated. Various $h_{\Theta^{(l-1)}}()$ functions can be adopted and some examples are listed below:

$$h_{\Theta^{(l-1)}}(\mathbf{F}_i^{(l-1)}, \mathbf{F}_j^{(l-1)}) = \alpha(\mathbf{F}_j^{(l-1)}\Theta^{(l-1)}), \quad (11.11)$$

$$h_{\Theta^{(l-1)}}(\mathbf{F}_i^{(l-1)}, \mathbf{F}_j^{(l-1)}) = \alpha\left(\left(\mathbf{F}_j^{(l-1)} - \mathbf{F}_i^{(l-1)}\right)\Theta^{(l-1)}\right), \quad (11.12)$$

where $\alpha()$ denotes a nonlinear activation function. Note that in Eq. (11.10), $\mathcal{N}^{(l-1)}(v_i)$ denotes the set of neighbors of v_i, which is the k-nearest neighbors (including node v_i itself) calculated based on the output features $\mathbf{F}^{(l-1)}$ from the previous layer. Specifically, $\mathcal{N}^{(0)}(v_i)$ is calculated based on $\mathbf{F}^{(0)}$, which are the associated coordinates of the points. Hence, during training, the graph is evolving as the node features are updated.

11.6 Conclusion

This chapter introduces GNN models in various computer vision tasks, including visual question answering, skeleton-based human action recognition, zero-shot image recognition, few-shot image recognition, multi-label image recognition, and point cloud learning. For each task, we briefly introduce the task and describe why and how GNNs can improve its performance with representative algorithms.

11.7 Further Reading

In addition to the computer vision tasks we introduced in this chapter, GNNs have been adopted to enhance many other tasks in computer vision. In Ling et al. (2019), graph neural networks are utilized to annotate objects from given images. Graph neural networks are adopted to deal with scene graphs and improve the performance of many tasks related to scene graphs, including scene graph generation (Chen et al., 2019a; Khademi and Schulte, 2020) and scene graph–based image captioning (Yang et al., 2019).

12

Graph Neural Networks in Data Mining

12.1 Introduction

Data mining aims to extract patterns and knowledge from large amounts of data (Han et al., 2011). Data from many real-world applications can be inherently represented as graphs. On the Web, relations among social media users such as friendships on Facebook and following relations on Twitter can be denoted as social graphs, and the historical interactions between e-commerce users and items can be modeled as a bipartite graph, with the users and items as the two sets of nodes and their interactions as edges. Roads or road sections in urban areas are often dependent on each other due to spatial relations between them. These spatial relations can be represented by a traffic network where nodes are roads or road sections and edges indicate the spatial relations. Therefore, graph neural networks (GNNs) have been naturally applied to facilitate various tasks of data mining. In this chapter, we illustrate how GNNs can be adopted for representative data mining tasks, including web data mining, urban data mining, and cybersecurity data mining.

12.2 Web Data Mining

Numerous Web-based applications, such as social media and e-commerce, have produced a massive volume of data. Web data mining is the application of data mining techniques to discover patterns from such data. This section demonstrates how GNNs advance two representative tasks of Web data mining; i.e., social network analysis and recommender systems.

12.2.1 Social Network Analysis

Social networks, which characterize relationships and/or interactions between users, are ubiquitous on the Web, especially social media. Social networks can be naturally modeled as graphs where users in the networks are the nodes and the relationships and/or interactions are the edges. GNNs have been adopted to facilitate various tasks on social networks such as social influence prediction (Qiu et al., 2018a), political perspective detection (Li and Goldwasser, 2019), and social representation learning (Wang et al., 2019a). Next, we detail some of these tasks.

Social Influence Prediction

In social networks, a person's emotions, opinions, behaviors, and decisions are affected by others. This phenomenon, which is usually referred to as social influence, is widely observed in various physical and/or online social networks. Investigating social influence is important for optimizing advertisement strategies and performing personalized recommendations. In Qiu et al. (2018a), GNNs were adopted to predict local social influence for users on social networks. More specifically, given the local neighborhood of a user and the actions of users in the neighborhood, the goal is to predict whether the user will take the actions in the future or not. For example, on the Twitter platform, the prediction task can be whether a user would retweet posts (the action) on a certain topic given the action status (whether retweet or not) of other closed users (local neighborhood).

The relations between users on a social network can be modeled as a graph $G = \{V, \mathcal{E}\}$, where V denotes the set of users on the social network and $\mathcal{E}$ denotes the relations between the users. For a node $v_i \in V$, its local neighborhood is defined as its r-ego network $G_{v_i}^r$ (Qiu et al., 2018a), which is a subgraph of G containing all nodes that are within an r-hop away from the node v_i. Formally, the node set $V_{v_i}^r$ and the edge set $\mathcal{E}_{v_i}^r$ for the r-ego network $G_{v_i}^r$ can be defined as

$$V_{v_i}^r = \left\{ v_j \in V \mid \mathrm{dis}(v_i, v_j) \leq r \right\},$$
$$\mathcal{E}_{v_i}^r = \left\{ (v_j, v_k) \in \mathcal{E} \mid v_j, v_k \in V_{v_i}^r \right\},$$

where $\mathrm{dis}(v_i, v_j)$ denotes the length of the shortest path between nodes v_i and v_j. Furthermore, for each node $v_j \in V_{v_i}^r / \{v_i\}$, there is an associated binary action state $s_j \in \{0, 1\}$. For example, in the case of Twitter, the action state $s_j = 1$ if the user v_j retweeted posts on a certain topic; otherwise, $s_j = 0$. The action statuses for all nodes in $v_j \in V_{v_i}^r / \{v_i\}$ can be summarized as $S_{v_i}^r = \left\{ s_j \mid v_j \in V_{v_i}^r / \{v_i\} \right\}$.

The goal of social influence prediction is to predict the action status of node v_i given $\mathcal{G}^r_{v_i}$ and $\mathcal{S}^r_{v_i}$, which is modeled as a binary classification problem.

To predict the action status s_i for node v_i, GNN models are applied to the ego network to learn the node representation for node v_i, which is then utilized to perform the classification. Specifically, the GCN-Filter and the GAT-Filter (see Subsection 5.3.2 for details on the GCN-Filter and GAT-Filter) were adopted as graph filters to build the GNNs in Qiu et al. (2018a). The following features shown in Eq. (12.1) are utilized as the initial input for the GNN models.

$$\mathbf{F}^{(0)}_j = [\mathbf{x}_j, \mathbf{e}_j, s_j, ind_j], v_j \in \mathcal{V}^r_{v_i}. \tag{12.1}$$

In Eq. (12.1), $\mathbf{x}_j$ denotes the pretrained embedding for node v_j learned by methods such as DeepWalk or LINE (see Subsection 4.2.1 for details on DeepWalk and LINE) over graph $\mathcal{G}$. The instance normalization trick, which normalizes the embeddings for nodes in $\mathcal{V}^r_{v_i}$, was adopted by Qiu et al. (2018a) to improve the performance of the model. The vector $\mathbf{e}_j$ contains other node features such as structural features, content features, and demographic features if available. For node v_j, s_j is initialized to be 0 because its action status is unknown. The last element $ind_j \in \{0, 1\}$ is a binary variable indicating whether a node v_j is the ego user; i.e., $ind_j = 1$ only if $v_j = v_i$ and 0 otherwise.

Social Representation Learning

With the rapid development of social media such as Facebook, a greater number of services have been provided to users on social networks. For example, users can express their preferences for various movies, sports, and books on Facebook. The availability of these different types of social network services leads to different categories of user behaviors. Users may have similar preferences in one category of behaviors but quite different preferences in other categories of behaviors. For example, two users may like the same kind of movies, but they like very different types of sports. To capture users' preference similarities in different categories of behaviors, multiple vectors are utilized to represent each user, where each vector corresponds to a specific category of behaviors (Wang et al., 2019a). In detail, for each user, these representations for different behaviors are conditioned on a general representation for this user. To learn these user representations, a GNN model is adapted to capture various preference similarities between users in different categories of behaviors (Wang et al., 2019a). Next, we formally describe the problem setting and then introduce the GNN model developed to learn conditional representations.

A social network can be modeled as a graph $\mathcal{G} = \{\mathcal{V}, \mathcal{E}\}$, where $\mathcal{V} = \{v_1, \ldots, v_N\}$ represents the set of nodes (social users) and $\mathcal{E}$ denotes the edges (social relations) connecting them. These relations between users can also be represented by the adjacency matrix of the graph $\mathbf{A}$. Furthermore, the users have interactions with items such as movies, books, and sports, which are organized in different categories. Specifically, the set of items for a category c (e.g., books) is denoted as $\mathcal{I}_c$ and the interactions between the users and these items are described by an interaction matrix $\mathbf{R}^c$, where $\mathbf{R}^c_{i,j} = 1$ only when the user v_i has interacted with the jth item in the category c and 0 otherwise. The goal of conditional representation learning is to learn a set of representations for each user v_j, where each conditional representation for a specific category c can capture the social structure information in $\mathbf{A}$ and also preference in category c described in $\mathbf{R}^c$. The representation learning framework is designed based on the message passing neural network (MPNN) framework introduced in Subsection 5.3.2. Its message function $M()$ and the update function $U()$ (for the lth layer) are described as follows. The message function $M()$ in the MPNN framework generates a message to pass to the center node v_i from its neighbor v_j. To capture various similarities between nodes v_i and v_j in different categories, the representations of these nodes are mapped to different categories as

$$\mathbf{F}^{(l-1)}_{j|c} = \mathbf{F}^{(l-1)}_j \odot \mathbf{b}^{(l-1)}_c,$$

where $\mathbf{b}^{(l-1)}_c$ is a learnable binary mask shared by all nodes to map the input representation $\mathbf{F}^{(l-1)}_j$ to the conditional representation $\mathbf{F}^{(l-1)}_{j|c}$ for category c. Then, the message from node v_j to node v_i is generated as

$$\mathbf{F}^{(l-1)}_{v_j \to v_i} = M(\mathbf{F}^{(l-1)}_i, \mathbf{F}^{(l-1)}_j) = \sum_{c=1}^{C} \alpha^{(l-1)}_{i,j|c} \cdot \mathbf{F}^{(l-1)}_{j|c},$$

where C denotes the number of categories and $\alpha^{(l-1)}_{i,j|c}$ is the attention score learned as

$$e^{(l-1)}_{i,j|c} = \mathbf{h}^{(l-1)^{\top}} \mathrm{ReLU}\left(\left[\mathbf{F}^{(l-1)}_{i|c}, \mathbf{F}^{(l-1)}_{j|c}\right] \Theta^{(l-1)}_a\right),$$

$$\alpha^{(l-1)}_{i,j|c} = \frac{\exp\left\{e^{(l-1)}_{i,j|c}\right\}}{\sum_{c=1}^{C} \exp\left\{e^{(l-1)}_{i,j|c}\right\}},$$

where $\mathbf{h}^{(l-1)}$ and $\Theta^{(l-1)}_a$ are parameters to be learned. The attention mechanism is utilized to ensure that more similar behaviors between users will contribute more when generating the message. After generating the messages, the representation for node v_i is updated with the update function as

$$\mathbf{m}_i^{(l-1)} = \sum_{v_j \in \mathcal{N}(v_i)} \mathbf{F}_{v_j \to v_i}^{(l-1)}, \tag{12.2}$$

$$\mathbf{F}^{(l)} = U(\mathbf{F}_i^{(l-1)}, \mathbf{m}_i^{(l-1)}) = \alpha\left(\left[\mathbf{F}_i^{(l-1)}, \mathbf{m}_i^{(l-1)}\right]\mathbf{\Theta}_u^{(l-1)}\right), \tag{12.3}$$

where $\mathbf{\Theta}_u^{(l-1)}$ are the parameters for the update function and $\alpha()$ denotes some activation functions. Note that, after stacking L layers of the above MPNN filtering operations, the final representations $\mathbf{F}_i^L$ can be obtained, which are then mapped to the conditional representation $\mathbf{F}_{i|c}^L$. The final conditional representation $\mathbf{F}_{i|c}^L$ is utilized to recover the interaction information $\mathbf{R}^c$, which serves as the training objective of the framework. Hence, the learned conditional representations capture both the social structure information and the user–item interaction information for a specific category.

12.2.2 Recommender Systems

Recommender systems have been widely applied to many online services such as e-commerce, video/music streaming services, and social media to alleviate the problem of information overload. Collaborative filtering (Goldberg et al., 1992; Resnick and Varian, 1997; Goldberg et al., 2001), which utilizes users' historical behavior data to predict their preferences, is one of the most important techniques for developing recommender systems. A key assumption of the collaborative filtering technique is that users with similar historical behaviors have similar preferences. Collaborative filtering approaches usually encode such information into vector representations of users and items, which can reconstruct the historical interactions (Koren et al., 2009; Wang et al., 2019h). When learning these representations, the historical interactions are usually not explicitly utilized but only serve as the ground truth for the reconstruction. These historical interactions between users and items can be modeled as a bipartite graph $\mathcal{G} = \{\mathcal{U} \cup \mathcal{V}, \mathcal{E}\}$. Specifically, the set of users can be denoted as $\mathcal{U} = \{u_1, \ldots, u_{N_u}\}$, the set of items can be indicated as $\mathcal{V} = \{v_1, \ldots, v_{N_v}\}$, and the interactions between them can be represented as $\mathcal{E} = \{e_1, \ldots, e_{N_e}\}$, where $e_i = (u_{(i)}, v_{(i)})$ with $u_{(i)} \in \mathcal{U}$ and $v_{(i)} \in \mathcal{V}$. These interactions can also be described by an interaction matrix $\mathbf{M} \in \mathbb{R}^{N_u \times N_v}$, where the i, jth element of $\mathbf{M}$ indicates the interaction status between the user u_i and item v_j. Specifically, $\mathbf{M}_{i,j}$ can be the rating value that user u_i gave to item v_j. It can also be a binary value, with $\mathbf{M}_{i,j} = 1$ indicating that user u_i interacted with item v_j. With the bipartite graph, the historical interactions can be explicitly utilized to model the representations for users and items by adopting GNN models (Berg et al., 2017; Ying et al., 2018b; Wang et al., 2019h). Furthermore, side information about users and items such as social networks for users and knowledge graphs for items can be modeled in the form of graphs. It is also incorporated for learning the representations with GNN models (Wang et al., 2019b,c,g; Fan et al., 2019). Next, we introduce representative collaborative filtering methods based on GNN models.

Collaborative Filtering

Typically, a collaborative filtering approach can be viewed as an encoder–decoder model, where the encoder is to encode each user/item into vector representations and the decoder is to utilize these representations to reconstruct the historical interactions. Hence, the decoder is usually modeled as a regression task (when reconstructing rating) or a binary classification task (when reconstructing the existence of the interactions). Thus, we mainly introduce the encoder part designed based on GNN models. Spatial graph filtering operations are adopted to update the representations for users and items. Specifically, for a given user, its representation is updated utilizing the information from its neighbors; i.e., the items the user has interacted with. Similarly, for a given item, its representation is updated utilizing the information from its neighbors; i.e., the users that have interacted with it. Next, we describe the graph filtering process from the perspective of a given user u_i because the graph filtering process for items is similar. The graph filtering process (for the l-th layer) can be generally described using the MPNN framework as introduced in Subsection 5.3.2 as follows:

$$\mathbf{m}_i^{(l-1)} = \text{AGGREGATE}\left(\left\{M(\mathbf{u}_i^{(l-1)}, \mathbf{v}_j^{(l-1)}, \mathbf{e}_{(i,j)}) \mid v_j \in \mathcal{N}(u_i)\right\}\right), \quad (12.4)$$
$$\mathbf{u}_i^{(l)} = U(\mathbf{u}_i^{(l-1)}, \mathbf{m}_i^{(l-1)}),$$

where $\mathbf{u}_i^{(l-1)}, \mathbf{v}_j^{(l-1)}$ denote the input representations of user u_i and item v_j for the lth layer, $\mathbf{e}_{(i,j)}$ is the edge information (for example, rating information if it is available), $\mathcal{N}(u_i)$ indicates the neighbors of user u_i i.e., the items the user has interacted with–and AGGREGATE(), $M()$, $U()$ are the aggregation function, message function, and update function to be designed, respectively. In Berg et al. (2017), different aggregation functions are proposed and one example is summation. The message function is designed to incorporate discrete ratings information associated with the interaction as follows:

$$M\left(\mathbf{u}_i^{(l-1)}, \mathbf{v}_j^{(l-1)}\right) = \frac{1}{\sqrt{|\mathcal{N}(u_i)||\mathcal{N}(v_j)|}} \mathbf{v}_j^{(l-1)} \mathbf{\Theta}_{r(u_i,v_j)}^{(l-1)},$$

where $r(u_i, v_j)$ denotes the discrete rating (e.g., 1–5) the user u_i gave to item v_j and $\mathbf{\Theta}_{r(u_i,v_j)}^{(l-1)}$ is shared by all interactions with this rating. The update function is implemented as

$$U(\mathbf{u}_i^{(l-1)}, \mathbf{m}_i^{(l-1)}) = \text{ReLU}(\mathbf{m}_i^{(l-1)}\Theta_{up}^{(l-1)}),$$

where $\Theta_{up}^{(l-1)}$ is the parameter to be learned.

In Wang et al. (2019h), summation was adopted as the AGGREGATE() function and the message function and the update function are implemented as

$$M\left(\mathbf{u}_i^{(l-1)}, \mathbf{v}_j^{(l-1)}\right) = \frac{1}{\sqrt{|\mathcal{N}(u_i)\|\mathcal{N}(v_j)|}}\left(\mathbf{v}_j^{(l-1)}\Theta_1^{(l-1)} + (\mathbf{u}_i^{(l-1)}\Theta_2^{(l-1)} \odot \mathbf{v}_j^{(l-1)})\right),$$

$$U(\mathbf{u}_i^{(l-1)}, \mathbf{m}_i^{(l-1)}) = \text{LeakyReLU}\left(\mathbf{u}_i^{(l-1)}\Theta_3^{(l-1)} + \mathbf{m}_i^{(l-1)}\right),$$

where $\Theta_1^{(l-1)}$, $\Theta_2^{(l-1)}$, and $\Theta_3^{(l-1)}$ are the parameters to be learned.

Collaborative Filtering with Side Information for Items

Knowledge graphs, which describe the relations between items, are utilized as another resource of information in addition to the historical interactions. GNN models have been adopted to incorporate the information encoded in knowledge graphs while learning representations for items (Wang et al., 2019c,b,g). Specifically, a knowledge graph with the set of items $\mathcal{V}$ as entities can be denoted as $\mathcal{G}_k = \{\mathcal{V}, \mathcal{E}_k, \mathcal{R}\}$, where $\mathcal{R}$ denotes the set of relations in the knowledge graph and each relational edge $e \in \mathcal{E}_k$ can be denoted as $e = (v_i, r, v_j)$ with $r \in \mathcal{R}$. For an item v_i, its connected items in the knowledge graph provide another resource to aggregate information. To aggregate the information while differentiating the importance of various relations, an attention mechanism is adopted. Specifically, in Wang et al. (2019g), the attention score α_{irj} for a relation (v_i, r, v_j) was calculated following the idea of the knowledge graph embedding method TransR (Lin et al., 2015) as

$$\pi(v_i, r, v_j) = \left(\mathbf{v}_j^{(0)}\Theta_r^{(l-1)}\right)^{\top} \tanh\left(\mathbf{v}_i^{(0)}\Theta_r^{(l-1)} + \mathbf{e}_r\right),$$

$$\alpha_{irj} = \frac{\exp(\pi(v_i, r, v_j))}{\sum\limits_{(r,v_j)\in\mathcal{N}^k(v_i)} \exp(\pi(v_i, r, v_j))},$$

where $\mathbf{v}_i^{(0)}, \mathbf{e}_r$, and $\Theta_r^{(l-1)}$ are the entity embedding, relation embedding, and the transformation matrix learned from TransR (Lin et al., 2015), and $\mathcal{N}^k(v_i)$ denotes the neighbors of v_i in the knowledge graph $\mathcal{G}_k$. The graph filtering process to update the representation for an item v_i (for the lth layer) is

$$\mathbf{m}_i^{(l-1)} = \sum\limits_{(r,v_j)\in\mathcal{N}^k(v_i)} \alpha_{irj}\mathbf{v}_j^{(l-1)},$$

$$\mathbf{v}_i^{(l)} = U(\mathbf{v}_i^{(l-1)}, \mathbf{m}_i^{(l-1)}) = \text{LeakyReLU}([\mathbf{v}_i^{(l-1)}, \mathbf{m}_i^{(l-1)}]\Theta_{up}^{(l-1)}), \qquad (12.5)$$

where $U()$ is the update function and $\Theta_{up}^{(l-1)}$ is the parameter to be learned. The embeddings $\mathbf{v}_i^{(0)}$ learned from TransR serve as the input for the first layer. Note that the entity embeddings, relation embeddings, and transformation matrix learned from TransR are fixed during the propagation described by Eq. (12.5). Hence, the attention score α_{irj} is shared in different graph filter layers. Furthermore, the interactions between users and items are incorporated into the knowledge graph as a special relation *interaction* (Wang et al., 2019g). Specifically, each $e_i = (u_{(i)}, v_{(i)}) \in \mathcal{E}$ is transformed to a relational edge $(u_{(i)}, r, v_{(i)})$ with $r = interaction$. Hence, both the user representations and the item representations can be updated utilizing Eq. (12.5).

On the other hand, in Wang et al. (2019b,c), the attention score was designed to be personalized for each user. In particular, when considering the impact from one entity v_j on another entity v_i, the user we want to recommend items to should also be considered. For example, when recommending movies to users, some users may prefer movies from certain directors and others might prefer to movies acted by certain actors. Hence, when learning item embeddings specifically for performing recommending items to a user u_k, the attention score for aggregation can be modeled as

$$\pi(v_i, r, v_j | u_k) = \mathbf{u}_k^T \mathbf{e}_r,$$

where $\mathbf{u}_k$ and $\mathbf{e}_r$ are the user embedding and the relation embedding, respectively. Specifically, this process can be regarded as inducing a knowledge graph for each user. Note that in Wang et al. (2019b,c), only the knowledge graph was explicitly utilized for learning representations, and the historical interactions only served as the ground truth for the reconstruction. Hence, the user representation $\mathbf{u}_k$ is just randomly initialized as that in matrix factorization (Koren et al., 2009).

Collaborative Filtering with Side Information for Users

Social networks, which encode the relations/interactions between users in $\mathcal{U}$, can serve as another resource of information besides the user–item interaction bipartite graph. The social network can be modeled as a graph $\mathcal{G}_s = \{\mathcal{U}, \mathcal{E}_s\}$, where $\mathcal{U}$ is the set of nodes (the users) and $\mathcal{E}_s$ is the set of edges describing the social relations between the users. In Fan et al. (2019), GNN models were adopted to learn representations for users and items utilizing both information. Specifically, the items' representations are updated by aggregating information from neighboring nodes (i.e., the users that have interacted with the item) in the interaction bipartite graph $\mathcal{G}$ similar to the GNN models with pure collaborative filtering introduced in the previous sections. For users, the information from the two resources (i.e., the user–item interaction bipartite graph $\mathcal{G}$ and the social network $\mathcal{G}_s$) are combined to generate the user representations as

$$\mathbf{u}_i^{(l)} = \left[\mathbf{u}_{i,\mathcal{I}}^{(l)}, \mathbf{u}_{i,S}^{(l)}\right]\boldsymbol{\Theta}_c^{(l-1)},$$

where $\mathbf{u}_{i,\mathcal{I}}^{(l)}$ denotes the representation for user u_i learned by aggregating information from the neighboring items in the interaction bipartite graph, and $\mathbf{u}_{i,S}^{(l)}$ indicates its representation learned by aggregating information from neighboring users in the social network. $\boldsymbol{\Theta}_c^{(l-1)}$ is the parameters to be learned. Specifically, $\mathbf{u}_{i,S}^{(l)}$ is updated with the parameter $\boldsymbol{\Theta}_S^{(l-1)}$ as

$$\mathbf{u}_{i,S}^{(l)} = \sigma\left(\sum_{u_j \in \mathcal{N}^s(u_i)} \mathbf{u}_j^{(l-1)}\boldsymbol{\Theta}_S^{(l-1)}\right),$$

where $\mathcal{N}^s(u_i)$ is the set of neighboring users of user u_i in the social network. In addition, $\mathbf{u}_{i,\mathcal{I}}^{(l)}$ is generated with the parameter $\boldsymbol{\Theta}_\mathcal{I}^{(l-1)}$ as

$$\mathbf{u}_{i,\mathcal{I}}^{(l)} = \sigma\left(\sum_{v_j \in \mathcal{N}(u_i)} \left[\mathbf{v}_j^{(l-1)}, \mathbf{e}_{r(i,j)}\right]\boldsymbol{\Theta}_\mathcal{I}^{(l-1)}\right), \qquad (12.6)$$

where $\mathcal{N}(u_i)$ is the set of items that user u_i has interacted with and $\mathbf{e}_{r(i,j)}$ is the rating information. In Fan et al. (2019), the ratings were discrete scores and the rating information $\mathbf{e}_{r(i,j)}$ was modeled as embeddings to be learned.

12.3 Urban Data Mining

The development of sensing technologies and computing infrastructures has enabled us to collect large volumes of data in urban areas such as data on air quality, traffic, and human mobility. Mining such urban data provides us with unprecedented opportunities to tackle various challenging problems introduced by urbanization, such as traffic congestion and air pollution. Next, we demonstrate how GNNs can advance urban data mining tasks.

12.3.1 Traffic Prediction

Analyzing and forecasting the dynamic traffic conditions are of great significance to the planning and construction of new roads and transportation management of smart cities in the new era. In traffic studies, traffic flow data can be usually treated as time series. It consists of traffic flow information such as traffic speed, volume, and density at multiple timesteps. In addition,

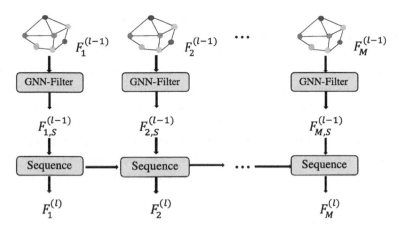

Figure 12.1 A learning layer in a typical framework for traffic prediction.

roads or road sections are not independent of each other because there exist spatial relations between them. These spatial relations between roads are typically represented by a traffic network, where roads or road sections are the nodes and spatial relations are encoded by the edges between them. To achieve better performance for traffic forecasting, it is desired to capture both the spatial and temporal information. GNN models are adopted for spatial relations, and temporal information is captured by sequential modeling methods such as convolutional neural networks, recurrent neural networks, and transformers (Yu et al., 2017; Guo et al., 2019; Wang et al., 2020a). Next, we describe how GNNs can capture spatial relations and be incorporated with sequential modeling methods for both the spatial and temporal information.

The traffic network can be denoted as a graph $\mathcal{G} = \{\mathcal{V}, \mathcal{E}\}$, where $\mathcal{V} = \{v_1, \ldots, v_N\}$ is the set of nodes (roads or road sections), with N the number of nodes in the traffic network and $\mathcal{E}$ the set of edges describing the spatial relations between nodes. The connections between the nodes can also be described by an adjacency matrix $\mathbf{A}$. The traffic status information such as traffic speed in the traffic network at a specific time t can be represented at a vector $\mathbf{x}_t \in \mathbb{R}^{N \times d}$, where the ith row of $\mathbf{x}_t$ corresponds to node v_i in the traffic network. The task of traffic forecasting is to predict the traffic status for the next H timesteps given the observations from the previous M timesteps. Specifically, it can be expressed as

$$(\hat{\mathbf{X}}_{M+1}, \ldots, \hat{\mathbf{X}}_{M+H}) = f(\mathbf{X}_1, \ldots, \mathbf{X}_M), \tag{12.7}$$

where $f()$ is the model to be learned and $\hat{\mathbf{X}}_t$ denotes the predicted traffic status at time step t. A typical framework to tackle this problem is first to learn refined node representations at each timestep by capturing both spatial and temporal information and then utilize node representations to perform predictions for the future timesteps. These representations are refined layer by layer where each learning layer updates the representations by capturing both spatial and temporal relations. The lth learning layer is shown in Figure 12.1, which consists of two components: (1) the spatial graph filtering operation to capture the spatial relations and (2) the sequence model to capture the temporal relations. The spatial graph filtering operation is applied to node representations in each timestep as follows:

$$\mathbf{F}_{t,S}^{(l)} = \text{GNN-Filter}(\mathbf{F}_t^{(l-1)}, \mathbf{A}), t = 1, \dots, M, \tag{12.8}$$

where $\mathbf{F}_t^{(l-1)}$ are the node representations at timestep t after the $(l-1)$st learning layer and $\mathbf{F}_{t,S}^{(l)}$ denotes the node representations after the lth spatial graph filtering layer, which serves as the input for the lth sequence model. Note that the GNN-Filter is shared by all timesteps. Different graph filtering operations can be adopted. For example, in Yu et al. (2017), the GCN-Filter (see details on the GCN-Filter in Subsection 5.3.2) was adopted, and in Guo et al. (2019) and Wang et al. (2020a), an attention mechanism is utilized to enhance the graph filtering operation. The output of the spatial graph filtering operation is a sequence–i.e., $(\mathbf{F}_{1,S}^{(l)}, \dots, \mathbf{F}_{M,S}^{(l)})$–which will be fed into a sequence model to capture the temporal relations as

$$\mathbf{F}_1^{(l)}, \dots, \mathbf{F}_M^{(l)} = \text{Sequence}(\mathbf{F}_{1,S}^{(l)}, \dots, \mathbf{F}_{M,S}^{(l)}), \tag{12.9}$$

where the output $\mathbf{F}_1^{(l)}, \dots, \mathbf{F}_M^{(l)}$ will in turn serve as the input to the next spatial graph filtering layer. Various sequence modeling methods can be adopted as the Sequence() function. For example, in Yu et al. (2017), 1D convolutional neural networks were adopted to deal with the temporal information. GRU model and the transformer were adopted in Wang et al. (2020a) to capture the temporal relations. The final representations $\mathbf{F}_1^{(L)}, \dots, \mathbf{F}_M^{(L)}$ are obtained by applying L learning layers as described above and then utilized to predict the traffic status in the future. Note that $\mathbf{F}_1^{(0)}, \dots, \mathbf{F}_M^{(0)}$ can be initialized with node information such as traffic status $\mathbf{X}_1, \dots, \mathbf{X}_M$.

12.3.2 Air Quality Forecasting

Air pollution has raised public concerns due to its adverse effects on the natural environment and human health. Hence, it is important to forecast air quality to provide public guidance for people affected by this issue. The air quality forecasting problem can be formulated in spatial–temporal form because the air quality in nearby locations is related, and the air quality in one location is temporally evolving. The spatial relations between different locations can be denoted as a graph $\mathcal{G} = \{\mathcal{V}, \mathcal{E}\}$, where the locations are the nodes and the edges describe the geographic relations between nodes. The air quality status includes different indices such as $PM_{2.5}$, PM_{10}, NO_2, SO_2, O_3, and CO. The air quality status measured at time t for all locations in $\mathcal{V}$ is denoted as $\mathbf{X}_t$, where the ith row of $\mathbf{X}_t$ corresponds to the air quality status of location $v_i \in \mathcal{V}$. In the task of air quality forecasting, we aim to predict air quality status for all locations in a future time slot given the historical status. Generally, we denote the air quality status we plan to predict at time t as $\mathbf{Y}_t$, where the ith row corresponds to the ith location v_i. Then, the air quality forecasting problem can be formulated as

$$(\mathbf{Y}_{M+1}, \ldots, \mathbf{Y}_{M+H}) = f(\mathbf{X}_1, \ldots, \mathbf{X}_M), \qquad (12.10)$$

where $(\mathbf{X}_1, \ldots, \mathbf{X}_M)$ is the observed air quality status from the previous M steps and $(\mathbf{Y}_{M+1}, \ldots, \mathbf{Y}_{M+H})$ is the air quality status we aim to forecast in the next H steps. The framework introduced in Subsection 12.3.1 can be used to forecast air quality. In Qi et al. (2019) where the goal is to predict only $PM_{2.5}$, a GCN-Filter was utilized to capture the spatial relations between different locations and a long short-term memory model is adopted to capture the temporal relations.

12.4 Cybersecurity Data Mining

With the growing use of the Internet, new vulnerabilities and attack schemes are discovered every day for computer and communication systems. These changes and dynamics have posed tremendous challenges to traditional security approaches. Data mining can discover actionable patterns from data and thus it has been employed to tackle these cybersecurity challenges. Given that cybersecurity data can be denoted as graphs, GNNs have facilitated various aspects of cybersecurity data such as spammer detection and fake news detection.

12.4.1 Malicious Account Detection

Cyber attackers aim to attack large-scale online services such as email systems, online social networks, e-commerce, and e-finance platforms by creating malicious accounts and propagating spamming messages. These attacks are harmful to these online services and could even cause a huge financial loss in certain circumstances. Hence, it is important to detect these malicious accounts effectively. GNN models have been utilized to facilitate the task of malicious account detection. In Liu et al. (2018b), two patterns for malicious accounts were observed. First, malicious accounts from the same attacker tend to sign up or log in to the same device or a common set of devices because of the attacker's limited resources. Second, malicious accounts from the same group tend to behave in batches; i.e., they sign up or log in in a burst of time. A graph between accounts and devices is built based on these two observations, and the malicious account detection task is treated as a binary semisupervised classification task on this graph, where the goal is to tell whether an account is malicious or not. Next, we first describe the graph construction process and then discuss how GNN models can be leveraged for malicious account detection.

Graph Construction

There are two types of objects involving in this task: accounts and devices. The concept of "device" can be very general, including IP addresses or phone numbers. We denote the set of types of devices as $\mathcal{D}$. Assume that there are N nodes, including accounts and devices. An edge is observed between an account and a device if an account has activities (e.g., signups and logins) in this specific device. This constructed graph can be denoted as $\mathcal{G} = \{\mathcal{V}, \mathcal{E}\}$, where $\mathcal{V}$ and $\mathcal{E}$ are the node and edge sets, respectively. The relations between these nodes in $\mathcal{V}$ can also be described by an adjacency matrix $\mathbf{A}$. $|\mathcal{D}|$ subgraphs $\{\mathcal{G}^{(d)} = \{\mathcal{V}, \mathcal{E}^{(d)}\}\}$ are extracted from the graph $\mathcal{G}$, where $\mathcal{G}^{(d)}$ is the subgraph consisting of all nodes but only edges involving type $d \in \mathcal{D}$ devices. We use $\mathbf{A}^{(d)}$ to denote the adjacency matrix of the subgraph $\mathcal{G}^{(d)}$. A feature vector $\mathbf{x}_i \in \mathbb{R}^{p+|\mathcal{D}|}$ is associated with each node $v_i \in \mathcal{V}$. Specifically, the first p elements in $\mathbf{x}_i$ denote the frequency of activities in p consecutive periods. For example, in Liu et al. (2018b), $p = 168$ and each time period is 1 hour. The last $|\mathcal{D}|$ elements in $\mathbf{x_i}$ indicate the type of the device. If the node is a device, it is a 1-hot indicator of its type, and it is all 0 if it is an account.

Malicious Account Detection with Graph Neural Networks

GNNs are utilized to refine the node features, which are then leveraged to perform malicious account detection (or the binary classification). The formulation of the semisupervised classification task is the same as that in Subsection 5.5.1. Hence, we mainly introduce the process of learning node features. More specifically, we introduce a graph filter dedicated to this task as follows:

$$\mathbf{F}^{(l)} = \sigma\left(\mathbf{X}\mathbf{\Theta}^{(l-1)} + \frac{1}{|\mathcal{D}|}\sum_{d\in\mathcal{D}}\mathbf{A}^{(d)}\mathbf{F}^{(l-1)}\mathbf{\Theta}_{(d)}^{(l-1)}\right),$$

where $\mathbf{X}$ denotes the input features of all nodes, $\mathbf{F}^{(l)}$ is the hidden representations after the lth graph filtering layer with $\mathbf{F}^{(0)} = \mathbf{0}$, and $\{\mathbf{\Theta}^{(l-1)}, \mathbf{\Theta}_{(d)}^{(l-1)}\}$ are parameters to be learned. Note that the graph filtering operation differs from that introduced in Subsection 5.3.2, because it utilizes the input features $\mathbf{X}$ in each graph filtering layer. The goal is to ensure that the account activity patterns encoded by $\mathbf{X}$ can be better preserved. After L graph filtering layers, these features are used to perform the binary classification. Because the malicious accounts (from the same attacker) tend to connect with the same set of device nodes, the graph filtering process will enforce them to have similar features. Meanwhile, the activity patterns of the accounts are captured by the input feature $\mathbf{X}$. Thus, the two aforementioned patterns can be captured by GNN models, which benefits the task of malicious account detection.

12.4.2 Fake News Detection

Online social media has become a critical source for people to obtain news because of its easy access and instant dissemination. Though extremely convenient and efficient, these platforms also significantly increase the risk of propagating fake news. Fake news could lead to many negative consequences or even severe societal issues and substantial financial loss. Hence, it is vital to detect fake news and prevent it from propagating through social media. Substantial empirical evidence has shown that fake news has different propagation patterns from real news in online social media (Vosoughi et al., 2018), which can be utilized to facilitate the task of fake news detection. In Monti et al. (2019), each story was modeled as a graph that characterizes its diffusion process and social relations in the social network platform such as Twitter. Then, the task of fake news detection is treated as a binary graph classification task, and GNN models are adopted to improve its performance. Next, we describe the process to form the graphs for the stories and then briefly introduce the GNN model designed for this task.

Graph Construction

We take the news diffusion process on Twitter as an example to illustrate the process of graph construction for each story. Given a story u with its corresponding tweets $\mathcal{T}_u = \{t_u^{(1)}, \ldots, t_u^{(N_u)}\}$ that mention u, the story u is described by a graph $\mathcal{G}_u$. The graph $\mathcal{G}_u$ consists of all of the tweets in $\mathcal{T}_u$

as nodes, and the edges either describe the news diffusion process or the social relations between the authors of these tweets. We next describe the two types of edges in this graph $\mathcal{G}_u$. We use $a(t_u^{(i)})$ to denote the author of a given tweet $t_u^{(i)}$. The first type of edge between the tweets is defined based on their authors; i.e., an edge exists between two tweets $t_u^{(i)}$ and $t_u^{(j)}$ if $a(t_u^{(i)})$ follows $a(t_u^{(j)})$ or $a(t_u^{(j)})$ follows $a(t_u^{(i)})$. The second type of edge is based on the diffusion process of this news u through the social network; i.e., an edge exists between two tweets $t_u^{(i)}$ and $t_u^{(j)}$ if the news u spreads from one to the other. The news diffusion path is estimated via the method proposed in Vosoughi et al. (2018), which jointly considers the timestamps of the tweets and the social connections between their authors. For convenience, we assume that the superscript of a tweet $t_u^{(i)}$ indicates its time-stamp information; i.e., all tweets with superscripts smaller than i are created before $t_u^{(i)}$ and the ones with superscripts larger than i are created after $t_u^{(i)}$. Then, for a given tweet $t_u^{(i)}$, we estimate its spreading path as follows:

- If $a(t_u^{(i)})$ follows at least one author of the previous tweets $\{a(t_u^{(1)}), \ldots, a(t_u^{(i-1)})\}$, we estimate that the news spreads to $t_u^{(i)}$ from the very last tweet whose author is followed by $a(t_u^{(i)})$.
- If $a(t_u^{(i)})$ does not follow any authors of the previous tweets $\{a(t_u^{(1)}), \ldots, a(t_u^{(i-1)})\}$, then we estimate that the news spreads to $t_u^{(i)}$ from the tweet in $\{t_u^{(1)}, \ldots, t_u^{(i-1)}\}$ whose author has the largest number of followers.

Fake News Detection as Graph Classification

We can build a graph for each story u as described above and then we treat the task of fake news detection as a binary graph classification task. The GNN framework for graph classification is introduced in Subsection 5.5.2, which can be directly applied to this task. Specifically, in Monti et al. (2019), two graph filtering layers were stacked to refine the node features, which are followed by a graph mean-pooling layer to generate a graph representation. The generated graph representation is then utilized to perform the binary classification.

12.5 Conclusion

This chapter describes how GNN models can be applied to advance various subfields of data mining, including Web data mining, urban data mining, and cybersecurity data mining. In Web data mining, we introduce representative methods using GNNs for social network analysis and recommender systems. In urban data mining, we discuss GNN-based models for traffic prediction and air quality prediction. In cybersecurity data mining, we provide representative algorithms built on GNNs to advance malicious account detection and fake news detection.

12.6 Further Reading

There are more methods than the representative ones we have detailed for the data mining tasks introduced in this chapter. For example, social information is encoded by GNNs to predict the political perspective (Li and Goldwasser, 2019), and GNNs are employed for fraud detection (Wang et al., 2019d; Liu et al., 2020), and anti-money laundering (Weber et al., 2019). In addition, GNNs were utilized to help more data mining tasks, such as community detection (Chen et al., 2017; Shchur and Günnemann, 2019) and anomaly detection (Wang et al., 2020b; Chaudhary et al., 2019).

13

Graph Neural Networks in Biochemistry and Health Care

13.1 Introduction

Graphs have been widely adopted to represent data in computational biochemistry and health care. For example, molecules and chemical compounds can be naturally denoted as graphs with atoms as nodes and bonds connecting them as edges. Protein–protein interactions, which record the physical contacts established between two or more proteins, can be captured as a graph. Furthermore, in the drug industry, drug–drug interactions, which describe the adverse outcomes when using certain combinations of drugs for complex diseases, can also be represented as graphs. Given the powerful capacity in learning graph representations, graph neural network (GNN) models have been adopted to facilitate many biochemistry and health care applications, including drug development and discovery, multiview drug similarity integration, polypharmacy side effect prediction, medication recommendation, and disease prediction. In this chapter, we discuss GNN models for representative applications in biochemistry and health care.

13.2 Drug Development and Discovery

GNNs have been adopted to advance many tasks that are important for drug development and discovery. Examples of these tasks include (1) molecular representation learning, which can facilitate downstream tasks such as molecular property prediction and therefore can help narrow down search space to find more promising candidates; (2) molecular graph generation, which aims to generate molecules with desired properties; (3) drug–target binding affinity prediction, which is to predict the drug–target interaction strength and thus can benefit the new drug development and drug repurposing; and (4) protein interface prediction, which targets prediction of the interaction interface of proteins and thus can allow us to understand molecular mechanisms. Next, we introduce the applications of GNNs in molecular representation learning, drug–target binding affinity prediction, and protein interface prediction. Note that we introduced representative methods that are partially based on GNN models to generate molecular graphs in Subsection 9.4.2 and Subsection 9.5.2.

13.2.1 Molecule Representation Learning

It is important to predict the properties of novel molecules for applications in material designs and drug discovery. Deep learning methods have been adopted to perform the predictions on molecular data. Typically, deep learning methods such as feedforward networks and convolutional neural networks cannot be directly applied to molecular data because the molecule can be of arbitrary size and shape. Hence, the prediction procedure usually consists of two stages: (1) feature extraction: extracting a molecular fingerprint, a vector representation encoding the structure information of the molecule, and (2) property prediction: performing prediction with deep learning methods using the extracted fingerprint as input. Traditionally the molecular fingerprint is extracted using some nondifferentiable off-the-shelf fingerprint software without guidance from the downstream prediction task. Thus, these extracted representations might not be optimal for the downstream tasks. In Duvenaud et al. (2015), an end-to-end framework was proposed to perform the predictions, where GNNs were adopted to learn the molecular fingerprints in a differentiable way. Specifically, a molecule can be represented as a graph $G = \{\mathcal{V}, \mathcal{E}\}$ where nodes are the atoms and edges represent the bonds between these atoms. Thus, the task of molecular property prediction can be regarded as graph classification or graph regression, which requires learning graph-level representations. Note that in the context of molecules, these representations are called molecular fingerprints. Hence, the GNN model adopted to perform this task consists of both graph filtering and graph pooling layers (see general framework in Chapter 5). Specifically, in Duvenaud et al. (2015), a global pooling method was adopted. Next, we introduce the graph filtering layers and then introduce the global pooling layer to obtain the molecular fingerprint. For a node $v_i \in \mathcal{V}$, the graph filtering operation (in the lth layer) can be described as

$$\mathbf{F}_i^{(l)} = \sigma\left(\left[\mathbf{F}_i^{(l-1)} + \sum_{v_j \in \mathcal{N}(v_i)} \mathbf{F}_j^{(l-1)}\right] \Theta_{|\mathcal{N}(v_i)|}^{(l-1)}\right), \tag{13.1}$$

where $\Theta_{|\mathcal{N}(v_i)|}^{(l-1)}$ is a transformation matrix depending on the size of the neighborhood $|\mathcal{N}(v_i)|$ of node v_i. Thus, the total number of transformation matrices in each layer is determined by the number of neighborhood size. In organic molecules, an atom can have up to five neighbors, and hence there are five transformation matrices in each layer. The molecular fingerprint $\mathbf{f}_\mathcal{G}$ for a molecule $\mathcal{G}$ can be obtained by the following global pooling operation:

$$\mathbf{f}_\mathcal{G} = \sum_{l=1}^{L} \sum_{v_i \in \mathcal{V}} \text{softmax}\left(\mathbf{F}_i^{(l)} \Theta_{pool}^{(l)}\right), \tag{13.2}$$

where L denotes the number of graph filtering layers, and $\Theta_{pool}^{(l)}$ is utilized to transform the node representations learned in the lth layer. The global pooling method in Eq. (13.2) aggregates the information from node representations learned in all of the graph filtering layers. The obtained molecular fingerprint $\mathbf{f}_\mathcal{G}$ can then be adopted for downstream tasks such as property prediction. Both the graph filtering process in Eq. (13.1) and the pooling process in Eq. (13.2) are guided by the given downstream task such as molecular property prediction (Liu et al., 2018a). In fact, in addition to the method we introduced above, any GNN designed for learning graph-level representations can be utilized to learn the molecular representations. Specifically, we can compose a GNN model with graph filtering layers and graph pooling layers, as introduced in Chapter 5. In particular, the MPNN-Filter discussed in Subsection 5.3.2 was introduced in the context of molecular representation learning (Gilmer et al., 2017).

13.2.2 Protein Interface Prediction

Proteins are chains of amino acids with biochemical functions (Fout et al., 2017) as shown in Figure 13.1. As shown in Figure 13.2, an amino acid is an organic compound. It contains amine ($-NH_2$) and carboxyl ($-COOH$) functional groups and a side chain (R group) that is specific to each amino acid. To perform their functions, proteins need to interact with other proteins. Predicting the interface where these interactions occur is a challenging problem with important applications in drug discovery and design (Fout et al., 2017). The protein interaction interface consists of interacting amino acid residues and nearby amino acid residues in the interacting proteins. Specifically, in Afsar Minhas et al. (2014), two amino acid residues from different proteins were considered to be a part of the interface if any non-hydrogen atom in one amino acid residue was within 6Å of any non-hydrogen atom in the other amino acid residue. Therefore, the protein interface prediction problem can be

Protein

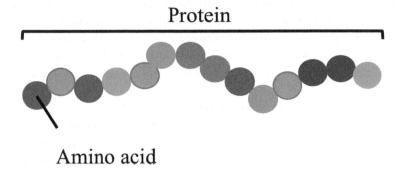

Amino acid

Figure 13.1 A protein consists of a chain of amino acids.

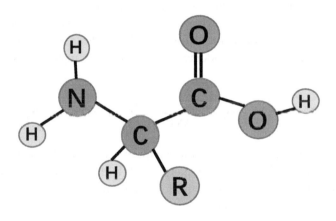

Figure 13.2 An illustrative example of amino acids.

modeled as a binary classification problem where a pair of amino acid residues from different proteins serves as the input. In Fout et al. (2017), a protein was modeled as a graph. In the graph, amino acid residues in the protein are treated as nodes, and relations between them are defined as edges. Then, GNN models are employed to learn node representations, which are then utilized for classification. Next, we describe how proteins are treated as graphs and then introduce the approach to perform the protein interface prediction.

Representing Proteins as Graphs
A protein can be represented as a graph $\mathcal{G} = \{\mathcal{V}, \mathcal{E}\}$. In detail, each amino acid residue in the protein is treated as a node. The spatial relations between the

amino acid residues are utilized to build the edges between them. Specifically, each amino acid residue node is connected to k closest amino acid residues determined by the mean distance between their atoms. Each node and edge in the graph is associated with some features. Specifically, features for node $v_i \in \mathcal{V}$ are denoted as $\mathbf{x}_i$ and features for an edge (v_i, v_j) are represented as $\mathbf{e}_{ij}$.

Protein Interface Prediction

Given a pair of amino acid residues, one from a ligand protein $\mathcal{G}_l = \{\mathcal{V}_l, \mathcal{E}_l\}$ and the other from a receptor protein $\mathcal{G}_r = \{\mathcal{V}_r, \mathcal{E}_r\}$, the task of protein interface prediction is to tell whether these two residues are in the protein interface. It is treated as a binary classification problem where each sample is a pair of amino acid residues (v_l, v_r) with $v_l \in \mathcal{V}_l$ and $v_r \in \mathcal{V}_r$. Graph filtering operations are applied to $\mathcal{G}_l$ and $\mathcal{G}_r$ to learn the node representations and then the node representations for v_l and v_r are combined to obtain a unified representation for this pair, which is then utilized for the classification by fully-connected layers. A graph filter similar to GCN-Filter (see details of GCN-Filter in Subsection 5.3.2) is adopted to learn the node representations as (for the lth layer)

$$\mathbf{F}_i^{(l)} = \sigma\left(\mathbf{F}_i^{(l-1)}\mathbf{\Theta}_c^{(l-1)} + \frac{1}{|\mathcal{N}(v_i)|}\sum_{v_j \in \mathcal{N}(v_i)} \mathbf{F}_j^{(l-1)}\mathbf{\Theta}_N^{(l-1)} + \mathbf{b}\right),$$

where $\mathbf{\Theta}_c^{(l-1)}$ and $\mathbf{\Theta}_N^{(l-1)}$ are learnable matrices specific to the centering node and the neighboring node, respectively, and $\mathbf{b}$ is the bias term. Furthermore, to incorporate the edge features, the following graph filtering operation was proposed in Fout et al. (2017):

$$\mathbf{F}_i^{(l)} = \sigma\left(\mathbf{F}_i^{(l-1)}\mathbf{\Theta}_c^{(l-1)} + \frac{1}{|\mathcal{N}(v_i)|}\sum_{v_j \in \mathcal{N}(v_i)} \mathbf{F}_j^{(l-1)}\mathbf{\Theta}_N^{(l-1)} + \frac{1}{|\mathcal{N}(v_i)|}\sum_{v_j \in \mathcal{N}(v_i)} \mathbf{e}_{ij}\mathbf{\Theta}_E^{(l-1)} + \mathbf{b}\right),$$

where $\mathbf{e}_{ij}$ denotes the edge features for the edge (v_i, v_j) and $\mathbf{\Theta}_E^{(l-1)}$ is the learnable transformation matrix for edges. Note that the edge features are fixed during the training process.

13.2.3 Drug–Target Binding Affinity Prediction

The development of a new drug is usually time-consuming and costly. The identification of drug–target interactions is vital in the early stage of drug development to narrow down the search space of candidate medications. It can also be used for drug repurposing, which aims to identify new targets for existing or abandoned drugs. The task of drug–target binding affinity

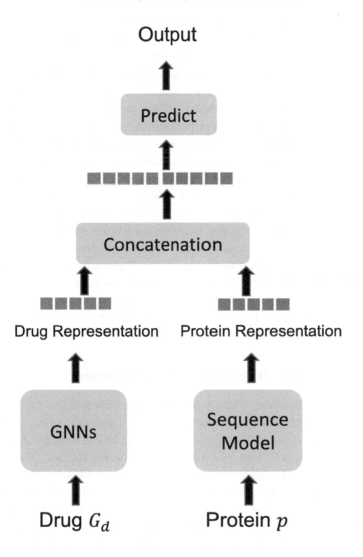

Figure 13.3 A general framework for drug–target binding affinity prediction.

prediction is to infer the strength of the binding between a given drug–target pair. It can be considered as a regression task. There are four main types of targets–i.e., protein, disease, gene, and side effects–frequently involved in the task of drug–target interaction prediction. In this section, we use protein as the target to illustrate how GNN models can be employed to facilitate this task.

A drug–protein pair is denoted as $(\mathcal{G}_d, p)$, with $\mathcal{G}_d$, p denoting the drug and protein, respectively. The drug $\mathcal{G}_d$ is represented as a molecular graph with atoms as nodes and the chemical bonds as edges. The protein can be denoted as either a sequence or a graph. In Nguyen et al. (2019), the proteins are represented as sequences of amino acids, which we adopt to illustrate the framework for drug–target binding affinity prediction. An overview of a general framework for drug–target binding affinity prediction is shown in Figure 13.3. In this framework, the drug $\mathcal{G}_d$ is fed into a GNN model to learn a graph-level drug representation, and the protein is fed into a sequence model to learn a protein representation. These two representations are concatenated to generate a combined representation for the pair, and it is then leveraged to predict the drug–target binding affinity. The GNN model consists of graph filtering and graph pooling layers, as introduced in Chapter 5. The GNN models introduced in Subsection 13.2.1 for molecular representation learning can also be used to learn the drug representation. Sequence models such as 1-D CNN, LSTM, and GRU, can learn the protein representation. Furthermore, if we model the protein as a graph, we can also use the GNNs to replace the sequence model in Figure 13.3 to learn its representation.

13.3 Drug Similarity Integration

With the rapid development of technology, drug data from multiple sources are collected for computational drug discovery research and drug safety studies. For example, the structural information of drugs can be extracted by chemical fingerprint software and drug indication information is extracted from drug packaging (Kuhn et al., 2016). To better facilitate downstream tasks such as drug–drug interaction prediction, it is necessary to fuse the drug data from multiple sources, because they contain information about drugs from various perspectives. These multiple data sources of drugs may encode different similarities between drugs and thus have different levels of association with targeting outcomes. For example, drugs' structural similarities could have more impact on their interaction profiles than drugs' indication similarities. In Ma et al. (2018c), an attentive algorithm based on GNNs was proposed to fuse the drug similarity information from various sources with the guidance of the downstream tasks. Specifically, each source of drug features was regarded as a view in Ma et al. (2018c). For view $t \in \{1, \dots, T\}$, the features for all nodes in this view are denoted as a matrix $\mathbf{X}_t \in \mathbb{R}^{N \times d_t}$, where N is the number of drugs and d_t is the dimension of the features in this view. Furthermore, the similarity information of the drugs in this view is encoded into a similarity matrix $\mathbf{A}_t \in \mathbb{R}^{N \times N}$. The goal of multiview drug similarity integration is to fuse the features and similarity matrices from different views to generate integrated features $\mathbf{Z} \in \mathbb{R}^{N \times d}$ and similarity matrix $\mathbf{A}$ across all views.

The similarity matrices from different views are combined as follows:

$$\mathbf{A} = \sum_{t=1}^{T} \text{diag}(\mathbf{g}_t)\mathbf{A}_t, \tag{13.3}$$

where $\mathbf{g}_t \in \mathbb{R}^N$ are the attention scores, which are learned as

$$\mathbf{g}_t' = \mathbf{\Theta}_t \mathbf{A}_t + \mathbf{b}_t, \forall t = 1, \ldots, T,$$
$$[\mathbf{g}_1, \ldots, \mathbf{g}_T] = \text{softmax}([\mathbf{g}_1', \ldots, \mathbf{g}_T']),$$

where $\mathbf{\Theta}_t, \mathbf{b}_t \in \mathbb{R}^N$ are parameters to be learned and the softmax function is applied to each row. With the fused similarity matrix $\mathbf{A}$, the fused features are obtained by applying a GNN-Filter on the multiview features as

$$\mathbf{Z} = \alpha(\text{GNN-Filter}(\mathbf{A}, \mathbf{X})), \tag{13.4}$$

where $\mathbf{X} = [\mathbf{X}_1, \ldots, \mathbf{X}_T]$ is the concatenation of the features from different views. Specifically, the GCN-Filter (see details about the GCN-Filter in Subsection 5.3.2) was adopted in Ma et al. (2018c) and $\alpha()$ is the softmax function (applied row-wise). A decoder is then used to reconstruct $\mathbf{X}$ from $\mathbf{Z}$ expecting that the fused representations contain as much information from $\mathbf{X}$ as possible. The decoder is also modeled by a GNN-Filter as

$$\mathbf{X}' = \alpha(\text{GNN-Filter}(\mathbf{A}, \mathbf{Z})), \tag{13.5}$$

where the GCN-Filter was again adopted as the graph filter and a sigmoid function is adopted as the nonlinear activation function $\alpha()$ in Ma et al. (2018c). The reconstruction loss is

$$\mathcal{L}_{ed} = \|\mathbf{X} - \mathbf{X}'\|^2.$$

The parameters in Eq. (13.3), Eq. (13.4), and Eq. (13.5) can be learned by minimizing the reconstruction loss. Furthermore, the fused representations $\mathbf{Z}$ can be used for downstream tasks and the gradient from the downstream tasks can also be leveraged to update the parameters in Eq. (13.3), Eq. (13.4), and Eq. (13.5).

13.4 Polypharmacy Side Effect Prediction

Many complex diseases cannot be treated by a single drug. A promising strategy to combat these diseases is polypharmacy, which means using a combination of several drugs to treat patients. However, a major adverse consequence of polypharmacy is that it is may introduce side effects due to drug–drug interactions. Hence, it is important to predict the side effects of polypharmacy when adopting novel drug combinations to treat diseases. The polypharmacy side effect prediction task is not only to predict whether a side effect exists between a pair of drugs but also to tell what type of side effect it is. Exploratory analysis in Zitnik et al. (2018) showed that co-prescribed drugs tend to have more target proteins in common than random drug pairs, which indicates that the interactions between drug and target proteins are important for polypharmacy modeling. Hence, the interactions between drug and target proteins and the interactions between the target proteins are incorporated for polypharmacy side effect prediction (Zitnik et al., 2018). In detail, a multi-modal graph is built on drug–drug interactions (polypharmacy side effects), drug–protein interactions, and protein–protein interactions. The task of polypharmacy prediction is thus modeled as a multirelational link prediction task over the multimodal graph. The goal is to predict whether a link exists between a pair of drugs and then what type of link it is if it exists. GNN models have been adopted to learn the node representations, which are then used to perform the prediction. Next, we describe the process to construct the multimodal graph and then introduce the framework to perform polypharmacy side effect prediction.

Multimodal Graph Construction

As shown in Figure 13.4, a two-layer multimodal graph with two types of nodes (drugs and proteins) is built upon three different interactions including drug–drug interactions, drug–protein interactions, and protein–protein interactions. Drug–drug interactions encode the observed polypharmacy side effects. For example, in Figure 13.4, the drugs doxycycline (node D) and ciprofloxacin (node C) are connected by the relation r_2 (bradycardia side effect), which indicates that taking a combination of these two drugs likely leads to the bradycardia side effect. The drug–protein interactions describe the proteins that a drug targets. For example, in Figure 13.4, the drug ciprofloxacin (node C) targets four proteins. The protein–protein interactions encode the physical binding relations between proteins in humans. In particular, this two-layer multimodal graph can be denoted as $\mathcal{G} = \{\mathcal{V}, \mathcal{E}, \mathcal{R}\}$. In $\mathcal{G}$, $\mathcal{V}$ is the set of nodes consisting of drugs and proteins and $\mathcal{E}$ denotes the edges. Each $e \in \mathcal{E}$ is in the form of $e = (v_i, r, v_j)$ with $r \in \mathcal{R}$ and $\mathcal{R}$ is the set of relations, which includes (1) protein–protein interactions, (2) a target relationship between a drug and a protein, and (3) various types of side effects between drugs.

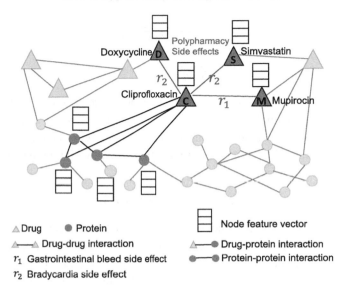

Figure 13.4 An illustrative example of the two-layer multimodal graph with drug–drug interactions, drug–protein interactions, and protein–protein interactions.

Polypharmacy Side Effect Prediction

The task of polypharmacy side effect prediction is modeled as a relational link prediction task on $\mathcal{G}$. In particular, given a pair of drugs $\{v_i, v_j\}$, we want to predict how likely an edge $e_{ij} = (v_i, r, v_j)$ of type $r \in \mathcal{R}$ exists between them. In Zitnik et al. (2018), graph filtering operations are adopted to learn the node representations, which are then utilized to perform the relational link prediction. Specifically, the graph filtering operation designed for knowledge graphs (Schlichtkrull et al., 2018) is adapted to update the node representations as

$$\mathbf{F}_i^{(l)} = \sigma\left(\sum_{r \in \mathcal{R}} \sum_{v_j \in \mathcal{N}_r(v_i)} c_r^{ij} \mathbf{F}_j^{(l-1)} \mathbf{\Theta}_r^{(l-1)} + c_r^i \mathbf{F}_i^{(l-1)}\right), \qquad (13.6)$$

where $\mathbf{F}_i^{(l)}$ is the hidden representation of node v_i after the lth layer, $r \in \mathcal{R}$ is a relation type, and $\mathcal{N}_r(v_i)$ denotes the set of neighbors of node v_i under the relation of r. The matrix $\mathbf{\Theta}_r^{(l-1)}$ is a transform matrix specific to the relation type r. c_r^{ij} and c_r^i are normalization constants defined as follows:

$$c_r^{ij} = \frac{1}{\sqrt{|\mathcal{N}_r(v_i)||\mathcal{N}_r(v_j)|}},$$

$$c_r^i = \frac{1}{|\mathcal{N}_r(v_i)|}.$$

The input of the first layer is the node features $\mathbf{F}_i^{(0)} = \mathbf{x}_i$. The final node representations are the output of the Lth layer – i.e., $\mathbf{z}_i = \mathbf{F}_i^{(L)}$ – where $\mathbf{z}_i$ denotes the final representation of node v_i. With the learned node representations, given a pair of drugs v_i, v_j, the probability of a relational edge with relation r existing between them is modeled as

$$p(v_i, r, v_j) = \sigma\left(\mathbf{z}_i^T \mathbf{D}_r \mathbf{R} \mathbf{D}_r \mathbf{z}_j\right), \tag{13.7}$$

where $\sigma()$ is the sigmoid function, $\mathbf{R}$ is a learnable matrix shared by all relations, and $\mathbf{D}_r$ is a learnable diagonal matrix specific to relation r. The reason for using a shared matrix $\mathbf{R}$ is that many relations (side effects) between drugs are rarely observed and learning specific matrices for them may cause overfitting. Introducing the shared parameter matrix $\mathbf{R}$ largely reduces the number of parameters of the model; hence, it can help prevent overfitting. During the training stage, the parameters in both the graph filters in Eq. (13.6) and the prediction model in Eq. (13.7) are optimized by maximizing the probability in Eq. (13.7) for those observed side effects between drugs. Note that in Zitnik et al. (2018), other types of relations – i.e., protein–protein interactions and drug–protein interactions – are also reconstructed during the training with their probabilities formulated similar to Eq. (13.7).

13.5 Disease Prediction

Increasing volumes of medical data, which usually consists of imaging, genetic and, behavioral data, are collected and shared to facilitate the understanding of disease mechanisms. The task of disease prediction is to tell whether a subject is diseased or not given its corresponding medical image and non-image data. The medical images are often magnetic resonance images, and the non-image data usually include phenotypic data such as age, sex, and acquisition site. These two types of information are complementary. Hence, facilitating both types of information effectively is necessary to enhance the performance of disease prediction. The image data directly provide the features corresponding to some diseases, and the phenotypic information provides between-subject association. For example, patients with similar ages tend to have more similar outcomes than those with very different ages when all other conditions are the same. Graphs provide an intuitive way of modeling these two types of information, where we treat subjects as nodes with their images as node features and the associations between them as edges. With the built graph, the disease prediction task can be treated as a binary semisupervised node classification task. It can be tackled using GNN models, as introduced in Subsection 5.5.1. Next, we briefly introduce the process of building the graph using the ABIDE database (Di Martino et al., 2014) as an illustrative example (Parisot et al., 2018).

The ABIDE database contains neuroimaging (functional magnetic resonance imaging) and phenotypic data from different international acquisition sites. With this database, we aim to predict whether a subject is healthy or has autism spectrum disorder. Each subject is modeled as a node v_i in the graph G, and $\mathbf{x}_i$ denotes the features extracted from the corresponding functional magnetic resonance image. To build the edges between the nodes (i.e., the adjacency matrix for the graph), we consider both the image data and the non-image phenotypic measures $\mathcal{M} = \{M_h\}_{h=1}^{H}$ as

$$\mathbf{A}_{i,j} = \text{sim}(\mathbf{x}_i, \mathbf{x}_j) \sum_{h=1}^{H} \gamma_h(M_h(v_i), M_h(v_j)),$$

where $\mathbf{A}$ denotes the adjacency matrix, $\text{sim}(\mathbf{x}_i, \mathbf{x}_j)$ computes the similarity between the features of two nodes v_i and v_j, $M_h(v_i)$ is the hth phenotypic measure of node v_i, and $\gamma_h()$ calculates their similarity. The similarity function $\text{sim}(\mathbf{x}_i, \mathbf{x}_j)$ can be modeled with Gaussian kernels, where nodes with a smaller distance have a higher similarity score. Three phenotypic measures, acquisition site, sex, and age, are utilized; i.e., we have $H = 3$ for the ABIDE database. The acquisition site is considered because the database is acquired from very different sites with diverse acquisition protocol, which results in fewer comparable images across different acquisition sites. Sex and age are considered because sex-related and age-related group differences have been observed (Werling and Geschwind, 2013; Kana et al., 2014). For sex and acquisition site, the function $\gamma_h()$ is defined as the Kronecker delta function, which takes a value of 1 if and only if the two inputs are the same (i.e., they are from the same acquisition site or they have the same sex) and 0 otherwise. For age, the function $\gamma_h()$ is defined as

$$\gamma_h\left(M_h(v_i), M_h(v_j)\right) = \begin{cases} 1 & \text{if } \left|M_h(v_i) - M_h(v_j)\right| < \theta \\ 0 & \text{otherwise} \end{cases},$$

where θ is a predefined threshold. This means that subjects with an age difference smaller than θ are considered to be similar.

13.6 Conclusion

In this chapter, we introduced various representative applications of GNN models in biochemistry and health care. We discuss the applications of GNN models in molecular representation learning, drug–target binding affinity prediction, and protein interface prediction. These tasks can facilitate the development and discovery of novel drugs. Next, we introduced an autoencoder based on graph filters to integrate multiview drug similarities. We also described how GNN models can be used for polypharmacy side effect prediction. In addition, we discussed how GNN models can be leveraged for disease prediction.

13.7 Further Reading

In addition to the applications we have detailed in this chapter, GNNs have been adopted or served as building blocks to benefit many other biochemistry tasks. They are employed as building blocks in models designed for medication recommendation (Shang et al., 2019b,c). In You et al. (2018a), GNN models were leveraged as policy networks for molecular graph generation with reinforcement learning. In addition, GNN models have been employed for computational phenotyping (Zhu et al., 2019b; Choi et al., 2020) and disease association prediction (Xuan et al., 2019; Li et al., 2019a).

Part IV

Advances

14

Advanced Topics in Graph Neural Networks

14.1 Introduction

In Part II, we discussed the most established methods of deep learning on graphs. On the one hand, with the increasingly deep understandings, numerous limitations have been identified for existing graph neural networks (GNNs). Some of these limitations are inherited from traditional deep neural networks (DNNs). For example, as DNNs, GNNs are often treated as black boxes and lack human-intelligible explanations, and they might present discrimination behaviors to protected groups that can result in unprecedented ethical, moral, and even legal consequences for human society. Others are unique to GNNs. For instance, increasing the number of layers of GNNs often leads to significant performance drop, and there are limitations on the expressive power of existing GNNs in distinguishing graph structures. On the other hand, recently, more successful experiences from traditional DNNs have been adapted to advance GNNs. For example, strategies have been designed to explore unlabeled data for GNNs, and there are attempts to extend GNNs from Euclidean space to hyperbolic space. We package these recent efforts in this chapter about advanced topics in GNNs with two goals. First, we aim to bring our readers near the frontier of current research on GNNs. Second, these topics can serve as promising future research directions. Some of the aforementioned advanced topics are relatively well developed, including deeper graph neural networks, exploring unlabeled data via self-supervised learning for GNNs, and the expressiveness of GNNs. We will detail them in the following sections. In contrast, others are just initialized, and we will provide corresponding references as further reading.

14.2 Deeper Graph Neural Networks

It is observed that increasing the number of graph filtering layers (such as GCN-Filter, GAT-Filter; see Subsection 5.3.2 for more graph filtering operations) often results in a significant drop in node classification performance. The performance drop is mainly caused by oversmoothing. It describes the phenomenon that the node features become similar and less distinguishable as the number of graph filtering layers increases (Li et al., 2018b). Next, we discuss the "oversmoothing" issue based on the GCN-Filter. Intuitively, from a spatial perspective, the GCN-Filter is to update a node's representation by "averaging" its neighbors' representations. This process naturally renders representations for neighboring nodes to be similar. Thus, deeply stacking graph filtering operations tends to make all of the nodes (assume that the graph is connected) have similar representations. In Li et al. (2018b), the oversmoothing phenomenon is studied asymptotically as the number of graph filtering layers goes to infinity. Specifically, when the number of filtering layers goes to infinity, the nodes' representations converge to the same regardless of their input features. For the ease of analysis, the nonlinear activation layers between the graph filtering layers are ignored in Li et al. (2018b). Without the nonlinear activation layers, repeatedly applying L GCN-Filters to the input features $\mathbf{F}$ can be expressed as

$$\widetilde{\mathbf{D}}^{-\frac{1}{2}}\widetilde{\mathbf{A}}\widetilde{\mathbf{D}}^{-\frac{1}{2}}\left(\cdots\left(\widetilde{\mathbf{D}}^{-\frac{1}{2}}\widetilde{\mathbf{A}}\widetilde{\mathbf{D}}^{-\frac{1}{2}}\left(\widetilde{\mathbf{D}}^{-\frac{1}{2}}\widetilde{\mathbf{A}}\widetilde{\mathbf{D}}^{-\frac{1}{2}}\mathbf{F}\Theta^{(0)}\right)\Theta^{(1)}\right)\cdots\right)\Theta^{(L-1)},$$

$$=\left(\widetilde{\mathbf{D}}^{-\frac{1}{2}}\widetilde{\mathbf{A}}\widetilde{\mathbf{D}}^{-\frac{1}{2}}\right)^{L}\mathbf{F}\Theta, \tag{14.1}$$

where Θ denotes the multiplication of $\Theta^{(0)},\ldots,\Theta^{(L-1)}$, $\widetilde{\mathbf{A}} = \mathbf{A}+\mathbf{I}$ as introduced in the GCN-Filter in Eq. (5.21) and $\widetilde{\mathbf{D}}$ is the corresponding degree matrix. The filtering process in Eq. (14.1) can be viewed as applying the operation $\left(\widetilde{\mathbf{D}}^{-\frac{1}{2}}\widetilde{\mathbf{A}}\widetilde{\mathbf{D}}^{-\frac{1}{2}}\right)^{L}$ to each column of $\mathbf{F}\Theta$.

The following theorem (Li et al., 2018b) demonstrates the oversmoothing phenomenon on single channel graph signals.

Theorem 14.1 *Let $\mathcal{G}$ denote a connected nonbipartite graph with $\mathbf{A}$ as its adjacency matrix. Then, for any input feature $\mathbf{f} \in \mathbb{R}^N$, we have*

$$\lim_{L\to\infty}\left(\widetilde{\mathbf{D}}^{-\frac{1}{2}}\widetilde{\mathbf{A}}\widetilde{\mathbf{D}}^{-\frac{1}{2}}\right)^{L}\mathbf{f} = \theta_1 \cdot \mathbf{u}_1, \tag{14.2}$$

where $\widetilde{\mathbf{A}} = \mathbf{A} + \mathbf{I}$ and $\widetilde{\mathbf{D}}$ denotes its corresponding degree matrix. Here $\widetilde{\mathbf{A}}$ can be regarded as the adjacency matrix of a modified version of graph $\mathcal{G}$ with self-loops. The vector $\mathbf{u}_1$ is the eigenvector of $\widetilde{\mathbf{D}}^{-\frac{1}{2}}\widetilde{\mathbf{A}}\widetilde{\mathbf{D}}^{-\frac{1}{2}}$ associated with its *largest eigenvalue and* $\theta_1 = \mathbf{u}_1^\top \mathbf{f}$. *In detail,* $\mathbf{u}_1 = \widetilde{\mathbf{D}}^{-\frac{1}{2}} \mathbf{1}$, *which only contains the information of the node degree.*

Proof Let $\widetilde{\mathbf{L}}_{nor} = \mathbf{I} - \widetilde{\mathbf{D}}^{-\frac{1}{2}} \widetilde{\mathbf{A}} \widetilde{\mathbf{D}}^{-\frac{1}{2}}$ denote the normalized Laplacian matrix corresponding to $\widetilde{\mathbf{A}}$. According to Lemma 1.7 in Chung and Graham (1997), $\widetilde{\mathbf{L}}_{nor}$ has a complete set of eigenvalues $0 = \lambda_1 < \lambda_2 \dots, \lambda_N < 2$ with their corresponding eigenvectors $\mathbf{u}_1, \dots, \mathbf{u}_N$. Specifically, in the matrix form, the eigendecomposition of $\widetilde{\mathbf{L}}_{nor}$ can be represented as $\widetilde{\mathbf{L}}_{nor} = \mathbf{U}\mathbf{\Lambda}\mathbf{U}^\top$, where $\mathbf{U} = [\mathbf{u}_1, \dots, \mathbf{u}_N]$ is the matrix that consists of all eigenvectors and $\mathbf{\Lambda} = \mathrm{diag}([\lambda_1, \dots, \lambda_N])$ is the diagonal eigenvalue matrix. The eigenvalues and eigenvectors of $\widetilde{\mathbf{D}}^{-\frac{1}{2}} \widetilde{\mathbf{A}} \widetilde{\mathbf{D}}^{-\frac{1}{2}}$ can be related to those of $\widetilde{\mathbf{L}}$ as

$$\widetilde{\mathbf{D}}^{-\frac{1}{2}} \widetilde{\mathbf{A}} \widetilde{\mathbf{D}}^{-\frac{1}{2}} = \mathbf{I} - \widetilde{\mathbf{L}}_{nor} = \mathbf{U}\mathbf{U}^\top - \mathbf{U}\mathbf{\Lambda}\mathbf{U}^\top = \mathbf{U}(\mathbf{I} - \mathbf{\Lambda})\mathbf{U}^\top.$$

Hence, $1 = 1 - \lambda_1 > 1 - \lambda_2 \dots, > 1 - \lambda_N > -1$ are the eigenvalues of $\widetilde{\mathbf{D}}^{-\frac{1}{2}} \widetilde{\mathbf{A}} \widetilde{\mathbf{D}}^{-\frac{1}{2}}$ with $\mathbf{u}_1, \dots, \mathbf{u}_N$ as its corresponding eigenvectors. Then, we have

$$\left(\widetilde{\mathbf{D}}^{-\frac{1}{2}} \widetilde{\mathbf{A}} \widetilde{\mathbf{D}}^{-\frac{1}{2}}\right)^L = \left(\mathbf{U}(\mathbf{I} - \mathbf{\Lambda})\mathbf{U}^\top\right)^L = \mathbf{U}(\mathbf{I} - \mathbf{\Lambda})^L \mathbf{U}^\top.$$

Because the eigenvalues of $\widetilde{\mathbf{A}}$ are in the range of $[0, 1)$, the limit in Eq. (14.2) can be expressed as

$$\lim_{k\to\infty} \left(\widetilde{\mathbf{D}}^{-\frac{1}{2}} \widetilde{\mathbf{A}} \widetilde{\mathbf{D}}^{-\frac{1}{2}}\right)^L \mathbf{f} = \lim_{k\to\infty} \mathbf{U}(I - \mathbf{\Lambda})^L \mathbf{U}^\top \mathbf{f}$$
$$= \mathbf{U}\mathrm{diag}([1, 0, \dots, 0])\mathbf{U}^\top \mathbf{f}$$
$$= \mathbf{u}_1 \cdot (\mathbf{u}_1^\top \mathbf{f})$$
$$= \theta_1 \cdot \mathbf{u}_1,$$

which completes the proof. □

Theorem 14.1 shows that repeatedly applying the GCN-Filters to a graph signal $\mathbf{f}$ results in $\theta_1 \cdot \mathbf{u}_1$, which captures information no more than the node degrees. For the multichannel case as shown in Eq. (14.1), each column of the matrix $\mathbf{F\Theta}$ is mapped to $\theta_1 \cdot \mathbf{u}_1$ with different θ_1. Hence, different columns contain the same information with different scales. Furthermore, the degree information contained in $\mathbf{u}_1$ is likely not be useful for most node classification tasks, which also explains why the node classification performance decreases as the number of graph filtering layers increases. Similar observations for the case where the nonlinear activation (limited to the rectified linear unit activation function) is included are made in Oono and Suzuki (2020). Specifically, it is shown in Oono and Suzuki (2020) that the rectified linear unit activation function accelerates the process of oversmoothing. The goal of the GCN-Filter is to update node representations with the information of neighboring nodes.

Stacking k GCN-Filters allows each node to access information from its k-hop neighborhood. To achieve good performance for node classification, it is necessary to aggregate the information from the local neighborhood for each node. However, as shown in above, stacking too many graph filtering layers leads to the oversmoothing issue. Various remedies have been proposed to alleviate the oversmoothing issue (Xu et al., 2018a; Rong et al., 2020; Zhao and Akoglu, 2019).

14.2.1 Jumping Knowledge

It is argued in Xu et al. (2018a) that different nodes require neighborhoods with different depths and thus different numbers of graph filtering layers are required for different nodes. Hence, a strategy called "jumping knowledge" was proposed in Xu et al. (2018a), which adaptively combines the hidden representations for each node from different layers as the final representations. Specifically, let $\mathbf{F}_i^{(1)}, \ldots, \mathbf{F}_i^{(L)}$ be the hidden representations for node v_i after the $1, \ldots, L$th layer. These representations are combined to generate the final representation for node v_i as follows:

$$\mathbf{F}_i^o = \mathrm{JK}\left(\mathbf{F}_i^{(0)}, \mathbf{F}_i^{(1)}, \ldots, \mathbf{F}_i^{(L)}\right),$$

where JK() is a function that is adaptive for each node. In particular, it can be implemented as the max pooling operation or attention-based long short-term memory.

14.2.2 DropEdge

Dropedge (Rong et al., 2019) is introduced to alleviate the oversmoothing issue by randomly dropping some edges in the graph during each training epoch. Specifically, before the training of each epoch, a fraction of edges $\mathcal{E}_p$ is uniformly sampled from $\mathcal{E}$ with a sampling rate p. These sampled edges are removed from the edge set, and the remaining edges are denoted as $\mathcal{E}_r = \mathcal{E}/\mathcal{E}_p$. The graph $\mathcal{G}' = \{\mathcal{V}, \mathcal{E}_r\}$ is then used for training in this epoch.

14.2.3 PairNorm

As discussed before, we desire some smoothness of the node representations to ensure good classification performance while preventing them from being too similar. An intuitive idea is to ensure that the representations of disconnected nodes are relatively distant. In Zhao and Akoglu (2019), PairNorm was proposed to introduce a regularization term to force representations of nodes that are not connected to be different.

14.3 Exploring Unlabeled Data via Self-Supervised Learning

Training good deep learning models usually requires a huge amount of labeled data. For a specific task, it is usually hard and expensive to collect/annotate massive labeled data. However, unlabeled data are typically rich and easy to obtain. For instance, if we are building a sentiment analysis model, the annotated data might be limited, and unlabeled texts are widely available. Thus, it is appealing to take advantage of unlabeled data. In fact, unlabeled data have been used to advance many areas, such as computer vision and natural language processing. In image recognition, deep convolutional neural networks pretrained on ImageNet such as Inception (Szegedy et al., 2016) and VGG (Simonyan and Zisserman, 2014) have been widely adopted. Note that images from ImageNet are originally labeled; however, they are considered as unlabeled data for a given specific image recognition task, which could have very different labels from those in the ImageNet data set. In natural language processing, pretrained language models such as GPT-2 (Radford et al., 2019) and BERT (Devlin et al., 2018) have been adopted to achieve the state-of-the-art performance for various tasks such as question answering and natural language generation. Therefore, they are promising and have the great potential to explore unlabeled data to enhance deep learning on graphs. This chapter discusses how GNNs can use unlabeled data for node classification and graph classification/regression tasks. For node classification, unlabeled data have been incorporated by GNNs via the simple information aggregation process. This process could be insufficient to make use of unlabeled data fully. Hence, we discuss strategies to leverage unlabeled data more thoroughly. In graph classification/regression tasks, labeled graphs could be limited, but many unlabeled graphs are available. For example, when performing classification/regression tasks on molecules, labeling molecules is expensive, and unlabeled molecules can be easily collected. Therefore, we present approaches to leverage unlabeled graphs for graph-focused tasks.

14.3.1 Node-Focused Tasks

The success of deep learning relies on massive labeled data. Self-supervised learning has been developed to alleviate this limitation. It often first designs a domain-specific pretext task and then learns better representations with the pretext task to include unlabeled data. As aforementioned, GNNs simply aggregate features of unlabeled data that cannot thoroughly take advantage of the abundant information. Thus, to fully explore unlabeled data, self-supervised learning has been harnessed for providing additional supervision for GNNs. The node-focused self-supervised tasks usually generate additional supervised signals from the graph structure and/or node attributes. Such generated self-supervised information can serve as the supervision of auxiliary tasks to improve the performance of GNNs on the node classification task. There are mainly two ways to utilize these generated self-supervised signals (Jin et al., 2020c): (1) two-stage training, where the self-supervised task is utilized to pretrain the GNN model and then the GNN model is fine-tuned for the node classification task and (2) joint training, where the self-supervised task and the main task are optimized together. Specifically, the objective of joint training can be formulated as follows:

$$\mathcal{L} = \mathcal{L}_{label} + \eta \cdot \mathcal{L}_{self},$$

where $\mathcal{L}_{label}$ denotes the loss of the main task – i.e., the node classification task – and $\mathcal{L}_{self}$ is the loss of the self-supervised task. Next, we briefly introduce some of the self-supervised tasks. In detail, we categorize these self-supervised tasks by the information they leverage to construct the self-supervised signals: (1) constructing self-supervised signals with graph structure information; (2) constructing self-supervised signals with node attribute information; and (3) constructing self-supervised signals with both graph structure and node attribute information.

Graph Structure Information

In this subsection, we introduce self-supervised tasks based on graph structure information.

- **Node Property** (Jin et al., 2020c). In this task, we aim to predict the node property using the learned node representations. These node properties can be node degree, node centrality, and local clustering coefficient.
- **Centrality Ranking** (Hu et al., 2019). In this task, we aim to preserve the centrality ranking of the nodes. Instead of directly predicting centrality as that in node property, the task aims to predict pair-wise ranking given any pair of nodes.
- **Edge Mask** (Jin et al., 2020c; Hu et al., 2019, 2020). In this task, we randomly mask (or remove) some edges from the graph and try to predict their existence using the node representations learned by GNNs.
- **Pair-wise Distance** (Jin et al., 2020c; Peng et al., 2020). In this task, we aim to utilize the node representations to predict the distance between pairs of nodes in the graph. Specifically, the distance between two nodes is measured by the length of the shortest path between them.

- **Distance2Clusters** (Jin et al., 2020c). Instead of predicting the distance between node pairs, in this task we aim to predict the distance between a node to the clusters in the graph, which can help learn the global position information of these nodes. Clustering methods based on graph structure information such as the METIS graph partitioning algorithm (Karypis and Kumar, 1998) are first utilized to generate a total of K clusters. Then, for each cluster, the node with the largest degree in this cluster is chosen as its center. The task of Distance2Cluster is to predict the distances between a node to the centers of these K clusters. Again, the distance is measured by the length of the shortest path between nodes.

Node Attribute Information

In this subsection, we introduce self-supervised tasks based on node attribute information.

- **Attribute Mask** (Jin et al., 2020c; You et al., 2020; Hu et al., 2020). In this task, we randomly mask (or remove) the associated attribute information of some nodes in the graph and aim to utilize the node representations learned from the GNN models to predict these node attributes.
- **PairwiseAttrSim** (Jin et al., 2020c). This task is similar to pair-wise distance in the sense that we also aim to predict pair-wise information between nodes. Specifically, we aim to predict the similarity between node attributes, where the similarity can be measured by cosine similarity or Euclidean distance.

Graph Structure and Node Attribute Information

In this subsection, we introduce self-supervised tasks based on both graph structure and node attribute information.

- **Pseudo Label** (Sun et al., 2019c; You et al., 2020). In this task, pseudo labels are generated for unlabeled nodes using the GNN model or other models. Then are utilized as supervised signals to re-train the model together with the labeled nodes. In You et al. (2020), clusters were generated using the learned node representations from the GNN model, and the clusters were used as the pseudo labels. In Sun et al. (2019c), these clusters were aligned with the real labels and then employed as the pseudo labels.
- **Distance2Labeled** (Jin et al., 2020c). This task is similar to the task of Distance2Cluster. Instead of predicting the distance between nodes and pre-calculated clusters, we aim to predict the distance between unlabeled nodes to the labeled nodes.

- **ContextLabel** (Jin et al., 2020c). The ContextLabel task is to predict the label distribution of the context for the nodes in the graph. The context of a given node is defined as all of its k-hop neighbors. The label distribution of the nodes in the context of a given node can then be formulated as a vector. Its dimension is the number of classes where each element indicates the frequency of the corresponding label in the context. Nevertheless, the label information of the unlabeled nodes is unknown. Hence, the distribution can not be accurately measured. In Jin et al. (2020c), methods such as label propagation (Zhu et al., 2003) and iterative classification algorithm (Neville and Jensen, n.d.) were adopted to predict the pseudo labels, which were then used to estimate the label distribution.

- **CorrectedLabel** (Jin et al., 2020c). This task is to enhance the ContextLabel task by iteratively refining the pseudo labels. Specifically, there are two phases in this task: the training phase and the label correction phase. Given the pseudo labels, the training phase is the same as the task of ContextLabel. The predicted pseudo labels in the training phase are then refined in the label correction phase using the noisy label refining algorithm proposed in Han et al. (2019). These refined (corrected) pseudo labels are adopted to extract the context label distribution in the training phase.

14.3.2 Graph-Focused Tasks

In graph-focused tasks, we denote the set of labeled graphs as $\mathcal{D}_l = \{(\mathcal{G}_i, y_i)\}$, where y_i is the associated label of the graph $\mathcal{G}_i$. The set of unlabeled graphs is denoted as $\mathcal{D}_u = \{(\mathcal{G}_j)\}$. Typically, the number of the unlabeled graphs is much larger than that of labeled graphs; i.e., $|\mathcal{D}_u| \gg |\mathcal{D}_l|$. Exploring unlabeled data aims to extract knowledge from $\mathcal{D}_u$ to help train models on $\mathcal{D}_l$. To take advantage of unlabeled data, self-supervision signals are extracted. As in the node-focused case, there are two main ways to leverage knowledge from $\mathcal{D}_u$. One is via two-stage training, where GNNs are pretrained on the unlabeled data $\mathcal{D}_u$ with the self-supervised objective and then fine-tuned on the labeled data $\mathcal{D}_l$. The other is through joint training, where the self-supervised objective is included as a regularization term to be optimized with the supervised loss. In this section, we introduce graph-level self-supervised tasks.

- **Context Prediction** (Hu et al., 2019). In context prediction, the pretraining task is to predict whether a given pair of *K-hop neighborhood* and *context graph* belongs to the same node. Specifically, for every node v in a graph $\mathcal{G}$, its *K-hop neighborhood* consists of all nodes and edges that are at most K-hops away from node v in $\mathcal{G}$, which can be denoted as $\mathcal{N}_{\mathcal{G}}^K(v)$. Meanwhile,

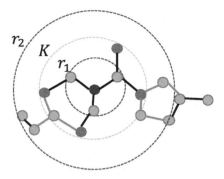

Figure 14.1 Context prediction.

the *context graph* of a node $v \in \mathcal{G}$ is defined by two hyperparameters r_1, r_2, and it is a subgraph that contains nodes and edges between r_1 and r_2 hops away from the node v in the graph $\mathcal{G}$. In detail, the context graph of node v in a graph $\mathcal{G}$ is a ring of width $r_2 - r_1$ as shown in Figure 14.1, which can be denoted as $C_{v,\mathcal{G}}$. Note that r_1 is required to be smaller than K to ensure that there are some nodes shared between the *neighborhood* and the *context graph* of node v. The task of context prediction is then modeled as a binary classification. It is to determine whether a particular neighborhood $\mathcal{N}_{\mathcal{G}}^{K}(v)$ and a particular *context graph* $C_{v,\mathcal{G}}$ belong to the same node. A similar task was proposed in Sun et al. (2019b) where, given a node and a graph, the goal is to predict whether the node belongs to the given graph.

- **Attribute Masking** (Hu et al., 2019). In attribute masking, some node/edge attributes (e.g., atom types in molecular graphs) in a given graph from $\mathcal{D}_u$ are randomly masked. Then GNN models are trained to predict these masked node/edge attributes. Note that the attribute masking strategy can only be applied to graphs with node/edge attributes.
- **Graph Property Prediction** (Hu et al., 2019). Though there might be no labels for graphs in $\mathcal{D}_u$ for the specific task we want to perform on $\mathcal{D}_l$, there could be other graph attributes available for them. These graph attributes can serve as the supervised signal to pretrain the GNN model.

14.4 Expressiveness of Graph Neural Networks

Increasing efforts have been made to analyze the expressiveness of GNN models. They aim to analyze the capability of GNN models to distinguish graph structures from the graph-level perspective. Hence, for the ease of discussion, we quickly recap the GNN models for graph-focused tasks. We write a general aggregation-based spatial graph filter of the lth layer of the GNN model as

$$\mathbf{a}_i^{(l)} = \text{AGG}\left(\left\{\mathbf{F}_j^{(l-1)}|v_j \in \mathcal{N}(v_i)\right\}\right),$$
$$\mathbf{F}_i^{(l)} = \text{COM}\left(\mathbf{F}_i^{(l-1)}, \mathbf{a}_i^{(l)}\right),$$

where $\mathbf{a}_i^{(l)}$ represents the information aggregated from the neighbors of node v_i with the function AGG() and $\mathbf{F}_i^{(l)}$ is the hidden representation of node v_i after the lth graph filtering layer. The function COM() combines the hidden representation of node v_i from the $(l-1)$st layer together with the aggregated information to generate the hidden representations in the lth layer. For graph-focused tasks, a pooling operation is usually operated on the representations $\{\mathbf{F}_i^{(L)}|v_i \in \mathcal{V}\}$ to generate the graph representation, where L is the number of graph filtering layers. Note that, in this chapter, for convenience, we only consider flat pooling operations and the process of pooling is described as

$$\mathbf{F}_\mathcal{G} = \text{POOL}\left(\left\{\mathbf{F}_i^{(L)}|v_i \in \mathcal{V}\right\}\right),$$

where $\mathbf{F}_\mathcal{G}$ denotes the graph representation. There are different choices and designs for the AGG(), COM(), and POOL() functions, which results in GNN models with different expressiveness. It was shown in Xu et al. (2019d) that no matter what kinds of functions are adopted, the GNN models are at most as powerful as the Weisfeiler–Lehman (WL) graph isomorphism test (Weisfeiler and Leman, n.d.) in distinguishing graph structures. The WL test is a powerful test that can distinguish a broad class of graph structures. Conditions are further established under which the GNN models can be as powerful as the WL test in distinguishing graph structures. Next, we briefly introduce the WL test and how GNN models are related. We then present some key results on the expressiveness of GNN models.

14.4.1 Weisfeiler–Lehman Test

Two graphs are considered to be topologically identical (or isomorphic) if there is a mapping between the node sets of the graphs such that the adjacency relations are the same. For example, two isomorphic graphs are shown in Figure 14.2, where the color and number indicate the mapping relations between the two sets of nodes. The graph isomorphism task aims to tell whether two given graphs $\mathcal{G}_1$ and $\mathcal{G}_2$ are topologically identical. It is computationally expensive to test graph isomorphism, and no polynomial-time algorithm has been found yet (Garey and Johnson, n.d.; Babai, 2016).

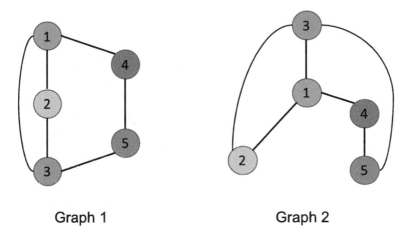

Graph 1   Graph 2

Figure 14.2 Two isomorphic graphs.

The Weisfeiler–Lehman test is an efficient and effective approach for the graph isomorphism task. It can distinguish a broad class of graphs while failing to distinguish some corner cases (Cai et al., 1992).

For convenience, we assume that each node in the two graphs is associated with labels (attributes). For example, in Figure 14.2, the numbers can be treated as the labels. In practice, the same labels could be associated with different nodes in the graph. A single iteration of the WL test can be described as follows:

- For each node v_i, we aggregate its neighbors' labels (including itself) into a multiset $\mathcal{NL}(v_i)$; i.e., a set with repeated elements.
- For each node v_i, we hash the multiset $\mathcal{NL}(v_i)$ into a unique new label, which is now associated with node v_i as its new label. Note that any nodes with the same multiset of labels are hashed to the same new label.

The above iteration is repeatedly applied until the sets of labels of two graphs differ from each other. If the sets of labels differ, then the two graphs are non-isomorphic and the algorithm is terminated. After N (or the number of nodes in the graph) iterations, if the sets of labels of the two graphs are still the same, the two graphs are considered to be isomorphic, or the WL test fails to distinguish them (see Cai et al. [1992] for the corner cases where the WL test fails). Note that the GNN models can be regarded as a generalized WL test. Specifically, the AGG() function in the GNNs corresponds to the aggregation step

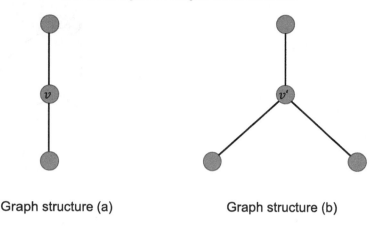

Graph structure (a)   Graph structure (b)

Figure 14.3 Graph structures that mean and max functions fail to distinguish.

in the WL test, and the COM() function corresponds to the hash function in the WL test.

14.4.2 Expressiveness

The expressiveness of the GNN models can be related to the graph isomorphism task. Ideally, a GNN model with sufficient expressiveness can distinguish graphs with different structures by mapping them into different embeddings. The following lemma shows that the GNN models are at most as powerful as the WL test in distinguishing nonisomorphic graphs.

Lemma 14.2   *(Xu et al., 2019d) Given any two nonisomorphic graphs G_1 and G_2, if a GNN model maps these two graphs into different embeddings, the WL test also decides that these two graphs are non-isomorphic.*

The power of the WL test is largely attributed to its injective aggregation operation; i.e., the hash function maps nodes with different neighborhoods to different labels. However, many popular aggregation functions in GNN models are not injective. Next, we briefly discuss some AGG() functions and provide examples of graph structures where these AGG() functions fail to distinguish. Both the mean function and max function introduced in Hamilton et al. (2017a) are not injective. As shown in Figure 14.3, assuming that all nodes have the same label (or the same feature), the local structures of nodes v and v' are distinct because they have different numbers of neighbors. However, if mean or max is adopted as the AGG() function, the same representation is obtained as the aggregation result for nodes v and v'. Hence, these two substructures shown in Figure 14.3 cannot be distinguished if mean or max is adopted as the AGG() function. To improve the expressiveness of the GNN models, it is important to design the functions carefully, including AGG(), COM(), and POOL() to be injective. Specifically, the GNN models are as powerful as WL test if all of these functions are injective as stated in the following theorem.

Theorem 14.3 *(Xu et al., 2019d) A GNN model with sufficient graph filtering layers can map two graphs that are tested as nonisomorphic by the WL test to different embeddings, if all AGG(), COM(), and POOL() functions in the GNN model are injective.*

Theorem 14.3 provides guidance on designing GNN models with high expressiveness. Though the GNN models are at most as powerful as the WL test in distinguishing graph structures, they have their advantages over the WL test. The GNN models can map graphs into low-dimensional embeddings, which capture the similarity between them. However, the WL test is not able to compare the similarity between graphs except for determining whether they are isomorphic or not. Hence, GNNs are suitable for tasks like graph classification, where graphs can have different sizes and nonisomorphic graphs with similar structures could belong to the same class.

14.5 Conclusion

In this chapter, we discuss advanced topics in GNNs. We describe the oversmoothing issue in GNNs and discuss some remedies to mitigate this issue. We introduce various self-supervised learning tasks on graph-structured data for both node- and graph-focused tasks. We demonstrate that GNN models are at most as powerful as the WL test in distinguishing graph structures and provide some guidance in developing GNNs with high expressiveness.

14.6 Further Reading

As aforementioned, there are more new directions on GNNs that are just initialized. Explainable GNN models have been developed in Ying et al.

(2019) and Yuan et al. (2020). Specifically, in Ying et al. (2019), sample-level explanations are generated for GNNs; i.e., generating explanations for each sample. In Yuan et al. (2020), model-level explanations have been studied for GNNs; i.e., understanding how the entire GNN model works. In Tang et al. (2020), the fairness issues of GNNs were investigated. It was observed that the node classification performance based on GNNs varies in terms of the node degree. In particular, nodes with low degrees tend to have a higher error rate than those with high degrees. In Chami et al. (2019) and Liu et al. (2019a), GNNs have been extended to hyperbolic space to facilitate both the expressiveness of GNNs and the hyperbolic geometry.

15

Advanced Applications in Graph
Neural Networks

15.1 Introduction

In Part III, we introduced representative applications of graph neural networks, including natural language processing, computer vision, data mining, and biochemistry and health care. Graph neural networks have been employed to facilitate more advanced applications because graphs are natural representations of data produced by many real-world applications and systems. Numerous combinational optimization problems on graphs such as minimum vertex cover and the traveling salesman problem (TSP) are NP-hard. Graph neural networks have been used to learn the heuristics for these NP-hard problems. Graphs can denote source code in programs from many perspectives, such as data and control flow. Thus, graph neural networks can be naturally leveraged to learn representations for source code to automate various tasks such as variable misuse detection and software vulnerability detection. For dynamical systems in physics, the objects and their relations can often be denoted as graphs. Graph neural networks have been adopted to infer future states of dynamic systems. This chapter discusses these advanced and sophisticated applications and then introduces how graph neural networks can be applied.

15.2 Combinatorial Optimization on Graphs

Many combinational optimization problems on graphs such as minimum vertex cover (MVC) and TSP are NP-hard. In other words, no polynomial-time solutions are available for them (under the condition P $\neq$ NP). These problems are hence usually tackled by approximation algorithms or heuristics. Designing good heuristics is usually a challenging and tedious process and requires significant problem-specific knowledge and trial-and-error. Hence,

281

it is desired to learn heuristics automatically. Graph neural networks have been utilized to learn these heuristics from given samples and then try to find solutions for unseen tasks. Next, we describe some combinatorial optimization problems on graphs and then briefly introduce how graph neural networks can be leveraged to facilitate these tasks.

- **Minimum Vertex Cover.** Given a graph $G = \{\mathcal{V}, \mathcal{E}\}$, a vertex cover $\mathcal{S} \subset \mathcal{V}$ is a subset of vertices that includes at least one endpoint for every edge in $\mathcal{E}$. The problem of MVC is to find a vertex cover that has the smallest amount of nodes.

- **Maximum Cut (MAXCUT).** Given a graph $G = \{\mathcal{V}, \mathcal{E}\}$, a cut $C = \{\mathcal{S}, \mathcal{V}/\mathcal{S}\}$ is a partition of $\mathcal{V}$ into two disjoint subsets $\mathcal{S}$ and $\mathcal{V}/\mathcal{S}$. Its corresponding cut set is the subset of edges $\mathcal{E}_c \in \mathcal{E}$ with one endpoint in $\mathcal{S}$ and the other endpoint in $\mathcal{V}/\mathcal{S}$. The problem of maximum cut is to find such a cut C, where the weights of its cut set $\mathcal{E}_c$ denoted as $\sum_{(u,v) \in \mathcal{E}_c} w(u, v)$ are maximized, where $w(u, v)$ denotes the weight of edge (u, v).

- **Traveling Salesman Problem.** Given a collection of cities connected through routes, the TSP problem is to find the shortest route that visits every city once and comes back to the starting city. It can be modeled as a graph $G = \{\mathcal{V}, \mathcal{E}\}$, where nodes are the cities and edges are the routes connecting them. The distance between cities can be modeled as weights on the edges.

- **Maximal Independent Set (MIS).** Given a graph G, an independent set is a subset of vertices $\mathcal{S} \subset \mathcal{V}$ where no pair of nodes is connected by an edge. The problem of MIS is to find the independent set with the largest number of nodes.

Some of these problems can often be modeled as a node/edge annotation problem, where the goal is to tell whether a node/edge is in the solution or not. For example, the problem of MVC can be modeled as a node annotation problem (or a node classification problem), where the node in the solution is annotated as 1. In contrast, those not in the solution are annotated as 0. Similarly, the TSP can be modeled as a problem of node selection or edge annotation. Graph neural networks are suitable to tackle these problems, given rich training samples. However, directly tackling these problems as purely node/edge annotation tasks may lead to invalid solutions. For example, in the task of MIS, two connected nodes might be annotated as 1 at the same time during the inference, which may lead to an invalid independent set. Hence, some search heuristics are usually utilized with graph neural networks to find valid solutions.

In Khalil et al. (2017), these problems are modeled as a sequential node selection task, which is tackled with reinforcement learning. The GNN model is utilized to model the state representations for the deep reinforcement learning framework. A solution is constructed by sequentially adding nodes to a partial solution. These nodes are sequentially selected greedily by maximizing some evaluation functions in the reinforcement learning framework, which is used to measure the quality of the solution (or partial solution). After the nodes are chosen, a helper function is employed to organize them into a valid solution of given tasks. For example, for the MAXCUT task, given the selected set S, its complementary set $\mathcal{V}/S$ is found, and the maximum cut set includes all edges with one endpoint in one set and the other endpoint in the other set.

Instead of sequentially choosing nodes with a reinforcement learning framework, the tasks were modeled as a node annotation task in Li et al. (2018e). During the training stage, nodes in each training sample are annotated with 1 or 0, where 1 indicates that nodes are in the set of solutions. After training, given a new sample, the GNN model can output a probability score for each node, indicating how likely it should be included in the solution. Then a greedy search algorithm is proposed based on these probability scores to build valid solutions recursively. For example, for the MIS task, nodes are first sorted by the probability scores in descending order. Then we iterate all nodes in this order and label each node with 1 and its neighbors with 0. The process stops when we encounter the first node labeled with 0. Next, we remove all labeled nodes (labeled with 1 or 0) and use the remaining nodes to build an induced subgraph. We repeat the process on the induced subgraph. The entire process is terminated until all nodes in the graph are labeled.

In Joshi et al. (2019), the GNN model is trained to annotate edges to solve the TSP. During training, edges in each training sample are annotated with 1 or 0, indicating whether the edge is in the solution or not. Then, during the inference stage, the model can predict probability scores for edges in the graph. These scores are combined with the beam search to find valid solutions for the TSP.

15.3 Learning Program Representations

Machine learning techniques have been adopted to automate various tasks on source code, such as variable misuse detection and software vulnerability detection. A natural way to denote the source code is to treat it as "articles" in a specific language. Then we can transfer the techniques designed for natural language processing to deal with source code. However, representing source code as a sequence of tokens usually fails to capture the syntactic and semantic relations in the code. There are increasing attempts to represent code as graphs, and graph neural networks have been employed to learn representations to facilitate downstream tasks. Next, we briefly introduce how source code can be denoted as graphs. Then, we describe some downstream tasks and how graph neural networks can be employed to handle these tasks.

There are various ways to construct graphs from source code. Representative ones are listed below (Zhou et al., 2019):

- **Abstract Syntax Tree (AST)**. One common graph representation for the program is the AST. It encodes the abstract syntactic structure of the source code. Usually, AST is used by code parsers to understand the code structures and find syntactic errors. Nodes in AST consist of syntax nodes (corresponding to nonterminals in the programming language's grammar) and syntax tokens (corresponding to terminals). Directed edges are adopted to represent the child–parent relations.

- **Control Flow Graph (CFG)**. The control flow graph describes all potential paths to be traversed in a program during the execution. CFGs consist of statements and conditions as nodes. Conditional statements such as *if* and *switch* are the key nodes for forming different paths. The edges in CFGs indicate the transfer of the control between statements.

- **Data Flow Graph (DFG)**. A data flow graph describes how variables are used through the program. It has the variables as its nodes, and the edges represent any access or modifications to these variables.

- **Natural Code Sequence (NCS)**. The natural code sequence is a sequence of the source code where the edges connect neighboring code tokens according to the order in the source code.

These graphs can further be combined to form a more comprehensive graph that encodes both syntactic and semantic information about the program. Different tasks can be performed with graph neural networks based on the built graphs for a given program. Graph neural networks are usually utilized to learn node representations or graph representations, which are then employed to perform these tasks. There are tasks focusing on nodes in the graphs such as variable misuse detection in a program (Allamanis et al., 2017) and tasks focusing on the entire program graph such as software vulnerability detection (Zhou et al., 2019).

15.4 Reasoning Interacting Dynamical Systems in Physics

Interacting systems are ubiquitous in nature, and dynamical systems in physics are representative. Inferring the future states or underlying properties of the dynamical system is challenging due to the complicated interactions between objects in the dynamical system. The objects and their relations in dynamical systems can be typically denoted as a graph, where the objects are the nodes and the relations between them can be captured as edges. We introduce some dynamical systems in physics and then briefly describe how graph neural networks can be used to infer these dynamical systems.

- **N-body**. In the N-body domain, there are N objects. All N objects in this dynamic system exert gravitational forces on each other dependent on their mass and pair-wise distance. Because the relations are pair-wise, there are in total $N(N-1)$ relations, which can be modeled as a fully connected graph. Predicting the dynamics of solar systems can be regarded as an N-body problem.
- **Bouncing balls**. In the domain of the bouncing ball, there are two types of objects; i.e., the balls and the walls. The balls are constantly moving and can collide with other balls and the static walls. Assuming that there are in total N objects including both balls and walls, $N(N-1)$ pair-wise relations exist, which again can be modeled as a fully connected graph.
- **Charged particles**. In the charged particles domain, there are N particles, and each of them carries a positive or negative charge. Each pair of particles interacts with each other; hence, there are $N(N-1)$ relations and the system can be modeled as a fully connected graph.

The goal of the task is to infer the future status, given the history (or the initial status) of the dynamical system. The status of the dynamical system can be represented by the trajectories of the objects $\mathcal{T} = \{\mathbf{x}_i, \ldots, \mathbf{x}_N\}$, where $\mathbf{x}_i = \{\mathbf{x}_i^{(0)}, \ldots \mathbf{x}_i^{(t)}\}$ with $\mathbf{x}_i^{(t)}$ denoting the status of node i at time t. Usually, the status information about an object includes its positions or velocity.

In Battaglia et al. (2016), a model called an interaction network is proposed to model and predict the future status of the dynamical system. The model can be viewed as a specific type of graph neural networks. It is also based on passing messages through the graphs to update the node representations. Specifically, there are relation-centric and node-centric functions in the interaction network model, where the relation-centric function is adopted to model the effect of the interactions between nodes and the node-centric function takes the output of the relation-centric function to update the status of the nodes. Hence, compared with the message passing neural network framework introduced in Subsection 5.3.2, the relation-centric function can be regarded as the message function and the node-centric function can be viewed as the update function. These functions are usually modeled with neural networks. Note that the interaction network can handle different types of objects and relations by designing various types of functions. A more general framework, caled a graph networks, was proposed in Battaglia et al. (2018).

The interaction network assumes that relations between the objects are known, which might not be practical. In Kipf et al. (2018), a model was proposed to infer the types of relations while predicting the future status of the dynamical system. It takes the form of variational autoencoder, where both the encoder and decoder are modeled by graph neural networks. The encoder, which is applied to the original input graph $\mathcal{G}$, takes the observed trajectories (the history of the dynamical system) as input and predicts the types of relations. The graph with the information of relation types from the encoder is denoted as $\mathcal{G}'$. It is used as the input graph for the decoder. The decoder is also modeled with graph neural networks, and its goal is to predict the future status of the interacting system.

15.5 Conclusion

In this chapter, we discussed some advanced applications of graph neural networks. We introduced their usage to produce heuristics for NP-hard combinatorial optimizations on graphs such as MVC, maximum cut, the TSP, and MIS set. We illustrated how source code can be denoted as graphs and how graph neural networks can be leveraged to learn program representations to facilitate downstream tasks. We also presented how to infer the future dynamics of interacting physical systems via graph neural networks.

15.6 Further Reading

Graph neural networks have been proven to be powerful in handling graph-structured data. They are continually being employed for new applications. In Jeong et al. (2019), musical scores were denoted as graphs, and graph neural networks were applied to these graphs to render expressive piano performance.

In Zhang et al. (2019c), graph neural networks were adopted to speed up the process of distributed circuit design. In Rusek et al. (2019), graph neural networks were utilized to facilitate network modeling and optimization in software-defined networks.

Bibliography

Abadi, Martín, Agarwal, Ashish, Barham, Paul, Brevdo, Eugene, Chen, Zhifeng, et al. 2015. *TensorFlow: Large-Scale Machine Learning on Heterogeneous Systems.* Software available from tensorflow.org.

Adamic, Lada A., and Adar, Eytan. 2003. Friends and neighbors on the web. *Social Networks*, **25**(3), 211–230.

Afsar Minhas, Fayyaz ul Amir, Geiss, Brian J., and Ben-Hur, Asa. 2014. PAIRpred: Partner-specific prediction of interacting residues from sequence and structure. *Proteins: Structure, Function, and Bioinformatics*, **82**(7), 1142–1155.

Aggarwal, Charu C. 2018. *Neural Networks and Deep Learning.* Springer.

Aggarwal, Charu C. 2020. *Linear Algebra and Optimization for Machine Learning.* Springer.

Allamanis, Miltiadis, Brockschmidt, Marc, and Khademi, Mahmoud. 2017. Learning to represent programs with graphs. *International Conference on Learning Representations.*

Andersen, Reid, Chung, Fan, and Lang, Kevin. 2006. Local graph partitioning using pagerank vectors. Pages 475–486 of: *2006 47th Annual IEEE Symposium on Foundations of Computer Science (FOCS'06).* IEEE.

Atwood, James, and Towsley, Don. 2016. Diffusion-convolutional neural networks. Pages 1993–2001 of: *Advances in Neural Information Processing Systems.*

Babai, László. 2016. Graph isomorphism in quasipolynomial time. Pages 684–697 of: *Proceedings of the Forty-Eighth Annual ACM Symposium on Theory of Computing.*

Bahdanau, Dzmitry, Cho, Kyunghyun, and Bengio, Yoshua. 2014. Neural machine translation by jointly learning to align and translate. *3rd International Conference on Learning Representations, (ICLR) 2015, San Diego, CA, USA, May 7–9, 2015, Conference Track Proceedings.*

Bai, Song, Zhang, Feihu, and Torr, Philip H. S. 2019. Hypergraph convolution and hypergraph attention. *Pattern Recognition*, **110**, 107637.

Banarescu, Laura, Bonial, Claire, Cai, Shu, Georgescu, Madalina, Griffitt, Kira, et al. 2013. Abstract meaning representation for sembanking. Pages 178–186 of:

Proceedings of the 7th Linguistic Annotation Workshop and Interoperability with Discourse.

Bastings, Joost, Titov, Ivan, Aziz, Wilker, Marcheggiani, Diego, and Sima'an, Khalil. 2017. Graph convolutional encoders for syntax-aware neural machine translation. Pages 1957–1967 of: *Proceedings of the 2017 Conference on Empirical Methods in Natural Language Processing.*

Battaglia, Peter W., Hamrick, Jessica B., Bapst, Victor, Sanchez-Gonzalez, Alvaro, Zambaldi, et al. 2018. Relational inductive biases, deep learning, and graph networks. *arXiv preprint arXiv:1806.01261.*

Battaglia, Peter W., Pascanu, Razvan, Lai, Matthew, Rezende, Danilo Jimenez, et al. 2016. Interaction networks for learning about objects, relations and physics. Pages 4502–4510 of: *Advances in Neural Information Processing Systems.*

Baytas, Inci M., Xiao, Cao, Wang, Fei, Jain, Anil K., and Zhou, Jiayu. 2018. Heterogeneous hyper-network embedding. Pages 875–880 of: *2018 IEEE International Conference on Data Mining (ICDM).* IEEE.

Beck, Daniel, Haffari, Gholamreza, and Cohn, Trevor. 2018. Graph-to-sequence learning using gated graph neural networks. Pages 273–283 of: *Proceedings of the 56th Annual Meeting of the Association for Computational Linguistics: Vol. 1. Long Papers.*

Belkin, Mikhail, and Niyogi, Partha. 2003. Laplacian eigenmaps for dimensionality reduction and data representation. *Neural Computation,* **15**(6), 1373–1396.

Berg, Rianne van den, Kipf, Thomas N., and Welling, Max. 2017. Graph convolutional matrix completion. *arXiv preprint arXiv:1706.02263.*

Berlusconi, Giulia, Calderoni, Francesco, Parolini, Nicola, Verani, Marco, and Piccardi, Carlo. 2016. Link prediction in criminal networks: A tool for criminal intelligence analysis. *PLoS One,* **11**(4), e0154244.

Bishop, Christopher M. 2006. *Pattern Recognition and Machine Learning.* Springer.

Bonacich, Phillip. 1972. Factoring and weighting approaches to status scores and clique identification. *Journal of Mathematical Sociology,* **2**(1), 113–120.

Bonacich, Phillip. 2007. Some unique properties of eigenvector centrality. *Social Networks,* **29**(4), 555–564.

Bonchev, Danail. 1991. *Chemical Graph Theory: Introduction and Fundamentals.* Vol. 1. CRC Press.

Bondy, John Adrian, et al. *Graph Theory with Applications.* Vol. 290.

Borgatti, Stephen P., Mehra, Ajay, Brass, Daniel J., and Labianca, Giuseppe. 2009. Network analysis in the social sciences. *Science,* **323**(5916), 892–895.

Bourigault, Simon, Lagnier, Cedric, Lamprier, Sylvain, Denoyer, Ludovic, and Gallinari, Patrick. 2014. Learning social network embeddings for predicting information diffusion. Pages 393–402 of: *Proceedings of the 7th ACM International Conference on Web Search and Data Mining.*

Boyd, Stephen, Boyd, Stephen P., and Vandenberghe, Lieven. 2004. *Convex Optimization.* Cambridge University Press.

Bracewell, Ronald Newbold. *The Fourier Transform and Its Applications.* Vol. 31999.

Bruna, Joan, Zaremba, Wojciech, Szlam, Arthur, and LeCun, Yann. 2013. Spectral networks and locally connected networks on graphs. *arXiv preprint arXiv:1312.6203.*

Cai, Hongyun, Zheng, Vincent W., and Chang, Kevin Chen-Chuan. 2018. A comprehensive survey of graph embedding: Problems, techniques, and applications. *IEEE Transactions on Knowledge and Data Engineering*, **30**(9), 1616–1637.

Cai, Jin-Yi, Fürer, Martin, and Immerman, Neil. 1992. An optimal lower bound on the number of variables for graph identification. *Combinatorica*, **12**(4), 389–410.

Cao, Shaosheng, Lu, Wei, and Xu, Qiongkai. 2015. GraRep: Learning graph representations with global structural information. Pages 891–900 of: *Proceedings of the 24th ACM International Conference on Information and Knowledge Management*.

Cao, Shaosheng, Lu, Wei, and Xu, Qiongkai. 2016. Deep neural networks for learning graph representations. *Thirtieth AAAI Conference on Artificial Intelligence*.

Cao, Yu, Fang, Meng, and Tao, Dacheng. 2019. BAG: Bi-directional attention entity graph convolutional network for multi-hop reasoning question answering. Pages 357–362 of: *Proceedings of the 2019 Conference of the North American Chapter of the Association for Computational Linguistics: Human Language Technologies: Vol. 1. Long and Short Papers*.

Carlini, Nicholas, and Wagner, David. 2017. Towards evaluating the robustness of neural networks. Pages 39–57 of: *2017 IEEE Symposium on Security and Privacy (SP)*. IEEE.

Cartwright, Dorwin, and Harary, Frank. 1956. Structural balance: A generalization of Heider's theory. *Psychological Review*, **63**(5), 277.

Cauchy, Augustin. *Méthode générale pour la résolution des systemes déquations simultanées*.

Chami, Ines, Ying, Zhitao, Ré, Christopher, and Leskovec, Jure. 2019. Hyperbolic graph convolutional neural networks. Pages 4868–4879 of: *Advances in Neural Information Processing Systems*.

Chan, T.-H. Hubert, and Liang, Zhibin. 2019. Generalizing the hypergraph Laplacian via a diffusion process with mediators. *Theoretical Computer Science*, **806**, 416–428.

Chan, T.-H. Hubert, Louis, Anand, Tang, Zhihao Gavin, and Zhang, Chenzi. 2018. Spectral properties of hypergraph Laplacian and approximation algorithms. *Journal of the ACM*, **65**(3), 15.

Chang, Shiyu, Han, Wei, Tang, Jiliang, Qi, Guo-Jun, Aggarwal, Charu C., and Huang, Thomas S. 2015. Heterogeneous network embedding via deep architectures. Pages 119–128 of: *Proceedings of the 21th ACM SIGKDD International Conference on Knowledge Discovery and Data Mining*.

Chaudhary, Anshika, Mittal, Himangi, and Arora, Anuja. 2019. Anomaly detection using graph neural networks. Pages 346–350 of: *2019 International Conference on Machine Learning, Big Data, Cloud and Parallel Computing (COMITCon)*. IEEE.

Chen, Jianfei, Zhu, Jun, and Song, Le. 2018a. Stochastic training of graph convolutional networks with variance reduction. Pages 941–949 of: *International Conference on Machine Learning*.

Chen, Jie, Ma, Tengfei, and Xiao, Cao. 2018b. FastGCN: Fast learning with graph convolutional networks via importance sampling. *International Conference on Learning Representations*.

Chen, Tianshui, Yu, Weihao, Chen, Riquan, and Lin, Liang. 2019a. Knowledge-embedded routing network for scene graph generation. Pages 6163–6171 of: *Proceedings of the IEEE Conference on Computer Vision and Pattern Recognition.*

Chen, Ting, and Sun, Yizhou. 2017. Task-guided and path-augmented heterogeneous network embedding for author identification. Pages 295–304 of: *Proceedings of the Tenth ACM International Conference on Web Search and Data Mining.*

Chen, Xia, Yu, Guoxian, Wang, Jun, Domeniconi, Carlotta, Li, Zhao, et al. 2019b. ActiveHNE: Active heterogeneous network embedding. Pages 2123–2129 of: *International Joint Conferences on Artificial Intelligence Organization.*

Chen, Zhao-Min, Wei, Xiu-Shen, Wang, Peng, and Guo, Yanwen. 2019c. Multi-label image recognition with graph convolutional networks. Pages 5177–5186 of: *Proceedings of the IEEE Conference on Computer Vision and Pattern Recognition.*

Chen, Zhengdao, Li, Xiang, and Bruna, Joan. 2017. Supervised community detection with line graph neural networks. *International Conference on Learning Representations.*

Cheng, Kewei, Li, Jundong, and Liu, Huan. 2017. Unsupervised feature selection in signed social networks. Pages 777–786 of: *Proceedings of the 23rd ACM SIGKDD International Conference on Knowledge Discovery and Data Mining.*

Chiang, Wei-Lin, Liu, Xuanqing, Si, Si, Li, Yang, Bengio, Samy, et al. 2019. Cluster-GCN: An efficient algorithm for training deep and large graph convolutional networks. Pages 257–266 of: *Proceedings of the 25th ACM SIGKDD International Conference on Knowledge Discovery & Data Mining.*

Cho, Kyunghyun, Van Merriënboer, Bart, Gulcehre, Caglar, Bahdanau, Dzmitry, Bougares, Fethi, et al. 2014a. Learning phrase representations using RNN encoder–decoder for statistical machine translation. Pages 1724–1734 of: *Proceedings of the 2014 Conference on Empirical Methods in Natural Language Processing (EMNLP).*

Cho, Minsu, Sun, Jian, Duchenne, Olivier, and Ponce, Jean. 2014b. Finding matches in a haystack: A max-pooling strategy for graph matching in the presence of outliers. Pages 2083–2090 of: *Proceedings of the IEEE Conference on Computer Vision and Pattern Recognition.*

Choi, Edward, Xu, Zhen, Li, Yujia, Dusenberry, Michael, Flores, Gerardo, et al. 2020. Learning the graphical structure of electronic health records with graph convolutional transformer. Pages 606–613 of: *Proceedings of the AAAI Conference on Artificial Intelligence.* Vol. 34.

Chung, Fan R. K., and Graham, Fan Chung. 1997. *Spectral Graph Theory.* American Mathematical Society.

Cui, Peng, Wang, Xiao, Pei, Jian, and Zhu, Wenwu. 2018. A survey on network embedding. *IEEE Transactions on Knowledge and Data Engineering*, **31**(5), 833–852.

Cygan, Marek, Pilipczuk, Marcin, Pilipczuk, Michał, and Wojtaszczyk, Jakub Onufry. 2012. Sitting closer to friends than enemies, revisited. Pages 296–307 of: *International Symposium on Mathematical Foundations of Computer Science.* Springer.

Dahl, George, Ranzato, Marc'Aurelio, Mohamed, Abdel-rahman, and Hinton, Geoffrey E. 2010. Phone recognition with the mean–covariance restricted Boltzmann machine. Pages 469–477 of: *Advances in Neural Information Processing Systems.*

Dai, Hanjun, Li, Hui, Tian, Tian, Huang, Xin, Wang, Lin, et al. 2018. Adversarial attack on graph structured data. *Proceedings of the 35th International Conference on Machine Learning, PMLR.* Vol. 80.

Damonte, Marco, and Cohen, Shay B. 2019. Structural neural encoders for AMR-to-text generation. Pages 3649–3658 of: *Proceedings of NAACL-HLT.*

De Cao, Nicola, and Kipf, Thomas. 2018. MolGAN: An implicit generative model for small molecular graphs. *arXiv preprint arXiv:1805.11973.*

De Cao, Nicola, Aziz, Wilker, and Titov, Ivan. 2019. Question answering by reasoning across documents with graph convolutional networks. Pages 2306–2317 of: *Proceedings of the 2019 Conference of the North American Chapter of the Association for Computational Linguistics: Human Language Technologies: Vol. 1. Long and Short Papers.*

Deerwester, Scott, Dumais, Susan T., Furnas, George W., Landauer, Thomas K., and Harshman, Richard. 1990. Indexing by latent semantic analysis. *Journal of the American Society for Information Science,* **41**(6), 391–407.

Defferrard, Michaël, Bresson, Xavier, and Vandergheynst, Pierre. 2016. Convolutional neural networks on graphs with fast localized spectral filtering. Pages 3844–3852 of: *Advances in Neural Information Processing Systems.*

Deng, Li, and Liu, Yang. 2018. *Deep Learning in Natural Language Processing.* Springer.

Deng, Li, Seltzer, Michael L., Yu, Dong, Acero, Alex, Mohamed, Abdel-rahman, and Hinton, Geoff. 2010. Binary coding of speech spectrograms using a deep auto-encoder. *Eleventh Annual Conference of the International Speech Communication Association.*

Derr, Tyler, Ma, Yao, and Tang, Jiliang. 2018. Signed graph convolutional networks. Pages 929–934 of: *2018 IEEE International Conference on Data Mining (ICDM).* IEEE.

Devlin, Jacob, Chang, Ming-Wei, Lee, Kenton, and Toutanova, Kristina. 2018. Bert: Pre-training of deep bidirectional transformers for language understanding. Pages 4171–4186 of: *Proceedings of the 2019 Conference of the North American Chapter of the Association for Computational Linguistics: Human Language Technologies, Volume 1 (Long and Short Papers).*

Dhillon, Inderjit S., Guan, Yuqiang, and Kulis, Brian. 2007. Weighted graph cuts without eigenvectors a multilevel approach. *IEEE Transactions on Pattern Analysis and Machine Intelligence,* **29**(11), 1944–1957.

Di Martino, Adriana, Yan, Chao-Gan, Li, Qingyang, Denio, Erin, Castellanos, Francisco X., et al. 2014. The autism brain imaging data exchange: Towards a large-scale evaluation of the intrinsic brain architecture in autism. *Molecular Psychiatry,* **19**(6), 659–667.

Dong, Yuxiao, Chawla, Nitesh V., and Swami, Ananthram. 2017. metapath2vec: Scalable representation learning for heterogeneous networks. Pages 135–144 of: *Proceedings of the 23rd ACM SIGKDD International Conference on Knowledge Discovery and Data Mining.* ACM.

Duchi, John, Hazan, Elad, and Singer, Yoram. 2011. Adaptive subgradient methods for online learning and stochastic optimization. *Journal of Machine Learning Research,* **12**a, 2121–2159.

Duvenaud, David K., Maclaurin, Dougal, Iparraguirre, Jorge, Bombarell, Rafael, Hirzel, Timothy, et al. 2015. Convolutional networks on graphs for learning molecular fingerprints. Pages 2224–2232 of: *Advances in Neural Information Processing Systems*.

Entezari, Negin, Al-Sayouri, Saba A., Darvishzadeh, Amirali, and Papalexakis, Evangelos E. 2020. All you need is low (rank) defending against adversarial attacks on graphs. Pages 169–177 of: *Proceedings of the 13th International Conference on Web Search and Data Mining*.

Fan, Wenqi, Ma, Yao, Li, Qing, He, Yuan, Zhao, Eric, et al. 2019. Graph neural networks for social recommendation. Pages 417–426 of: *The World Wide Web Conference*. ACM.

Feller, William. 1957. An Introduction to Probability Theory and Its Applications.

Feng, Fuli, He, Xiangnan, Tang, Jie, and Chua, Tat-Seng. 2019a. Graph adversarial training: Dynamically regularizing based on graph structure. *IEEE Transactions on Knowledge and Data Engineering*. 1.

Feng, Yifan, You, Haoxuan, Zhang, Zizhao, Ji, Rongrong, and Gao, Yue. 2019b. Hypergraph neural networks. Pages 3558–3565 of: *Proceedings of the AAAI Conference on Artificial Intelligence*. Vol. 33.

Fernandes, Patrick, Allamanis, Miltiadis, and Brockschmidt, Marc. 2018. Structured neural summarization. *International Conference on Learning Representations*.

Fey, Matthias, and Lenssen, Jan E. 2019. Fast graph representation learning with PyTorch Geometric. *ICLR Workshop on Representation Learning on Graphs and Manifolds*.

Finn, Chelsea, Abbeel, Pieter, and Levine, Sergey. 2017. Model-agnostic meta-learning for fast adaptation of deep networks. Pages 1126–1135 of: *Proceedings of the 34th International Conference on Machine Learning*. Vol. 70.

Fouss, Francois, Pirotte, Alain, Renders, Jean-Michel, and Saerens, Marco. 2007. Random-walk computation of similarities between nodes of a graph with application to collaborative recommendation. *IEEE Transactions on Knowledge and Data Engineering*, **19**(3), 355–369.

Fout, Alex, Byrd, Jonathon, Shariat, Basir, and Ben-Hur, Asa. 2017. Protein interface prediction using graph convolutional networks. Pages 6530–6539 of: *Advances in Neural Information Processing Systems*.

Frobenius, Georg, Frobenius, Ferdinand Georg, Frobenius, Ferdinand Georg, Frobenius, Ferdinand Georg, and Mathematician, Germany. 1912. Über Matrizen aus nicht negativen Elementen.

Fu, Tsu-Jui, Li, Peng-Hsuan, and Ma, Wei-Yun. 2019. GraphRel: Modeling text as relational graphs for joint entity and relation extraction. Pages 1409–1418 of: *Proceedings of the 57th Annual Meeting of the Association for Computational Linguistics*.

Gao, Hongyang, and Ji, Shuiwang. 2019. Graph U-nets. Pages 2083–2092 of: *Proceedings of the 36th International Conference on Machine Learning, ICML 2019, 9–15 June 2019, Long Beach, California, USA*.

Gao, Hongyang, Wang, Zhengyang, and Ji, Shuiwang. 2018a. Large-scale learnable graph convolutional networks. Pages 1416–1424 of: *Proceedings of the 24th ACM SIGKDD International Conference on Knowledge Discovery & Data Mining*.

Gao, Hongyang, Wang, Zhengyang, and Ji, Shuiwang. 2020. Kronecker Attention Networks. Pages 229–237 of: *Proceedings of the 26th ACM SIGKDD International Conference on Knowledge Discovery & Data Mining.*

Gao, Ming, Chen, Leihui, He, Xiangnan, and Zhou, Aoying. 2018b. Bine: Bipartite network embedding. Pages 715–724 of: *The 41st International ACM SIGIR Conference on Research & Development in Information Retrieval.*

Garey, Michael R., and Johnson, David S. *Computers and Intractability.* Vol. 174.

Gidaris, Spyros, and Komodakis, Nikos. 2019. Generating classification weights with GNN denoising autoencoders for few-shot learning. Pages 21–30 of: *Proceedings of the IEEE Conference on Computer Vision and Pattern Recognition.*

Gilmer, Justin, Schoenholz, Samuel S., Riley, Patrick F., Vinyals, Oriol, and Dahl, George E. 2017. Neural message passing for quantum chemistry. Pages 1263–1272 of: *Proceedings of the 34th International Conference on Machine Learning, ICML 2017, Sydney, NSW, Australia, 6–11 August 2017.*

Goldberg, David, Nichols, David, Oki, Brian M., and Terry, Douglas. 1992. Using collaborative filtering to weave an information tapestry. *Communications of the ACM,* **35**(12), 61–70.

Goldberg, Ken, Roeder, Theresa, Gupta, Dhruv, and Perkins, Chris. 2001. Eigentaste: A constant time collaborative filtering algorithm. *Information Retrieval,* **4**(2), 133–151.

Goldberg, Yoav. 2016. A primer on neural network models for natural language processing. *Journal of Artificial Intelligence Research,* **57**, 345–420.

Goodfellow, Ian, Bengio, Yoshua, and Courville, Aaron. 2016. *Deep Learning.*

Goodfellow, Ian, Pouget-Abadie, Jean, Mirza, Mehdi, Xu, Bing, Warde-Farley, David, et al. 2014a. Generative adversarial nets. Pages 2672–2680 of: *Advances in Neural Information Processing Systems.*

Goodfellow, Ian J., Shlens, Jonathon, and Szegedy, Christian. 2014b. Explaining and harnessing adversarial examples. *International Conference on Learning Representations.*

Goyal, Palash, and Ferrara, Emilio. 2018. Graph embedding techniques, applications, and performance: A survey. *Knowledge-Based Systems,* **151**, 78–94.

Grover, Aditya, and Leskovec, Jure. 2016. node2vec: Scalable feature learning for networks. Pages 855–864 of: *Proceedings of the 22nd ACM SIGKDD International Conference on Knowledge Discovery and Data Mining.* ACM.

Gu, Quanquan, and Han, Jiawei. 2011. Towards feature selection in network. Pages 1175–1184 of: *Proceedings of the 20th ACM International Conference on Information and Knowledge Management.*

Gu, Yupeng, Sun, Yizhou, Li, Yanen, and Yang, Yang. 2018. Rare: Social rank regulated large-scale network embedding. Pages 359–368 of: *Proceedings of the 2018 World Wide Web Conference.*

Guo, Zhijiang, Zhang, Yan, and Lu, Wei. 2019. Attention guided graph convolutional networks for relation extraction. Pages 241–251 of: *Association for Computational Linguistics.*

Gutmann, Michael U., and Hyvärinen, Aapo. 2012. Noise-contrastive estimation of unnormalized statistical models, with applications to natural image statistics. *Journal of Machine Learning Research,* **13–**, 307–361.

Hagberg, Aric, Swart, Pieter, and Schult, Daniel. 2008. Exploring network structure, dynamics, and function using NetworkX. Technical Report, Los Alamos National Laboratory, Los Alamos, NM.

Hamaguchi, Takuo, Oiwa, Hidekazu, Shimbo, Masashi, and Matsumoto, Yuji. 2017. Knowledge transfer for out-of-knowledge-base entities: A graph neural network approach. Pages 1802–1808 of: *Proceedings of the 26th International Joint Conference on Artificial Intelligence*. AAAI Press.

Hamilton, Will, Ying, Zhitao, and Leskovec, Jure. 2017a. Inductive representation learning on large graphs. Pages 1024–1034 of: *Advances in Neural Information Processing Systems*.

Hamilton, William L., Ying, Rex, and Leskovec, Jure. 2017b. Representation learning on graphs: Methods and applications. *arXiv preprint arXiv:1709.05584*.

Han, Jiangfan, Luo, Ping, and Wang, Xiaogang. 2019. Deep self-learning from noisy labels. Pages 5138–5147 of: *Proceedings of the IEEE International Conference on Computer Vision*.

Han, Jiawei, Pei, Jian, and Kamber, Micheline. 2011. *Data Mining: Concepts and Techniques*. Elsevier.

He, Chaoyang, Xie, Tian, Rong, Yu, Huang, Wenbing, Li, Yanfang, et al. 2019. Bipartite graph neural networks for efficient node representation learning. *arXiv preprint arXiv:1906.11994*.

He, Kaiming, Zhang, Xiangyu, Ren, Shaoqing, and Sun, Jian. 2016. Deep residual learning for image recognition. Pages 770–778 of: *Proceedings of the IEEE Conference on Computer Vision and Pattern Recognition*.

Heider, Fritz. 1946. Attitudes and cognitive organization. *The Journal of Psychology*, **21**(1), 107–112.

Hochreiter, Sepp, and Schmidhuber, Jürgen. 1997. Long short-term memory. *Neural Computation*, **9**(8), 1735–1780.

Hoffman, Kenneth, and Kunze, Ray. 1971. *Linear Algebra*. NJ.

Hu, Weihua, Liu, Bowen, Gomes, Joseph, Zitnik, Marinka, Liang, Percy, et al. 2019. Pre-training graph neural networks. *International Conference on Learning Representations*.

Hu, Ziniu, Dong, Yuxiao, Wang, Kuansan, Chang, Kai-Wei, and Sun, Yizhou. 2020. GPT-GNN: Generative pre-training of graph neural networks. Pages 1857–1867 of: *Proceedings of the 26th ACM SIGKDD International Conference on Knowledge Discovery & Data Mining*.

Huang, Qiang, Xia, Tingyu, Sun, Huiyan, Yamada, Makoto, and Chang, Yi. 2020. Unsupervised nonlinear feature selection from high-dimensional signed networks. Pages 4182–4189 of: *Proceedings of the AAAI Conference on Artificial Intelligence*.

Huang, Wenbing, Zhang, Tong, Rong, Yu, and Huang, Junzhou. 2018. Adaptive sampling towards fast graph representation learning. Pages 4558–4567 of: *Advances in Neural Information Processing Systems*.

Ioffe, Sergey, and Szegedy, Christian. 2015. Batch normalization: Accelerating deep network training by reducing internal covariate shift. Pages 448–456 of: *Proceedings of the 32nd International Conference on Machine Learning*.

Jeong, Dasaem, Kwon, Taegyun, Kim, Yoojin, and Nam, Juhan. 2019. Graph neural network for music score data and modeling expressive piano performance. Pages 3060–3070 of: *International Conference on Machine Learning*.

Jiang, Jianwen, Wei, Yuxuan, Feng, Yifan, Cao, Jingxuan, and Gao, Yue. 2019. Dynamic hypergraph neural networks. Pages 2635–2641 of: *International Joint Conferences on Artificial Intelligence Organization*.

Jin, Hongwei, and Zhang, Xinhua. 2019. Latent adversarial training of graph convolution networks. *ICML Workshop on Learning and Reasoning with Graph-Structured Representations*.

Jin, Wei, Derr, Tyler, Liu, Haochen, Wang, Yiqi, Wang, Suhang, et al. 2020c. Self-supervised learning on graphs: Deep insights and new direction. *arXiv preprint arXiv:2006.10141*.

Jin, Wei, Li, Yaxin, Xu, Han, Wang, Yiqi, and Tang, Jiliang. 2020a. Adversarial attacks and defenses on graphs: A review and empirical study. *arXiv preprint arXiv:2003.00653*.

Jin, Wei, Ma, Yao, Liu, Xiaorui, Tang, Xianfeng, Wang, Suhang, et al. 2020b. Graph structure learning for robust graph neural networks. *arXiv preprint arXiv:2005.10203*.

Jin, Wengong, Barzilay, Regina, and Jaakkola, Tommi. 2018. Junction tree variational autoencoder for molecular graph generation. Pages 2323–2332 of: *Proceedings of the 35th International Conference on Machine Learning*.

Joshi, Chaitanya K., Laurent, Thomas, and Bresson, Xavier. 2019. An efficient graph convolutional network technique for the travelling salesman problem. *arXiv preprint arXiv:1906.01227*.

Joyce, James M. 2011. *Kullback–Leibler Divergence*.

Jurafsky, Daniel, and Martin, James H. *Speech and Language Processing: An Introduction to Natural Language Processing, Computational Linguistics, and Speech Recognition*.

Kamath, Uday, Liu, John, and Whitaker, James. 2019. *Deep Learning for NLP and Speech Recognition*. Vol. 84. Springer.

Kampffmeyer, Michael, Chen, Yinbo, Liang, Xiaodan, Wang, Hao, Zhang, Yujia, et al. 2019. Rethinking knowledge graph propagation for zero-shot learning. Pages 11487–11496 of: *Proceedings of the IEEE Conference on Computer Vision and Pattern Recognition*.

Kana, Rajesh K., Uddin, Lucina Q., Kenet, Tal, Chugani, Diane, and Müller, Ralph-Axel. 2014. Brain connectivity in autism. *Frontiers in Human Neuroscience*, **8**, 349.

Karypis, George, and Kumar, Vipin. 1998. A fast and high quality multilevel scheme for partitioning irregular graphs. *SIAM Journal on Scientific Computing*, **20**(1), 359–392.

Khademi, Mahmoud, and Schulte, Oliver. 2020. Deep generative probabilistic graph neural networks for scene graph generation. Pages 11237–11245 of: *Proceedings of the AAAI Conference on Artificial Intelligence*.

Khalil, Elias, Dai, Hanjun, Zhang, Yuyu, Dilkina, Bistra, and Song, Le. 2017. Learning combinatorial optimization algorithms over graphs. Pages 6348–6358 of: *Advances in Neural Information Processing Systems*.

Kingma, Diederik P., and Ba, Jimmy. 2014. Adam: A method for stochastic optimization. *arXiv preprint arXiv:1412.6980*.

Kingma, Diederik P., and Welling, Max. 2013. Auto-encoding variational bayes. *arXiv preprint arXiv:1312.6114*.

Kipf, Thomas, Fetaya, Ethan, Wang, Kuan-Chieh, Welling, Max, and Zemel, Richard. 2018. Neural relational inference for interacting systems. Pages 2688–2697 of: *International Conference on Machine Learning*.

Kipf, Thomas N., and Welling, Max. 2016a. Semi-supervised classification with graph convolutional networks. *International Conference on Learning Representations (ICLR)*.

Kipf, Thomas N., and Welling, Max. 2016b. Variational graph auto-encoders. *arXiv preprint arXiv:1611.07308*.

Koren, Yehuda, Bell, Robert, and Volinsky, Chris. 2009. Matrix factorization techniques for recommender systems. *Computer*, **42**(8), 30–37.

Krizhevsky, Alex, Sutskever, Ilya, and Hinton, Geoffrey E. 2012. Imagenet classification with deep convolutional neural networks. Pages 1097–1105 of: *Advances in Neural Information Processing Systems*.

Kuhn, Michael, Letunic, Ivica, Jensen, Lars Juhl, and Bork, Peer. 2016. The SIDER database of drugs and side effects. *Nucleic Acids Research*, **44**(D1), D1075–D1079.

Kunegis, Jérôme, Lommatzsch, Andreas, and Bauckhage, Christian. 2009. The slashdot zoo: Mining a social network with negative edges. Pages 741–750 of: *Proceedings of the 18th International Conference on World Wide Web*. ACM.

Lai, Yi-An, Hsu, Chin-Chi, Chen, Wen Hao, Yeh, Mi-Yen, and Lin, Shou-De. 2017. Prune: Preserving proximity and global ranking for network embedding. Pages 5257–5266 of: *Advances in Neural Information Processing Systems*.

Le Cun, Yann, and Fogelman-Soulié, Françoise. 1987. Modèles connexionnistes de l'apprentissage. *Intellectica*, **2**(1), 114–143.

Lee, John Boaz, Rossi, Ryan, and Kong, Xiangnan. 2018. Graph classification using structural attention. Pages 1666–1674 of: *Proceedings of the 24th ACM SIGKDD International Conference on Knowledge Discovery & Data Mining*.

Lee, Junhyun, Lee, Inyeop, and Kang, Jaewoo. 2019. Self-attention graph pooling. Pages 3734–3743 of: *Proceedings of the 36th International Conference on Machine Learning, ICML 2019, 9–15 June 2019, Long Beach, California, USA*.

Lee, Kenton, He, Luheng, Lewis, Mike, and Zettlemoyer, Luke. 2017. End-to-end neural coreference resolution. Pages 188–197 of: *Proceedings of the 2017 Conference on Empirical Methods in Natural Language Processing*.

Leskovec, Jure, Huttenlocher, Daniel, and Kleinberg, Jon. 2010a. Predicting positive and negative links in online social networks. Pages 641–650 of: *Proceedings of the 19th International Conference on World Wide Web*. ACM.

Leskovec, Jure, Huttenlocher, Daniel, and Kleinberg, Jon. 2010b. Signed networks in social media. Pages 1361–1370 of: *Proceedings of the SIGCHI Conference on Human Factors in Computing Systems*. ACM.

Leskovec, Jur, and Krevl, Andrej. 2014. *SNAP Datasets*.

Leskovec, Jure, and Sosič, Rok. 2016. SNAP: A general-purpose network analysis and graph-mining library. *ACM Transactions on Intelligent Systems and Technology*, **8**(1).

Li, Chang, and Goldwasser, Dan. 2019. Encoding social information with graph convolutional networks for political perspective detection in news media. Pages 2594–2604 of: *Proceedings of the 57th Annual Meeting of the Association for Computational Linguistics*.

Li, Chaolong, Cui, Zhen, Zheng, Wenming, Xu, Chunyan, and Yang, Jian. 2018a. Spatio-temporal graph convolution for skeleton based action recognition. *Thirty-Second AAAI Conference on Artificial Intelligence*.

Li, Chunyan, Liu, Hongju, Hu, Qian, Que, Jinlong, and Yao, Junfeng. 2019a. A novel computational model for predicting microRNA–disease associations based on heterogeneous graph convolutional networks. *Cells*, **8**(9), 977.

Li, Jundong, Cheng, Kewei, Wang, Suhang, Morstatter, Fred, Trevino, Robert P. et al. 2017b. Feature selection: A data perspective. *ACM Computing Surveys*, **50**(6), 1–45.

Li, Jundong, Dani, Harsh, Hu, Xia, Tang, Jiliang, Chang, Yi, and Liu, Huan. 2017a. Attributed network embedding for learning in a dynamic environment. Pages 387–396 of: *Proceedings of the 2017 ACM on Conference on Information and Knowledge Management*. ACM.

Li, Jundong, Guo, Ruocheng, Liu, Chenghao, and Liu, Huan. 2019b. Adaptive unsupervised feature selection on attributed networks. Pages 92–100 of: *Proceedings of the 25th ACM SIGKDD International Conference on Knowledge Discovery & Data Mining*.

Li, Jundong, Hu, Xia, Jian, Ling, and Liu, Huan. 2016. Toward time-evolving feature selection on dynamic networks. Pages 1003–1008 of: *2016 IEEE 16th International Conference on Data Mining (ICDM)*. IEEE.

Li, Maosen, Chen, Siheng, Chen, Xu, Zhang, Ya, Wang, Yanfeng, et al. 2019c. Actional-structural graph convolutional networks for skeleton-based action recognition. Pages 3595–3603 of: *Proceedings of the IEEE Conference on Computer Vision and Pattern Recognition*.

Li, Qimai, Han, Zhichao, and Wu, Xiao-Ming. 2018b. Deeper insights into graph convolutional networks for semi-supervised learning. Pages 3538–3545 of: McIlraith, Sheila A., and Weinberger, Kilian Q. (eds.), *Proceedings of the Thirty-Second AAAI Conference on Artificial Intelligence, (AAAI-18), the 30th innovative Applications of Artificial Intelligence (IAAI-18), and the 8th AAAI Symposium on Educational Advances in Artificial Intelligence (EAAI-18), New Orleans, Louisiana, USA, February 2–7, 2018*. AAAI Press.

Li, Ruoyu, Wang, Sheng, Zhu, Feiyun, and Huang, Junzhou. 2018c. Adaptive graph convolutional neural networks. *Thirty-Second AAAI Conference on Artificial Intelligence*.

Li, Yaxin, Jin, Wei, Xu, Han, and Tang, Jiliang. 2020a. DeepRobust: A PyTorch library for adversarial attacks and defenses. *arXiv preprint arXiv:2005.06149*.

Li, Ye, Sha, Chaofeng, Huang, Xin, and Zhang, Yanchun. 2018d. Community detection in attributed graphs: An embedding approach. *Thirty-Second AAAI Conference on Artificial Intelligence*.

Li, Yu, Tian, Yuan, Zhang, Jiawei, and Chang, Yi. 2020b. Learning signed network embedding via graph attention. *Proceedings of the Thirty-Fourth AAAI Conference on Artificial Intelligence.*

Li, Yujia, Tarlow, Daniel, Brockschmidt, Marc, and Zemel, Richard. 2015. Gated graph sequence neural networks. *arXiv preprint arXiv:1511.05493.*

Li, Zhuwen, Chen, Qifeng, and Koltun, Vladlen. 2018e. Combinatorial optimization with graph convolutional networks and guided tree search. Pages 539–548 of: *Advances in Neural Information Processing Systems.*

Liang, Xiaodan, Shen, Xiaohui, Feng, Jiashi, Lin, Liang, and Yan, Shuicheng. 2016. Semantic object parsing with graph lstm. Pages 125–143 of: *European Conference on Computer Vision.* Springer.

Liao, Renjie, Li, Yujia, Song, Yang, Wang, Shenlong, Hamilton, Will, et al. 2019. Efficient graph generation with graph recurrent attention networks. Pages 4255–4265 of: *Advances in Neural Information Processing Systems.*

Lin, Yankai, Liu, Zhiyuan, Sun, Maosong, Liu, Yang, and Zhu, Xuan. 2015. Learning entity and relation embeddings for knowledge graph completion. *Twenty-Ninth AAAI Conference on Artificial Intelligence.*

Ling, Huan, Gao, Jun, Kar, Amlan, Chen, Wenzheng, and Fidler, Sanja. 2019. Fast interactive object annotation with curve-gcn. Pages 5257–5266 of: *Proceedings of the IEEE Conference on Computer Vision and Pattern Recognition.*

Liu, Huan, and Motoda, Hiroshi. 2007. *Computational Methods of Feature Selection.* CRC Press.

Liu, Huan, and Motoda, Hiroshi. 2012. *Feature Selection for Knowledge Discovery and Data Mining.* Vol. 454. Springer Science & Business Media.

Liu, Ke, Sun, Xiangyan, Jia, Lei, Ma, Jun, Xing, Haoming, et al. 2018a. Chemi-net: A graph convolutional network for accurate drug property prediction. *International Journal of Molecular Sciences*, **20**(14).

Liu, Qi, Nickel, Maximilian, and Kiela, Douwe. 2019a. Hyperbolic graph neural networks. Pages 8230–8241 of: *Advances in Neural Information Processing Systems.*

Liu, Zhiwei, Dou, Yingtong, Yu, Philip S., Deng, Yutong, and Peng, Hao. 2020. Alleviating the inconsistency problem of applying graph neural network to fraud detection. Pages 1569–1572 of: *Proceedings of the 43rd International ACM SIGIR Conference on Research and Development in Information Retrieval.*

Liu, Ziqi, Chen, Chaochao, Yang, Xinxing, Zhou, Jun, Li, Xiaolong, et al. 2018b. Heterogeneous graph neural networks for malicious account detection. Pages 2077–2085 of: *Proceedings of the 27th ACM International Conference on Information and Knowledge Management.*

Liu, Ziqi, Chen, Chaochao, Li, Longfei, Zhou, Jun, Li, Xiaolong, et al. 2019b. Geniepath: Graph neural networks with adaptive receptive paths. Pages 4424–4431 of: *Proceedings of the AAAI Conference on Artificial Intelligence.* Vol. 33.

Ma, Lingxiao, Yang, Zhi, Miao, Youshan, Xue, Jilong, Wu, Ming, et al. 2018a. Towards efficient large-scale graph neural network computing. *arXiv preprint arXiv:1810.08403.*

Ma, Lingxiao, Yang, Zhi, Miao, Youshan, Xue, Jilong, Wu, Ming, et al. 2019a. Neugraph: parallel deep neural network computation on large graphs. Pages 443–458 of: *2019 {USENIX} Annual Technical Conference ({USENIX}{ATC} 19)*.

Ma, Tengfei, Chen, Jie, and Xiao, Cao. 2018b. Constrained generation of semantically valid graphs via regularizing variational autoencoders. Pages 7113–7124 of: *Advances in Neural Information Processing Systems*.

Ma, Tengfei, Xiao, Cao, Zhou, Jiayu, and Wang, Fei. 2018c. Drug similarity integration through attentive multi-view graph auto-encoders. Pages 3477–3483 of: *Proceedings of the 27th International Joint Conference on Artificial Intelligence*.

Ma, Yao, Wang, Suhang, Ren, ZhaoChun, Yin, Dawei, and Tang, Jiliang. 2017. Preserving local and global information for network embedding. *arXiv preprint arXiv:1710.07266*.

Ma, Yao, Ren, Zhaochun, Jiang, Ziheng, Tang, Jiliang, and Yin, Dawei. 2018d. Multi-dimensional network embedding with hierarchical structure. Pages 387–395 of: *Proceedings of the Eleventh ACM International Conference on Web Search and Data Mining*.

Ma, Yao, Wang, Suhang, Aggarwal, Charu C., and Tang, Jiliang. 2019b. Graph convolutional networks with eigenpooling. Pages 723–731 of: Teredesai, Ankur, Kumar, Vipin, Li, Ying, Rosales, Rómer, Terzi, Evimaria, et al. (eds.), *Proceedings of the 25th ACM SIGKDD International Conference on Knowledge Discovery & Data Mining, KDD 2019, Anchorage, AK, USA, August 4–8, 2019*. ACM.

Ma, Yao, Wang, Suhang, Aggarwal, Chara C., Yin, Dawei, and Tang, Jiliang. 2019c. Multi-dimensional graph convolutional networks. Pages 657–665 of: *Proceedings of the 2019 SIAM International Conference on Data Mining*. SIAM.

Ma, Yao, Wang, Suhang, Derr, Tyler, Wu, Lingfei, and Tang, Jiliang. 2020. *Attacking Graph Convolutional Networks via Rewiring*.

Maas, Andrew L., Hannun, Awni Y., and Ng, Andrew Y. 2013. Rectifier nonlinearities improve neural network acoustic models. *Proceedings of the International Conference on Machine Learning*.

Marcheggiani, Diego, and Titov, Ivan. 2017. Encoding sentences with graph convolutional networks for semantic role labeling. Pages 1506–1515 of: *Proceedings of the 2017 Conference on Empirical Methods in Natural Language Processing*.

Marcheggiani, Diego, Bastings, Joost, and Titov, Ivan. 2018. Exploiting semantics in neural machine translation with graph convolutional networks. Pages 486–492 of: *Proceedings of the 2018 Conference of the North American Chapter of the Association for Computational Linguistics: Human Language Technologies, Volume 2 (Short Papers)*.

McCulloch, Warren S, and Pitts, Walter. 1943. A logical calculus of the ideas immanent in nervous activity. *The Bulletin of Mathematical Biophysics*, **5**(4), 115–133.

Menon, Aditya Krishna, and Elkan, Charles. 2011. Link prediction via matrix factorization. Pages 437–452 of: *Joint European Conference on Machine Learning and Knowledge Discovery in Databases*. Springer.

Mikolov, Tomas, Sutskever, Ilya, Chen, Kai, Corrado, Greg S., and Dean, Jeff. 2013. Distributed representations of words and phrases and their compositionality. Pages 3111–3119 of: *Advances in Neural Information Processing Systems*.

Miller, George A. 1998. *WordNet: An Electronic Lexical Database*. MIT press.

Mishra, Pushkar, Del Tredici, Marco, Yannakoudakis, Helen, and Shutova, Ekaterina. 2019. Abusive language detection with graph convolutional networks. Pages 2145–2150 of: *Proceedings of the 2019 Conference of the North American Chapter of the Association for Computational Linguistics: Human Language Technologies, Volume 1 (Long and Short Papers)*.

Miwa, Makoto, and Bansal, Mohit. 2016. End-to-end relation extraction using LSTMs on sequences and tree structures. Pages 1105–1116 of: *Association for Computational Linguistics*.

Monti, Federico, Bronstein, Michael, and Bresson, Xavier. 2017. Geometric matrix completion with recurrent multi-graph neural networks. Pages 3697–3707 of: *Advances in Neural Information Processing Systems*.

Monti, Federico, Frasca, Fabrizio, Eynard, Davide, Mannion, Damon, and Bronstein, Michael M. 2019. Fake news detection on social media using geometric deep learning. *arXiv preprint arXiv:1902.06673*.

Morin, Frederic, and Bengio, Yoshua. 2005. Hierarchical probabilistic neural network language model. Pages 246–252 of: *Proceedings of the Tenth International Workshop on Artificial Intelligence and Statistics*.

Morris, Christopher, Ritzert, Martin, Fey, Matthias, Hamilton, William L, Lenssen, Jan Eric, et al. 2019. Weisfeiler and Leman go neural: Higher-order graph neural networks. Pages 4602–4609 of: *Proceedings of the AAAI Conference on Artificial Intelligence*. Vol. 33.

Nastase, Vivi, Mihalcea, Rada, and Radev, Dragomir R. 2015. A survey of graphs in natural language processing. *Natural Language Engineering*, **21**(5), 665–698.

Nathani, Deepak, Chauhan, Jatin, Sharma, Charu, and Kaul, Manohar. 2019. Learning attention-based embeddings for relation prediction in knowledge graphs. Pages 4710–4723 of: *Proceedings of the 57th Annual Meeting of the Association for Computational Linguistics*.

Neville, Jennifer, and Jensen, David. 2000. Iterative classification in relational data. Pages 13–20 of: *Proc. AAAI-2000 workshop on learning statistical models from relational data*.

Newman, Mark E.J. 2006. Modularity and community structure in networks. *Proceedings of the National Academy of Sciences*, **103**(23), 8577–8582.

Ng, Andrew, et al. 2011. Sparse autoencoder. **72**(2011), 1–19.

Ng, Andrew Y., Jordan, Michael I., and Weiss, Yair. 2002. On spectral clustering: Analysis and an algorithm. Pages 849–856 of: *Advances in Neural Information Processing Systems*.

Nguyen, Giang Hoang, Lee, John Boaz, Rossi, Ryan A., Ahmed, Nesreen K., et al. 2018. Continuous-time dynamic network embeddings. Pages 969–976 of: *Companion Proceedings of the the Web Conference 2018*.

Nguyen, Thin, Le, Hang, and Venkatesh, Svetha. 2019. GraphDTA: prediction of drug–target binding affinity using graph convolutional networks. *BioRxiv: 684662*.

Nickel, Maximilian, Murphy, Kevin, Tresp, Volker, and Gabrilovich, Evgeniy. 2015. A review of relational machine learning for knowledge graphs. *Proceedings of the IEEE*, **104**(1), 11–33.

Niepert, Mathias, Ahmed, Mohamed, and Kutzkov, Konstantin. 2016. Learning convolutional neural networks for graphs. Pages 2014–2023 of: *International Conference on Machine Learning*.

Norcliffe-Brown, Will, Vafeias, Stathis, and Parisot, Sarah. 2018. Learning conditioned graph structures for interpretable visual question answering. Pages 8334–8343 of: *Advances in Neural Information Processing Systems.*

Nwankpa, Chigozie, Ijomah, Winifred, Gachagan, Anthony, and Marshall, Stephen. 2018. Activation functions: Comparison of trends in practice and research for deep learning. *arXiv preprint arXiv:1811.03378.*

Olshausen, Bruno A., and Field, David J. 1997. Sparse coding with an overcomplete basis set: A strategy employed by V1? *Vision Research*, **37**(23), 3311–3325.

Oono, Kenta, and Suzuki, Taiji. 2020. Graph neural networks exponentially lose expressive power for node classification. *International Conference on Learning Representations.*

Ou, Mingdong, Cui, Peng, Pei, Jian, Zhang, Ziwei, and Zhu, Wenwu. 2016. Asymmetric transitivity preserving graph embedding. Pages 1105–1114 of: *Proceedings of the 22nd ACM SIGKDD International Conference on Knowledge Discovery and Data Mining.*

Owen, Art B. 2013. *Monte Carlo Theory, Methods and Examples.*

Pan, Shirui, Hu, Ruiqi, Long, Guodong, Jiang, Jing, Yao, Lina, et al. 2018. Adversarially regularized graph autoencoder for graph embedding. *arXiv preprint arXiv:1802.04407.*

Pareja, Aldo, Domeniconi, Giacomo, Chen, Jie, Ma, Tengfei, Suzumura, Toyotaro, et al. 2019. Evolvegcn: Evolving graph convolutional networks for dynamic graphs. Pages 5363–5370 of: *Proceedings of the AAAI Conference on Artificial Intelligence.*

Parisot, Sarah, Ktena, Sofia Ira, Ferrante, Enzo, Lee, Matthew, Guerrero, Ricardo, et al. 2018. Disease prediction using graph convolutional networks: Application to autism spectrum disorder and Alzheimers disease. *Medical Image Analysis*, **48**, 117–130.

Park, Namyong, Kan, Andrey, Dong, Xin Luna, Zhao, Tong, and Faloutsos, Christos. 2019. Estimating node importance in knowledge graphs using graph neural networks. Pages 596–606 of: *Proceedings of the 25th ACM SIGKDD International Conference on Knowledge Discovery & Data Mining.*

Paszke, Adam, Gross, Sam, Chintala, Soumith, Chanan, Gregory, Yang, Edward, et al. 2017. 2019. PyTorch: An imperative style, high-performance deep learning library. *Advances in Neural Information Processing Systems.* **32**, 8024–8035.

Peixoto, Tiago P. 2014. The graph-tool python library. *figshare.*

Peng, Zhen, Dong, Yixiang, Luo, Minnan, Wu, Xiao-Ming, and Zheng, Qinghua. 2020. Self-supervised graph representation learning via global context prediction. *arXiv preprint arXiv:2003.01604.*

Perozzi, Bryan, Al-Rfou, Rami, and Skiena, Steven. 2014. Deepwalk: Online learning of social representations. Pages 701–710 of: *Proceedings of the 20th ACM SIGKDD International Conference on Knowledge Discovery and Data Mining.* ACM.

Perraudin, Nathanaël, Paratte, Johan, Shuman, David, Martin, Lionel, Kalofolias, Vassilis, et al. 2014. GSPBOX: A toolbox for signal processing on graphs. *arXiv preprint arXiv:1408.5781.*

Perron, Oskar. 1907. Zur theorie der matrices. *Mathematische Annalen*, **64**(2), 248–263.

Peters, Matthew E., Neumann, Mark, Iyyer, Mohit, Gardner, Matt, Clark, Christopher, et al. 2018. Deep contextualized word representations. Pages 2227–2237 of: *Proceedings of the 2018 Conference of the North American Chapter of the Association for Computational Linguistics: Human Language Technologies, Volume 1 (Long Papers)*.

Pillai, S. Unnikrishna, Suel, Torsten, and Cha, Seunghun. 2005. The Perron–Frobenius theorem: some of its applications. *IEEE Signal Processing Magazine*, **22**(2), 62–75.

Qi, Yanlin, Li, Qi, Karimian, Hamed, and Liu, Di. 2019. A hybrid model for spatiotemporal forecasting of PM2. 5 based on graph convolutional neural network and long short-term memory. *Science of the Total Environment*, **664**, 1–10.

Qiu, Jiezhong, Tang, Jian, Ma, Hao, Dong, Yuxiao, Wang, Kuansan, et al. 2018a. Deepinf: Social influence prediction with deep learning. Pages 2110–2119 of: *Proceedings of the 24th ACM SIGKDD International Conference on Knowledge Discovery & Data Mining*.

Qiu, Jiezhong, Dong, Yuxiao, Ma, Hao, Li, Jian, Wang, Kuansan, et al. 2018b. Network embedding as matrix factorization: Unifying DeepWalk, LINE, PTE, and node2vec. Pages 459–467 of: *Proceedings of the Eleventh ACM International Conference on Web Search and Data Mining*. ACM.

Radford, Alec, Wu, Jeff, Child, Rewon, Luan, David, Amodei, Dario, et al. 2019. Language models are unsupervised multitask learners. *OpenAI blog*, **1**(8), 9.

Ren, Kui, Zheng, Tianhang, Qin, Zhan, and Liu, Xue. 2020. Adversarial attacks and defenses in deep learning. *Engineering*. **6**(3), 346–360.

Resnick, Paul, and Varian, Hal R. 1997. Recommender systems. *Communications of the ACM*, **40**(3), 56–58.

Ribeiro, Leonardo F.R., Saverese, Pedro H.P., and Figueiredo, Daniel R. 2017. struc2vec: Learning node representations from structural identity. Pages 385–394 of: *Proceedings of the 23rd ACM SIGKDD International Conference on Knowledge Discovery and Data Mining*. ACM.

Rong, Yu, Huang, Wenbing, Xu, Tingyang, and Huang, Junzhou. 2019. Dropedge: Towards deep graph convolutional networks on node classification. *International Conference on Learning Representations*.

Rong, Yu, Huang, Wenbing, Xu, Tingyang, and Huang, Junzhou. 2020. DropEdge: Towards deep graph convolutional networks on node classification. *International Conference on Learning Representations*.

Rosenblatt, Frank. 1958. The perceptron: A probabilistic model for information storage and organization in the brain. *Psychological Review*, **65**(6), 386.

Rossi, Ryan A., and Ahmed, Nesreen K. 2015. The network data repository with interactive graph analytics and visualization. *Proceedings of the Twenty-Ninth AAAI Conference on Artificial Intelligence*.

Rossi, Ryan A., Ahmed, Nesreen K., Koh, Eunyee, Kim, Sungchul, Rao, Anup, et al. 2018. HONE: Higher-order network embeddings. Pages 3–4 of: *Companion Proceedings of the The Web Conference 2018*.

Roweis, Sam T., and Saul, Lawrence K. 2000. Nonlinear dimensionality reduction by locally linear embedding. *Science*, **290**(5500), 2323–2326.

Rumelhart, David E., Hinton, Geoffrey E., and Williams, Ronald J. 1986. Learning representations by back-propagating errors. *Nature*, **323**(6088), 533–536.

Rusek, Krzysztof, Suárez-Varela, José, Mestres, Albert, Barlet-Ros, Pere, and Cabellos-Aparicio, Albert. 2019. Unveiling the potential of graph neural networks for network modeling and optimization in SDN. Pages 140–151 of: *Proceedings of the 2019 ACM Symposium on SDN Research.*

Sahu, Sunil Kumar, Christopoulou, Fenia, Miwa, Makoto, and Ananiadou, Sophia. 2019. Inter-sentence relation extraction with document-level graph convolutional neural network. Pages 4309–4316 of: *Proceedings of the 57th Annual Meeting of the Association for Computational Linguistics.*

Sailer, Lee Douglas. 1978. Structural equivalence: Meaning and definition, computation and application. *Social Networks*, 1(1), 73–90.

Salvador, Stan, and Chan, Philip. 2007. Toward accurate dynamic time warping in linear time and space. *Intelligent Data Analysis*, 11(5), 561–580.

Sankar, Aravind, Wu, Yanhong, Gou, Liang, Zhang, Wei, and Yang, Hao. 2018. Dynamic graph representation learning via self-attention networks. Pages 519–527 of: *Proceedings of the 13th International Conference on Web Search and Data Mining.*

Scarselli, Franco, Gori, Marco, Tsoi, Ah Chung, Hagenbuchner, Markus, and Monfardini, Gabriele. 2008. The graph neural network model. *IEEE Transactions on Neural Networks*, 20(1), 61–80.

Scarselli, Franco, Yong, Sweah Liang, Gori, Marco, Hagenbuchner, Markus, Tsoi, Ah Chung, et al. 2005. Graph neural networks for ranking web pages. Pages 666–672 of: *Proceedings of the 2005 IEEE/WIC/ACM International Conference on Web Intelligence*. IEEE Computer Society.

Schlichtkrull, Michael, Kipf, Thomas N., Bloem, Peter, Van Den Berg, Rianne, Titov, Ivan, et al. 2018. Modeling relational data with graph convolutional networks. Pages 593–607 of: *European Semantic Web Conference*. Springer.

Seide, Frank, Li, Gang, and Yu, Dong. 2011. Conversational speech transcription using context-dependent deep neural networks. *Twelfth Annual Conference of the International Speech Communication Association.*

Sen, Prithviraj, Namata, Galileo, Bilgic, Mustafa, Getoor, Lise, Galligher, Brian, et al. 2008. Collective classification in network data. *AI Magazine*, 29(3), 93–93.

Shang, Chao, Tang, Yun, Huang, Jing, Bi, Jinbo, He, Xiaodong, et al. 2019a. End-to-end structure-aware convolutional networks for knowledge base completion. Pages 3060–3067 of: *Proceedings of the AAAI Conference on Artificial Intelligence*. Vol. 33.

Shang, Junyuan, Ma, Tengfei, Xiao, Cao, and Sun, Jimeng. 2019b. Pre-training of graph augmented transformers for medication recommendation. *arXiv preprint arXiv:1906.00346.*

Shang, Junyuan, Xiao, Cao, Ma, Tengfei, Li, Hongyan, and Sun, Jimeng. 2019c. Gamenet: Graph augmented memory networks for recommending medication combination. Pages 1126–1133 of: *Proceedings of the AAAI Conference on Artificial Intelligence*. Vol. 33.

Shchur, Oleksandr, and Günnemann, Stephan. 2019. Overlapping community detection with graph neural networks. *arXiv preprint arXiv:1909.12201.*

Shi, Chuan, Hu, Binbin, Zhao, Wayne Xin, and Philip, S. Yu. 2018a. Heterogeneous information network embedding for recommendation. *IEEE Transactions on Knowledge and Data Engineering*, 31(2), 357–370.

Shi, Jianbo, and Malik, Jitendra. 2000. Normalized cuts and image segmentation. *IEEE Transactions on Pattern Analysis and Machine Intelligence*, **22**(8), 888–905.

Shi, Lei, Zhang, Yifan, Cheng, Jian, and Lu, Hanqing. 2019a. Skeleton-based action recognition with directed graph neural networks. Pages 7912–7921 of: *Proceedings of the IEEE Conference on Computer Vision and Pattern Recognition*.

Shi, Lei, Zhang, Yifan, Cheng, Jian, and Lu, Hanqing. 2019b. Two-stream adaptive graph convolutional networks for skeleton-based action recognition. Pages 12026–12035 of: *Proceedings of the IEEE Conference on Computer Vision and Pattern Recognition*.

Shi, Yu, Han, Fangqiu, He, Xinwei, He, Xinran, Yang, Carl, et al. 2018b. mvn2vec: Preservation and collaboration in multi-view network embedding. *arXiv preprint arXiv:1801.06597*.

Shuman, David I., Narang, Sunil K., Frossard, Pascal, Ortega, Antonio, and Vandergheynst, Pierre. 2013. The emerging field of signal processing on graphs: Extending high-dimensional data analysis to networks and other irregular domains. *IEEE Signal Processing Magazine*, **30**(3), 83–98.

Si, Chenyang, Chen, Wentao, Wang, Wei, Wang, Liang, and Tan, Tieniu. 2019. An attention enhanced graph convolutional lstm network for skeleton-based action recognition. Pages 1227–1236 of: *Proceedings of the IEEE Conference on Computer Vision and Pattern Recognition*.

Si, Chenyang, Jing, Ya, Wang, Wei, Wang, Liang, and Tan, Tieniu. 2018. Skeleton-based action recognition with spatial reasoning and temporal stack learning. Pages 103–118 of: *Proceedings of the European Conference on Computer Vision (ECCV)*.

Simonovsky, Martin, and Komodakis, Nikos. 2017. Dynamic edge-conditioned filters in convolutional neural networks on graphs. Pages 3693–3702 of: *Proceedings of the IEEE Conference on Computer Vision and Pattern Recognition*.

Simonovsky, Martin, and Komodakis, Nikos. 2018. Graphvae: Towards generation of small graphs using variational autoencoders. Pages 412–422 of: *International Conference on Artificial Neural Networks*. Springer.

Simonyan, Karen, and Zisserman, Andrew. 2014. Very deep convolutional networks for large-scale image recognition. *International Conference on Learning Representations*.

Song, Linfeng, Peng, Xiaochang, Zhang, Yue, Wang, Zhiguo, and Gildea, Daniel. 2017. AMR-to-text generation with synchronous node replacement grammar. Pages 7–13 of: *Proceedings of the 55th Annual Meeting of the Association for Computational Linguistics (Volume 2: Short Papers)*.

Song, Linfeng, Wang, Zhiguo, Yu, Mo, Zhang, Yue, Florian, Radu, et al. 2018a. Exploring graph-structured passage representation for multi-hop reading comprehension with graph neural networks. *arXiv preprint arXiv:1809.02040*.

Song, Linfeng, Zhang, Yue, Wang, Zhiguo, and Gildea, Daniel. 2018b. A graph-to-sequence model for AMR-to-text generation. Pages 1616–1626 of: *Proceedings of the 56th Annual Meeting of the Association for Computational Linguistics (Volume 1: Long Papers)*.

Song, Linfeng, Zhang, Yue, Wang, Zhiguo, and Gildea, Daniel. 2018c. N-ary relation extraction using graph state LSTM. Pages 2226–2235 of: *Proceedings of the 2018 Conference on Empirical Methods in Natural Language Processing*.

Srivastava, Nitish, Hinton, Geoffrey, Krizhevsky, Alex, Sutskever, Ilya, and Salakhutdinov, Ruslan. 2014. Dropout: A simple way to prevent neural networks from overfitting. *The Journal of Machine Learning Research*, **15**(1), 1929–1958.

Sun, Changzhi, Gong, Yeyun, Wu, Yuanbin, Gong, Ming, Jiang, Daxin, et al. 2019a. Joint type inference on entities and relations via graph convolutional networks. Pages 1361–1370 of: *Proceedings of the 57th Annual Meeting of the Association for Computational Linguistics*.

Sun, Fan-Yun, Hoffmann, Jordan, and Tang, Jian. 2019b. InfoGraph: Unsupervised and semi-supervised graph-level representation learning via mutual information maximization. *arXiv preprint arXiv:1908.01000*.

Sun, Ke, Lin, Zhouchen, and Zhu, Zhanxing. 2019c. Multi-stage self-supervised learning for graph convolutional networks on graphs with few labels. Pages 5892–5899 of: *Proceedings of the AAAI Conference on Artificial Intelligence*.

Sundararajan, Mukund, Taly, Ankur, and Yan, Qiqi. 2017. Axiomatic attribution for deep networks. Pages 3319–3328 of: *Proceedings of the 34th International Conference on Machine Learning*. Vol. 70.

Sutskever, I., Vinyals, O., and Le, Q.V. 2014. Sequence to sequence learning with neural networks. *Advances in NIPS*. **27**.

Sutton, Richard S., McAllester, David A., Singh, Satinder P., and Mansour, Yishay. 2000. Policy gradient methods for reinforcement learning with function approximation. Pages 1057–1063 of: *Advances in Neural Information Processing Systems*.

Szegedy, Christian, Vanhoucke, Vincent, Ioffe, Sergey, Shlens, Jon, and Wojna, Zbigniew. 2016. Rethinking the inception architecture for computer vision. Pages 2818–2826 of: *Proceedings of the IEEE Conference on Computer Vision and Pattern Recognition*.

Tai, Kai Sheng, Socher, Richard, and Manning, Christopher D. 2015. Improved semantic representations from tree-structured long short-term memory networks. Pages 1556–1566 of: *Proceedings of the 53rd Annual Meeting of the Association for Computational Linguistics and the 7th International Joint Conference on Natural Language Processing (Volume 1: Long Papers)*

Tan, Pang-Ning, Steinbach, Michael, and Kumar, Vipin. 2016. *Introduction to Data Mining*. Pearson Education India.

Tang, Jian, Qu, Meng, Wang, Mingzhe, Zhang, Ming, Yan, Jun, et al. 2015. Line: Large-scale information network embedding. Pages 1067–1077 of: *Proceedings of the 24th International Conference on World Wide Web*. International World Wide Web Conferences Steering Committee.

Tang, Jiliang, Aggarwal, Charu, and Liu, Huan. 2016a. Node classification in signed social networks. Pages 54–62 of: *Proceedings of the 2016 SIAM International Conference on Data Mining*. SIAM.

Tang, Jiliang, Alelyani, Salem, and Liu, Huan. 2014a. Feature selection for classification: A review. *Data classification: Algorithms and applications*, 37.

Tang, Jiliang, Chang, Yi, Aggarwal, Charu, and Liu, Huan. 2016b. A survey of signed network mining in social media. *ACM Computing Surveys (CSUR)*, **49**(3), 1–37.

Tang, Jiliang, Gao, Huiji, Hu, Xia, and Liu, Huan. 2013a. Exploiting homophily effect for trust prediction. Pages 53–62 of: *Proceedings of the Sixth ACM International Conference on Web Search and Data Mining*.

Tang, Jiliang, Hu, Xia, Gao, Huiji, and Liu, Huan. 2013b. Unsupervised feature selection for multi-view data in social media. Pages 270–278 of: *Proceedings of the 2013 SIAM International Conference on Data Mining*. SIAM.

Tang, Jiliang, Hu, Xia, and Liu, Huan. 2014b. Is distrust the negation of trust? The value of distrust in social media. Pages 148–157 of: *Proceedings of the 25th ACM Conference on Hypertext and Social Media*.

Tang, Jiliang, and Liu, Huan. 2012a. Feature selection with linked data in social media. Pages 118–128 of: *Proceedings of the 2012 SIAM International Conference on Data Mining*. SIAM.

Tang, Jiliang, and Liu, Huan. 2012b. Unsupervised feature selection for linked social media data. Pages 904–912 of: *Proceedings of the 18th ACM SIGKDD International Conference on Knowledge Discovery and Data Mining*.

Tang, Lei, and Liu, Huan. 2009. Relational learning via latent social dimensions. Pages 817–826 of: *Proceedings of the 15th ACM SIGKDD International Conference on Knowledge Discovery and Data Mining*. ACM.

Tang, Xianfeng, Li, Yandong, Sun, Yiwei, Yao, Huaxiu, Mitra, Prasenjit, et al. 2019. Robust Graph Neural Network against Poisoning Attacks via Transfer Learning. Pages 600–608 of: *Proceedings of the 13th International Conference on Web Search and Data Mining*.

Tang, Xianfeng, Yao, Huaxiu, Sun, Yiwei, Wang, Yiqi, Tang, Jiliang, et al. 2020. Graph convolutional networks against degree-related biases. Pages 1435–1444 of: *Proceedings of the 29th ACM International Conference on Information & Knowledge Management*.

Tenenbaum, Joshua B., De Silva, Vin, and Langford, John C. 2000. A global geometric framework for nonlinear dimensionality reduction. *Science*, **290**(5500), 2319–2323.

Teney, Damien, Liu, Lingqiao, and van den Hengel, Anton. 2017. Graph-structured representations for visual question answering. Pages 1–9 of: *Proceedings of the IEEE Conference on Computer Vision and Pattern Recognition*.

Trinajstic, Nenad. 2018. *Chemical Graph Theory*. Routledge.

Tu, Ke, Cui, Peng, Wang, Xiao, Wang, Fei, and Zhu, Wenwu. 2018. Structural deep embedding for hyper-networks. *Thirty-Second AAAI Conference on Artificial Intelligence*.

Tu, Ming, Wang, Guangtao, Huang, Jing, Tang, Yun, He, Xiaodong, et al. 2019. Multi-hop reading comprehension across multiple documents by reasoning over heterogeneous graphs. Pages 2704–2713 of: *Proceedings of the 57th Annual Meeting of the Association for Computational Linguistics*.

Vashishth, Shikhar, Sanyal, Soumya, Nitin, Vikram, and Talukdar, Partha. 2019. Composition-based multi-relational graph convolutional networks. *International Conference on Learning Representations*.

Vaswani, Ashish, Shazeer, Noam, Parmar, Niki, Uszkoreit, Jakob, Jones, Llion, et al. 2017. Attention is all you need. Pages 5998–6008 of: *Advances in Neural Information Processing Systems*.

Veličković, Petar, Cucurull, Guillem, Casanova, Arantxa, Romero, Adriana, Lio, Pietro, et al. 2017. Graph attention networks. *International Conference on Learning Representations*.

Vinyals, Oriol, and Le, Quoc. 2015. A neural conversational model. *arXiv preprint arXiv:1506.05869.*

Vosoughi, Soroush, Roy, Deb, and Aral, Sinan. 2018. The spread of true and false news online. *Science,* **359**(6380), 1146–1151.

Wang, Daixin, Cui, Peng, and Zhu, Wenwu. 2016. Structural deep network embedding. Pages 1225–1234 of: *Proceedings of the 22nd ACM SIGKDD International Conference on Knowledge Discovery and Data Mining.* ACM.

Wang, Fei, Li, Tao, Wang, Xin, Zhu, Shenghuo, and Ding, Chris. 2011. Community discovery using nonnegative matrix factorization. *Data Mining and Knowledge Discovery,* **22**(3), 493–521.

Wang, Hao, Xu, Tong, Liu, Qi, Lian, Defu, Chen, Enhong, et al. 2019a. MCNE: An end-to-end framework for learning multiple conditional network representations of social network. Pages 1064–1072 of: *Proceedings of the 25th ACM SIGKDD International Conference on Knowledge Discovery & Data Mining.*

Wang, Hongwei, Wang, Jia, Wang, Jialin, Zhao, Miao, Zhang, Weinan, et al. 2018a. Graphgan: Graph representation learning with generative adversarial nets. *Thirty-Second AAAI Conference on Artificial Intelligence.*

Wang, Hongwei, Zhang, Fuzheng, Zhang, Mengdi, Leskovec, Jure, Zhao, Miao, et al. 2019b. Knowledge-aware graph neural networks with label smoothness regularization for recommender systems. Pages 968–977 of: *Proceedings of the 25th ACM SIGKDD International Conference on Knowledge Discovery & Data Mining.*

Wang, Hongwei, Zhao, Miao, Xie, Xing, Li, Wenjie, and Guo, Minyi. 2019c. Knowledge graph convolutional networks for recommender systems. Pages 3307–3313 of: *The World Wide Web Conference.* ACM.

Wang, Jianyu, Wen, Rui, Wu, Chunming, Huang, Yu, and Xion, Jian. 2019d. Fdgars: Fraudster detection via graph convolutional networks in online app review system. Pages 310–316 of: *Companion Proceedings of the 2019 World Wide Web Conference.*

Wang, Minjie, Yu, Lingfan, Zheng, Da, Gan, Quan, Gai, Yu, et al. 2019e. Deep graph library: Towards efficient and scalable deep learning on graphs. *arXiv preprint arXiv:1909.01315.*

Wang, Peifeng, Han, Jialong, Li, Chenliang, and Pan, Rong. 2019f. Logic attention based neighborhood aggregation for inductive knowledge graph embedding. Pages 7152–7159 of: *Proceedings of the AAAI Conference on Artificial Intelligence.* Vol. 33.

Wang, Suhang, Aggarwal, Charu, Tang, Jiliang, and Liu, Huan. 2017a. Attributed signed network embedding. Pages 137–146 of: *Proceedings of the 2017 ACM on Conference on Information and Knowledge Management.*

Wang, Suhang, Tang, Jiliang, Aggarwal, Charu, Chang, Yi, and Liu, Huan. 2017b. Signed network embedding in social media. Pages 327–335 of: *Proceedings of the 2017 SIAM International Conference on Data Mining.* SIAM.

Wang, Xiang, He, Xiangnan, Cao, Yixin, Liu, Meng, and Chua, Tat-Seng. 2019g. KGAT: Knowledge graph attention network for recommendation. Pages 950–958 of: *Proceedings of the 25th ACM SIGKDD International Conference on Knowledge Discovery & Data Mining.*

Wang, Xiang, He, Xiangnan, Wang, Meng, Feng, Fuli, and Chua, Tat-Seng. 2019h. Neural graph collaborative filtering. Pages 165–174 of: *Proceedings of the 42nd International ACM SIGIR Conference on Research and Development in Information Retrieval.*

Wang, Xiao, Cui, Peng, Wang, Jing, Pei, Jian, Zhu, Wenwu, et al. 2017c. Community preserving network embedding. *Thirty-First AAAI conference on Artificial Intelligence.*

Wang, Xiao, Ji, Houye, Shi, Chuan, Wang, Bai, Ye, Yanfang, et al. 2019i. Heterogeneous graph attention network. Pages 2022–2032 of: *The World Wide Web Conference.*

Wang, Xiaolong, Ye, Yufei, and Gupta, Abhinav. 2018b. Zero-shot recognition via semantic embeddings and knowledge graphs. Pages 6857–6866 of: *Proceedings of the IEEE Conference on Computer Vision and Pattern Recognition.*

Wang, Xiaoyang, Ma, Yao, Wang, Yiqi, Jin, Wei, Wang, Xin, Tang, et al. 2020a. Traffic flow prediction via spatial temporal graph neural network. Pages 1082–1092 of: *Proceedings of the Web Conference 2020.*

Wang, Xuhong, Du, Ying, Cui, Ping, and Yang, Yupu. 2020b. OCGNN: One-class classification with graph neural networks. *arXiv preprint arXiv:2002.09594.*

Wang, Yaping, Jiao, Pengfei, Wang, Wenjun, Lu, Chunyu, Liu, Hongtao, et al. 2019j. Bipartite network embedding via effective integration of explicit and implicit relations. Pages 435–451 of: *International Conference on Database Systems for Advanced Applications.* Springer.

Wang, Yue, Sun, Yongbin, Liu, Ziwei, Sarma, Sanjay E., Bronstein, Michael M., et al. 2019k. Dynamic graph cnn for learning on point clouds. *ACM Transactions on Graphics (TOG),* **38**(5), 1–12.

Wang, Zhichun, Lv, Qingsong, Lan, Xiaohan, and Zhang, Yu. 2018c. Cross-lingual knowledge graph alignment via graph convolutional networks. Pages 349–357 of: *Proceedings of the 2018 Conference on Empirical Methods in Natural Language Processing.*

Watkins, Christopher J.C.H, and Dayan, Peter. 1992. Q-learning. *Machine Learning,* **8**(3–4), 279–292.

Weber, Mark, Domeniconi, Giacomo, Chen, Jie, Weidele, Daniel Karl I., Bellei, Claudio, et al. 2019. Anti-money laundering in bitcoin: Experimenting with graph convolutional networks for financial forensics. *arXiv preprint arXiv:1908.02591.*

Wei, Xiaokai, Cao, Bokai, and Philip, S Yu. 2016. Unsupervised feature selection on networks: a generative view. *Thirtieth AAAI Conference on Artificial Intelligence.*

Wei, Xiaokai, Xie, Sihong, and Yu, Philip S. 2015. Efficient partial order preserving unsupervised feature selection on networks. Pages 82–90 of: *Proceedings of the 2015 SIAM International Conference on Data Mining.* SIAM.

Weisfeiler, B., and Leman, A. 1968. A reduction of a graph to a canonical form and an algebra arising during this reduction, *Nauchno-Technicheskaya Informatsiya,* **2**(9), 12–16 (in Russian).

Welbl, Johannes, Stenetorp, Pontus, and Riedel, Sebastian. 2018. Constructing datasets for multi-hop reading comprehension across documents. *Transactions of the Association for Computational Linguistics,* **6**, 287–302.

Wen, Yu-Hui, Gao, Lin, Fu, Hongbo, Zhang, Fang-Lue, and Xia, Shihong. 2019. Graph CNNs with motif and variable temporal block for skeleton-based action recognition. Pages 8989–8996 of: *Proceedings of the AAAI Conference on Artificial Intelligence*. Vol. 33.

Werbos, Paul John. 1994. The Roots of *Backpropagation: From Ordered Derivatives to Neural Networks and Political Forecasting*. John Wiley & Sons.

Werling, Donna M., and Geschwind, Daniel H. 2013. Sex differences in autism spectrum disorders. *Current Opinion in Neurology*, **26**(2), 146.

Widder, David Vernon, and Hirschman, Isidore Isaac. 2015. *Convolution Transform*. Vol. 2153. Princeton University Press.

Wu, Huijun, Wang, Chen, Tyshetskiy, Yuriy, Docherty, Andrew, Lu, Kai, et al. 2019. Adversarial examples for graph data: Deep insights into attack and defense. Pages 4816–4823 of: Kraus, Sarit (ed.), *Proceedings of the Twenty-Eighth International Joint Conference on Artificial Intelligence, IJCAI 2019, Macao, China, August 10–16, 2019*.

Wu, Zonghan, Pan, Shirui, Chen, Fengwen, Long, Guodong, Zhang, Chengqi, et al. 2020. A comprehensive survey on graph neural networks. *IEEE Transactions on Neural Networks and Learning Systems*.

Xu, Bingbing, Shen, Huawei, Cao, Qi, Qiu, Yunqi, and Cheng, Xueqi. 2019a. Graph wavelet neural network. *International Conference on Learning Representations*.

Xu, Han, Ma, Yao, Liu, Haochen, Deb, Debayan, Liu, Hui, et al. 2019b. Adversarial attacks and defenses in images, graphs and text: A review. Pages 151–178 of: *International Journal of Automation and Computing*.

Xu, Jian. 2017. Representing big data as networks: New methods and insights. *arXiv preprint arXiv:1712.09648*.

Xu, Kaidi, Chen, Hongge, Liu, Sijia, Chen, Pin-Yu, Weng, Tsui-Wei, et al. 2019c. Topology attack and defense for graph neural networks: an optimization perspective. Pages 3961–3967 of: Kraus, Sarit (ed.), *Proceedings of the Twenty-Eighth International Joint Conference on Artificial Intelligence, IJCAI 2019, Macao, China, August 10–16, 2019*.

Xu, Keyulu, Hu, Weihua, Leskovec, Jure, and Jegelka, Stefanie. 2019d. How powerful are graph neural networks? *7th International Conference on Learning Representations, ICLR 2019, New Orleans, LA, USA, May 6–9, 2019*.

Xu, Keyulu, Li, Chengtao, Tian, Yonglong, Sonobe, Tomohiro, Kawarabayashi, Ken-ichi, et al. 2018a. Representation learning on graphs with jumping knowledge networks. Pages 5449–5458 of: Dy, Jennifer G., and Krause, Andreas (eds.), *Proceedings of the 35th International Conference on Machine Learning, ICML 2018, Stockholmsmässan, Stockholm, Sweden, July 10–15, 2018*.

Xu, Kun, Wang, Liwei, Yu, Mo, Feng, Yansong, Song, Yan, et al. 2019e. Cross-lingual knowledge graph alignment via graph matching neural network. Pages 349–357 of: *Proceedings of the 2018 Conference on Empirical Methods in Natural Language Processing Computational Linguistics*.

Xu, Kun, Wu, Lingfei, Wang, Zhiguo, Feng, Yansong, Witbrock, Michael, et al. 2018b. Graph2seq: Graph to sequence learning with attention-based neural networks. *arXiv preprint arXiv:1804.00823*.

Xuan, Ping, Pan, Shuxiang, Zhang, Tiangang, Liu, Yong, and Sun, Hao. 2019. Graph convolutional network and convolutional neural network based method for predicting lncRNA-disease associations. *Cells*, **8**(9), 1012.

Yadati, Naganand, Nimishakavi, Madhav, Yadav, Prateek, Nitin, Vikram, Louis, Anand, et al. 2019. HyperGCN: A new method for training graph convolutional networks on hypergraphs. Pages 1509–1520 of: *Advances in Neural Information Processing Systems*.

Yan, Sijie, Xiong, Yuanjun, and Lin, Dahua. 2018. Spatial temporal graph convolutional networks for skeleton-based action recognition. *Thirty-Second AAAI Conference on Artificial Intelligence*.

Yanardag, Pinar, and Vishwanathan, SVN. 2015. Deep graph kernels. Pages 1365–1374 of: *Proceedings of the 21th ACM SIGKDD International Conference on Knowledge Discovery and Data Mining*.

Yang, Bishan, Yih, Wen-tau, He, Xiaodong, Gao, Jianfeng, and Deng, Li. 2014. Learning multi-relational semantics using neural-embedding models. *arXiv preprint arXiv:1411.4072*.

Yang, Jaewon, and Leskovec, Jure. 2015. Defining and evaluating network communities based on ground-truth. *Knowledge and Information Systems*, **42**(1), 181–213.

Yang, Xu, Tang, Kaihua, Zhang, Hanwang, and Cai, Jianfei. 2019. Auto-encoding scene graphs for image captioning. Pages 10685–10694 of: *Proceedings of the IEEE Conference on Computer Vision and Pattern Recognition*.

Yao, Liang, Mao, Chengsheng, and Luo, Yuan. 2019. Graph convolutional networks for text classification. Pages 7370–7377 of: *Proceedings of the AAAI Conference on Artificial Intelligence*. Vol. 33.

Ying, Rex, He, Ruining, Chen, Kaifeng, Eksombatchai, Pong, Hamilton, William L., et al. 2018a. Graph convolutional neural networks for web-scale recommender systems. Pages 974–983 of: *Proceedings of the 24th ACM SIGKDD International Conference on Knowledge Discovery & Data Mining*. ACM.

Ying, Zhitao, Bourgeois, Dylan, You, Jiaxuan, Zitnik, Marinka, and Leskovec, Jure. 2019. Gnnexplainer: Generating explanations for graph neural networks. Pages 9244–9255 of: *Advances in Neural Information Processing Systems*.

Ying, Zhitao, You, Jiaxuan, Morris, Christopher, Ren, Xiang, Hamilton, Will, et al. 2018b. Hierarchical graph representation learning with differentiable pooling. Pages 4800–4810 of: *Advances in Neural Information Processing Systems*.

You, Jiaxuan, Liu, Bowen, Ying, Zhitao, Pande, Vijay, and Leskovec, Jure. 2018a. Graph convolutional policy network for goal-directed molecular graph generation. Pages 6410–6421 of: *Advances in Neural Information Processing Systems*.

You, Jiaxuan, Ying, Rex, Ren, Xiang, Hamilton, William L., and Leskovec, Jure. 2018b. Graphrnn: Generating realistic graphs with deep auto-regressive models. Pages 5708–5717 of: *International Conference on Machine Learning*.

You, Yuning, Chen, Tianlong, Wang, Zhangyang, and Shen, Yang. 2020. When Does self-supervision help graph convolutional networks? Pages 10871–10880 of: *International Conference on Machine Learning*.

Yu, Bing, Yin, Haoteng, and Zhu, Zhanxing. 2017. Spatio-temporal graph convolutional networks: A deep learning framework for traffic forecasting. Pages 3634–3640 of: *Proceedings of the Twenty-Seventh International Joint Conference on Artificial Intelligence, (IJCAI-18)*.

Yu, Dong, and Deng, Li. 2016. *Automatic Speech Recognition*. Springer.

Yuan, Hao, and Ji, Shuiwang. 2019. StructPool: Structured graph pooling via conditional random fields. *International Conference on Learning Representations.*

Yuan, Hao, Tang, Jiliang, Hu, Xia, and Ji, Shuiwang. 2020. XGNN: Towards model-level explanations of graph neural networks. Pages 430–438 of: *Proceedings of the 26th ACM SIGKDD International Conference on Knowledge Discovery & Data Mining.*

Yuan, Shuhan, Wu, Xintao, and Xiang, Yang. 2017. SNE: Signed network embedding. Pages 183–195 of: *Pacific-Asia Conference on Knowledge Discovery and Data Mining.* Springer.

Yuan, Xiaoyong, He, Pan, Zhu, Qile, and Li, Xiaolin. 2019. Adversarial examples: Attacks and defenses for deep learning. *IEEE Transactions on Neural Networks and Learning Systems,* **30**(9), 2805–2824.

Zeiler, Matthew D. 2012. ADADELTA: An adaptive learning rate method. *arXiv preprint arXiv:1212.5701.*

Zeng, Hanqing, Zhou, Hongkuan, Srivastava, Ajitesh, Kannan, Rajgopal, and Prasanna, Viktor. 2019. Graphsaint: Graph sampling based inductive learning method. *International Conference on Learning Representations.*

Zhang, Chuxu, Song, Dongjin, Huang, Chao, Swami, Ananthram, and Chawla, Nitesh V. 2019a. Heterogeneous graph neural network. Pages 793–803 of: *Proceedings of the 25th ACM SIGKDD International Conference on Knowledge Discovery & Data Mining.*

Zhang, Fanjin, Liu, Xiao, Tang, Jie, Dong, Yuxiao, Yao, Peiran, et al. 2019b. Oag: Toward linking large-scale heterogeneous entity graphs. Pages 2585–2595 of: *Proceedings of the 25th ACM SIGKDD International Conference on Knowledge Discovery & Data Mining.*

Zhang, Guo, He, Hao, and Katabi, Dina. 2019c. Circuit-GNN: Graph neural networks for distributed circuit design. Pages 7364–7373 of: *International Conference on Machine Learning.*

Zhang, Jiani, Shi, Xingjian, Xie, Junyuan, Ma, Hao, King, Irwin, and Yeung, Dit-Yan. 2018a. Gaan: Gated attention networks for learning on large and spatiotemporal graphs. *arXiv preprint arXiv:1803.07294.*

Zhang, Ningyu, Deng, Shumin, Sun, Zhanlin, Wang, Guanying, Chen, Xi, et al. 2019d. Long-tail relation extraction via knowledge graph embeddings and graph convolution networks. Pages 1331–1339 of: *Proceedings of the 2019 Conference of the North American Chapter of the Association for Computational Linguistics: Human Language Technologies, Volume 1 (Long and Short Papers).*

Zhang, Wei Emma, Sheng, Quan Z., Alhazmi, Ahoud, and Li, Chenliang. 2020. Adversarial attacks on deep-learning models in natural language processing: A survey. *ACM Transactions on Intelligent Systems and Technology (TIST),* **11**(3), 1–41.

Zhang, Yizhou, Xiong, Yun, Kong, Xiangnan, Li, Shanshan, Mi, Jinhong, et al. 2018b. Deep collective classification in heterogeneous information networks. Pages 399–408 of: *Proceedings of the 2018 World Wide Web Conference.*

Zhang, Yuhao, Qi, Peng, and Manning, Christopher D. 2018c. Graph convolution over pruned dependency trees improves relation extraction. Pages 2205–2215 of: *Proceedings of the 2018 Conference on Empirical Methods in Natural Language Processing.*

Zhao, Lingxiao, and Akoglu, Leman. 2019. PairNorm: Tackling oversmoothing in GNNs. *International Conference on Learning Representations.*

Zhou, Jie, Cui, Ganqu, Zhang, Zhengyan, Yang, Cheng, Liu, Zhiyuan, et al. 2018a. Graph neural networks: A review of methods and applications. *arXiv preprint arXiv:1812.08434.*

Zhou, Lekui, Yang, Yang, Ren, Xiang, Wu, Fei, and Zhuang, Yueting. 2018b. Dynamic network embedding by modeling triadic closure process. *Thirty-Second AAAI Conference on Artificial Intelligence.*

Zhou, Yaqin, Liu, Shangqing, Siow, Jingkai, Du, Xiaoning, and Liu, Yang. 2019. Devign: Effective vulnerability identification by learning comprehensive program semantics via graph neural networks. Pages 10197–10207 of: *Advances in Neural Information Processing Systems.*

Zhu, Dingyuan, Zhang, Ziwei, Cui, Peng, and Zhu, Wenwu. 2019a. Robust graph convolutional networks against adversarial attacks. Pages 1399–1407 of: *Proceedings of the 25th ACM SIGKDD International Conference on Knowledge Discovery & Data Mining.*

Zhu, Hao, Lin, Yankai, Liu, Zhiyuan, Fu, Jie, Chua, Tat-seng, et al. 2019b. Graph neural networks with generated parameters for relation extraction. Pages 1331–1339 of: *Proceedings of the 57th Annual Meeting of the Association for Computational Linguistics.*

Zhu, Rong, Zhao, Kun, Yang, Hongxia, Lin, Wei, Zhou, Chang, et al. 2019c. Aligraph: A comprehensive graph neural network platform. *arXiv preprint arXiv:1902.08730.*

Zhu, Shenghuo, Yu, Kai, Chi, Yun, and Gong, Yihong. 2007. Combining content and link for classification using matrix factorization. Pages 487–494 of: *Proceedings of the 30th Annual International ACM SIGIR Conference on Research and Development in Information Retrieval.*

Zhu, Xiaojin, Ghahramani, Zoubin, and Lafferty, John D. 2003. Semi-supervised learning using Gaussian fields and harmonic functions. Pages 912–919 of: *Proceedings of the 20th International Conference on Machine Learning (ICML-03).*

Zitnik, Marinka, Agrawal, Monica, and Leskovec, Jure. 2018. Modeling polypharmacy side effects with graph convolutional networks. *Bioinformatics*, **34**(13), i457–i466.

Zügner, Daniel, and Günnemann, Stephan. 2019. Adversarial attacks on graph neural networks via meta learning. *International Conference on Learning Representations.*

Zügner, Daniel, Akbarnejad, Amir, and Günnemann, Stephan. 2018. Adversarial attacks on neural networks for graph data. Pages 2847–2856 of: *Proceedings of the 24th ACM SIGKDD International Conference on Knowledge Discovery & Data Mining.*

Index

Index